Get Your Knee Off Our Necks

Bruce E. Johansen • Adebowale Akande
Editors

Get Your Knee Off Our Necks

From Slavery to Black Lives Matter

Editors
Bruce E. Johansen
Communication and Native American Studies
University of Nebraska at Omaha
Omaha, NE, USA

Adebowale Akande
IR Globe Cross-Cultural Inc
Vancouver, BC, Canada

ISBN 978-3-030-85154-5   ISBN 978-3-030-85155-2   (eBook)
https://doi.org/10.1007/978-3-030-85155-2

© The Editor(s) (if applicable) and The Author(s), under exclusive licence to Springer Nature Switzerland AG 2022
This work is subject to copyright. All rights are reserved by the Publisher, whether the whole or part of the material is concerned, specifically the rights of translation, reprinting, reuse of illustrations, recitation, broadcasting, reproduction on microfilms or in any other physical way, and transmission or information storage and retrieval, electronic adaptation, computer software, or by similar or dissimilar methodology now known or hereafter developed.
The use of general descriptive names, registered names, trademarks, service marks, etc. in this publication does not imply, even in the absence of a specific statement, that such names are exempt from the relevant protective laws and regulations and therefore free for general use.
The publisher, the authors and the editors are safe to assume that the advice and information in this book are believed to be true and accurate at the date of publication. Neither the publisher nor the authors or the editors give a warranty, expressed or implied, with respect to the material contained herein or for any errors or omissions that may have been made. The publisher remains neutral with regard to jurisdictional claims in published maps and institutional affiliations.

This Springer imprint is published by the registered company Springer Nature Switzerland AG.
The registered company address is: Gewerbestrasse 11, 6330 Cham, Switzerland

Contents

1 *"I Can't Breathe:"* Dying While Black in America: Today's
   Lynchings and Ending the Heritage of Slavery   1
   Bruce E. Johansen

2 *The Perils of Populism, Racism, and Sexism*: The Trump
   Lesson Plan for African Americans and Women   83
   Mamie E. Locke

3 *Penal Populism*: The End of Reason   111
   John Pratt and Michelle Miao

4 White Supremacy and the Politics of Race   141
   Ronald E. Goodwin

5 *The Civil Rights Movement in Urban Microcosm*: Omaha,
   Nebraska   169
   Bruce E. Johansen

6 *Blackfacing, White Shaming, and Yellow Journalism*: A
   Jaundiced View of How Contemporary PC Erodes First
   Amendment Principles   191
   Kenneth Lasson

7 *In the Spirit of Queen Araweelo*: An Analysis of Congresswoman Ilhan Omar's Disruption of Nativism and White Supremacy 229
Dorian Brown Crosby

8 *Australia*: Tainted Blood—Scientific Racism, Eugenics and Sanctimonious Treatments of Aboriginal Australians: 1869–2008 253
Greg Blyton

9 *Brazil and Australia*: Indigenous Peoples and the Fires This Time 275
Bruce E. Johansen

10 *Though the Heavens Should Fall*: The Mansfield Decision (1772) 313
Barbara Alice Mann

Index 327

Introduction

From different interdisciplinary angles, this scholarly collection's central theme examines a rising wave of White supremacy and racism inundating all facets of American life from the slaves' first landings at Jamestown (1619), to the murder of George Floyd in 2020, and beyond. We focus on contemporary murders in the United States, often of Black men by police, along with historical context that ties these murders to past practices, such as lynching

Each murder is an example of what has come before, and after. It is the "why" that we are after. Why, for example, was Ahmaud Arbery, a Black man out for a jog, shot to death by whites? They had assumed that he had robbed an empty (under construction) home that he had jogged through. Many such deaths occur because of whites' negative (and usually mistaken) stereotypes of Blacks. Once such a blunder has been made, it takes on a life of its own. For Arbery (as well as Floyd, and many others) an assumed act of petty theft, or even merely running from an officer, can make a Black man liable for summary execution. These are not incidental incidents. On an average of one a day, a Black man or woman has been shot to death by police in recent years.

We dissect the recent history of Black–White relationships in the United States. For example, in Chap. 1, "'I Can't Breathe:' Dying While Black in America: Today's Lynchings and Ending the Heritage of Slavery," We begin on the streets of America's inner cities, with its jails and prisons, where, nearly without fail, young men come into contact (some for extended periods of time) with a vast criminal "justice" complex, the heritage of slavery. The slaves, one learns, were legally freed in 1865 by Abraham Lincoln. However, in our time, there are more young Black men in prisons and jails than in colleges and universities, in a country that incarcerates, by proportion of population, more people (mainly, but not all, men) than any other national jurisdiction on Planet Earth, half or more of whom are Black, Latino, or Native American.

We analyze a wave of Black shootings by police during 2020 and 2021, the most publicized of which was the murder of George Floyd in May 2020. Floyd's murder was followed by a month of mass marches that involved about a million people in the United States and other countries, the largest civil-rights marches in U.S. history. We analyze these events in the context of dozens of other shootings of similar characters. The service revolver has become the new lynching rope. The assassination of young Blacks continued long after Floyd was murdered, and his murderer, former Minneapolis police officer Derek Chauvin was convicted and sentenced. Following much talk about police reform, very little has changed.

The murder of Floyd was not unique, even in 2020, even in its horrific brutality. What *had* changed was the ability of modern communication's technology to place in the hands of ordinary people small, portable machines that may be used to capture the images and sounds of a Black man's neck being crushed by an ample knee belonging to a Minneapolis police officer, then send those images around the world to similar machines in a fraction of a second. One wonders how history might have been changed if these machines had been available during lynchings centuries ago, as the first slaves were being forced ashore along what is now the United States East Coast, or as Native American hunting lands were being converted to cotton fields harvested by Black slaves, during the battles over Reconstruction and Jim Crow, the growth and the genocidal nature of White nationalism through the Ku Klux Klan, the Dixiecrat movement. How did people in other nations (Europe and Africa) see Blacks' oppression? Welcoming arms were extended from Africa even as Adolph Hitler used the United States' oppression of freed slaves and Native Americans as examples for the "Jew codes" of the Third Reich. Your Mississippi will be our Volga! Hitler proclaimed.

Be prepared to be surprised and sometimes shocked by a new narrative that will challenge previous interpretations of color lines in American history to the present day: The opening of the South after the U.S. Civil War, the U.S. political parties' Southern Strategy as formulized by an ever-more conservative Republican Party, W.E.B. DuBois' Black reconstruction, Martin Luther King, Jr., Malcolm X, and the civil rights movements during the 1950s and 1960s, desegregated schools, Richard Nixon's groundwork for Donald Trump versus the Democratic Strategy (Jimmy Carter to Bill Clinton), cumulating to this day, with a massive racist reaction against Barack Obama's presidency, From lynching, "rape as a badge of slavery," systematic exclusion, and southern oppression, discrimination in employment, education to voter suppression, against police abuses of power, the struggle continues a century and a half after the abolition of slavery, into the Black Lives Matter and the #Me Too movements. Our contributors dissect the social construction of whiteness and racial domination around race, gender, and class in American politics.

* * *

In **Chap. 1**, we dissect the recent history of Black–White relationships in the United States in **"'*I Can't Breathe:*' Dying While Black in America: Today's Lynchings and Ending the Heritage of Slavery."** We begin on the streets of America's inner cities, with its jails and prisons, where, nearly without fail, young men come into contact (some for extended periods of time) with a vast criminal "justice" complex, the heritage of slavery.

On the street, among the half of Black men who are not serving time, prudent young people are having "the conversation" with their parents, which boils down to this: do *not* give the police any lip. Never run, no matter what the circumstances or temptation, because, in so doing, you may become a rabbit giving a bad cop a moving target. A quick sprint away from an officer may become an on-the-spot assumption of guilt and an instant sentence of execution, often carried out by a shot in the back or, once captured, by the fatal crushing of a thorax. In many such cases, the service revolver or the crushing knee may again become today's hanging rope. It is more productive to *march* with many thousands of people of all races around you.

By the early years of the twenty-first century, such deaths had become so frequent that, like dry tinder, they were waiting for a spark. This chapter describes the popular uprising that followed the killing of George Floyd, in Minneapolis, as his neck was crushed on nearly live television provided by a civilian with a cell phone. This was, of course, not the first time, and it was not the last, but the brutality was so unforgiving, and so lacking in provable criminal intent on Floyd's part, that the tinder was lit around the world. Tens, then hundreds of thousands of people, Black, White, Brown, and Red, coursed into the streets of the United States and many other countries. After almost a month of marches, it became the largest display of demonstrations and demands for basic change in United States history.

In **Chap. 2**, *"The Perils of Populism, Racism, and Sexism*: **The Trump Lesson Plan for African Americans and Women." By Mamie E. Locke, Ph.D.** of Hampton University, examines the motives of Donald J. Trump, including racial overtones. The indifference shown to women and African Americans is part and parcel of the Trump lesson plan as he has preyed on the anxieties of his base to make anyone who disagrees with him so-called "enemies of the American people." Using the politics of insecurity and insult, Trump mobilized his base to undermine the political and socioeconomic voices of African Americans and women, especially women of color. Donald Trump used nationalistic rhetoric, insults, and foul language to create a frenzy with his base to instigate backlash against those he considered to be enemies of the people.

Trump's non-stop political campaigns demonstrated a continuation of a race-based, nationalistic appeal that began as far back as the mid-nineteenth century in various iterations, which continued with Theodore Roosevelt in 1912 and resurfaced with former presidential candidate and Alabama Governor George Wallace in the 1960s and 1970s. An underlying theme of this ideology is the designation of a common enemy that must be castigated in order to uplift the purveyor of the message. The difference was that Roosevelt and Wallace were not able to solidify the popular appeal in such a way to propel themselves to the White House (although Roosevelt had previously served two terms as President as a Republican). Donald Trump, with no political experience, found himself on the stage in Cleveland, Ohio accepting the Republican nomination for President in 2016. Trump is remarkably ignorant of history, including his ideology's roots and past practice. Once, taken to Pearl Harbor, having witnessed a ceremony, Trump asked his staff what was so important about Pearl Harbor, anyway.

This chapter explores Trump's racist and nationalistic messaging, not only during his 2016 and 2020 campaigns, but also within his overall history, his administration, and his politics of changing the narrative rather than engaging in public policy. Given that Trump has mastered this lesson plan of criticism by insult, he has reshaped the Republican Party, leaders, and members such that his is the voice that dominates and controls Republican ideology. By 2020, with a new election looming, along with the killing coronavirus, economic depression, and mass protests, the question became: could Trump's old tactics survive fast-moving events? Trump and his obvious racism lost, but he maintained victory, right down to an armed trashing of the U.S. Capitol on January 6, 2021.

In **Chap. 3, "*Penal Populism*: The End of Reason," John Pratt** (Professor of Criminology, Victoria University of Wellington, Wellington, New Zealand) **and Michelle Miao,** (Assistant Professor of Law, The Chinese University of Hong Kong), analyze the phenomenon of "penal populism," which was first identified as characteristic of English-speaking Western democracies around the end of the twentieth century—specifically, the United States, the United Kingdom, New Zealand, Australia, and Canada. Since that time, however, various strands of it—the exact form that it takes and the impact it has vary from society to society—have been identified in a diverse range of countries. Generally, it demands a much more punitive approach to law-breaking. This has been manifested in the form of dramatically rising imprisonment rates, as in the Anglophone world; but it has also led to clamorings for a more vigorous use of the death penalty in some Asian societies, particularly Japan, or chemical castration of child sex offenders, as in South Korea and the Czech Republic.

With each society that it touches, it is as if penal populism undermines the very kernel on which modern punishment had been built: the way in which, from the time of the Enlightenment, science, rationality, and expert knowledge were expected to outweigh emotive, uninformed common-sense, thereby ensuring that reason outweighed anti-reason in the development of penal policy. Now, however, slamming the door in the face of reason, penal populism drives up imprisonment rates when the detrimental effects—social and economic—of imprisonment are well known; or it reaffirms the place of capital punishment in modern penal systems when it is well known that there is no conclusive evidence about its deterrent effect; or it targets the bodies of offenders, in a reversion to punishment of the pre-modern era, rather than compelling them to forfeit time or money in line with the expectations of punishment in the modern world.

Most analyses of these developments have treated penal populism as a kind of localized event within the social body, as an aberration from the direction of punishment in modern society, as an infection that can be diagnosed, provided with treatment and exorcized: at which point, it is thought, the voice of reason will once again be allowed to drive modern penal arrangements in a progressive, humane direction and away from such excesses.

This, however, is a matter of little consequence to populism and its forces. What drives it is not any legacy of reason and the Enlightenment, but anger, resentment, and the construction of a magical politics around these emotive forces that promises to eliminate at a stroke all of the demons and devils it identifies. In taking back control, in making a nation (such as the United States) great again, who then needs former President Barack Obama's commitment to tolerance, compromise, and our common humanity, the values of liberal democracy.

Who needs evidence, rationality, facts, science, and all the other attributes on which modernity itself has been built? Yet, as Jonathan Freedland writes, evidence, facts and reason are the building blocks of civilization. Without them we plunge into darkness. And as this darkness falls, so it brings with it the end of Reason and all its light.

Ronald E. Goodwin (Prairie View, Texas A&M University), in Chap. 4, **"White Supremacy and the Politics of Race,"** writes that "Many in our society believed Barack Obama's first election as United States president in 2008 was a sign that it had finally evolved beyond its racist past." Sadly, writes Goodwin, this was not the case: "White supremacists continue to use racially influenced political policies to maintain their particular view of society: a view in which people of color are relegated to the margins." As a result, racial politics continue to undermine the theoretical principles of democracy by advancing the goals of specific groups over others.

According to Goodwin, U.S. history has been marked by many instances of racial politics. Four hundred years after captured Africans arrived on the banks of the James River and "more than two hundred and thirty years after the Founding Fathers conceded to Blacks being considered less than a whole person," he writes. "Some still regard the Black community as inferior and endorse policies that reinforce these absurd notions of race. After Jim Crow, after the revival of the Ku Klux Klan, after enduring segregation, and police shootings, and extreme right-wing persecution, so it remains in some political circles today, among Donald Trump and his base. Trump purposefully spoke to this group like two old friends over a game of dominoes," says Goodwin. He was seeking to expose that part of conservatism that could easily be confused with racism. Even though the Republican leadership saw Trump as merely a political neophyte, his acumen in riling his audiences during rallies could not be ignored, nor could his appeal to White nationalists. Trump's White nationalistic rhetoric intensified along with his primary victories. Soon, signs touting White nationalism were appearing prominently at rally after rally. Instead of racial stereotypes portraying Black men as lazy except for mainly imagined violence toward whites (often women), Trump's twenty-first-century southern strategy emphasized rhetoric that disparaged Muslim and Latino immigrants. His claims that Mexico would pay for a wall along the Mexico—United States border sent his "base" into a frenzy, although only a small fraction of his precious wall was built, and Mexico paid for none of it. Racial politics was suddenly front-and-center again as he pummeled Barack Obama.

Goodwin concludes that, by definition, a post-racial society is one in which the racism that once defined American society would no longer exist. Racist policies used to benefit one group over another will have been eradicated. Symbols of race-based hate will no longer appear in public. And, as Martin Luther King, Jr. once said, a post-racial society is one where everyone would be judged by the content of character over the color of skin.

Many thought this society had evolved to that point with Obama's election as president in November 2008. Sadly, this was not the case. In the presidential campaign of 2016, the politics of race that many thought no longer existed returned with a vengeance. Two hundred and twenty-one years (2652 months) after the Founding Fathers compromised with their slave-holding contemporaries to limit Blacks to a status of three-fifths of a White man, a Black man was elected to the presidency of the United States. The political backlash of this event was vicious. As a result, Goodwin closes, the politics of race continue to be a defining feature of this republic—to a lethal point where the police service revolver can become a new lynching tool.

In **Chap. 5, "*The Civil Rights Movement in Urban Microcosm*: Omaha, Nebraska,"** we face another widespread stereotype: that Nebraska comprises nothing except corn, beef (e.g., "Omaha Steaks"), pigs, and White farmers. How could a vibrant Black community exist in a place such as this? While the state *does* have plenty of corn, beef, hogs, and White farmers, Omaha, its largest city (metropolitan population about 800,000), also contains a long-enduring Black community, the birthplace of such historic figures as Malcolm X and Ernie Chambers. Omaha also includes a rapidly growing Latino community, with a renovated main shopping street. Meatpacking, once Omaha's staple industry has since moved out of the city. Most of the Blacks and Latinos have remained.

Relatively small Midwestern cities that include Black communities such as Omaha's, offer some unusual distinctions. Omaha hosted some of the United States' first lunch-counter sit-ins and bus boycotts before this civil-rights tactic became better known in the South in the 1950s. It also has been home to Ernie Chambers, probably the longest-serving Black member of a statehouse in the United States. In 2020, Chambers had served 50 years, interrupted only by a term-limits law.

Another such city is Tulsa, Oklahoma, which contained a mostly Black business district that came known as the "Black Wall Street," until it was burned out by mainly White mobs.

The Tulsa race massacre took place there on May 31 and June 1, 1921, as at least 300 Blacks were killed, and the area was bombed from the air, the earliest (and very likely *only*) airborne gutting of American people, their homes, churches, and businesses by other Americans within the United States.

Like Tulsa and other turn-of-the-century working-class cities, Omaha's history also has been marred by eruptions of anti-Black racial violence. In 1890, several hundred European Americans formed a mob that seized Joe Coe, a Black worker, from a jail cell after he had been accused of kidnapping a five-year-old White child. Coe was killed and lynched as thousands of whites danced with glee. The same city, however, was the home of Ernie Chambers, a state legislator who became the longest-serving person ever to serve in its Unicameral (statehouse), and a city institution.

Chapter 6, in "*Black-facing, White Shaming, and Yellow Journalism*: A Jaundiced View of How Contemporary 'Political Correctness' Erodes First Amendment Principles." Kenneth Lasson, Professor of Law, University of Baltimore School of Law, dissects conflicts concerning different interpretations of free speech. "In a world of rapidly changing norms, standards, and sensitivities," writes Lasson, "it has become increasingly difficult to state one's opinions without fear of repercussion. The idea that what happened years ago can so easily come back to haunt current status and career ambitions is troubling on a number of levels, not the least of which is the danger it poses for traditional American notions of due process and civil liberties."

Lasson continues by saying that the twenty-first century has presented new challenges to the traditional ways that free speech in America has been encouraged and protected. This is particularly so on college and university campuses, the very places that pride themselves as being relatively open forums for ideas. Numerous campus speech codes substantially limit First Amendment rights. They come with new catch-phrases like "trigger warnings," "safe spaces," and "cultural appropriation"—all calculated in one way or another to shelter students and others from the honest give-and-take of discussion and debate about topics that might be controversial. Lasson asserts that those with opinions that might challenge campus orthodoxies are rarely invited, and sometimes disinvited after having been scheduled, or even shouted down or otherwise disrupted. According to Lasson, when protestors disrupt campus events, administrators often choose to look the other way, and students rarely face disciplinary actions.

Lasson writes that the latter-day dilution of free speech has been generated at least in part by the rise of postmodernism—generally defined as skepticism, irony, or distrust toward traditional narratives, ideologies, Enlightenment rationality, perceptions of human nature, morality, social progress, objective reality, absolute truth—in short, the whole concept of reasoned discourse.

On the other hand, postmodernism itself is difficult to define because to do so would violate its proponents' premise that there are no definite terms, boundaries, or absolute truths. During the past few years, scholars have come to espouse distinctly opposing views regarding the rights and responsibilities of colleges and universities toward their students regarding freedom of speech on campus. "Nationalism" has become a byword that divides. So has the term "identity politics," which has come to signify a wide range of political activity and theory based on the shared perceptions of injustice toward members of certain social groups.

Of the many examples that can be cited to illustrate the somewhat bizarre manifestations of liberal angst are the phenomena of "Blackfacing" and "White shaming." Citing U.S. founder James Madison, Lasson says that every American has his or her right to say, write, and read what he or she wants. Opinions conflict, of course, and on person's truths may be another's "alternative facts."

"Don't be misled," said Scott Pelley, a CBS News anchor, "Any constraint on 'the press' applies to every citizen's voice." Is this the voice on an "enemy of the people," in ex-President Trump's (or Josef Stalin's) phrase? We are the American people. Journalists bring vitality to the national conversation. We bridge differences, serve public safety, expose corruption, constrain power and give voice to the voiceless. As Madison might say today, freedom of the press is the right that guarantees all our other rights. Or, as Thomas Jefferson, writing to Edward Carrington in 1787, with elegant phrasing much beloved by newspaper editors and journalism professors: "The basis of our governments being the opinion of the people, [its] very first object should be to keep that right; and were it left to me to decide whether we should have a government without newspapers, or newspapers without a government, I should not hesitate a moment to prefer the latter." Or, writes Lasson, "No mail bomb, no president, no Congress, can alter one enduring fact of freedom—there is no democracy without journalism."

However, in the real world, there exists no such thing as completely unbiased news. One's truth may be another's "fake news." As Lasson writes: "Even if a journalist tries to report only facts, he or she must still decide which ones to include and in what order. Phrasing also differs subjectively." And: "Consumers of news should seek opposing points of view and draw their own conclusions. They should recognize that many of today's media outlets rely on a business model that encourages them to sensationalize news; they rely on advertising, which pays more money when they get more viewers or clicks. These types of outlets should be used only to *confirm a source*. **They should understand that the sole purpose of many** sites is to amass viewership and profits. And, yes, some seek to spread false information for political purposes. Journalists and editors are not unlike anyone else, but they are subject to pressures that confine their narratives and reporting. Would objective and ethical news coverage yield better results?"

Politics always involves causes and comparisons of policies and personalities—but fairer coverage would mean more healthy debate—and perhaps a better outcome for the nation and its collective psyche. And debate, most assuredly, is what Lasson finds on his scholarly tour of journalistic fits and misfits.

In **Chap. 7, "*U.S. House of Representative Ilhan Omar*: Fighting Nativism and White Supremacy in the Spirit of Queen Araweelo,"** Dorian Brown Crosby, assistant professor, Department of Political Science, Spelman College, places a newsworthy spotlight on Ilhan Omar, the first Somali refugee elected to the U.S. Congress. She is also one of the first two Muslim Congresswomen. Before heading to Washington, D.C., she became the first of two Somali women elected to a state legislature, winning the Minnesota House of Representative seat vacated by Keith Ellison, an African American, and a Muslim. While her elections on state and national levels of government "were cheered by Somalis in the United States and on the Diaspora, this news was less than welcomed by resentful White supremacists and nativists. Some outright hated her," writes Crosby. "Anti-refugee, anti-Somali sentiments and stereotypes of Somalis." "Some as terrorists in Europe and around the globe are the same negative narratives and images produced in the United States to fuel resistance to resettling Somali refugees."

Omar's elections also were a case in point in an amazingly polarized United States, where *E Pluribus Unum* ("Out of many, one," the United States' traditional motto) has been tested in practice nearly every day in our national conversation. While such a conversation may have been (slightly) more genteel in the past, today, writes Crosby, "Such conflict underlies social attitudes, immigration, as well as foreign and domestic public policies." "Exhibit A" may be [or have been] behind ex-President Trump's unvarnished favoritism toward one side of the spectrum, on which Omar Ilhan found herself on the other side. One can hardly imagine Trump quoting that motto as he orders the locking Latino children in cages, away from their parents, awaiting deportation.

Trump's Tweets and rhetoric against Representative Omar are indicative of White supremacists' and nativists' rejection of her as a person and as an elected official. Thus, this essay is a political-sociological analysis of the attacks that House member Ilhan Omar endures from President Donald Trump. It explores the fact that her racial, gender, religious, ideological, and class identities do not represent whom nativist and White supremacists envision as an American and power player.

"Currently," Crosby writes, with unusual insight, "the United States is structured to operate as a liberal democracy. It strives to uphold its ideals of freedom, equality, and justice for everyone. However, it fails miserably in many instances, especially regarding citizens pushed to the periphery of society. Previous presidents—regardless of their political ideology and their shortcomings—have always upheld the United States as a democracy. Under President Donald Trump, however, these principles are being tested. It is safe to say that for the first time in history, Americans are experiencing an aggressive, unapologetic, move away from liberal democracy toward authoritarian rule."

The legend of Queen Araweelo dates back centuries in Somali history. For men, she represents agitation against a patriarchal society. For women, however, she is the epitome of the strength and intellect a patriarchal system dismisses or restrains. There are different versions of her story. The most often recounted one places her in early Somalia around the fifteenth century. As the oldest of the king's three daughters, she automatically assumed the throne. As a child, she rejected Somalia's socially constructed gender roles. She wanted the same opportunities to gain an education as Somali boys.

In **Chap. 8, "Tainted Blood: Scientific Racism, Eugenics and Sanctimonious Treatments of Aboriginal Australians: 1869–2008,"** Australian scholar Greg Blyton writes that the Eugenics movement that emerged in England in the latter half of the nineteenth century was a continuance of European scientific racism sustained by a flotilla of political and academic ignorance that defined human credibility by hereditary traits, including color and race. The movement may be defined as a European intellectual promotion to scientifically improve western societies through state systems that regulated human reproduction.

In Australia, the foundations of the eugenics movement were heavily influenced by two former Cambridge University students, English scientists, Sir Francis Galton (1822–1911) and Charles Robert Darwin (1809–1882). It was a case of intellectual imperialism with colonial policymakers in Australia willingly adopting eugenic ideologies from their two English tutors. However, it would be unfair to blame a single man for the sanctimonious ways his concepts and theories were applied in policy and practice in relation to the treatment of Aboriginal Australians by Australian federal and state governments. The exploitable resources here were an entire continent and its resources, as well as the human capital of its indigenous peoples. Even more tempting to the invaders were natural resources such as coal, the world's main source of climate change, and, well into the twentieth century, uranium.

There appears to be a strong tendency to downplay the influence of the Eugenics movement in Australian history with a counter-claim that policymakers were motivated by humanitarian reasons regarding the governance of Aboriginal Australians. This well-meaning cliché is also found in histories in countries outside Australia where draconian measures were used to manage indigenous and other minority group populations. Despite many negative impacts of Eugenics, policymakers believed they were doing the right thing when the movement started, "…in the early part of the twentieth century by seemingly well-intended scientists and policy makers, particularly in the United States, Britain, and the Scandinavian countries."

In **Chap. 9,** "*Brazil and Australia*: **The Fires This Time,**" **Bruce E. Johansen** combines the science of climate change with the insidiousness of racial and cultural conquest that propels national borders. In this case, the causal agent is intense wildfire, which victimizes the entire living array in Australia and Brazil—plants, animals, indigenous peoples, and (mainly) European immigrants. While everyone and everything suffers from this apocalyptic amalgam, the longest-lived plants, creatures, and human beings are among the first in line to be extinguished by the ruination of the environment by fire.

In 2019, 2020, and 2021, the signature malady of the global climate crisis became raging wildfires. They occurred with previously unknown size and ferocity in California, the Amazon Valley, and Australia (as well as many other places, from Chile, to Siberia)—and even, perhaps as an indication of things to come, along the west coast of Greenland. In each of the wildfires' major sites, environmentalists have run smack into political systems dominated by established nationalistic interests with mindsets (whether the U.S.A.'s Donald Trump, Brazil's Jair Bolsonaro, or Australia's Scott Morrison) at least a century and a half old—which is to say able, with straight faces, to deny that greenhouse gases are a problem at all. In each case, this denial has been fed by copious amounts of political cash from established interests that have become very good at combining oil, gas, and coal to produce corporate profits. If carbon dioxide had a sense of irony (or even a sense of humor), it would have been roaring with laughter. As it is, in our world, greenhouse gases have no political preferences, no emotions, no envy, and no sense of guilt about ruining Planet Earth. All they do is hold heat.

Similarly, when the worldwide COVID virus crisis exploded in March 2020, Bolsonaro extended his adamant denial to it, comparing the disease that already had killed tens of thousands of people to the common cold. Bolsanaro also said that anyone who took a COVID-19 vaccine would turn into a crocodile. Was Bolsanaro exercising a warped sense of humor, or displaying the intelligence of a peanut when he said that Brazilians had a unique ability to resist the virus because they had been steeped in prayer and sewage. Soak them in enough sewage, and they will survive anything, he inferred. "God is Brazilian!" he told supporters. "The cure is right there". When vaccines became available, Bolsanaro turned them down, asserting that they would turn his compatriots into crocodiles. This is not stand-up comedy. Bolsanaro is the elected leader of one of the Planet's largest national entities, one who makes Donald J. Trump look like Albert Einstein. One supposes that the crocodiles should be consulted.

Many Brazilians rose *en masse*, pounding pots and pans in the streets to oppose what they regarded as insane statements by Bolsonaro. An impeachment movement grew apace. Several state governors instituted stay-at-home orders. Twitter, Facebook, and Instagram deleted Bolsonaro's rants against social distancing as a threat to public health. In the *favelas* (slums) of Rio de Janeiro, drug gangs and community leaders imposed nighttime curfews and urged residents to restrict outdoor movements to essential tasks. Bolsonaro accused the news media of inciting panic to undermine his influence. By May 2020, the undertakers could not commission burial places fast enough to accommodate the dead who were collapsing in the hundreds per hour.

And, summoned by their respective dry seasons, as in both Brazil and Australia, the wildfires turned increasing swaths of both countries into piles of ashes as the wealthy continued old habits, such as turning coal, uranium, and oil into profits. All over the earth, it seemed that the cultural pull of old habits was running head-on into a brick wall of urgent necessity, old assumptions against new realities that will not be optional for our planet, or its peoples.

In Chap. 10, Barbara Alice Mann, a professor of Honors at the University of Toledo, traces the history of slavery in the United Kingdom, which also is outlined in its seminal Mansfield decision. Briefly stated, the holding of slaves was (and remains, of course) illegal there. Slaves did stop in British ports, locked below decks in ships making the infamous trade triangle between Africa, Europe, and North America where the market in human beings provided the second-largest class of asset, after the trade in land. The trade in slaves was such an attractive asset despite the fact that about a quarter of them died, their lifeless bodies thrown overboard.

Having read this book, we have an intellectual exercise to propose. What would have happened if Great Britain's Mansfield decision also had covered the Americas? This short question could elicit some long answers.

Omaha, NE Bruce E. Johansen
Cape Town, Union of South Africa (USA) Ad Akande
November, 2021

1

"I Can't Breathe:" Dying While Black in America: Today's Lynchings and Ending the Heritage of Slavery

Bruce E. Johansen

The murder of George Floyd on May 25, 2020, and the ensuing trial of Derek Chauvin almost a year later rubbed raw the bloodiest stain on the United States' history and its world reputation. The 9 minutes and 29 seconds during which Chauvin's knee crushed the spark of life out of Floyd was not unusual in the history of the United States. Before the U.S. Civil War, disobedient slaves were routinely beaten to death for evading orders or for running away, then lynched.

At that time, human beings, as a group, comprised the second most valuable class of assets in the soon-to-be severed United States of America. The most valuable class of assets was land. As a large-scale owner of both these assets, president-to-be Andrew Jackson sometimes bet the lives of slaves in poker games. In almost two centuries after Jackson's two terms as U.S. president, Blacks have achieved nominal freedom but as this chapter and expert essays that follow indicate, it is a freedom that has been conditional on inequity of wealth, social, and legal discrimination.

The strength and severity of this repressive system are not well known by most European American people. The USA has by far the largest incarceration system of any country on Earth. Taken as a percentage of population, Black, Latino/as, and Indigenous peoples (especially men) make up a large majority

---

B. E. Johansen (✉)
Communication and Native American Studies, University of Nebraska at Omaha, Omaha, NE, USA
e-mail: bjohansen@unomaha.edu

© The Author(s), under exclusive license to Springer Nature Switzerland AG 2022
B. E. Johansen, A. Akande (eds.), *Get Your Knee Off Our Necks*,
https://doi.org/10.1007/978-3-030-85155-2_1

of prisoners, who often are held for minor crimes for which many whites would not be arrested. The lynching rope has often been replaced by the service revolver. None of this is new in the United States; what is new is the number of people rising up in protest, a figure in the millions around the world after Floyd's murder. Even with so many miles marched and voices raised, life-threatening crimes against Blacks and other minorities *increased* in the United States after Floyd's murder. On average, three people have been dying per day (2019–2021) in police shootings within the United States.

If you are doing time in New Orleans, or many other of the United States of America, you are very likely Black, more often than not crowded into prisons and jails overloaded beyond capacity, without adequate air flow or air conditioning during some of the hottest, most humid summers on Earth. As a prisoner, you are very likely taking medications for psychiatric conditions (22%), or hypertension (18%); you may have asthma (18%), or diabetes (6%). All of these medical conditions make people more vulnerable to heat (Prison Policy, 2018). You are also in a prime location for pandemic diseases, such as COVID-19. "For a large number of inmates," according to one expert observer, "prison terms became death sentences" (Aviv, 2020, p. 56).

Cummins Unit, a penitentiary in southeastern Arkansas, was not unusual when, by April 25, 2020, test results indicted that 826 inmates of about 3000, as well as 33 staff members, tested positive for COVID-19, less than 2 months after the first death occurred in the United States (Aviv, 2020, p. 59). By August 2020, San Quentin prison in California reported more than 2200 cases and 25 deaths among a prison population of 3265. In Arkansas, hospitals outside prison walls at Cummins Unit refused to treat dying inmates, who often died in their beds in makeshift wards. Staff and government officials routinely under-reported deaths. Dozens of inmates who had died were reported as having recovered. At one point, the governor of Arkansas was told that Cummins had only 12 positive cases (Aviv, 2020, pp. 62–64).

In 2018, the United States had the highest incarceration rate in the world, at about 700 per 100,000 people; Russia had about 400 behind bars; the United Kingdom had 139 inmates, Canada, 114; France, 102; Italy, 96; Norway, 74; Germany, about 70; the Netherlands, 59; Denmark, 59, and Iceland, 38. Louisiana, at 1050, was consistently among the highest in the United States, along with Mississippi, Alabama, Arkansas, Arizona, Georgia, and Oklahoma. African Americans were incarcerated in the United States at more than five times the rate of whites. Louisiana was one of 12 states in which more than half of state inmates were Black. Around the world, per 100,000 people, The United States makes up about 5% of the world's population but had 21% of the world's prisoners (Prison Policy, 2018).

The prisons in Louisiana are among the most notorious in the U.S. South. Their "alumni" include Archie Williams, who served 37 years of a life sentence for a murder he did not commit. He was exonerated with DNA evidence and help from the Innocence Project. After his release, Williams became nationally famous for singing on "America's Got Talent," and also as an inmates' rights activist.

A high incarceration rate inflicts widespread societal damage. As David Leonard and Yaryna Serkev wrote in the *New York Times* (2020): "Time in prison casts a long shadow, leaving people with lingering health problems as well as permanently damaging their ability to find decent-paying work. Mass incarceration is a major reason that, even before the [COVID] pandemic hit, about 30 percent of middle-aged Black men were not working in a typical week. Many of them do not count as unemployed because they are incarcerated or because they have stopped looking for work."

By July 2021, when the Coronavirus killed more than 600,000 people in the United States (600,000 as of June 3), jails and prisons were identified as one of its major vectors, with Blacks and Latinos its major victims. Because of the swift nature and speed of COVID-19 infection and spread, Eric Reingart, a Ph.D. candidate in anthropology at Harvard University, found that "for each person cycled [arrested, charged for a minor, non-violent crime], and released from the Cook County Jail [in Chicago] an additional 2149 cases of COVID-19 appeared in their ZIP code within three to four weeks after the inmate's discharge…Cook County Jail cycles about 100,000 people through its doors every year, approximately 75 percent of them Black" (Reinhart, 2020, p. A-19). All in all, 94% of offenders at the same jail were booked for non-violent offenses.

Quit Harassing Black People "for Petty-Ass Shit"

Typically, the inmates are Black, young men or women, who are found guilty for a string of minor offenses and lack the money to post bail, stuck in a maze of legal bureaucracy, losing their families as they are shuffled around a network of Louisiana or other state prisons. *The New Yorker* personalized these elements with the life of Roslyn Crouch, mother of 12, who was living in New Orleans with six of her children and her mother; one of her children had sickle-cell anemia. Crouch, age 42 in 2020, had chronic bronchitis and was very afraid that she would get coronavirus. Her neighborhood had little competent medical care; while Blacks made up about 30% of Louisiana's population, they suffered 60% of the state's documented coronavirus deaths

(Stillman, 2020, p. 16). In late March 2020, Louisiana was experiencing the highest coronavirus infection rate in the world; the state also had the highest incarceration rate in the United States (Stillman, 2020, p. 16). The crowded and rarely sanitized prisons and jails had become sinks for the coronavirus.

On March 14, 2020, with coronavirus endemic all around her, Crouch drove to a dollar store with her 2-year-old son, Kyi, to stock up on canned food and toilet paper so that she could shelter in place. She ran a stop sign, and was pulled over by a police officer, who ran a rap sheet on his cruiser's computer, and found a string of minor offenses, including lack of registration for the car, driving with a stolen license and a 9-year-old warrant for possession of marijuana (Stillman, 2020, p. 16). Crouch was hauled off to the Jefferson Parish Jail while her daughter Tae took Kyi. The New Orleans police had not yet adopted an experiment in "decarceration" which advised judges to vacate minor warrants against hundreds of non-violent inmates, especially in California, to reduce exposure to coronavirus, as well as to reduce crowding and expense.

A Family's Story

Meanwhile, in New Orleans, Crouch's children had raised enough money to bail her out, and the family celebrated. They thought that Mom would be home for dinner. The police then refused to release her for reasons that no one in her family understood. Later, Thomas Frampton, a public defense lawyer, found that police were acting on the basis of a 4-year old material witness warrant to extend Crouch's incarceration. Such a warrant is issued on people who may have no charges levied against them (or may even be victims of a crime) to insure that they will be available to testify (Stillman, 2020, p. 19).

Appeals for Crouch's release went unanswered as the number of coronavirus cases rose, and prosecutors told judges that public defenders were using the disease as an excuse to get their clients out of jail. The police continued to arrest mainly Black young people for minor crimes, crowding them into prisons and jails that were already overcrowded and rife with coronavirus. People familiar with the prison system recalled Hurricane Katrina, in 1995, when the prisons' staffs abandoned the 6500 inmates, who remained locked in their cells without food, water, or ventilation as dirty water rose around them (Stillman, 2020, p. 19). After the hurricane passed, Human Rights Watch reported that more than 500 inmates had not been accounted for; children being held in the prison found some soggy dog food and ate it (Stillman, 2020, p. 19).

In 2020, what ravaged the Orleans Parish Jail was not a hurricane, but a rising tide of coronavirus. More than 100 inmates became sick with the virus, and two sheriff's deputies died. Crouch herself experienced aches and shivers, as she lost her sense of smell, a hallmark symptom of the virus. Frampton, meanwhile, confronted police and judges, and, on March 19, won Crouch's release. She walked out of a jail filled with hundreds of people, mainly Black, who could not afford bail, raked by the virus. She felt immensely lucky to be free—and alive.

She told Sarah Stillman of *The New Yorker* (2020, p. 120) that if she ever crossed paths with the Orleans Parish district attorney, she would tell him (or her): "I want to thank you for getting me out of the dog cage. But, Lord, there are other things for you to worry about right now rather than harassing people for petty-ass shit."

Blacks and Mass Incarceration

Beginning in the 1970s, "the United States undertook a national project of over-criminalization that has put more than two million people behind bars at any given time, and brought the U.S. incarceration rate far above that of any other nation in the world. A closer look at which communities are most heavily impacted by mass incarceration reveals stark racial and ethnic disparities in U.S. incarceration rates in every region of the country." (Wagner & Sakala, 2014). As of April 18, 2020, Blacks, 13% of the population, made up 40% of the jail and prison population, according to the U.S. Census. Latinos, with 16% of the population, had 19%; whites had 64% of the population and 39% of inmates according to the Census Bureau's correctional facility data, which includes individuals incarcerated in federal prisons and detention centers as well as in state and local facilities.

According to the US Department of Justice, African Americans accounted for 52.5% of all homicide offenders from 1980 to 2008, with Whites 45.3% and "Other" 2.2%. The offending rate for African Americans was almost 8 times higher than Whites, and the victim rate was six times higher. Most homicides were intra-racial, with 84% of White victims killed by Whites, and 93% of African American victims were killed by African Americans (Sakala, 2014a). In addition, in New York City, police kill Blacks at 7.8 times as many as whites on a per capita basis; in Chicago, this figure is 27.4; in St. Louis, it is 14 times, according to a database compiled by Mapping Police Violence (Finnegan, 2020, p. 51). The figures are averages for 5 years ending in 2019,

Then there is the sheer cost of incarceration, which has been accelerating. In Juvenile Hall, the cost of a room is about as much as a very fancy suite in a luxury hotel. "The average state cost for the secure confinement of a young person is now $588 per day, or $214,620 per year, a 44 percent increase from 2014" (Sticker Shock, 2020).

Torture by Temperature

Air conditioning has become nearly universal across the U. S. South during the last 30 years, with one exception: in prisons. Although 95% of households in the South use air conditioning, including 90% of households that make below $20,000 per year. The reason for this is heat and humidity during summer months that have been aggravated by global warming. Conditions can become lethal. In Texas, a state that has air conditioning for all inmate housing areas in only 30 of its 109 prisons, a high percentage of incarcerated people are particularly vulnerable to heat. "The lack of air conditioning in Southern prisons creates unsafe—even lethal—conditions. Prolonged exposure to extreme heat can cause dehydration and heat stroke, both of which can be fatal. It can also affect people's kidneys, liver, heart, brain, and lungs, which can lead to renal failure, heart attack, and stroke" (Jones, 2019). "Conditions such as diabetes and obesity can limit people's ability to regulate their body heat, as can high blood pressure medications and most psychotropic medications (including Zoloft, Lexapro, Prozac, Cymbalta, and others but excluding the benzodiazepines). Old age also increases risk of heat-related illness, and respiratory and cardiovascular illnesses, such as asthma, are exacerbated by heat," said one analysis (Jones, 2019).

The structure of prisons and prison life can also make incarcerated people more vulnerable to heat. Prisons are mostly built from heat-retaining materials that can increase internal prison temperatures. Because of this, the temperatures inside prisons can often exceed outdoor temperatures. Moreover, people in prison do not have the same cooling options as people on the outside. As *Prison Legal News* disclosed in a 2018 article on prison air conditioning litigation, "People outside of prison who experience extreme heat have options that prisoners often lack—they can take a cool shower, drink cold water, move into the shade or go to a place that is air conditioned. For prisoners, those options are generally unavailable." Even fans may be inaccessible. For example, despite the fact that incarcerated people in Texas are not paid for their labor, a fan in the Texas prison commissary costs an unaffordable $20.

The lack of air conditioning in prisons has already had fatal consequences. In 2011, an exceptionally hot summer in Texas, 10 incarcerated people died from heat-related illnesses during a month-long heat wave. (It is not only incarcerated people who get sick from the heat in the state's prisons. In August 2018, 19 prison staff and incarcerated people had to be treated for heat-related illnesses.) As David Fathi, director of the American Civil Liberties Union National Prison Project, explained to *The Intercept*, "Everyone understands that if you leave a child in a car on a hot day, there's a serious risk this child could be injured or die. And that's exactly what we're doing when we leave prisoners locked in cells when the heat and humidity climb beyond a certain level." An incarcerated man in Texas described how torturous heat becomes in prisons: "It routinely feels as if one's sitting in a convection oven being slowly cooked alive. There is no respite from the agony that the heat in Texas prisons inflicts" (Jones, 2019).

Refusing to install air conditioning is a matter not only of short-term cost savings but of appearing tough on crime. State and local governments go to astonishing lengths to avoid installing air conditioning in prisons. In 2016, Louisiana spent more than $1 million in legal bills in an attempt to avoid installing air conditioning on death row, an amount four times higher than the actual cost of installing air conditioning, according to an expert witness (Jones, 2019). Similarly, in 2014, the people of Jefferson Parish (New Orleans) voted to build a new jail only after local leaders promised there would be no air conditioning.

With air conditioning nearly universal in the South (as are brutally hot and humid summers), it should not be considered a privilege or amenity, but rather a human right. States and counties that deny air conditioning to incarcerated people should understand that, far from withholding a "luxury," they are subjecting people to cruel and unusual punishment, and even, in effect, handing out death sentences. Courts in Wisconsin, Arizona, and Mississippi have ruled that incarceration in extremely hot or cold temperatures violates the Eighth Amendment. However, these court cases have not had a national impact on air conditioning in prisons under the federal aegis.

Inmates and staff are living in an environment that is a petri dish for the spread of disease, most notably easily transmitted maladies such as the coronavirus that began to ravage not only prisons, but also meat packing plants, U.S. Navy aircraft carriers, and nursing homes by March of 2020. Within less than three months, more than 100,000 people had died of coronavirus in the United States, many in nursing homes, packing plants, and prisons. Some states by May 22, 2020, had expedited releases for non-violent inmates due to the corona virus. Examples included:

- Massachusetts jails in Plymouth and Norfolk counties reduced their prison populations by around 20%.
- County jails in Colorado and Florida are reporting population decreases by over 30% over a few months.
- On May 19th, a federal judge ordered the federal Bureau of Prisons to "expedite the release" of 837 people.
- Only three states had not suspended medical co-pays for people in state prisons: Nevada, Hawaii, and Delaware.
- Prisons and jails are amplifiers of infectious diseases such as the coronavirus, because social distancing is impossible inside and movement in and out of facilities is common. But criminal justice officials have the power to prevent coronavirus deaths.
- Some state and local governments have been taking meaningful steps to protect people behind bars (and the general public). "We've also published a detailed guide to what the criminal justice system should be doing, as well as several other resources about the coronavirus in prisons and jails," according to one source (Responses, 2020a, b).

Prejudice May Wear a Black Robe

- An investigative series in the *Sarasota Herald-Tribune* said that: "Justice has never been blind when it comes to race in Florida. Blacks were first at the mercy of slave masters. Then came Jim Crow segregation and the Ku Klux Klan. Now, prejudice may wear a black robe. Half a century after the civil rights movement, trial judges throughout Florida sentence Blacks to harsher punishments than whites. They offer Blacks fewer chances to avoid jail or scrub away felonies. They give Blacks more time behind bars—sometimes double the sentences of whites accused of the same crimes under identical circumstances" (Salman et al., 2016).
- The same report found that Florida judges were sentencing Black defendants to far longer prison sentences than whites for the same offenses. For the same drug possession crimes, Blacks were sentenced to double the time of whites (Salman et al., 2016) Blacks were given longer sentences in 60% of felony cases, 68% of the most serious first-degree crimes, 45% of burglary cases, and 30% of battery cases. For third-degree felonies (the least serious types of felonies in Florida), White judges sentenced Blacks to 20% more time than whites, whereas Black judges gave more balanced sentences (Salman et al., 2016). One judge responded by noting that about 98% of sentences are the result of plea-bargaining and that sentencing is a compli-

cated issue given the various facts involved, thus no two cases can be compared (Salman et al., 2016). Some attorneys note that poorer defendants often rely on public defenders who often receive less favorable plea offers than defendants with private counsel because private attorneys have lighter case loads, are less likely to go to trial with prosecutors, and defendants with means are more likely to present mitigating factors (Williams, n.d.).

The Engrained Nature of U.S. Racism

The engrained nature of U.S. racism, especially in the U.S. South, is especially evident in the names of avowed White supremacists that have been affixed to U.S. Army bases. A *New York Times* editorial (Why Does, 2020) described the deep roots of racism on the nomenclature of U.S. military history:

> The White supremacist who murdered nine Black churchgoers in Charleston, S.C., [in 2015] dispensed with the fiction that the Confederate battle flag was an innocuous symbol of "Southern pride." A murderer's manifesto describing the killings as the start of a race war, combined with photos of the killer brandishing a pistol and a rebel flag, made it impossible to ignore the connection between Confederate ideology and a blood-drenched tradition of racial terrorism that dates back to the mid-nineteenth century in the American South.

Defense Secretary Mark T. Esper said he was open to discussions that could lead to name changes for ten Army bases named after Confederate generals, among them Fort Hood, Fort Lee, and Fort Bragg. *New York Times* columnist Paul Krugman wrote (2020, p. A-24) "These bases honor men who stood for slavery, the opposite of freedom, and as it happens, two of the biggest bases are named for generals famed not for victories, but for defeats. Bragg, whose army suffered an epic rout at Chattanooga, was one of the Civil War's worst-regarded generals. John Bell Hood squandered his men's lives in futile attacks at Atlanta and Franklin, then led what was left of his army to annihilation at Nashville."

The "stars and bars" has come off several southern states' flags; by June 2020, the last one came down, at least for a time. A resolution to do so passed both houses of the Mississippi legislature on June 29, 2020, and later was signed by the governor, Tate Reeves, to redesign the 126-year-old flag without the Confederate battle flag symbol. "Still embraced by many White Mississippians as a proud display of Old South heritage, the flag increasingly has come to evoke segregation, racial violence, and a war that had a central aim of preserving slavery," Rick Rojas wrote in the *New York Times* (2020, p. A-19).

The notorious nature of police behavior in the South had some recalling that many police departments began as slave patrols. Mississippi now has the United States' highest percentage of Black residents. The legislators took the action after a barrage of mail, phone calls, and testimony by a wide array of people of all ethnicities, inside and outside Mississippi, that the flag's retirement date was overdue. "This entire state is screaming for a change," said Phillip Gunn, a Republican who is speaker of the House (Rojas, 2020, p. A-17). The new design was ready in September 2020 for a popular referendum on the November ballot. Polls showed that nearly half of Mississippians still supported the old banner. In 2001, voters emphatically supported the retention of the stars-and-bars flag. Since then, many cities and towns and all of Mississippi's eight state colleges and universities have taken the old flag down.

Confederate symbols could be found in some unusual places, and easily missed if one was not looking closely. For example, Washington, D.C.'s National Cathedral dismantled stained-glass windows displaying Confederate general Robert E. Lee (the commanding general) "in saintly poses" (Why Does, 2020). Another example is the Edmund Pettus Bridge in Selma, Alabama, which is best known today as the site of significant civil-rights marches during the 1960s. Less well known is Pettus' biography; he was a U.S. Senator, a Confederate general during the Civil War, and a Grand Dragon in the Ku Klux Klan. Momentum has been building to rename the bridge after John Lewis, 80, the long-serving "conscience" of the U.S. House of Representatives, in which he served several terms. Lewis, who died July 17, 2020, at age 80, had his skull cracked by Alabama State Troopers as he and roughly 600 other people walked across that bridge seeking voting rights on March 7, 1965.

Lewis lost consciousness during the beating in which the troopers attacked with tear gas, bullwhips, and clubs. At that point, he later said "I thought I was going to die" (Remnick, 2020, p. 8). Lewis had been a civil-rights activist since very early in his life, raised on histories such as this: Jesse Thornton, manager of a nearby chicken farm, called a police officer by his first name, not "mister." For that, he was pursued by a mob, stoned and shot, then lynched. Thornton's body was dumped into a swamp, where it was found two weeks later, having been ripped apart by vultures.

Criminalization of Black Peoples

When Blacks win release from jail or prison, they face more than the usual adjustment problems. They also face a United States where, among other obstacles to maintaining life and limb while Black, there is constant, unsolicited attention from the police. Shootings by police, often fatal, have become the new lynchings.

The day-to-day nature of anti-Black racism in the United States is not confined to the U.S. South, although it may have been most frequently displayed there. Enough Blacks (most often, but not always men) have been murdered so often by police across the country—North and South—that thumbnail sketches of each case's circumstances could fill an encyclopedia. One will recall that the following people who were assassinated, murdered, and framed during the civil-rights movement included Medgar Evans (1963, Mississippi), Hattie Carroll (1963, Baltimore), and Rubin Carter (1966, New Jersey).

Today's shootings have roots in the stark class differences of slavery, which were turned on their heads following the Civil War, under Reconstruction. Suddenly, whites who had been slave masters found themselves challenged by Blacks, who were buying farms and starting businesses. By the end of the nineteenth century, the whites were forming the Ku Klux Klan and other supremacist groups in an attempt to recapture their former status by terrorizing Blacks. During Reconstruction, an effort to constitute a multi-racial legislature in Louisiana was destroyed by an alliance of the embryonic Ku Klux Klan and other White supremacist groups, whose members "In broad daylight…stabbed or shot to death nearly two hundred Black supporters of multi-racial democracy" (Lucas, 2020, p. 74). Thus began the "Jim Crow" era (named after a genre of minstrel show in which whites smeared their faces with black color and staged demeaning skits, such as Step 'n Fetchit). As an accompaniment to "blackface," any attempt at political or economic assertion by Blacks was crushed.

From about 1880 until the passage of civil-rights laws during the 1960s, Jim Crow included a wide variety of laws (often called Black Codes) meant to deny Blacks the right to vote, hold any jobs except the most menial, get an education, or engage in many acts of personal or group improvement. Those who attempted to violate Jim Crow laws often faced arrest, fines, jail sentences, violence, and death. Stereotypes of Blacks also were enhanced "as inferior, lazy, dangerous, sub-human animals, and Black men in particular as 'Black beasts,'" wrote Cynthia L. Robinson, chair of the Black Studies Department at the University of Nebraska at Omaha. "This narrative of Black inferiority encourages a post-slavery criminalization of Black people that allows police brutality and killings of Black people to go unpunished" (Robinson, 2020, p. 5-B).

George Floyd's Murder Lights a Fuse

Witness, notably, George Floyd, 46, who was seized by a half-dozen Minneapolis police officers Monday night, May 25, 2020. They handcuffed Floyd, then shoved his head between the wheel rim of a police cruiser and a paved street, and suffocated him. Officer Derek Chauvin rammed his beefy knee onto Floyd's throat and pressed progressively harder as Floyd said, then moaned "I can't breathe!" twenty times, becoming weaker and weaker. Floyd called out to his deceased mother and children, and then gasped his last words: "Momma, I love you. Tell my kids I love them. They'll kill me! They'll kill me....I'm dead!" One of the officers told Floyd to "Stop talking. Stop yelling. It takes a hell of a lot of oxygen to talk" (Oppel & Barker, 2020, p. A-1). Chauvin continued to press his knee against Floyd's throat for 9 minutes and 29 seconds, rolling it back and forth, crushing Floyd's neck, depriving his brain of oxygen. Soon, Floyd's body was limp and lifeless. An ambulance was called, and Floyd was pronounced dead at a nearby hospital. The ambulance was delayed because drivers had been told that they were being called for a minor injury.

The first police report asserted that Floyd had been "under the influence" (of *what* was left to the imagination of the reader) and that he had "physically resisted officers" and appeared to be "suffering medical distress" (Burch & Eligon, 2020, p. A-1). The report further asserted, without proof, that Floyd had been carrying a forged $20 bill. How the police had determined on the basis of a few minutes of observation on a public street that the bill was faked also was left to imagination. How did they know that Floyd had done the faking? Again, such things were left to observers' imaginations. And even if Floyd had somehow faked the bill, since when is the punishment for possession of a fake twenty-dollar bill grounds for summary execution, punishable by asphyxiation? "Every bit of what I saw was wrong," said Minneapolis Mayor Jacob Frey. Minneapolis Police Chief Medaria Arradondo fired four of the officers within hours of the incident as a small crowd gathered at the site, shouting that the officer who had crushed Floyd's throat should be charged with first-degree murder (Burch & Eligon, 2020, p. A-1).

The police did not know at the time that a bystander had video-recorded the entire sequence of events on a cellphone. By Tuesday, the video and sound were burning a screaming trail across the Internet around the world, contradicting the police report, as anger intensified. Once again, a Black man had been shot, whipped, or crushed to death in the United States by police whose monumentally flawed reports had been undercut by cellphone audio and video.

Within a few hours after Floyd's death, rioting broke out in Minneapolis, and demonstrations spread across the United States. Simmering anger propelled fires and looting for several nights beginning May 27, along miles of streets in Minneapolis' sprawling inner city, including a police precinct station, which burned after officers fled in an area that could be compared to Los Angeles' Watts. The National Guard was deployed. While Minneapolis is generally known beyond its borders as a livable city, Blacks there earn one-third as much as whites and graduate from high school at much lower rates. Unemployment is much higher among Blacks than whites; 70% of whites own their homes; 27% of Blacks do. Household assets (savings, home ownership, etc.) display a stark color line more similar to that of a Southern city. The police force in Minneapolis in 2020 was 91% White, and well known among Blacks for its brutality. The murder of Floyd was not an isolated incident or an accident, but part of a pattern. The 19% of Minneapolis residents who are Black in 2020 found themselves on the receiving end of between 56% and 68% of police use-of-force incidents, neck restraints, takedowns and joint locks, attacks by service dogs, use of chemical irritants, and taserings (Oppel & Gamio, 2020).

The death of Floyd was *more* than part of a pattern. It was unusually brutal, with no resistance by Floyd whatsoever, except to ask for his mother and then gasp, several times, "I can't breathe!" In addition to its witness by hundreds of millions of people around the world, the asphyxiation of Floyd was the proverbial straw that broke the camel's back. Thus the ferocity and widespread number of the demonstrations and riots. On the scene of the riots, outside a looted Target store, Cynthia Montana said that Blacks often are treated as inferior or mentally ill. "It's like layer and layer and layer of gunpowder building over a long time. And when you become an adult, it's this stick of dynamite" (Furber et al., 2020, p. A-1).

Participants in demonstrations seemed to come in several varieties: the vast majority, of mixed ethnicity, and mainly young, were peacefully exercising their rights to assemble and petition their government, usually before sunset; a minority who mainly came out after sunset, many of whom were ideological anarchists, or people looking to break windows to score a wide-screen TV, jewelry, clothing, et al. Others were White supremacists who were aiming to tarnish the peaceful *bona fides* of the peaceful majority, bait that was very quickly swallowed by such political luminaries as President Trump and his attorney general, William Barr, as well as self-professed members of Trump's base who had convinced themselves that the whole thing was set up (as Trump and Barr characterized them), by "domestic terrorists." Several months later, Barr had lost none of his venom toward the demonstrators. If they had been involved in "sedition," said Barr, that is, according to legal doctrine, "conduct or speech inciting people to rebel against the authority of a state or monarch." Trump also came out for punishing Black-history advocates when he said while speaking at the National Archives on September 17, 2020, that schools had become "infested" (a word usually used in reference to insects) with "Marxists" who are "indoctrinating" students with such things as the wicked nature of slavery. Trump, it would seem, advocated "Patriotic" education based only on curriculum without discussion of racism or other unsettling concepts ("critical race theory"). This is part of a line of attack that would forbid teaching regrettable episodes of U.S. history. The teaching of history thus becomes an ice cream of sugary delights (Crowley, 2020, p. A-19).

The killing of Floyd and its graphic portrayal on media around the world brought out crowds comprising hundreds of thousands of people, then a total, around the world, of millions, of all races and ages, calling for an end to police brutality. So it was across the United States, day after day: In New York City, Austin, Texas, Portland, Oregon, Boston, Denver, Los Angeles, Atlanta, Boston, Miami, Philadelphia, Washington, D.C., Chicago, San Francisco, Seattle, Houston, and many other urban areas. Hundreds of thousands of people, mainly young, and surprisingly multi-ethnic, marched peacefully, as a small minority, mainly White and advocates of anarchy, smashed store windows and stripped shelves empty, threw Molotov cocktails at police, and torched some of their squad cars. Streets of buildings burned, giving President Trump and his toady attorney general William Barr reason to proclaim that the whole thing had been set off by anarchist agitators (Antifa was most of often named), ignoring the genuine rage behind the anger.

The entire United States National Guard was called out across the nation to repress the United States' largest expression of "street heat" in its history. After a week of righteous protests and anarchistic pillage, Trump swore to call out the U.S. Army to quell the tide of demonstrations, although the law on this subject (written in 1813) allows dispatch of troops only after requests from individual states' governors. When governors refused to provide the requests that he demanded, Trump slathered them with one of his favorite insults: weak jerks. Senior officers at the Pentagon also criticized the deployment of troops against U.S. citizens. Others said that such a thing had never before occurred. In fact, it had. President Abraham Lincoln sent federal troops to New York City during the early 1860s to suppress anti-draft riots during the Civil War; in 1967, almost 5000 Federal troops were dispatched to Newark, N.J. during racial riots. Fourteen square miles of the city were blocked off, and about 7000 people were arrested. In February 1965, Watts, part of Los Angeles, burned during protests of anti-Black police brutality. Federal troops were not called in, but the National Guard and police arrested about 4000 people (Lepore, 2020, p. 24).

The huge rallies, marchers, and small riots of 2020 were different. They were mainly (but not completely) peaceful, of mixed ethnicity, and national (and, after a few days, worldwide). The *New York Times* tallied all of the demonstrations in the United States in support of George Floyd. The total for two weeks (May 26 through June 9) was estimated at 2000 to 2500 (Where Two Weeks, 2020, F-4-F-5.) In Salt Lake City, population 200,000, overwhelmingly Republican and Mormon, 2% Black, several thousand people marched and shouted for several nights, several thousands at a time. So many people became involved that medical experts warned that a new wave of coronavirus might emerge, as many people ignored social distancing and many did not wear masks. Rallies of 50,000 or more for several days running were not unusual in some large cities such as New York, Boston, Philadelphia, Washington, D.C., Houston (Floyd's hometown), Los Angeles, San Francisco, and Seattle. According to four national polling organizations (The Kaiser Family Foundation, Civis Analytics, N.O.R.C [previously, the National Opinion Research Center], and the Pew Foundation, between 16 million and 26 million people marched in June, making this the largest group of demonstrations on the same issue in United States history (Buchanan et al., 2020, p. A-15). National civil rights and anti-Vietnam war marches during the 1960s were smaller and less frequent, said professor Deva Woodly, associate professor of politics at the New School in New York City. "Really, it's hard to overstate the scale of this movement," said Woodly. [In the 1960s and early 1970s] "We [were] talking about hundreds of thousands of people, but not millions" (Buchanan et al., 2020).

The coincident invention of cell phones and the rise of Black Lives Matter was no accident. The killing of Trayvon Martin, 17, of Florida, by a Neighborhood Watch volunteer in 2012, was an early observable victim, followed by Michael Brown, 18, in Ferguson, Mo. in 2014. Many others also were killed, but not much publicized. All of that changed with the death of George Floyd in 2020, which precipitated national and world outrage, described below. Three months later, it was Jacob Blake, as Portland, Oregon was convulsed by protests and riots the day that Floyd's neck was crushed.

When Blake was shot seven times in the back, the nightly unrest had continued for 3 months.

The protests had an immediate, arresting impact on nationwide public opinion. According to several polls, Trump's approval feel sharply, between 4 and 12 percentage points. Joe Biden, the presumptive Democratic nominee in the fall, 2020 presidential election, was nearly invisible, standing by, watching Trump flail and implode with racist rage. In the polls, approval of Black Lives Matter soared, perhaps because of the evident justice of its cause, fortified by the fact that while it targeted Black issues, participants in their two weeks-plus of rallies were elegantly inter-racial—the Blacks welcomed everyone. *Everyone's lives mattered.*

Their cause also was eminently adaptable. Thousands of scientists, for example, called a one-day strike on June 10 in support of the cause. Minneapolis public schools and the University of Minnesota terminated their contracts with the Minneapolis Police Department. The National Football League reversed its ban on "taking a knee" during the National Anthem before the beginning of games. And, as discussed elsewhere in this chapter, the U.S. Army came on board to discuss changing the bases' named after Confederate generals because they were traitors who were fighting for the maintenance of slavery. Speaker of the House of Representatives Nancy Pelosi pledged to remove eleven statues of Confederate luminaries from the U.S. Capitol, including Jefferson Davis, president of the Confederacy, and Robert E, Lee, its commanding general. The list goes on, for example, to the U.S. Military Academy at West Point, where Lee, who was a student there and later West Point's superintendent, "is honored throughout the academy. His name adorns a gate, a road, and a barracks as well as portraits on the walls" (Baker & Cooper, 2020, p. A-22). Trump adamantly refused to even consider changing the bases' names. If Congress tried to change the names, said Trump, he would veto the annual defense authorization bill. The next day, the Republican-controlled Senate Armed Services Committee passed the authorization bill with a clause attached that would require renaming bases, equipment, monuments, or symbols referring to the Confederate States of America within 3 years.

Black Lives Matter's message also became adaptable over time and space, over the Earth, from Sydney to Tokyo, London, South and North America. A major reason that response was so large, fast, and furious was that so many cities have their own roll calls of fatal encounters with police, usually, but not always, including Black men. This was true in smaller cities as well. For example, in Omaha, Nebraska, a small city about 250 miles southwest of Minneapolis, several thousand people gathered in protest at one of Omaha's busiest intersections, 72d and Dodge streets, recalling previous police shootings in its inner city, north of downtown. The crowds grew after President Donald J. Trump, playing this usual role as incendiary-in-chief, posted a condemnation of the demonstrators on Twitter, which the social media platform censured as incitement to violence: "When the looting starts, the shooting starts." The looting had already started in Minneapolis, as many people took Trump's comment to suggest that the demonstrators should be shot.

Protesters in Omaha blocked the intersection as police used tear gas to disperse them. The next evening, a Saturday, several hundred people assembled at the same location, planning a march eastward along Dodge Street about a mile to Memorial Park. Police confronted the marchers with tear gas. The scene then turned into a riot, with some demonstrators breaking windows of shops along Dodge Street. Police formed a phalanx and arrested several who rained rocks and bottles on them.

So why such an outpouring of anger in a small city? Peoples' reasons for protesting were very similar to those in larger cities:

> Many people complained that mass incarceration of Black and Hispanic inmates has replaced slavery as a way to maintain racial inequality, and some Black men told stories of being pulled over and questioned by police for "driving [while] Black." About 26 per cent of Nebraska prison inmates are Black, but only 5 per cent of the state's population is Black.

Trump meanwhile was itching for a fight, as he called for the deployment of the U.S. armed forces against American citizens, something that their commanders, including Defense Secretary Mark T. Esper, refused to do. Mark A. Milley, chairman of the Joint Chiefs of Staff, sent a letter to Trump, and to all men and women under his command (18% of whom are Black) that they had all taken an oath to defend the Constitution, not Trump, and that includes the First Amendment. Milley did not mention Trump by name, but he wrote, in his own hand, at the bottom of the letter addressed to the president: "We all committed our lives to the idea that [this] is America—[and] we will stay true to that oath and the American people" (Schmitt et al., 2020, p. A-1). The message was clear: if Trump wanted to impose martial law on the United States, he would have to do it without the U.S. armed forces. It took some guts, no doubt, to pull rank on the commander in chief in favor of The U.S. Constitution.

In Washington, D.C. on June 1, Trump ordered about 100 armed officers in riot gear from several federal agencies to push peaceful protestors out of Lafayette Park near the White House gates, using tear gas, flash-bang grenades, and rubber bullets, so that he could walk to St. John's Church, a landmark historical site, holding a *Bible*, for a photo opportunity that was meant for use in campaign advertising. Some witnesses asked sardonically how many armed men were required to escort a grown man one block to have his picture taken with a *Bible*. Others noted that in some of his poses, Trump's *Bible* was being held upside down. The Episcopal diocese of Washington, D.C., whose jurisdiction includes the church, criticized Trump severely for not asking permission to use it. Rev. Mariann Budde said Trump was using a church as a prop for a message that was "antithetical to the teachings of Jesus and everything that our churches stand for" (Antithetical, 2020).

The next day and evening, the protests around the United States became larger yet, for the eighth afternoon in a row. Moreover, protests were spreading around the world: London, Paris, Berlin, and Sydney, Australia, where 3000 people marched in solidarity with Americans, as well as indigenous Australians (Cooper, 2020).

Seattle's "No Cop Co-op"

In Seattle, protesters took over a police precinct house on Capitol Hill, east of downtown, then cordoned off five or six blocks and declared it an Autonomous Zone, or, to the more ideologically inclined, "The Peoples Republic of Capitol Hill"…[A Cop-Free Co-op]. By June 13, the area had been occupied for a week. President Trump was hiss-spittingly enraged, firing off tweets demanding that Seattle Mayor Jenny Durkan and Washington Gov. Jay Inslee "crack down" on the "domestic terrorists" who had "taken over Seattle" (Baker, 2020a, p. A-20). If Durkan and Inslee did not deal with this affront to Trumpian Law and Order, he vowed to take care of it himself. Trump did not deal with how he came to declare the occupation of an area five blocks long and two streets wide as "taking over" an urban area about 50 miles north-south by 20 miles east-west.

> Take back your city NOW. If you don't do it, I will. This is not a game. These ugly Anarchists must be stooped [*sic*] IMMEDIATELY. MOVE FAST!" "Domestic Terrorists have taken over Seattle, run by Radical Left Democrats, of course. LAW & ORDER!" said Trump. Inslee responded with a tweet of his own, telling Trump to stay out of the state and, mocking the president's Twitter typo: "A man who is totally incapable of governing should stay out of Washington state's business. 'Stoop' [*sic*] tweeting," Inslee said. (Cummings, 2020)

As might befit a city that had voted 8% for Trump in 2016, just about everyone laughed him off. The fire chief stopped by the liberated zone and had an amiable chat. Durkan shot back to Trump on Twitter: "Make us all safe. Go back to your bunker" (Baker, 2020, p. A-20). Durkan's June 11 tweet continued: "Lawfully gathering and expressing First Amendment rights, demanding we do better as a society and provide true equity for communities of color is not terrorism—it is patriotism…. The Capitol Hill Autonomous Zone #CHAZ [Later changed to the Capitol Hill Organized Protest zone] (CHOP) is not a lawless wasteland of anarchist insurrection. It is a peaceful expression of our community's collective grief and… desire to build a better world. Given his track record, it's not hard to believe that Trump is wrong, yet again."

City workers brought potted flowers and made sure that everyone had access to porta-potties. Carmen Best, the chief of police, ordered her officers to stand down, after a clash the previous week in which police had used tear gas, flash-bangs, and pepper spray during a Black Lives Matter march. This time, the police had chosen to be more careful. Occupants painted a Black Lives Matter mural on a block-long stretch of street, and bought hot dogs from vendors, as they sought to turn the police station into a community center, and the police department's funding toward health and social services (A Look, 2020, p. 5-A).

This was not the first time that citizens of Seattle had occupied real estate in defiance of the police. The tactic has a storied history. During 1970, an alliance of ethnic groups led by Native Americans occupied parts of what was Ft. Lawton, which was being declared surplus by the U.S. Army, an extension of many similar occupations led by the American Indian Movement in places such as Alcatraz. The occupants at Ft. Lawton engaged in three pitched battles with Army military police but won several acres on which they built what became the internationally acclaimed Daybreak Star Center, where everyone is welcomed to take part in social services, workshops, and indigenous entertainment.

In October 1972, a multi-racial alliance led by Latinos occupied the empty, decrepit Beacon Hill School and began to renovate it with their own hands, becoming El Centro de la Raza ("The Center for Peoples of All Races"), while Seattle Police kept a respectful distance. The building was eventually leased from the City of Seattle for $1 a year, as services for the poor were begun, as well as businesses and community groups. As it had in other Seattle demonstrations, income inequity had been something of a silent partner in these protests, beginning with El Centro's founding, because Black family net worth in the United Stated was roughly one-tenth that of whites. Income inequity in the United States by 2020 was more skewed than it had been for more than

100 years, the Gilded Age. Jeff Bezos, co-founder of Amazon.com in 2020 was worth roughly $200 billion. On one day (July 19, 2020) he added a record $13 billion to his fortune. *By then Bezos was personally worth more than Exxon Mobil, Nike and McDonald's, combined.* Young whites, who often marched with Black Lives Matter, also realized that wealth is skewed age-wise as well as race-wise.

Later, El Centro de la Raza renovated all three floors of its old building, as it was listed in the National Register of Historic Places. Affordable Housing was added, adding to a roster of services that include multi-lingual child development, and many others, which are described in a book (Johansen, 2020).

As police stood down in Seattle again in June 2020, and as President Trump blew his orange-tinged top over what he regarded as a takeover of the city by anarchists while the mayor and governor told Trump to keep hands-off. The number of people in the "No Cop Co-op" swelled to several thousand, who inscribed a street with "BLACK LIVES MATTER" in bright yellow block letters. Most stores in the zone remained open. On June 15, seriously right-wing news outlets carried notices that a group of "patriotic bikers" were preparing to crash the party at the CHAZ ("American Patriots Re-take the Seattle Occupation Zone for America" July 4). They invited anyone with a Harley Hog, a flag, and a serious case of ass-whupping right-wing attitude to join them.

Anyone who read their press releases (which characterized the occupiers as "anarchist-dominated…unruly Barbarians…[with] crazed craniums." might surmise that the pseudo-patriotic bikers were not planning a holiday picnic (A Real Life, 2020). On June 20, a 19-year-old man was shot inside the occupied zone after confrontations among people turned violent. Volunteer medics rushed the man to a hospital in a pickup truck, where he died. When police and an aid car arrived in the occupied zone, they were denied entry; the police did not force the point. Another man, age 33, was shot, but not fatally, near the same site at about the same time. Sunday evening, a 17-year old was shot and sustained minor injuries. After the shootings, the size of crowds inside CHOP diminished, as "Others continued to sit on couches and chat at the Decolonization Café" (Baker, 2020, p. A-17). On June 29, two more people, both boys, aged 16 and 14, were shot inside the zone, one fatally, the other critically. Leaders of CHOP were reported by the *Seattle Times* as "trying to reorganize" the Zone, perhaps moving it to a public park. Multiple shootings were not helping CHOP's image as a peaceful frolic.

On July 1, more than 100 heavily equipped Seattle Police officers and tactical vehicles, moved into the CHOP zone to evict the occupants, arresting at least 44 people (At Least 100, 2020). After several shootings in one week, The

CHOP zone was starting to look like South Chicago on a Friday night. After having called the occupation a playful romp a few days earlier, Mayor Durkan, endorsed the police raid, declaring CHOP "an unlawful assembly requiring immediate action" (At Least 100, 2020).

In the department of duplicity, however, while opponents of CHOP cheered lustily when police broke it up on grounds of public safety, the cheering stopped when a 27-year-old man, Dawit Kelete killed one person (Summer Taylor) and seriously injured another (Diaz Love) as he rammed his car into a Black Lives Matter march on Interstate Five in Seattle three days later. This incident was one of 66 intentional car attacks on protestors nationwide that may have been partially spurred by Internet hate speech. In Seattle, the King County Sheriffs Office said that one officer had been placed on administrative leave after he posted an image of a vehicle hitting someone under the words "BLACK LIVES SPLATTER" (MacFarquhar, 2010, p. A-15).

In Washington, D.C., protestors attempted to set up an "autonomous zone" in Lafayette Park near the White House, calling it the "Black House Autonomous Zone." In a tweet, President Trump then said he would use "serious force" against anyone who tried to erect such a zone. Twitter then slapped a warning label on Trump's tweet, saying that it violated company policy against "abusive behavior" (Twitter Puts, 2020, p. B-2). The D.C. "Zone" was short-lived.

In New York City, demonstrators set up an encampment in front of City Hall for several days and nights as the City Council held hearings on the Police Department's budget. The police were not excluded, and no one claimed the property as a special zone. The City Council did cut the NYPD budget by just under $1 billion, redirecting much of the money to social programs. No one was shot, nor arrested.

"We All Breathe the Same Air"

Including Seattle's uncharacteristic fatal shootings, events in the rest of the United States continued to be occasionally grim and bloody. At a standoff in Las Vegas, Nevada, an armed man worked his way into a protest rally, hauled out a firearm, and killed a police officer. The police shot back, killing him.

On Saturday, June 12, officers tazed and then fatally shot a Black man in Atlanta in circumstances that resembled the killing of George Floyd, with bullets replacing a knee to the neck. Rayshard Brooks, age 27, was waiting to be served at an Atlanta Wendy's at about 10 p.m. Saturday, June 13, when he fell asleep at the wheel. Employees at the Wendy's called the police. Two officers,

Garrett Rolfe and Devin Brosnan answered the call. They administered a field sobriety test, which Brooks failed. After that, police video showed Brooks engaging the officers in what appeared to be a casual conversation for more than 25 minutes before they moved to arrest him. A scuffle then ensued, during which Rolfe tazed Brooks. Despite his allegedly inebriated state, Brooks threw a punch, took one of the officers' tasers, eluded both of them, and began running. At one point, Brooks turned and fired a wild taser shot at the officers, missing by a large margin, then resumed running. Rolfe then fatally shot Brooks in the back two times, according to an autopsy, approached Brooks' limp body, and shouted "I got him!" He then kicked Brooks' dying body. The second officer then stood on one of Brooks' shoulders. Suddenly realizing, perhaps, that they had murdered a man, both officers fell to their knees and tried to administer CPR. It was too late. Brooks died in a local hospital after surgery. As word spread that Brooks had been killed, a crowd formed, blocking local roads and an interstate highway. The Wendy's was torched. Within a few hours, Rolfe was told to surrender his badge. Atlanta's police chief, Erika Shields, resigned at the request of Atlanta Mayor Keisha Lance Bottoms.

Within days, a world speed record of procedures what used to take prosecutors weeks or even months, Rolfe was indicted on felony murder and eleven other counts. In Georgia, felony murder can carry a sentence of life in prison without parole, or death. "Mr. Brooks never presented himself as a threat," said District Attorney Paul Howard (Officer Who Killed, 2020, p. 7-A). The other officer, Howard Brosnan, was indicted on a half dozen lesser charges, including aggravated assault. Brosnan also agreed to testify for the prosecution, the first time in 40 such cases that a police officer has turned state's witness in Atlanta.

So what had Brooks done to deserve summary execution by former Officer Rolfe? Falling asleep in his car? Blocking traffic at a Wendy's? Failing a sobriety test? Resisting arrest? Firing an officer's Taser and not hitting anyone or anything? Or, much like George Floyd, being in the wrong place at the wrong time while being Black? Both Atlanta's mayor and the local NAACP leaders agreed that Brooks did not deserve to be killed. By Sunday, June 15, 2020, Brooks' death was ruled as a homicide by the coroner, opening the way for a murder charge against Rolfe.

Similar questions were being raised across the United States. At a rally in Omaha, Anthony Baker, one of the Omaha rally's organizers, asked "Since when does the [alleged] crime of forgery end with the sentence of death? [for George Floyd]" "George Floyd was put 'on trial' in the streets of Minneapolis, and so often…the streets are so often the court of law for Black people.

[Officer] Derek Chauvin was the judge, the jury, and the executioner" (Cole, 2020, p. A-3). Jean Young of Omaha wrote to the *Omaha World-Herald* (May 30, 2020, p. 8-B), "I long for the day when being Black and breathing was not a capital offense." Ernie Chambers, long the Nebraska Unicameral's [state legislature's] only Black member of 49 senators, said that people should pay attention to local deaths at the hands of police not only of Blacks, but also others, such as Zachary Bear Heels, a Native American, who died in police custody during June 2017. The Omaha *World-Herald* published an editorial cartoon (May 29, 2020, p. 5-B) depicting George Floyd's headstone with words from John F. Kennedy: "If we cannot end now our differences, at least we can make the world safe for diversity. For, in the final analysis, our most common link is that we all inhabit this small planet, we all breathe the same air."

Demonstrations Grow Worldwide

On June 3, charges for ex-officer Chauvin and the three ex-officers who stood by and watched Floyd's murder were charged with 2d degree aiding and abetting murder. At the same time, Plans are being made for Floyd's funeral—with a police escort. Demonstrations continued countrywide and internationally for a tenth straight day.

By June 5, the demonstrators had painted BLACK LIVES MATTER in vibrant, visible-at-all-hours bright yellow, on a city street leading to the White House, as close as they could get without running into Trump's Great Wall of armed police in riot gear, which now took up most of Lafayette Park, near St. John's Church, where Trump had held his *Bible* upside down a few days earlier. The mayor of the District of Columbia, Muriel Bowser, going head-to-head with Trump, had authorized the street painting. The mayor also had authorized the renaming of one nearby street George Floyd Avenue, and another Black Lives Matter Plaza. Both are within sight of the White House.

The mayor also told Trump to get all troops and police without jurisdiction in the District of Columbia to march or drive across the Potomac and get out of town. Trump, holding a press conference in the Rose Garden at which no reporters were allowed to ask questions, pointed an unsteady right index finger upward somewhere between the Big Dipper and the Washington Monument, and said that George Floyd was looking down from heaven and giving thanks that he was showering Black people with jobs. (The Black unemployment rate for April, reported the same day, was 16.8%.) This was the 12th consecutive day of protests, with more to come.

On Day 13th, June 7th, crowds swelled to their largest, and nearly wholly peacefully around the world once again, with minimal looting, and few arrests. The police stood down, as a memorial service was held for Floyd in Raeford County, N.C. (He had been born in nearby Fayetteville, and later moved to Texas, near Houston, where he had grown up.)

The next day, people took to the streets once again, in what had by then become the longest consecutive string of protests in United States history. Most of them were peaceful, except for clashes with gas and club-wielding police in Seattle and Portland, Oregon. News about international protests came from Madrid, Spain to Osaka, Japan. "As Barack Obama pointed out in his recent town hall," wrote Jennifer Senior in the *New York Times* (2020, p. A-25), "a far more representative cross-section of America is out protesting in the streets than in the 1960s." Trump and his apologists (as well as Republican campaign advertising) made Black Lives Matter look like a huge pack of bomb-throwing, baby-strangling, blood-thirsty super-hoodlums, but in fact, 93% of BLM-sponsored events harmed no one and damaged no property (Harpers, 2020, p. 11).

Protesters were beginning to define goals. One that went almost without saying was organizing voting campaigns to get rid of Trump. Another was to redirect the funding of police departments in their present form, to reduce their roles as paramilitary organizations and increase funding for community services' role in law enforcement. The proposals also sought more emphasis on rehabilitation over punishment in U.S. jails and prisons, which by 2020 had incarceration rates that were by far the highest in the world.

On June 8, Floyd's funeral was held in Houston, Texas. On the day before the funeral, 14 days after protests had begun, 50,000 people marched in Los Angeles, with smaller rallies nationwide, as voices rose across the country to retrain police officers to adopt ties with the communities they serve, and to fire officers who display violent tendencies by violating acts that should be deemed illegal, such as chokeholds. The *New York Times* on June 8 carried a front-page article describing how some protesters had given up or lost their jobs to make new lives with the movement.

In Minneapolis, Mayor Jacob Frey was hissed offstage on June 7 after he said that the city needed a police force in its present form. Minneapolis' nine-member City Council passed a veto-proof resolution to defund the police. These proposals were being made by people living in communities where policing as it is now conducted has dismally failed to a point that it requires fundamental change. This has been the enduring goal propelling the protests. Those who protested daily acquired a sense of belonging, and a sense that they were making history while seeking justice was being made with their participation, a required next chapter in the United States' long-overdue emergence from its heritage of slavery.

At about the same time, The NASCAR stock car racing association forbade the display of the Confederate battle flag at its races, heretofore a common practice by admirers of the Stars and Bars as a symbol of southern White resurgence. "Gone With the Wind" was pulled from movie streaming services, and the "reality" Television show "COPS" was removed from network air after 32 years of police heroics as prime-time entertainment.

Instead of mourning Floyd's death as his hearse was transporting him to burial, President Trump tweeted a wildly distorted conspiracy theory to his 80 million followers that 75-year-old Martin Gugino, a White peace organizer, who had been shoved onto a concrete sidewalk and critically injured by police during a protest in Buffalo, New York, was an Antifa provocateur attempting to monitor police communications on his cellphone. As Trump sent his tweet, Gugino was about to be released from Intensive Care (ICU) but was still in a hospital in critical condition. (Police communications may be easily tracked using an inexpensive cellphone app. There exists no reason to be shoved to the cement by an officer's nightstick to get access.)

The next day, the conspiracy theorists "doubled down" (one of Trump's favorite phrases) on Gugino, asserting that the blood seen gushing out of his right ear was fake. (Might the doctors in the ICU have noticed?) Lying is one thing. Lying *badly* to gullible people is quite another. From Trump there was no apology, no acknowledgment of error, and certainly no dignity or empathy. No, not ever. George Orwell rolled over in his grave once again, as Trump and his enablers again flunked out of elementary school in the Ministry of Alt-facts. Instead, Trump defended the Stars and Bars and criticized NASCAR for forbidding the display of it at races.

Symbols and Stereotypes

One irony of the stars-and-bars crowd is that its members seemed to *love* stereotypical Native American professional sports mascots, such as the 87-year-old Washington Redskin and the century-old Cleveland Indian. Somehow, such stereotypes have become standard-bearers of White-identity politics. The debate, which first arose during the occupation of Wounded Knee by the American Indian Movement (AIM) in 1973, resurfaced during the debate over ethnic respect *vis a vis* Black Lives Matter. As team owners began to talk about retiring the (R-word), President Trump stepped in, endorsing both as glorious pillars of American popular culture.

The owners of both sports teams this time decided to differ, with a little help from their money-bearing corporate sponsors. Federal Express, for example, said it would take its name off the R-word's stadium (worth $8 million a year) if the (R-word) was not removed. In one week in late June and early July, more than 87 investment firms and shareholders that handle accounts worth a collective $620 billion sent letters asking Nike, FedEx, and PepsiCo to end their financial arrangements with the (R-words) (Cohen, 2020). The issue had swiftly jumped from the sports pages to the financial section, as Amazon. com, Target, Wal-mart, and other retailing giants prepared to remove (R-----'s) merchandise from their shelves. After almost 50 years of resisting change in the face of innumerable protests, at the intersection of cold hard cash and massive protest, on July 13, the owners decided to retire both the name and the mascot. A week later, the Mutual of Omaha retired its 70-year-old Indianhead logo. No one had complained about the Plains Indian-style figure, which was originally adopted "as a symbol of strength and respect," said Mutual's CEO James Blackledge (Cordes, 2020, p. A-1). It was just time to great ahead of the game, he said.

On June 21, with Black Lives Matter's demonstrations entering their third week, the Minnesota Freedom Fund, which pays bail for arrested marchers and allied charitable organizations, reported that almost a million people had donated $30 million, or 300 times what the group had received during the entire previous year. ActBlue, which funds Democratic Party candidates and liberal causes, hauled in more than $250 million during the period that Black Lives Matter and its allies were hitting the bricks (Goldmacher, 2020). This flood of donations was inundating a mainly young, multiethnic coalition in the midst of the coronavirus pandemic, a worldwide economic crash, and relentless Twitter sliming by President Trump, who appeared to be losing the public relations battle to Black Lives Matter, as his job approval polls continued to plunge, along with the margin by which Trump was losing ground to this presumptive Democratic opponent Joe Biden. In fact, many polls indicated that BLM was "moving the needle" in the national conversation over race relations, as well as police behavior. For America, it was a tutorial in a world turned upside down. The coronavirus was a constant reminder of Trump's inane attachment to ridiculous medical hokum. His latest at the time was cure by imbibing industrial disinfectants, such as Lysol. Yes, Lysol might kill the virus, but with certain noxious side-effects, such as also killing the patient.

In the meantime, Black Lives Matter continued to rearrange many Americans' cultural attitudes toward race and racism. Questions about abuses of Black people seeped into all parts of American life. The 11-Worth, an old-fashioned diner in Omaha, closed after demonstrators raised questions about a breakfast entry named after Robert W. Lee. A pair of work boots inscribed with the names of White men who had been killed by police, dripping with ersatz blood, was featured on fashion runways in New York City. Other participants in New York fashion shows raised clenched fists and "took a knee." Quaker Oats retired its brand icon Aunt Jemima from syrup bottles after 131 years. Uncle Ben's rice also (as current biz-buzz has it) was "evolving." Neel Kashkari, president of the Federal Reserve Bank of Minneapolis deplored racism and police brutality, as the King County Labor Council (which includes Seattle) expelled the Seattle Police Officers Guild for making insufficient progress against institutional racism. Lloyd's of London, the venerable insurance firm, agreed to pay reparations for its involvement in the slave trade during the eighteenth and nineteenth centuries.

Police Killings Continue

As the United States and parts of the world convulsed over the death of Floyd, other accounts of police killings on the slimmest of provocations arose, often with videotapes, months or even years old. The number of such killings plus memories indicated that such street killings by police had been excruciatingly common practice across the United States.

In Tucson, Arizona, for example, two months before Floyd's death, Carlos Ingram Lopez, 27, was stopped for questioning while he was walking to his grandmother's house. Police knocked Lopez to the ground, face down, and handcuffed him. He pleaded for water a dozen times and called out for his grandmother ("nana!") as he died. The entire episode took about 12 minutes. A Pima County Medical Examiner's autopsy found that Lopez had died of cardiac arrest, with physical restraint by the officers as a contributing cause (Lopez also had cocaine in his system). According to Bodycam evidence, Lopez said "I can't breathe properly" as he died. Officials equivocated over whether Lopez's death was of natural causes or a homicide. His mother said that Lopez was undergoing a "mental health crisis" that "caused him to behave erratically" (Romero et al., 2020, p. A-22).

A year earlier, Vicente Villela had died as officers held him down in an Albuquerque jail. Villela also said that he could not breathe, laying on his stomach as officers pressed their knees into his back and legs. An autopsy said he had died of mechanical asphyxia, with physical restraint and the presence of methamphetamine in his system as contributing factors. His death was ruled a homicide. The three officers involved in the death resigned, and Albuquerque's police chief offered to resign, but his request was not accepted.

The Death of Breonna Taylor

In Louisville, Kentucky, Breonna Taylor, 26, an emergency medical technician, was shot to death by three Louisville police officers who knocked down her apartment's door on a no-knock warrant on March 20, 2020. Taylor's boyfriend Kenneth Walker shot back, believing that the officers were intruders—which, in a sense, they were. Following intense national criticism over the incident, Police Chief Steve Conrad announced his retirement effective June 30. After a Black business owner, David McAtlee, was fatally shot by police on June 1, Conrad was fired. The fact that the officers had not been charged with murder provoked several days of marches in Louisville by hundreds of people shouting "No justice, no peace; prosecute police." The police announced on June 10 that it would change how its officers serve warrants. No-knock search warrants were banned. On May 29, during a protest march, seven people were injured by gunfire. Several dozen protesters established a camp from which to press for murder charges. On June 28, a gunman sprayed the camp with bullets, killing one person.

During several more weeks of marches against police misconduct that sometimes turned violent, the family filed a wrongful-death lawsuit, as Taylor's name became an icon (with George Floyd and others) in nation-wide protests of police brutality, her family filed a wrongful death lawsuit, which on September 15, 2020, won an award of $12 million and pledges from the city and Louisville police to avoid the kinds of no-knock warrants (including other behavior) which led to her death. On September 14, Taylor's family received a $12 million settlement from the City of Louisville. The use of cash settlements was not unusual in these days of itchy police trigger fingers. For example, the family of Alton Sterling, father of five, who was fatally shot in Baton Rogue, Louisiana July 5, 2016, received a $4.5 million settlement that was not cleared for distribution until almost 5 years after his death. Simmering tension over Sterling's death, plus that of Philando Castile in Minnesota the next day helped to set a tone of incipient violence following the gruesome murder of George Floyd in Minneapolis.

After Taylor was killed, Louisville braced for a ruling on whether any of the six officers involved in the break-in in which Taylor was killed would be criminally charged by the state attorney general. (Two of them were involved in the shooting barrage that killed her.) Downtown businesses were boarded up and police stationed around courthouse grounds. On September 23, after more than 100 nights of demonstrations, a report, recommended no charges directly connected to the fatal shooting of Taylor, bringing demonstrators back onto the streets of downtown Louisville, between cordons of police and National Guard in armed personnel carriers who arrested anyone who stepped the least bit out of line (127 people were arrested) bracketed by boarded windows. The size of demonstrations grew in Louisville, New York, Los Angeles, and several other cities as darkness fell, marching past some of two-dozen billboards bought in her honor by Oprah Winfrey. Taylor also appeared on the cover of Oprah's magazine "O," the first time that space was filled by Winfrey herself. At ground level, as darkness fell and a 9 p.m. curfew came into force, two police officers were injured by gunfire.

On December 29, 2020, more than nine months after Taylor's death in what became widely regarded as a badly botched police raid, two Louisville police officers who were involved in the raid were told they would be fired. One of them was Detective Myles Cosgrove, in his 15th year on the Louisville police force, who had fired three shots at Taylor inside her apartment, killing her. The other was officer Joshua Jaynes, who had arranged the night-time raid on Taylor's apartment. They joined Bret Hankison, also a detective, who had been fired in June for violating the department's deadly force policy, by shooting ten rounds into Taylor's apartment from the outside. The shots also entered a neighboring apartment, for which a grand jury in September had indicted him on three counts of wanton endangerment. The firings came only after months of persistent demonstrations in Louisville and around the world asking "who was safe from the police if officers could kill a promising young woman in her own home and remain on the payroll" (Bogel-Burroughs, 2020, p. A-17).

Taylor had been an emergency-room technician; she received no medical care for half an hour after the fatal shooting. None of the seven officers who took part in the faux raid were wearing body cameras, a violation of Louisville Police Department policy (Browne et al., 2020, p. A-11).

When Taylor is seen on the body-cams shouting, several times, "You've got the wrong place!" she was correct. The target of the raid, Jamarcus Glover, who lived on Elliott Avenue, in West Louisville, ten miles from Taylor's home. A raid by a SWAT team also arrested Glover and others, seizing drugs and other evidence.

Another point of contention and confusion during the raid on Taylor's apartment was the police's method of entry. They had a "knock and announce" warrant. Some of the neighbors said they entered that way. More heard no announcement of police presence, just what amounted to a break-in

45 seconds after the knock, which convinced Taylor's boyfriend, Kenneth Walker, that a break-in was in progress, prompting him to pick up his handgun and shoot at the supposed invaders. The police then shot back with considerably more firepower (Browne et al., 2020, pp. A-11, A-13).

Taylor's death was investigated by the FBI for civil-rights violations and other crimes, as requested, but as of January 2021, the U.S. Justice Department had made no indictments, even as allegations surfaced that Jaynes had lied while the operation was being set up, by saying that a postal inspector had told him that boxes containing drugs were being sent to Taylor's apartment in the name of her boyfriend. According to the grand jury's transcripts, Jaynes had fabricated the story that a postal inspector was sending boxes filled with illegal drugs to Taylor's apartment under the name of her ex-boyfriend. Additionally, Kentucky's attorney general, Daniel Cameron, had told three of the grand jurors that three of the officers who fired their weapons could not be subject to homicide charges.

Another fatal shooting of a Black man near Atlanta contained eerie parallels to the death of Breonna Taylor. As the Associated Press reported from Atlanta: "Johnny Lorenzo Bolton was lying with his eyes closed on a couch in his apartment [near Atlanta] when police serving a narcotics search warrant burst through the front door with guns drawn and no warning. Bolton stood up and at least one of the officers fired, sending two bullets into Bolton's chest. The 49-year-old Black man died from his injuries [in December, 2020]" (Brumback, 2021). However, Bolton's case seemed to get lost in the cacophony of bullets that slew George Floyd, Breonna Taylor and many others in this season of hot lead, shooting first and asking questions later. Local police stonewalled the case and most of the media all but ignored it, excerpt for a detrailed Associated Press report long after the shooting (Brumback, 2021).

"For almost six months, we gave them quiet," Bolton's sister Daphne Bolton told the Associated Press in mid-June, 2021. "That lets me know that's not what gets a response." Now, Bolton said, "I want my brother's name to ring beside Breonna Taylor's. When they say Breonna Taylor, I want them to say Breonna Taylor and Johnny Lorenzo Bolton. I want them to be simultaneous."

Johnny Bolton had run into trouble with the law over the years, usually for drug and misdemeanor offenses, and occasionally was locked up for short periods. He often called his sister, to ask for money. "He always told me, he said, 'Baby Sis, I'm gonna get better.' I said, 'I know you are,'" Daphne Bolton said through tears. "I never gave up hope that he would get better. Now I, unfortunately, will never get to see that day" (Brumback, 2021).

The Killing of Eligah McClain

And—say their names, again, and again, and again. This incomplete roll of the dead by police bullets continues. Next is Eligah McClain, of Aurora, Colorado, 23 years of age, who stopped at a Shell gasoline and convenience store to buy a soft drink for his brother during the evening of August 24, 2019. He paid for the drink and began to walk home, singing and dancing, wearing a black ski mask. Someone in a nearby apartment called 9-11, complaining that he was acting strangely.

A police cruiser arrived, blocking McClain's path. His singing stopped as one of the three officers in the cruiser told McClain he was under suspicion. For what, he asked, by which time McClain was on the pavement, handcuffed, face down, a tight chokehold around his neck, cutting off blood to his brain. McClain's life being crushed out of him. McClain said he was just going home. An officer said, without evidence, that he was "on something," but had incredible strength. An aid car arrived, McClain was sedated, then taken to a hospital, where he died three days later. Summary execution: for what? Buying a soft drink while Black? Wearing a black ski mask while Black? Dancing while Black? Singing while Black? Whatever "suspicion" meant this time, it was yet another twenty-first-century lynching. The police hierarchy said the officers had done nothing "legally wrong." The killing of a young Black man who had done nothing legally wrong seemed, as in so many other incantations, not to cross the legal bar as "wrong."

By the time of George Floyd's death, two million people had signed petitions asserting that McClain's case be re-opened. After the massive reaction to Floyd's death, the state's attorney general announced an investigation, after thousands of protestors assembled in Aurora, Denver, and elsewhere. The three officers who had been involved in McClain's death had been reassigned to desk duty—*for their own safety*. Safety from what? possible attack from a young dead man suspected of being Black? Yes, that's what the police chief's office told reporters, with no apparent irony intended. Try to find another such case with a White man's life terminated in this manner. Try, and try again. Thus, does a very thick book acquire yet another new chapter.

Naming and Shaming: Images and Words of Racism Come Down

As ghosts arose from graves, BLM continued to demonstrate, opening new cases and demanding that statues of Confederate "heroes" come down. A statue of Robert E. Lee in Richmond, Virginia, the former capital of the Confederacy, was retired June 3, 2020, by the state's governor, Ralph Northam. This statue was in a circle at the terminus of a road with similar statues called Monument Avenue. Richmond's Mayor Levoy Staney introduced a measure to have all of the statues removed. By June 10, with Staney's proposal stalled, Black Lives Matter beat the city to the punch, toppling Jefferson Davis, once president of the Confederate States, as police looked on. A statue of Christopher Columbus also was torn down and set on fire in Richmond. Staney, who is Black, later proposed that "Stonewall" Jackson's statue be removed as well. A ten-foot-high statue of Columbus also was removed from the Minnesota State Capitol in St. Paul, about ten miles from where George Floyd had been killed. Other statues of Columbus went down in Columbus, Ohio, and near Columbus State Community College, In Philadelphia, a bronze statue of Frank Rizzo, an infamously racist mayor of Philadelphia during most of the 1970s, also came down.

Meanwhile, four more Confederate statues were beheaded and pulled down in Portsmouth, Virginia. One of the protesters was hit on the head by a falling statue and sent to a hospital unconscious, with his head cut open. The same site had been used as a slave market and whipping post. The protesters gave a sword and rifle that they had ripped from the monument to 73-year-old Vietnam veteran John Hooks. "You've kept your foot on our neck for 401 damn years. When are you going to get the hell off?" Hooks said to what remained of the statue. A brass band played as the statues came down (Ley et al., 2020).

In New Mexico, officials removed a bronze statue of Juan de Oñate y Salazar, the first conquistador to arrive in Nuevo Mexico in 1598. Oñate and a small band of Spaniards killed several thousand native Pueblos and Navajos, and also cut off the right feet of 24 others in retaliation for the murder of Oñate's nephew.

Memories are long in New Mexico; 400 years later, Latinos, Latinas, and Native Americans severed an Oñate's statue's right foot in 1998 (Romero, 2020, p. A-18). One of the protesters was taken to a hospital in critical but stable condition after being shot by a member of a right-wing militia group. At about the same time, activists in northern New Mexico celebrated the removal of another likeness of Oñate that was on public display at a cultural center in the town of Alcalde.

Notre Dame University in about 2018 covered several murals in the main hallway of its nineteenth-century administration building that depicted Columbus. (For those who know the Notre Dame campus, this is the building under the iconic Golden Dome.) It was not until mid-2020 that the U.S. Marine Corps took down the last confederate flag at its installations. Shortly after that, the Pentagon forbade the public display of the Stars and Bars from at any of its installations (that is, any property operated by the U.S. armed forces).

During the first half of the twentieth century, ten U.S. military bases in the U.S. South were still named for Confederate Army officers. Fort Benning, Ga., was named for Henry Lewis Benning, one such general, who argued when the Supreme Court of Georgia "that African-Americans were not really human and could never be trusted with full citizenship" (Why Does, 2020). Benning asserted that the abolition of slavery would lead to the horror of "black governors, black legislatures, black juries, black everything." Benning also believed that legal equality would place White women at the mercy of African-Americans with equal rights to sexual intercourse with them. "We will be completely exterminated," he said, "and the land will be left in the possession of the Blacks, and then it will go back into a wilderness" (Why Does, 2020).

After several Confederate figures' statues were dumped, the movement expanded to include U.S. presidents who had owned slaves. Ulysses S. Grant, for example, was the Union's major military figure and, as president, supervised Reconstruction. A statue of him went down in San Francisco. Theodore Roosevelt was given one slave, whom he freed. Roosevelt was too young to own any slaves before they were freed, but a statue of him at the main entrance to the American Museum of Natural History in New York City was taken down because Roosevelt, mounted on a large equine charger, was flanked by much smaller figures of a Native American on the left, and a Black man, on the right. Roosevelt's statue, 24 feet high (including an eight-foot base), sculpted by James Earl Fraser and mounted in 1940, depicted Roosevelt armed with pistols, "his face alert, resolute, forward-directed; theirs [The Native American and Black men] passive, [eyes] withdrawn [and] cast down (Cotter, 2020, p. C-1). The Museum's directors agreed to the removal of the statue because several indoor venues are named for Roosevelt. Even Theodore Roosevelt IV, 77 years of age in 2020, great-grandson of "TR," a well as a trustee of the museum, consented to the statue's removal.

Princeton University decided to remove President Woodrow Wilson's name from its well-known public policy school. The university also removed his name from a residential college that had been slated for closing. The name was removed for Wilson's racist views on important issues. He believed in eugenics, for example, a pseudo-science holding that intelligence and racial attributes should be bred in or out of a given group. Wilson shared these beliefs with a resurgent KKK. The same doctrines also attracted a surprisingly large following among otherwise genteel White men into the 1930s, when Adolph Hitler and the Nazis' brutal application of its doctrines made eugenics so ugly that its former popularity shriveled to almost zero. Wilson also expelled all non-whites from the federal civil service, after it had been integrated following the Civil War. The civil service had become a major source for Blacks' employment before and after Wilson's presidency; this is why Washington, D.C. is overwhelmingly majority Black today.

Also in the line of fire were statues of George Washington and Thomas Jefferson, who, aside from their major roles in the founding of the United States, owned plantations in Virginia kept running by hundreds of slaves—600 over Jefferson's lifetime. Across the Potomac from Mt. Vernon and Monticello, the U.S. Capitol and White House were built largely with slave labor. Members of the New York City Council also argued for the removal of a Jefferson statue from City Hall. In addition to being a slave owner, Washington also signed a fugitive slave act and freed his slaves in his will, after he no longer had any use for them.

In 2020, journalist and author Lucian K. Truscott IV, a direct descendant of Jefferson, made a case in the *New York Times* that the statue of Jefferson in his memorial dome near the Tidal Basin in Washington, D.C. should be removed, and replaced by a memorial to abolitionist Harriet Tubman. Truscott wrote that the Washington, D.C. memorial has little to teach visitors, whereas his home at Monticello had become a museum describing Jefferson's home life, with rebuilt slave quarters, as well as a restored bedroom that he used to procreate at least six children with Sally Hemings, one of his slaves. "Monticello," wrote Truscott (2020, p. A-19) "is an almost perfect memorial because it reveals him with his moral failings in full, an imperfect man, a flawed founder…a man who wrote that 'all men are created equal,' and yet never did much to make those words come true." An artist with words, Jefferson was a miserable manager of money. After he died, most of Jefferson's slaves were sold to pay his debts.

A statue of another former president, Andrew Jackson, was attacked on June 23 in Washington, D.C.'s Lafayette Park, near the White House. Protesters sprayed "Indian Killer" and "Slaveholder" on the base, strung a rope around its neck and the horse it was riding and were rocking it back and forth when police moved in.

Jackson became infamous among many people (especially Native Americans) for ordering mass emigration of the Cherokees, and others, from the Southeastern United States to "Indian Territory" (now Oklahoma). The mass marches, which killed thousands of people, came to be known as trails of tears. Jackson also bet the lives of Black slaves in poker games but also was acclaimed by many poor whites as a leader who brought democracy to the masses. He had a major role in founding the Democratic Party. When Jackson's opponents called him an "ass," he adopted a donkey as his political symbol. Today, the donkey remains the Democrats' trademark.

The same day that demonstrators nearly toppled the statue of Jackson, one of Trump's favorite presidents, Trump said that he would sign an executive order to make damage to or "tampering with" statues a crime carrying a penalty of up to 10 years in prison. "We're going to do an executive order. We're going to make the cities guard their monuments [with] long-term jail sentences for these vandals and these hoodlums and these anarchists and agitators," Trump said on June 23 (Haberman & Martin, 2020, p. A-24). In the meantime, Donald Trump, Jr. suggested (perhaps half in jest) that toppled statues should be replaced by "more sturdy" monuments to his father (Phillips, 2020).

The marches of 2020 gave rise to narratives recalling the lives of slaves in the "Middle Passage" between Africa and the slave markets of Eastern North America by the likes of Rev. Robert Walsh: small ships carrying 500 or more people crammed below the main deck in space about three feet high, meant for cargo, "packed together so tight that they were sitting up between one another's legs, everyone completely nude....There was no possibility of their lying down or at all changing their position by night or day....[They] sat in their own vomit, urine, and feces, and that of others… Those who died were thrown overboard, [only] so much human flesh…that sharks learned to trail them" (Blow, 2020, p. 21).

Even as Trump fumed over the removal of Confederacy-era statues, Robert E. Lee IV said that monuments to his famous ancestor should go. Lee, who is pastor at Unifour Church and author of *A Sin by Any Other Name: Reckoning With Racism and the Heritage of the South*, said: "Take down his statue, and let his cause be lost" (Lee, 2020). Based on his own writings, the general himself probably would not have wanted a statue of himself hoisted. Such things, he said, "keep open the sores of war" (Boyette, 2017).

Names of other historical figures also became fair game, a history lesson for anyone who was familiar with them who had never looked at the small print in their biographies. "Yale," for example, the Ivy League university was founded on the riches of a slave-trader… (Kimball, 2020, p. A-5). Elihu Yale was an active slave trader who was very good at buying human cargo low and selling high. Born in the United States, turned British, Yale built his wealth as an administrator in India who smuggled slaves to Europe in cargo holds. He was far from alone. A half-dozen of Yale's residential colleges were named after slave owners, including John C. Calhoun, whose name was being removed as this is being written. Among this number are some surprises, including New England firebrand preacher Jonathan Edwards, and F.B. Morse, inventor of the telegraph and Morse Code. Calhoun and Morse thought that slavery was *good* for the human merchandise, as well as ordained by God. Mr. Yale "made a gift that supported the founding" of the university—800 British pounds worth of books and goods, enough to get his name on the marquee. Kimball writes that Mr. Yale, in a cruel time, judging by how often slaves met the whip, had slaves flogged for minor offenses, and hung a boy for stealing a horse (Kimball, 2020, p. A-5).

The people of Black Lives Matter were doing their homework, made easier by the fact that many men of means, especially in the Southern states, owned slaves before Lincoln's Emancipation Proclamation turned the ownership of human beings into a felony. No plantation could have existed without them. The master was not going to pick his *own* cotton. In fact, before the industrial revolution, the two largest types of property in the United States were real estate and human beings. (Francis Scott Key, who wrote "The Star-Spangled Banner," also was a slave owner.) By mid-century, however, slaves were becoming obsolete as fossil fuels replaced their labor, without sociopolitical onus, long before the climate crisis indicted them with destroying the Earth.

Trump continued implicitly to endorse racism and even slavery as he called Black Lives Matter activists hoodlums and anarchists. It is probably no excuse, for Trump did not know why the demonstrators paid such attention to statues. After all, he was the only U.S. president (after December 7, 1941) who couldn't find "Pearl Harbor" in a U.S. history textbook. Trump would rather tell bald-faced lies that members of his "base" cheered loudly at various rallies. He also erroneously accused the demonstrators of pulling down statues of Jesus Christ. All of this was tied into Trump's very tenuous hold on anything even vaguely resembling the truth. He refused to wear a mask or observe social distancing as the number of coronavirus cases raced upwards in California, Texas, Florida, and other states. Trump declared the pandemic over when the U.S. death toll passed 130,000—the same thing he had said when it was at 15. When deaths in the United States grew past about 200,000, he finally said it was a problem. Given usual practice, Trump might have changed his position in 15 minutes. At the same time, Trump's poll numbers in the presidential race were tanking. Against Joe Biden, on June 23, he was behind 50 to 36% in a *New York Times* poll. Trump, as is his custom if a poll finds him behind, said that the polls were being manufactured—fake news. His "internal polls" were said to be much better—but no one was allowed to see them or to examine their sources.

Statues Fall in Europe

Statues feel in Europe, as well. King Leopold II of Belgium, who supervised the colonization of what was until 1960 called the Belgian Congo was memorialized in Antwerp until May of 2020, when 10,000 people supporting Black Lives Matter first defaced, and then removed it. Leopold II's forces seized the Congo, which is 76 times the size of Belgium, and brought in extractive industries that mined a rich trove of minerals and metals, including gold, and diamonds, enslaved the Congolese, and killed about 10 million people who resisted Belgium's rule. No records were kept, so no one knows the exact number killed. Leopold, who was born in 1835 and became king in 1865, gave up his claim to the Congo in 1908 (independence followed in 1960). In 1908, Leopold denied accusations of atrocities but admitted that "most likely cruelties, even crimes" had been committed in his name (Pronczuk & Zaveri, 2020, p. A-16). Another statue of Leopold was painted red, then removed in Ghent.

In England, several slave traders' statues were removed in Bristol and London, as well. These included Edward Colston and Robert Milligan. Colston's company shipped roughly 100,000 Black people from West Africa to the Caribbean and North America. Each was branded with the company's trademark, "RAC," on his chest. Nearly 20,000 died of diseases and lack of water en route, their lifeless bodies dumped overboard. The statue that was dumped into Bristol's harbor honored him as one of the city's "most virtuous and wise sons" (Bhambra, 2020, p. A-25).

The statue of Colston later was replaced very briefly by another of Jen Reid, a Black Lives Matter activist who had climbed atop the base of the former Colston statue, her right fist elevated, after it came down. Artist Marc Quinn created her likeness from black resin and steel, from a photo taken by Reid's husband. Bristol's mayor, Marvin Rees, said that the new statue was erected without city permission and would have to be removed, pending a vote. It was removed the next day, 1/45,625th the length of time that Colston's likeness had stood on the same pedestal.

A statue of Cecil Rhodes (re: Rhodes scholarships), an imperialist whose views helped lay the ideological basis for Apartheid in South Africa, was taken down at Oxford University after several days of large rallies in London. Rhodes' name as applied to Rhodesia, then changed to Zimbabwe in 1979. Earlier, it was a British colony named Southern Rhodesia. Northern Rhodesia, carved out of land claimed by Rhodes' company in 1911, was a British "protectorate" until it became independent in 1964. Today, most of it lies within Zambia. Winston Churchill also came in for criticism for his role in maintaining the British Empire at a time when it was said that the sun never set upon it. Even today, anyone who wants to take part in the world conversation on almost any subject does so in the English language. More people *study* English in China than *speak* it in the United States of America.

As evidence of the world's English heritage, substantial protests in memory of George Floyd reached Australia and New Zealand, where Statues of Capt. James Cook, who first told the English about Australia and New Zealand, were defaced as an oppressor whose explorations brought Europeans to their shores, where aboriginal peoples, including the Maoris, today face issues similar to those of Blacks, Native Americans, and Latinos in the United States (Olsen, 2020).

On July 18, 2020, a John Wayne exhibit at the University of Southern California School of Cinematic Arts was dismantled after racist comments of his came to light a half-century after their initial publication. Among them: "I believe in White supremacy until the Blacks are educated to a point of responsibility" (Sweeney, 2020). Wayne also said, in the same interview, that: "I don't believe in giving authority and positions of leadership and judgment to irresponsible people" (Williams, 2020). Wayne's comments were originally published in a 1971 edition of *Playboy* magazine, which, aside from its infamous photographs of nude women, published some revealing journalism. Calls also were made to remove a statue of Wayne under a huge United States flag in a main foyer of Orange County's John Wayne Airport, returning its name to Orange County Airport.

Wayne also said that White immigrants had a right to push indigenous people off their lands. "I don't feel we did wrong in taking this great country away from them. [O]ur so-called stealing of this country from them was just a matter of survival," he said. "There were great numbers of people who needed new land, and the Indians were selfishly trying to keep it for themselves" (Williams, 2020). Wayne called Orange County home for many years before he died in 1979.

Marches in Portland, Oregon Night After Night, Month After Month

President Trump, meantime, made abundantly clear that he did not regard a month of demonstrations that had swept the world as a reaction to 400 years of Black oppression, but—as he took just about everything that is out of line with his stubborn beliefs—as a personal insult to be ripped into pieces. Trump then began to dispatch squadrons of Federal agents dressed in camouflage and tactical gear, including what looked like colorful toy machineguns to corral what he considered to be an overenthusiastic protest. By August 15, 2020, Oregon, which was experiencing its 80th straight day of protests and occasional violence had become ground zero for Trump's show of force, unleashing tear gas, bloodying protesters with rubber bullets, and pulling some people into unmarked vans in what Governor Kate Brown of Oregon called "a blatant abuse of power." Christopher David, 53, a U.S. Navy veteran, left one night of protests with two broken bones in his hands after the "police" beat him with batons and covered his face with pepper spray.

Portland Mayor Ted Wheeler said, "This is an attack on our democracy." Oregon's United States senators agreed. Mark Pettibone, 29, a demonstrator who was roughed up and then thrown into an unmarked van, said "I felt as if I was being hunted for no reason. It feels like fascism" (Olmos et al., 2020a, p. A-1). A few minutes later, Pettibone was just as quickly thrown out of the van after he refused to waive his *Miranda* rights as he was being questioned about other people.

Protesters often said that the federal "police" were being interjected into Portland's fray to scare them, or provide photo ops for Trump's increasingly unpopular campaign. All of this, in turn, provoked a stiffening of the demonstrators' spines and drew more opponents of Trump's policies to the scene. The lack of training among the "police" and their chaotic nature, which injured several protesters, spread anger, and intensified the conflict. The protesters often seemed more organized than the "police," as volunteers handed out earplugs, eye wash, and hand sanitizer from a van circulated with snacks and Gatorade.

At the same time, protestors created some poignant moments, as when several hundred laid in ranks, face down, on Portland's Burnside Bridge for nine minutes and 29 seconds, the amount of time that George Floyd's neck had been crushed in Minneapolis. After the second night of clashes between demonstrators and the unmarked "police," Saturday evening, July 18, a large group of women formed a "wall of moms," all wearing T-shirts of egg-yolk yellow, to protect the demonstrators, chanting "Moms are here, feds stay clear." Early Sunday morning, the "feds" shoved the women aside with their nightsticks and tear-tear-gassed them (Miller, 2020). Portland police distanced themselves from the federal "police," and said in a statement on Sunday that they did not engage with anyone and did not deploy any tear gas against their fellow citizens. The feds were the outside agitators, nearly all of whom told the "Feds," Get out of our city! Local Walls of Moms also popped up at demonstrations in Seattle, Oakland, and Albuquerque, without federal "police" in sight.

Soon the Wall of Moms in Portland grew to well over a hundred, despite the "Feds'" gassing. They were joined by a Wall of Dads, who brought their suburban leaf-blowers, which they found to be very useful at turning tear gas around. Next came a wall of nurses, in blue scrubs to tend the injured. Other people swept up the debris. After a veteran had been roughed up by "Feds" for asking them a question about the Constitution, a wall of veterans appeared, with the stated purpose of protecting everyone's First Amendment rights. The crowd grew into the thousands as sympathy rallies popped up in other cities, coast to coast.

Oregon governor Kate Brown said that she had requested the removal of the "Feds," but Trump's Department of Homeland Security refused her request, complaining that Portland's federal courthouse was under threat from the demonstrators. Brown speculated that footage was being readied for campaign photo-ops featuring law-and-order tough-guy Trump versus the supposed Antifa hordes. The trigger-finger-in chief was using his 84 million followers to wage a propaganda battle with "sick and deranged anarchists & agitators" who were intent, he said, to inflict damage on Portland that would leave it "burned and beaten to the ground" (Baker & Kanno-Youngs, p. A-1). The next day, U.S. Senator Joni Ernest, Republican of Iowa, who originally had been elected partially because of her self-proclaimed ability to castrate pigs, broadcast a campaign ad claiming that, if re-elected, she would keep America's streets clear of "Antifa mobs." The same theme was pumped out to Trump's 80 million Twitter followers. That middle-aged mom—Antifa! That suburban guy with a beer belly and a leaf blower? Antifa! Those thousands of people behind them? All candidates for a Twitter bombing raid by Trump.

Meanwhile, several hundred people stormed a statue of Columbus in Chicago's Grant Park before a large phalanx of city police shoved, beat, and pepper-sprayed them away. Back in Portland, officials said the presence of federal agents with no identifying markings was making the situation worse, not better, as the agents chased and clubbed, and gassed anyone they could reach for a second straight night, late July 19th and early July 20th Angry demonstrators torched a police union office, as Oregon's attorney general, Ellen Rosenblum, prepared a lawsuit alleging that citizens were being taken into custody without due cause, violating their civil rights. Rosenblum also opened a criminal investigation into circumstances surrounding one protester who sustained a head injury. A week later, a federal judge denied the suit; on Friday night, July 26, several thousand demonstrators once again took out their wrath on the federal courthouse, which was now surrounded by a tall chain-length fence.

By now, the "Feds" and the demonstrators had been doing battle almost every night. The mayor was doused with tear gas one evening, leaving him temporarily blinded as he waded into the battle for a "listening session." "They knocked the hell out of him," Trump cackled on Fox News. "That was the end of him" (Kristof, 2020). He told the Feds that Portland might be only their opening act. "You're doing a fantastic job," Trump enthused. At about the same time, his beloved little goon squad had shot a protester, Donovan La Bella, in the face with "non-lethal" munitions that fractured his skull and required facial reconstruction surgery (Kristof, 2020). In the midst of all of this, some of the protesters burned a *Bible*, an act later attributed to Russian disinformation agents to push observant *Bible* readers toward the Trump campaign. The act also raised an intriguing question: How many of the other acts during the Portland clashes that Trump attributed to the "mobs" of "Antifa" were actually performed by Russian infiltrators to help swing electoral opinion in Trump's favor?

The "Feds" built a tall wire fence around the U.S. Courthouse, which the demonstrators tried (and failed) to topple. They settled for tossing firecrackers over the fence. A group of war veterans formed a protective "wall" between the Feds and the demonstrators. In the meantime, by Saturday, July 27, the crowd had grown into uncounted thousands, as militants, supporters of both sides, tourists, and teenage boys looking for some action surrounded the actual players on both sides. The same day, much smaller left-wing and right-wing "militias" converged in Louisville, Kentucky, and spent much of the afternoon looking at each other, except for one accidental volley of gunshots that injured three people. No one seemed to know who had shot whom. In Seattle, meanwhile, police sprayed tear gas and projectiles into a sizable rally called to support demonstrators in Portland.

Nancy Pelosi, in a tweet dated July 17 said: "Unidentified stormtroopers. Unmarked cars. Kidnapping protesters and causing severe injuries in response to graffiti. These are not the actions of a democratic republic. @DHSgov's [Department of Homeland Security's] actions in Portland undermine its mission. Trump & his stormtroopers must be stopped" (Olmos et al., 2020).

In the White House, Trump said that Portland, Oregon's demonstration of federal force was just the beginning. *Any* large city in the United States that was represented by "radical liberal" Democrats could expect a visit from well-armed emissaries of various federal agencies in unmarked uniforms. Names floated were New York City, Chicago, Philadelphia, and others. As the week went on, the Feds and demonstrators, as conflicts between demonstrators and police (not Feds, yet) broke out coast to coast: Seattle, Los Angeles, Oakland, CA, Richmond, VA, Austin, Texas, et al.

Larry Krasner, the district attorney of Philadelphia compared the conflict to the fight against fascism during World War II, with Trump playing the role of Hitler and Mussolini, and said he would criminally charge any federal agents who exceeded their authority in his jurisdiction "Anyone, including federal law enforcement who unlawfully assaults and kidnaps people will face criminal charges from my office," Krasner said. "At trial, they will face a Philadelphia jury" (Kanno-Youngs, 2020, p. A-1; 2020, p. A-17).

In Portland, targets of the prospective raids generally said that Trump was deflecting attention from the collapsing U.S. economy and his mismanagement of the surging coronavirus pandemic, with a U.S. death toll of 150,000 and counting (766,000 as of November 18, 2021). Here we saw growing a corps of United States storm troopers—a secretive, nationwide police force—created without congressional input or authorization, formed from highly politicized agencies, tasked with rooting out vague threats and answerable only to the president. Trump's dark, self-aggrandizing state of mind had conjured up a monster. A cardboard sign upwind from the Trump troupe read: "FEDS GET OUT NOW! BLACK LIVES MATTER. HERE TO STAY."

After more than two weeks of battles, on July 29, Trump and Portland's mayor seemed ready for a truce (or, as the "Feds" put it, a "phased withdrawal.") "We know where we are headed: complete withdrawal of federal troops from the city and the state" said Gov. Brown. Hey, however, U.S. executive tough-guy twitter-finger had already nixed the agreement. "You hear all sorts of reports about us leaving….We're not leaving until they've secured their city. We told the governor. We told the mayor. Secure their city. If they don't secure their city soon, we have no choice. We're going to have to go in there and clean it out" (Baker & Kanno-Youngs, 2020, p. A-17).

By the end of July, the Feds had departed the scene, leaving the demonstrators to the local police, who were then engaged night after night in a running battle of cat-and-mouse. Only hours before police and activists faced off during the evening of Saturday, August 8, for example. on Portland's East Side, roughly 300 protesters faced off with police outside the Multnomah County Sheriff's Office.

The officers tried to break up the crowd with stun grenades, pepper spray, impact munitions and physical force, but the crowd pushed back by throwing eggs. A few were detained and a photojournalist was arrested for trespassing, the Portland *Oregonian* reported. Later, police claimed they had decided to end the standoff because protesters started throwing rocks and explosive devices (what *kind* of devices was not revealed). In other "direct action" rallies at police buildings, smaller groups of protesters started fires in trashcans, damaged property, and threw various small objects at police, the *Oregonian* reported. Police dressed in riot gear responded "in force" every night, once using tear gas. Trump again and again sounded his familiar alarm on Twitter: "anarchists" and "mobs" were orchestrating the demonstrations. Over and over, he accused local political figures of surrendering Portland to "the mob."

The situation in Portland was considerably more complex than Mob versus The People. For example, on May 19, 2020, about a week before George Floyd had been killed. Multnomah County had elected Mike Schmidt, 39 years of age, as district attorney. Schmidt won the election three-to-one against an experienced opponent. Upon assuming office on August 1, one of Schmidt's first major actions was to dismiss charges against roughly half of the protesters who had been involved in previous protests. He dropped charges against people who were not involved in intentional violence, property damage or theft, upholding their rights to engage in "people's righteous anger and grief and fury over a system that has not been responsive enough for decades and centuries" (Oppel, 2020, p. A-1). The police and county sheriff then expressed their own righteous anger and grief, and fury.

Right-wing talking heads around the country continued to echo Trump's simplistic analysis of Mob versus People while, on the streets of Portland, right-and-left-wing protesters brawled, throwing punches and water bottles. Right-wing extremists showed up with very high caliber assault weapons, showing them off, looking like a heavy-metal fashion show. Black Lives Matter supporters brought wooden shields and paintball guns. "This is a city that likes to protest," said Aliza Kaplan, professor and director of the criminal justice reform clinic at the Northwestern School of Law of Lewis and Clark College in Portland (Oppel, 2020, p. A-13).

Trump Casts Himself on Mount Rushmore

On the eve of Independence Day 2020, standing in front of 7500 fervent supporters in a natural amphitheater at the base of Mt. Rushmore beneath the stone-etched gaze of Washington, Jefferson, Lincoln, and Roosevelt, atop the infamously stolen crown of the Lakotas' Black Hills, Trump had blasted the Black Lives Matter demonstrators and their allies as assassins of classic American culture and heritage, a "mob" (his word) of leftist fascists (a rare breed in world history), "bad, evil people," defacing "our most sacred memorials," who were leaving America "tyrannized" (Karni, 2020). The next evening, Trump repeated the speech nearly verbatim at the national Fourth of July celebration in Washington, D.C., as demonstrators pulled down a statue of Columbus a few dozen miles away, and dumped it in Baltimore's Inner Harbor.

The guests facing Trump at Mt. Rushmore sat in plastic chairs strapped together, offering the occupants a few inches less social-distancing room as the middle seats of a jet aircraft. Trump barely mentioned cases of the COVID-19 virus that had almost doubled in two weeks. Practically no one was wearing masks, as the COVID-19 crisis reached unprecedented levels. Trump, with no evidence, as usual, but a great deal of apparent self-certainty, declared that 99% of COVID cases were harmless.

As the U.S. Navy's Blue Angels roared overhead, Trump made it evident that the preceding months had taught him nothing. Instead, Trump's campaign workers (eight of whom had tested positive for COVID-19) were circulating on social media a fake bust of Trump "carved" into the top of Mt. Rushmore next to the other four presidents. One may have asked: *who* was defacing *what*?

Thursday, September 3, Michael Forest Reinoehi, a self-described antifascist and prime suspect in the fatal shooting of a Trump supporter days earlier, was killed by police and state patrol during a hail of gunfire in Lacy, Washington, about 100 miles north of Portland, after Reinoehi refused arrest. Two days later, protesters in Portland marked 100 consecutive days of marches and raids there with the usual 100 to 200 people seeking reductions in the police budget for reallocation to Black residents and businesses. One day earlier, Trump had instructed the federal government to cease funding for any federal government sensitivity training that contained content that held whites responsible for systematic racism. He called such content anti-American. Within a week, Trump had showcased selected Blacks and Latinos at the Republican National Convention, "and made it clear that, in his view, the country's real race problem is bias against white Americans" (Baker, September 7, 2020, p. A-13). Trump drove the point into the ground during a day and a half of relentless tweeting. "This is a sickness that cannot be allowed to continue, [and should be] quickly extinguished....How to be anti-White 101 is permanently cancelled!" To Trump, Black Lives Matter was a "symbol of hate" (Baker, September 7, 2020, p. A-13).

Within a few days of these tweets, Michael Cohen, Trump's former attorney and "fixer" released a book, *Disloyal:* A Memoir, in which he wrote that Trump allegedly had told him: "I will never get the Hispanic vote. Like the Blacks, they are too stupid to vote for Trump" (Baker, September 7, 2020, p. A-13. This, after Trump's often-repeated but utterly questionable opinion that he has done more for Black people than any U.S. president since Abraham Lincoln. "Tell me one country run by a Black person that isn't a shithole," Cohen said Trump told him (having let slip the fact the Barack Obama was president of the United States for 8 years, since he was "consumed with hate for…Obama" (Haberman, 2020, p. A-13).

On August 23, marked 3 months since the killing of George Floyd, a stark reminder that the days had not passed when some police considered the lives of young Black men as cheap. During those 3 months, several other Black men had been shot to death. On that date, yet another horribly unnecessary shooting again brought angry demonstrators into the streets.

Abut 5 p.m., Sunday, April 23, in Kenosha, Wisconsin, a small city of about 100,000, 40 miles south of Milwaukee, Jacob Blake, Jr., 29, was approaching his SUV, containing three of his six children in a back seat, after having unsuccessfully tried to stop an argument between two women. Police officers, having been called to quell a domestic disturbance, drew up near Blake's SUV as he was opening the driver's side door. What happened next is not entirely clear because the officers had no bodycams. Some neighbors did have phones, however, and what they recorded was one officer reaching for Blake's T-shirt as one of the others, a seven-year veteran of the Kenosha Police Rusten Sheskey, pumped seven shots into Blake's back. Blake, who was working as a security guard (but was off duty), was unarmed (except for a small knife on the floor of the SUV). He was carrying toys for the birthday of one son, who was sitting in the car's back seat with two of his brothers. Blake had done nothing that could have been construed as a crime.

In Kenosha, where about 12% of its 100,000 residents are Black, the police force keeps itself very busy by arresting Blacks for just about anything. The African-American incarceration rate in Kenosha is 80% higher than in Milwaukee, which itself has the third-highest rate of major U.S. cities, according to Marc V. Levine, acting director of the Center for Economic Development at the University of Wisconsin. Black Kenosha residents are 12 times as likely to be locked up as whites (Eligon et al., 2021a, p. A-11).

The videos rocketed onto the Internet. Within 3 hours, Kenosha's small downtown was enveloped in rioting by hundreds of people who destroyed several cars and shops. Within a day, other demonstrations and minor property damage had taken place in Chicago, Seattle, Madison, Wisconsin (where

4000 people rallied near the State Capitol), a well as Portland, Oregon, New York City, Minneapolis, and other urban areas. State police had released so little information by August 25 that the public did not even know the identity of the officer who had shot Blake. It was a "senseless attempted murder," said Jacob Blake, Sr., the younger Blake's father, as he cried. The officer had been placed on administrative leave.

At the same time, Blake was in surgery, fighting for his life, facing a probability that (at best) because the bullets had severed his spinal cord, that he would be paralyzed for the rest of his life, from the waist down. At one point, Jacob was with his mother in a hospital room and shared prayers. Jacob stopped the conversation and asked a police officer in the room if he was a man of faith. "Yes," he said. Jacob then asked that all of them pray, and they did (CNN, Situation Room, 8/25/2020).

Several vehicles were set ablaze and windows smashed along city thoroughfares in Kenosha as crowds faced off with police. Officers in riot gear stood in lines and SWAT vehicles remained on the streets to move people away from city buildings despite the declaration of an overnight curfew. Tear gas was used to disperse groups of people, according to reporters at the scene. (Protests Erupt, 2020). By the early morning of August 26, during a third night of protests in Kenosha, Two were killed and one injured shortly after midnight by gunshots. A few hours later, a 17-year old White juvenile Kyle Rittenhouse was arrested. He had been photographed during the disturbance carrying a gun nearly as long as was tall.

Kyle Rittenhouse, the Kenosha gun fanatic and probable killer of Joseph Rosenbaum, 36, and Anthony Huber, 26, at a Black Lives Matter rally on August 23, hardly got a close look from several police on the scene while the muzzle of his very long assault rifle was still smoking. Neither did several other armed whites with long guns who stood on sidewalks in downtown Kenosha, with the announced mission of saving the city from any more looting. In Wisconsin, it is illegal to carry a gun under age 18. Ja'Mal Green, a community organizer from Chicago, asked Neil MacFarquhar, a reporter for the *New York Times*, to consider what kind of reception a young *Black* man would have received from the same police officers after midnight, on the same street. "If they have an umbrella, if they have any object, they are deemed as armed," Green replied (MacFarquhar, 2020, p. A-19).

The same evening, in honor of Jacob Blake, the Milwaukee Bucks did not take the court for Game Five of the National Basketball Association playoffs. The basketball players already had painted "BLACK LIVES MATTER" on the court. The Bucks' opponents, the Orlando Magic, whose members had been warming up on the court, joined the Bucks in solidarity. The rest of that day's playoff games were soon postponed as well. As the sun rose on August 26, Major League Baseball called off its games as an appreciation that Black lives matter. The air was electric, reminding many people of 1968, when Martin Luther King had been assassinated. In the summer of 1968, at the Mexico City Olympics, two United States track stars celebrated their victories by raising clenched fists while receiving their medals. Fists were raised again in August of 2020, 52 years later, with an outpouring of support for Blake. The Women's NBA called off their games, wearing T-shirts spelling out Jacob Blake's name, with seven bullet-like pockmarks on the back of each one. Baseball and soccer players joined the boycott, as did the mainly White NHL (National Hockey League). Tennis notable Naomi Osaka sounded a call for racial justice as several other players and tennis organizations joined. "I don't expect anything drastic to happen with me not playing," Osaka said. "But if I can get a conversation started in a majority white sport, that's a step in the right direction," she continued, concluding: "Watching the continued genocide of Black people at the hands of the police is honestly making me sick to my stomach" (Osaka Withdraws, 2020, p. 2-B).

Doc Rivers, head coach of the Philadelphia 76ers, said: "We're the ones getting shot. We're the ones who were denied to live in certain communities. We've been hung. We've been shot. And all you do is keep hearing about fear. It's amazing why we keep loving this country, and this country does not love us back. And it's just, it's really so sad." And Jeanie Buss, the Governor of the Los Angeles Lakers, added: "After more than 400 years of cruelty, racism, and injustice, we all need to work together to say: 'Enough is enough'" (Players, 2020, p. 2-B).

At the same time, a search of Rittenhouse's social media posts revealed an intense devotion to "guns, law enforcement, and President Trump" (Bosman & Mervosh, 2020). At the Republican National Convention, ongoing at the same time, Vice President Mike Pence and Trump blamed the violence on Democrats, especially presidential nominee Joe Biden, even though it was occurring on Trump's watch. The events in Kenosha fit finely into Trump's often-repeated narrative that Democratic-run cities were awash in violence and crime. Trump tweeted that he would send federal law enforcement to Kenosha, in addition to several hundred National Guard already there. "LAW AND ORDER!" he announced (Bosman & Mervosh, 2020, p. A-18). No one at the RNC wanted to discuss the fact that an avid devotee of Trump appeared to be fulfilling his fantasy of making the streets of Kenosha run with Black people's blood. Visiting Kenosha the next week, Trump said that Rittenhouse probably acted in self-defense. As for Blake, whose family refused to stand with Trump for a photo op, Trump said that sometimes police make mistakes, like a golfer missing a short putt. Joe Biden, whom Trump was now calling "slow Joe" did meet with the Blake family.

Within a few days of Blake's shooting, Trump all but forced his way into Kenosha, pointedly uninvited by the city's mayor and Wisconsin's governor. Members of Blake's family refused to share a photo-op with Trump, as did owners of businesses destroyed in the riots that followed Blake's shooting. Trump did meet with local law enforcement. Within 48 hours of Trump's self-invitation to Kenosha, Joe Biden (whom Trump had taken to calling "Slow Joe," visited with Blake's family and held a community forum.

While the aftermath of Blake's shooting was covered minute by minute on national television, the toll of Black deaths mounted coast to coast. In Los Angeles, Dion Kizzee, 29, a Black man, was shot to death by police after having been stopped for a traffic violation on a bicycle. It was yet another example of a Black man being subjected to summary execution for what is known on the street as a "petty-assed" crime. After the stop, Kizzee scuffled with an officer, then took off running, shedding a coat, out of which rolled a small gun. The police, now in pursuit, said that Kizzee was reaching for his gun as he stumbled and fell—and in yet another case of shoot-first-and-ask questions—police work. Family said that, having stumbled and fallen, Kizzee had no chance of reaching the gun before he was shot to death for a misdemeanor.

In interviews with the Associated Press (September 2), family members remembered the 29-year-old Kizzee as an energetic man with many friends. "You guys [police] take care of dogs. You don't take care of us," said Kizzee's aunt, Fletcher Fair, addressing the Sheriff's Department. "He was a sweet and loving young man. He had his whole life ahead of him, and it was cut short by rogue sheriffs" (ASP, September 2, 2020).

In Rochester, New York, Daniel Prude, a Black man in Rochester, New York, died of asphyxiation after a group of seven police officers put a hood over his head, then pressed his face into the pavement for two minutes, according to video and records released by Prude's family. This death occurred on March 30, 2020, after he was taken off life support, seven days after the encounter with officers, but was not made public until September 1, 2020. Prude died March 30 Police body-camera video of the arrest was released Wednesday, September 1, five months after he was killed. His death had received no public attention until then. "I placed a phone call for my brother to get help. Not for my brother to get lynched," Prude's brother, Joe Prude, said at a news conference (AP, September 2, 2020).

Prude apparently was killed for acting erratically, which is not a capital crime. He had been running naked through the streets of Rochester in a wet snow. An autopsy found low levels of oxygen and high levels of PCP in Prude's blood. His family said that the encounter with police had provoked a resigned.

Trump ignored these events; at campaign stops he invented tales of airplanes full of "thugs" "dressed in black uniforms and gear, and this and that," purportedly traveling from city to city (Seattle, Portland, Oregon, and New York City were mentioned) to coordinate protests and damage his re-election prospects. Trump then pledged to cut off federal funds to cities governed by Democrats. Mario Cuomo, governor of New York City, said that if Trump wants to walk the streets of New York City, he had better bring an army.

Trump's ravings were partly scraps of conspiracy theories picked up from the disinformation sewers of the Internet, enhanced by Trump's imagination. It all sounded just plausible enough that the owner of a limo service in Michigan had to deny that his bus fleet had been hijacked with money provided by left-wing activist and billionaire George Soros (Trump Says, 2020, p. 6-A). Trump also said that Biden was "being controlled by people you've never heard of—powerful people in the dark shadows" (Trump Says, 2020, p. 6-A). "The radical left is out to get you and destroy the American way of life," Trump said repeatedly. "They're already here…just a short plane ride away. They're scary. They wear black" (Trump Says, 2020).

The country's summer of blood and fire continued into the fall. On September 30 (in one egregious example of many), a Texas police officer, Shaun Lucas killed Jonathan Price, a Black man who had been known as a pillar of his community in Wolfe City, Tex., a town of 1400 people about 60 miles northeast of Dallas. Lucas tasered and then shot Price, who later died at a nearby hospital. Price, who had been trying to stop an argument at a convenience store, made no attempt to resist Officer Lucas, who complained as Price was dying that he had been resisting arrest. Quickly, outraged crowds assembled, and the question became not whether Price, had resisted arrest, but whether resisting arrest (as in so many such shootings) was grounds for the summary execution of a vibrant, peaceful, young Black man. Again, a service revolver had become the rope for a twenty-first-century hanging. Lucas within 24 hours was fired from the force and charged with murder.

As summer waned, leftist radicals continued to wear out their welcome in Portland. On September 7, the 102nd consecutive night of marches and riots in Portland, Anitfa threw gasoline bombs around prior targets. The same day, a large caravan of Trump-affiliated pickup trucks headed for Portland in late afternoon.

On October 11, a Sunday evening, during the 136th straight night of small-scale rioting in Portland, about 200 demonstrators toppled statues of former presidents Theodore Roosevelt and Abraham Lincoln and shattered the entrance to the Oregon Historical Society in Portland's South Park neighborhood before moving into other areas of downtown, smashing storefronts and engaging in other acts of destruction. The group showed the same dichotomy as many other demonstrators around the country during previous months. While the majority was peaceful, a small group set out to smash windows and grab merchandise.

BLM indicted Lincoln and Roosevelt for historical reasons. In Lincoln's case, Lincoln had ordered the hanging of 38 Native people in 1862 (thereafter known as the "Dakota 38")—the largest mass hanging in U.S. history. At the same time, Lincoln, who was concerned about sloppy prosecution, commuted the death sentences of 362 others. Roosevelt had favored Eugenics, a school of pseudoscience that asserted the superiority of Europeans and their progeny in America. The race law of the Nazis implemented Eugenic doctrines on a mass scale which killed its reputation as any kind of science. Before Hitler adopted it, Eugenics was known as a form of discussion-point racism subscribed to by many upper-class whites. Theodore Roosevelt, however, took his racism more seriously, subscribing to an American "final solution" argument holding that the only "good Indian" was a dead Indian.

President Trump, not a man for nuance, called all of the protestors "animals": and a good reason to vote for him in national elections three weeks away at that time (Baker, 2020, p. A-21). Trump offered federal troops to crush the rebellion, as had been tried before, even as local elected officials objected to their uninvited presence. The problem was that federal "troops," who came in unmarked uniforms and vehicles, drew several thousand mainly anti-Trump demonstrators and made the problem much worse. By that point, the riots were mainly supplying Republican election campaigns with film footage for television attack ads blaming the riots on their political foes in places such as Nebraska and Iowa—a long way to go for an evening watching a two-bit riot.

In addition to well-publicized police killings of Black men and women, the epidemic of Black men dying in unprovoked killings did not stop after all the protests of George Floyd's (and others') killings. Many others were killed as well. A national survey about the time Floyd was killed indicated that his was hardly the only mistaken Black man on woman to fall prey to police bullets aimed in incompetence.

Was It a Gun, a Cell Phone, or a Subway Sandwich?

Police continued to express rotten judgment when it came to confusing just about anything that was flat or pointed and could fit inside a pants pocket with a gun. An unarmed Black man standing in an open garage carrying a cell phone (an officer assumed it was a gun) was shot to death in Columbus, Ohio. The penalty for carrying a cell phone is *not* grounds for summary execution. Officer Adam Coy was stripped of his badge and gun (and later charged with murder) after killing Maurice Hill, 47, who was walking toward the officer with the cell phone in his left hand and his right hand not visible when Coy opened fire, authorities said.

City officials in Columbus, Ohio, later agreed to pay $10 million to the family of Hill, a Black man who was fatally shot in December 2020. In addition to being fired (for failing to immediately turn on his Bodycam and not rendering aid to Hill), Coy was charged with murder, as well as felonious assault and two counts of dereliction of duty. The $10 million was the city's largest. A month before Hill was killed, Ma'Khia Bryant, age 16, was shot to death in Columbus shortly before a jury in Minneapolis convicted Derek Chauvin of killing George Floyd. Two other Blacks had been killed by police in Columbus within a few months.

"It's very emotional because every day you turn on the T.V., you see a new killing," Karissa Hill, Mr. Hill's daughter, said at a news conference about her reactions to police killings after her father's death. "It retriggers, because no matter how it happened or justified, non-justified, you see it, and it just brings back a trigger that my dad's not here" (Morales, 2021). All four killings had not involved any major crimes; the Blacks had simply found themselves in the paths of Columbus' cops' bullets.

In one case, an officer had been responding to a non-emergency disturbance call from a neighbor, according to the Columbus Department of Public Safety. The shooting was the latest involving law enforcement in Columbus, where less than three weeks before, another Black man, Casey Goodson, Jr., had been fatally shot by a Franklin County sheriff's deputy. Speaking at a news conference on December 23, 2020, hours after attending Goodson's funeral, Columbus Mayor Andrew Ginther said that Hill had been an expected guest at the home where he was shot. He had committed no crime.

Goodson, 23, was shot to death with three bullets to his torso after he engaged in contretemps with a deputy in front of Goodson's grandmother and two very young children. The police said he had a gun; the family said he was carrying Subway sandwiches after returning from a dentist. We have asked this before: when does carrying Subway sandwiches and having words with a deputy cause for summary execution? If cops can't tell the difference between a gun and a sandwich, what are they doing on a police force with a gun?

Determining how and why Goodson was fatally shot was complicated by the fact that law enforcement officers in Columbus were not wearing body cameras at the time of the shooting although the purchase of them was under consideration by municipal authorities. The Columbus Police, having said that Goodson waved a gun at them, as of two weeks after the shooting, was unable to produce a weapon, disclose where it had been found, or even provide a plausible description of one. Protesters in Columbus waved Subway Sandwiches in the air as they marched.

What *was* known is this: as Goodson was entering his home, placing his key into the door's lock, three men in plainclothes (who turned out to be law-enforcement officers) converged on him. After a confrontation, Jason Meade, one of the officers, shot Goodson several times. The three men were assigned to a fugitive task force associated with the U.S. Marshals, looking for someone else who had no connection to Goodson. His family said that Goodson was "a gentle soul who had never been in trouble with the law" (Walinchus & Oppel, 2020, p. A-16). Tensions have risen between police and Black people in Columbus, where about a third of the city's 900,000 residents are Black. They are pulled over 84% more often by police per capita than whites (Walinchus & Oppel, 2020, p. A-16).

Anjanette Young was standing in her Chicago apartment after having taken a shower, wrapped in a towel, but otherwise naked, when police, acting on fake information, broke down her door, shooting her fatally. "Justice has to be served. Not only for Ms. Young, but for any other woman in the city of Chicago, no matter what ward they live in. This is wrong," Chicago Alderman Stephanie Coleman said. "It's not easy to put this type of exposure out there," she said outside of police headquarters in Bronzeville, a Chicago neighborhood. "I'm somewhat of a private person, so this is not something that I enjoy doing, but this is something that's very necessary." "If you ask me what I want from this, I want accountability," Young said. "I don't need social media followers, I don't need that type of stuff" (Charles, 2020), over objections from the city's Law Department. Young tried to obtain the footage herself through the Freedom of Information Act, but she was denied.

The video's release forced Chicago City Hall to confront the reality that Mayor Lori Lightfoot's administration fought to keep the footage under wraps, though Lightfoot denied having knowledge of the raid until a week before it became public. "It's unacceptable. It tells me they don't care about me, a person who lives in this city. I work. I pay my taxes. I vote," Young said, her voice shaking as a tear rolled down her cheek. "And so to have my home invaded the way it was, for over 40 minutes to have to deal with police officers yelling at me, pointing guns at me, telling me to calm down, making me stand in front of them naked, putting handcuffs on me while I was naked. No one should have to experience that. And there's no way for that to go away" (Charles, 2020).

Young told reporters that she had voted for Mayor Lightfoot, who, as a candidate, visited Young's church in the Armour Square neighborhood just a few blocks west of CPD headquarters. Addressing Lightfoot directly, Young said: "I was there when you came to my church and you campaigned, and I was all on board for voting for you, and I did vote for you. I told my friends to vote for you. I believed in you as a Black woman that was running for mayor in the city of Chicago. So I want you to come back to my church and I want you to respond to this because that's where you asked me to vote for you. So come back and tell me and the people at my church how you're gonna fix this so this never happens again to me or to anyone else. It's not OK" (Charles, 2020).

Within a few days, another Black man was fatally shot in Oregon after a dispute over the volume of his music in a hotel parking lot. Local activists said that race was a factor in the shooting, in the small community of Ashland.

Kenneth Jones, 35, a Black man was fatally shot during a traffic stop in Omaha on November 19, 2020, at 7:27 p.m. during a traffic stop. Three women were in the car with him. The reason for the stop was not immediately available. Police asked the man to get out of the car, and he initially refused. The police later said they saw a weapon. A struggle ensued, at which time the man was shot. A police body-cam showed several shots quickly discharged. No one else was harmed.

On November 20, 2020, at about 7:30 p.m., about 50 people marched in front of Omaha police's central headquarters to protest the shooting death of Jones, 35. Police said Jones had reached for a gun before he was fatally shot. The protestors demanded the release of police bodycam evidence of what had occurred during the confrontation. Two demonstrators were detained and tear gas was released after police declared the march an unlawful assembly. Peyton Zyla, ProBLAC spokesman, said: "Until [police] prove that they didn't murder a Black man, we're not shutting up—not one bit" (Wade, 2020, p. B-1). Witnesses said that Jones was hauled out of the car after an officer broke the driver's side window with a flashlight, then hauled him out of the car. Jones was told to keep his hands in the air. At that point, he dug his right hand into a coat pocket as one officer shouted that he was reaching for a gun. At that point, one officer fatally shot him four times.

The Black Wall Street: The First Bombing of Americans by Americans

In the midst of Jim Crow, with the Ku Klux Klan metastasizing like an aggressive tumor across the United States, in 1921, the Black people of Tulsa, Oklahoma did something unusual. Mainly with their own hands, in the north end of town, they built a hometown in the Green that was so successful that everyone called it "The Black Wall Street."

And what did the White neighbors surrounding this exemplar of American free enterprise do? They burned and bombed it to the ground, and killed at least 300 people. We say "at least" because, even in 2021, a century later, unmarked graves were being uncovered. The city of Tulsa, in 2020, after 99 years of silence and denial, began excavating places, such as old cemeteries, that may contain coffins of dead individuals who have heretofore been unknown. One mass grave contained 12 skeletons. In a year, city excavators found 27 such coffins, as searches continued (Robertson, 2021, p. A-18).

This was a race massacre that was made to be forgotten, although its authors did a sloppy job of it. Moving pictures (still a novelty) were taken, and some of them showed private aircraft (*very* novel in 1921) strafing Greenwood with hand-made turpentine bombs that exploded and sparked fires upon impact. This may well have been the first (and possibly the only) mass bombing of Americans by Americans.

As happens so often (as with the lynching of Emmett Till in 1955), the 1921 Tulsa race massacre was a massive over-reaction by whites to a perceived Black slight. In this case, the riot was precipitated by allegations of assault, purportedly of a White woman by Dick Rowland, 19 years of age. Rowland may have stepped on the foot of a White woman in a downtown elevator. When he was accused of sexual assault, he ran, and rumors grew, as did the inflamed mob. Answering unproven allegations of assault brought a White mob to rage through Greenwood, burning, looting, and killing anyone whom its members could catch, with the avowed purpose of "running the Negro out of Tulsa" (Brown, 2021, p. 65). Thus, Blacks who took so much pride in their hand-hewn neighborhood found themselves dodging machine-gun fire. Many people on both sides were veterans of World War I; Blacks who served the bombing, fires, and machine-gun fire were confined to internment camps.

These murderous acts of intemporary insanity of what became known as Tulsa's "red summer" were shrouded from the city's collective memory for 80 years. Newspapers containing accounts of the massacre were systematically cut out of archives at the University of Tulsa Library with razors. In 2001, the Tulsa Race Riot Commission compiled the first organized inquiry into the bloody assault by White Tulsans on what may have been the first large, organized Black community. White rioters had rampaged through many medium-sized cities in the Midwest (usually because of competition for jobs or alleged rape of White women by Blacks). In Omaha, for example, in 1919, A White mob, perhaps 3000 or more, lynched Will Brown, 41, a Black worker, whose body was mutilated and burned, after he was accused of raping a White woman. This riot also resulted in the deaths of two White men and an attempted lynching of Omaha mayor Edward Parsons Smith. The White mob set fire to the Douglas County Courthouse. It was one of more than 20 riots in major U.S. industrial cities during the "Red Summer" of 1919.

Tulsa, however, was the only riot in which a White mob all but wiped a prosperous Black community off the map—about 10,000 homes, pharmacies, four doctors' offices (sometimes with doctors incinerated inside, two dozen grocery stores, a public library, two newspaper offices, a dozen churches, schools, 31 restaurants, five hotels, and more than 1000 houses (Brown, 2021, p. 77.) Tulsa's fire department was routed when its members tried to put out fires in Greenwood. Material losses from the riot totaled $26,752,705 in 2021 dollars (Brown, 2021, p. 71). Close to 10,000 people were left homeless, nearly all of Tulsa's Blacks as well as whites)

Police Behavior: Life, Death, and Little Change

The behavior of police across the United States in many cases has been impervious to change, even in the face of a year and more of steady protests in the names of George Floyd and many others who have been targets of uncalled-for fatal shootings. Consider a Rochester, N.Y., police officer who tackled and used pepper spray on a woman who had been accused of shoplifting, according to police body-camera videos. She was traveling with her three-month-old daughter, who was seized by police. Also in Rochester, a nine-year-old girl was targeted by pepper spray. Another nine-year-old girl had earlier been targeted by the same chemical irritant. Both incidents occurred in the shadow of the death of Daniel Prude, a Black man who was asphyxiated by Rochester police. "It feels like our officers are out of control," said Mary Lupien, a Rochester City Council member told the *New York Times* (Maslin-Nir, 2021).

Before that, Ronald Greene, who was Black and 49 years of age in 2019, was chased by police in Louisiana, hit a tree, and was beaten to death by police. Police said his death was caused by a collision with the tree.

The Associated Press reported:

> A Louisiana State Police trooper was suspended without pay for kicking and dragging a handcuffed Black man whose in-custody death remained unexplained and the subject of a federal civil rights investigation. Body camera footage shows Master Trooper Kory York dragging Ronald Greene "on his stomach by the leg shackles" following a violent arrest and high-speed pursuit, according to internal State Police records obtained by The Associated Press.
>
> The records are the first publicly acknowledgement by State Police that Greene was mistreated, and they confirm details provided by an attorney for Greene's family who viewed graphic body camera footage of the May 2019 arrest and likened it the police killing of George Floyd. The video shows troopers choking and beating the man, repeatedly jolting him with stun guns and dragging him face-down across the pavement, the attorney told AP.
>
> "It is now undisputed that Trooper York participated in the brutal assault that took Ronald Greene's life," said Mark Maguire, a Philadelphia civil rights attorney who represents Greene's family. "This suspension is a start but it does not come close to the full transparency and accountability the family continues to seek." (Mustian, 2021a, b).
>
> Greene's family's account was supported when bodycam footage [was] finally released after 474 days during May of 2021 displayed the full brutality of Greene's treatment after his arrest.

The 46-minute clip showed one trooper wrestling Greene to the ground, putting him in a chokehold and punching him in the face while another can be heard calling him a "stupid motherf------ as "Greene wails "I'm sorry!" as another trooper delivers another stun gun shock to his backside and warns, "Look, you're going to get it again if you don't put your f------ hands behind your back!" Another trooper can be seen briefly dragging the man facedown after his legs had been shackled and his hands cuffed behind him. Instead of rendering aid, the troopers leave the heavyset man unattended, facedown and moaning for more than nine minutes, as they use sanitizer wipes to wash the blood off their hands and faces. "I hope this guy ain't got f------ AIDS," one of the troopers can be heard saying....Andrew Scott, a former Boca Raton, Florida, police chief who often testified as an expert witness in use-of-force cases, [said that] While noting Greene "was not without fault" and appeared to resist the troopers' orders...dragging the handcuffed man facedown by his ankle shackles was "malicious, sadistic, completely unnecessary" (Mustian, 2021).

Following accumulating evidence that Louisiana state troopers lied about circumstances leading to Greene's death, authorities ordered an internal investigation to test the behavior of all state troopers through examination of body-cam footage. The investigation was ordered after "three other violent stops of Black men: one who was punched, stunned and hoisted to his feet by his hair braids…another who was beaten after he was handcuffed, and yet another who was slammed 18 times with a flashlight.…Every time I told him to stop he'd hit me again," said Aaron Bowman, whose flashlight pummeling left him with three broken ribs, a broken jaw, a broken wrist and a gash to his head that required six staples to close. "I don't want to see this happen to nobody—not to my worst enemy" (Mustian, 2021).

The audit involved several thousand body-cam videos involving as many as 12 suspect troopers, all of whom were White, of which four had taken part in the assault and death of Greene. The probe involved Troop F, with 66 members, a usual number of whom had been cited for brutality involving felony charges.

The AP played a leading role in this case, documenting police lies about circumstances before Greene's arrest. Bodycam footage obtained by the AP "show[ed] troopers converging on Greene's car, repeatedly jolting the…unarmed man with stun guns, putting him in a chokehold, striking him on the head and dragging him by his ankle shackles". Greene can be heard apologizing to the officers, telling them he is scared and moaning and gasping for air.

One 30-minute clip, "troopers order[d] the heavyset Greene to remain facedown with his hands and feet restrained for more than nine minutes—a tactic use-of-force experts criticized as dangerous and likely to have restricted his breathing" (Mustian, 2021), a reminder of a tactic that killed George Floyd.

In Minnesota, a new federal grand jury was empaneled during February 2021 to call new witnesses in its investigation of Derek Chauvin, the Minneapolis police officer who had used his knee to kill George Floyd. Chauvin was scheduled to go on trial in Minneapolis for second-degree murder at the state level. A federal investigation into Chauvin's actions began in 2020 but languished under the Trump administration's Department of Justice. It picked up under Joe Biden's administration. At about the same time, no charges were brought against anyone in Rochester who was involved in Prude's death after a grand jury refused to indict them.

The same day, according to the Associated Press (February 24, 2021), "family and friends of a Black man, Ahmaud Arbery, 25, marked the anniversary of his slaying in Georgia. Arbery's father led about 100 people in a memorial procession to the spot where armed White men chased and shot the 25-year-old Black man as he was jogging on a residential street outside the city of Brunswick on Feb. 23, 2020. Arbery's mother visited his grave before a church vigil. Hours earlier, she had filed a civil lawsuit accusing the men charged in her son's death and local authorities who first responded to the shooting of violating his civil rights. The defendants continued to maintain that they had committed no crimes. Three men were charged with murder. A year later, all were awaiting a trial on those shootings." (No charges, 2021). The defendants were using a 158-year-old state citizens' arrest law.

Georgia Gov. Brian Kemp, a conservative Republican, wrote in an *Atlanta Journal-Constitution* op-ed column that "The horrid killing of Ahmaud Arbery shook a Georgia community to its very core….[Arbery was] was the victim of a vigilante-style of violence that has no place in our state, and some tried to justify their actions of his killers by claiming that they had the protection of an antiquated law that is ripe for abuse" (Fausset, 2021a, p. A-12). On April 28, 2012, the three White men who were involved in this case (Travis McMichael, Gregory McMichael, and William Bryan, Jr.) were charged with federal hate crimes and affiliated offenses.

From a nationwide perspective, such news piles on with such frequency and power that it becomes a blur. New deaths occur with news, for example, that no charges were filed against Rochester officers involved in Daniel Prude's death. At the same time, Patrick Warren, 52, was shot to death on January 14, 2021, by a police officer in Killeen, Texas. The officer, *Ronaldo Contreras*, did not understand that he was mentally challenged. Warren needed a mental health worker, not a young, hot-headed police officer. About the same time, No charges were brought against police whose shots paralyzed Jacob Blake in Kenosha, Wisconsin. He was still paralyzed from the waist down.

Near Vancouver, Washington, two Black teenagers in a car that police thought was stolen (it wasn't) were shot to death by police. The night of October 26/27, 2020, tensions in Philadelphia increased following the killing of Walter Wallace, Jr., a young Black man, by police. According to police (using the most over-ripe trope in modern-day police practice for such a murder), Walter refused to drop a knife. Demonstrations and rioting followed as 30 officers, as well as an untold number of rioters, were injured. National Guard troops were called in. The next night, looting continued as more than 1000 people clashed with police; 170 were arrested and 50 officers injured.

* * *

A Statistical Interlude

The United States has the highest incarceration rate in the world: 700 per 100,000. The United Kingdom's rate is a fifth of that; most European countries are much lower than that. "What's most unsettling to foreign eyes," wrote Hari Kunzru in *Harper's Magazine*, is not just the continuation of mass incarceration in a country with a falling crime rate, but

> the sheer cruelty with which [this] state is administered. From the use of solitary confinement, which amounts to torture, to the punitive charges for phone calls, every aspect of the American system, major or minor, seems to be motivated not by the desire to prevent crime, or to rehabilitate prisoners, but by the impulse to inflict spectacular, exemplary pain for the satisfaction of a general public that derives furtive pleasure from its proximity to suffering....The majority [of] Prisons are dangerous across the world, but Americans accept staggeringly high rates of rape and assault. According to one estimate, around 180,000 men currently incarcerated in the United States have been sexually assaulted. (Kunzru, 2021, p. 5)

While 13.2% of the United States' population is Black, 41.4% of inmates on death row are. The majority of this very high incarceration rate is black and brown, especially among men, an *in situ* retooling of slavery. Many are killed by police before they even reach prison or jail. British police, who carry guns only under extraordinary circumstances, killed 75 men in 30 years (1990–2020); In the United States, 1100 "officer-involved shootings" occurred in one recent year (2019). In the United States, heavily armed police find themselves amidst a population that owns more than 400 million firearms, slightly less than half the world's total.

Louisiana and Mississippi usually rank as the two poorest states in the United States. Louisiana has been in the bottom five 37 of the last 40 years; it also has been number 49 of 50 nineteen times in that period. Mississippi's rankings were similar. Louisiana also has been called "the world's prison capitol," by the *New Orleans Times-Picayune* with the highest or second-highest incarceration rate in the United States for each of the last 19 years, according to the U.S. Bureau of Justice Statistics. Louisiana's murder rate, at 17.5 per 100,000 was the nation's highest in 1996. The former slave-holding states all rank within the United States' top 20 for murder rates, typically four times those of states that had no slavery. The rates for murder also are similar—more evidence that Blacks often live in an America separate, and more dangerous to them than whites (Asher et al., 2021, p. A-16).

Along these lines of color, the shackles of slavery have taken new forms, enforced by heat-bearing police officers and the penal system. As mentioned earlier, the service revolver is the new lynching rope. Being Black, Latino, or Native American is to be in the "wrong" place, at the "wrong" time; mouthing off in ways that officers deem inappropriate can be, *ipso facto*, a sentence to many years' incarceration, or death on the streets. Many of these deaths are never shown on national media.

For example, there was a police shooting of a Black man in Omaha in November 2020, but the Dashcam video was not released until April of 2021, about two months before George Floyd's neck was crushed. The sequence of events followed the usual pattern, starting with a minor traffic stop. Cops order young man out of the car. Young man says there's no reason for this kind of over-reaction; it's just a routine stop. Cops convince themselves that he has a gun, although no gun is visible. Cop breaks the driver-side window and fatally shoots man, blasting him with several shots: Another case of a little Black lip turning into grounds for summary execution.

"Believe Your Eyes: It's Homicide"

On March 12, 2021, the City of Minneapolis announced, in a joint press conference that $27 million was being awarded to George Floyd's family to settle a lawsuit. His family said they would give it all to have him back. At the same time, a jury was being selected for the trial of Officer Derek Chauvin, who had crushed his neck. The settlement was the largest ever in a pre-trial civil suit.

The explosive nature of ex-officer Derek Chauvin's trial began early on its first day, with opening statements, March 26. "You can believe your eyes, that it's homicide," Jerry W. Blackwell, one of the prosecutors, told jurors. "It's murder." (Eligon et al., 2021a, p. A-1). The defense emphasized that Chauvin "did exactly what he had been trained to do over the course of his 19-year career," Eric J. Nelson, one of Chauvin's attorneys, told the court, in his opening statement. "The use of force is not attractive, but it is a necessary component of policing" (Eligon et al., March 30, 2021b, p. A-1). According to a *New York Times* account, "The prosecution said it would present reams of evidence that Mr. Chauvin violated policy, his training, and widely accepted practice" (Eligon, 2021, p. A-16). The trial was expected to utilize testimony of more than 200 civilian witnesses and at least 50,000 pieces of evidence, according to the *Times* account. Blackwell said that he would make a case that

Floyd had died of asphyxia due to Chauvin's pressure on his neck, something that a forensic pathologist would not be able to easily detect.

Following opening statements, Minneapolis firefighter Genevieve Hansen, who had been heard on video repeatedly asking the officers to take Floyd's pulse, testified that she was "desperate" to help him. She said, however, that officers would not allow her to provide medical assistance, leaving her feeling frustrated, helpless, and totally distressed. Hansen described Floyd as "going limp on the pavement [with a] woman screaming that the officers were killing him. There's a man being killed, and had I had access to a call similar to that, I would have been able to provide medical attention to the best of my ability, and this human [being] was denied that right," said Hansen, who is also an emergency medical technician (Eligon et al., 2021a, p. A-17).

While Chauvin was crushing Floyd's neck, a small group of people assembled around them, Black and White, offering help, aghast when Chauvin and other police officers refused their offers. During the trial's second day, March 30, the prosecution put several of these people on the witness stand. Darnella Frazier, 18, spoke softly and frequently wiped her eyes with tissues as she described taking a cell-phone video that shot around the world on social media and helped to ignite millions of people around the world to march in protest. She "sometimes lies awake at night," reported the *New York Times*, "apologizing to George Floyd, for not doing more and not physically interacting[,] and not saving his life" (Eligon et al., 2021a, p. A-1). Similarly, several other bystanders shouted at the officers on the scene to render aid to Floyd, but none of them moved to intervene. Chauvin's counsel asserted that the "crowd" was growing, becoming hostile, "and diverted their [the officers'] attention from caring for Floyd" (Eligon et al., 2021a, p. A-1). Video of the scene showed a group of about ten who were angry, but not threatening. On the contrary, they were pleading with the police to intervene with Chauvin to get his knee off of Floyd's neck and allow oxygen to reach his brain. Instead, Chauvin pressed harder.

Several witnesses told the court that bystanders grew increasingly angry as Chauvin refused to remove his knee from Floyd's neck. Frazier said that Chauvin directed a "cold" and "heartless" stare at them instead: "He didn't care. It seemed as if he didn't care what we were saying," Frazier said (Karnowski & Forliti, 2021a, p. A-4). Officer Chauvin's supervising sergeant, David Pleoger, told the court that by keeping his knee on Floyd's throat until he was obviously unresponsive (had stopped resisting, or breathing) constituted excessive force on Chauvin's part. According to a *USA Today* report, "Two paramedics [Derek Smith and Seth Bravinder] told jurors that Floyd appeared to be in severe medical distress, and probably dead when they arrived at the scene" (Bragg et al., 2021). "If your restrain somebody or leave somebody on their chest and stomach for too long, their breathing can become compromised, so you want to get them up out of that position after a while," Pleoger said, adding that the prone position can be dangerous even if there is no additional pressure (Bragg et al., 2021).

During the first few days of the trial, two very different narratives of Floyd's death came into stark relief. The prosecution built a case that Floyd was killed by asphyxia as Chauvin's knee applied increasing amounts of eventually fatal force to his throat for nine minutes and 29 seconds. This case was built methodically up the MPD's chain of command to the chief of police. No one even began to argue that Chauvin's behavior could be justified for any reason.

The defense, on the other hand, attempted to make its case on reports that Floyd died loaded with meth, fentanyl, and perhaps heroin, not from having Chauvin's big, beefy knee crushing his throat. If so, then, why was a 9-1-1 operator asked for help from her supervisor? If Floyd's choking to death was drug-related, why did not the police call an ambulance instead of making it all worse as Chauvin crushed every last breath out of Floyd's lungs?

Beginning on the trial's first day, continuing on the morning of the second, Donald Williams, 33, a former wrestler who said that he was trained in mixed martial arts, including chokeholds, described seeing Floyd struggle for air as his eyes rolled back into his head, saying he saw Floyd "slowly fade away … like a fish in a bag" (Karnowsky & Forliti, March 27, 2021). Williams recognized that Chauvin was doing a blood choke, which is used to render an opponent unconscious. Williams became so angry that he cursed Chauvin. "Then," reported *The New York Times*, "He took a highly unusual step: he called the police on the police" (Eligon et al., 2021a, p. A-17). Wiping his eyes, Williams told a 911 contact that he was witnessing a murder.

Williams testified that he thought Chauvin had used a shimmying motion several times to drive his knee into Floyd's neck, increasing pressure. Williams shouted from the curb that Chauvin was cutting off Floyd's blood supply. According to an Associated Press report, Williams recalled that Floyd's voice grew thicker, his breathing became more labored, and he eventually stopped moving. "From there on he was lifeless," Williams said. "He didn't move, he didn't speak, he didn't have no life in him…" (Karnowsky & Forliti, March 27, 2021). During the nine minutes and 29 seconds that Chauvin pushed his knee into Floyd's throat, "he said he couldn't breathe 27 times and then went limp," Prosecutor Jerry Blackwell said. "He put his knees upon his neck and his back, grinding and crushing him, until the very breath—no, ladies and gentlemen—until the very *life* was squeezed out of him," (Karnowsky & Forliti, 2021).

One of Chauvin's attorneys, Eric Nelson, argued: "Derek Chauvin did exactly what he had been trained to do over his 19-year career." Nelson did not disclose that during those years Chauvin had accumulated 18 complaints for variations of unprofessional conduct. The prosecution then built a case up the chain of command indicating strongly that Chauvin was violating MPD procedure in several ways.

The defense, however, pressed its case that Floyd had not been fatally harmed by Chauvin. Nelson argued that Floyd "had none of the telltale signs of asphyxiation and he had fentanyl and methamphetamine in his system. He said that Floyd's drug use, combined with his heart disease, high blood pressure, and the adrenaline flowing through his body, caused a heart rhythm disturbance that killed him. The defense also argued from time to time that Chauvin wasn't even crushing Floyd's neck, but had placed his knee on one of Floyd's shoulders.

Minneapolis police dispatcher Jena Scurry testified that she saw part of Floyd's arrest unfolding via a city surveillance camera and was so disturbed that she called a duty sergeant. "You can call me a snitch if you want to," Scurry said in her call to the sergeant, which was played in court. She said she would not normally call the sergeant about the use of force because it was beyond the scope of her duties, but "my instincts were telling me that something is wrong" (Karnowsky & Forliti, 2021).

Before Floyd went mute, silent and motionless, he pleaded for relief one last time. "My stomach hurts. My neck hurts. Everything hurts," Floyd said in a video that was played in court, and, for the last time "I can't breathe, officer." About a dozen people had gathered on the sidewalk a few feet from the police cruiser where Chauvin's knee was crushing Floyd's throat. Several of them shouted at Chauvin to get off of Floyd because he was not breathing, resisting, or even moving. During the fourth day of testimony, Thursday, April 1, Philonise Floyd, one of George Floyd's brothers, told NBC News, outside the courtroom, that he was being "tortured to death."

On the witness stand, Floyd's former girlfriend for 3 years, Courteney Ross, after they met at a Salvation Army shelter where he was a security guard, described his kindness, and the pain he endured from injuries to his back. She also endured chronic pain in her neck. She described Floyd as a caring partner and a father devoted to his children and all others, who liked to ride his bike with neighborhood youngsters. He and Ross both took opiates to relieve their pain. It was this pain that led to opiates, including oxycontin and heroin, to which they became addicted and were unable to quit. "We tried really hard to break that addiction many times," Ross said (Floyd's Girlfriend, 2021, p. A-5).

On day 5 of the trial, April 2, Lt. Richard Zimmerman, one of the MPD's highest-ranking officers, who had served on the force longer than anyone else, told the court that the degree of force used against Floyd by Chauvin was "uncalled for" and "totally unnecessary," and violated department policy (Sanchez & Cooper, 2021). Ray Sanchez and Aaron Cooper of the Cable News Network (CNN) said, The Minneapolis Police Department's top homicide detective testified that kneeling on George Floyd's neck after he had been handcuffed "could kill [him]." (Sanchez & Cooper, 2021). Police are not trained to kneel on a person's neck, Zimmerman said.

Zimmerman, head of the MPD's homicide division for more than 12 years, said that "Once the person is cuffed, the threat level goes down all the way…. If your knee is on someone's neck—that could kill them," the lieutenant said. Sanchez and Cooper wrote that "Chauvin at that point raised his head at the defense table and shot a look at Zimmerman," as he heard this potentially devastating testimony by the department's most senior officer.

The Police Chief Takes the Stand

On Monday, April 6, day six of the trial, in what may have been the most damaging testimony directed at Chauvin, Minneapolis Police Chief Medaria Arradondo, having been called to the witness stand by the prosecution, said emphatically that holding a suspect captive in handcuffs with a knee against his neck was "absolutely" a violation of departmental policy, training, and ethics, especially after he had ceased to be responsive. Arradondo, the MPD's first Black chief, had said previously that Floyd was murdered by Chauvin. The testimony by the MPD chief completed a complete chain of command up the line from former officer Chauvin that ran counter to the usual "blue line" by which police protect each other in legal proceedings.

In another statement from the stand, the emergency room doctor who struggled to save Floyd's life, Dr. Bradford T. Wankhede Langenfeld, who had pronounced Floyd dead, said that lack of oxygen (asphyxia) was the most probable major cause ("one of the more likely"), repudiating defense allegations that drugs in Floyd's bloodstream were the most likely cause of his death. Langenfeld said that many different things—including taking fentanyl and methamphetamines—can cause a death that would still be considered asphyxiation. His testimony followed that of two paramedics who said that Mr. Floyd's heart had stopped by the time they arrived at the scene of his arrest and death (Will et al., 2021).

During Thursday, April 8, a noted pulmonologist, Martin Tobin, testified that Chauvin's knee had remained on Floyd's neck for more than 3 minutes after his blood oxygen level had fallen to zero—that is, when the lack of oxygenated blood caused his death by asphyxiation. Tobin also said that fentanyl and methamphetamine levels in Floyd's blood, while they did exist, were much too low to have been a factor in his death.

On Friday, April 9, day 10 of the trial, Andrew Baker, the Hennepin County medical examiner who performed the initial autopsy on Floyd, cited principally the same evidence and came up with the same conclusions as the many other experts whose profession it is to decide how and why a person dies. It was homicide by Derek Chauvin, Baker said. Once again, fentanyl and methamphetamines were mentioned in this autopsy, but at levels far too low to kill him. What killed him, all of the experts agreed, was 90 pounds of Chauvin's knee and police gear crushing Floyd's neck until he, literally, ran out of oxygen. He could not breathe. Period. Full stop.

A Demand for Complete Submission

A major reason that public reaction to George Floyd's death was so sudden and so visceral, over and above the fact that it was cruel beyond measure, was its resemblance to lynching, both in appearance and purpose. As the police service revolver had become the new hanging rope, so had the knee on the neck. Charles M. Blow commented in the *New York Times*:

> The application of force, a deadly force, even after he was handcuffed, even after he became unresponsive, is to me emblematic of an attempt not only to punish Floyd's body, but also to demonstrate and demand complete submission. The treatment of Floyd's body was a message to those in his community: any perceived disorder or disobedience will be crushed, literally. (Blow, 2021, p. A-19)

Such disobedience, it may be added, as begging to breathe, or calling for his mother. Repression was *complete*, as if a lynching had been imported (say, of Nat Turner) from 1831, as his skin turned into purses (Blow, 2021, p. A-19). The rolling of Jewish skin into lampshades by the Nazis a century later may be too much for White Americans to bear. Emmett Till, in 1955, at age 14, was pistol-whipped, "forced to stand naked on the banks of the Tallahatchee River…shot through the face, then tied to a cotton gin [on his neck] by barbed wire," and shoved into [the] river—all for *allegedly* making eyes at a young White woman in 1955 (Blow, 2021, p. A-19). Concluded Blow:

"Motionless Black bodies have been the tableau upon which the American story has unfolded, and Floyd's body is sadly but one of the latest examples" (2021, p. A-19). Blow's words sent a chill down my spine as I calculated how *recent* Till's tortuous murder (of which lynching was but *one* part) had been. In 1955, I was five years of age, 13 years before men landed on the Moon and Martin Luther King was assassinated.

Demonstrations grew in Minneapolis as the trial progressed. They also sprang up in Chicago as a 13-year-old-boy was shot in the back by police while fleeing along an alley. The fatal shooting had occurred March 29 but was not disclosed until the middle of April, as the murder trial of Chauvin was drawing to a close. In Brooklyn Center, a suburb of Minneapolis, 10 miles from the Floyd murder, site another fatal shooting by police had killed 20-year-old Daunte Wright.

Court in the Chauvin case resumed with closing statements. Anger and grief laced the courtroom's air like static as Daunte Wright's family members spoke up about him. After Wright's shooting, police found an outstanding warrant for a misdemeanor gun charge on his record—not usually the kind of evidence of which summary executions are made, especially if you are not White. Brooklyn Center's mayor, Mike Elliott, who is Black, told members of the media that he had been tailed by police, not realizing he was mayor, looking for reasons to stop a Black man who was driving a nice car. Was it stolen? Was he a drug dealer? When it came out that he was an affluent Black man who owned a nice car and also had an important job in City Hall, the officers flashed shit-eating grins and backed away—*ahem, Mr. Mayor!* Daunte Wright had not been nearly so lucky.

During a third night of demonstrations and looting in Brooklyn Center, 40 were arrested and the National Guard was called in. By April 19, 270 people had been arrested in one week in Brooklyn Center. Minneapolis had fewer arrests, but razor wire and boarded windows as well as National Guard troops on nearly every street corner gave downtown Minneapolis a sense of lockdown. This was the atmosphere at the Hennepin County Courthouse as lawyers made their final statements and the jury was escorted into a deliberation room on the afternoon of Monday, April 19. People milled around public areas on a seasonally cold afternoon in an area bristling with anticipatory tension.

In Wright's case, how was it that an officer with 26 years on the force could not seem to tell the the the difference between a Taser and a service revolver? Could she have told the difference between the Sun and the Moon? Or a dog and a cat? She could have saved a lot of grief by looking at what she had pulled out of her holster. Two seconds would have sufficed.

Within days, videos were released about the fatal killing of a 13-year-old Latino boy, Adam Toledo, who had been killed by Chicago police on March 29; body-cam footage was released on April 16. The nine-minute video from Eric Stillman's body camera showed the 34-year-old officer getting out of his squad car and running along an alley after Toledo at 2:30 a.m. on March 29 in Little Village, a mainly Latinx neighborhood on the city's West Side. The video then showed Stillman yelling "Stop" to Toledo before he caught up to him and ordered him to show his hands. Toledo appeared to raise his hands right before Stillman fired one shot and then ran to the boy as he fell to the ground. "Shots fired, shots fired. Get an ambulance over here now," the police officer was heard saying in the video. "Stay with me, stay with me," Stillman said. "Somebody bring the medical kit now!"

The Chicago Police Department said immediately following the incident that Toledo had a gun in his hand. The gun had been dropped long before Stillman shot Toledo, after Toledo had put his hands into the air. "838 milliseconds between gun shown in hand and single shot," the Chicago Police Department said. About five minutes and 30 seconds into the video, the officer shined a flashlight on a handgun several feet from where officers worked frantically to save Toledo's life, giving him CPR. An attorney for the Toledo family, Adeena Weiss Ortiz, told a news conference after the release of the video that Toledo complied with Officer Stillman's orders, dropped his weapon and turned around, hands up, before the officer opened fire.

Demonstrations were held every evening in Brooklyn Center, peaceful by evening, often violent overnight, as some stores were looted and larger crowds marched in peace. Following a second night of disturbances in Brooklyn Center. Each night, protesters surrounded the barricaded Brooklyn Center Police Station, shouted profanities, launched fireworks, shook a security fence surrounding the building, and lobbed water bottles at police officers, who drove people away with tear gas grenades, rubber bullets, flash-bang grenades, and long lines of riot police. Brooklyn Center city officials passed a resolution banning the city's officers from using tear gas and other chemicals, and chokeholds to arrest demonstrators. The city's resolution did not apply to many other types of police who flooded Brooklyn Center under what they called Operation Safety Net, most notably Hennepin County Sheriff's Department and the Minnesota National Guard. Meanwhile, the families of George Floyd and Daunte Wright met outside the Hennepin County Courthouse in Minneapolis, hugged, and shared condolences.

One last witness at the Chauvin trial, Jonathan Rich, a cardiologist, was called to testify on April 12, 2021. Like the others, he said that George Floyd was killed by a lack of oxygen caused by police restraint. On Tuesday, April 13, in the Chauvin trial, the prosecution rested.

The defense began presenting witnesses Tuesday, April 13, who argued that Floyd did not die of Chauvin's actions and that his actions were "by the book." The defense put an ex-medical examiner on the stand who blamed Floyd's death on just about everything except Chauvin's knee—a massive cardiac arrest, the exhaust from the squad car, et al. Chauvin took the fifth.

Between March 29, when the Chauvin trial began, and April 17, when the *New York Times* published an investigative story on police killings of civilians an average of three people a day had been killed by police in the United States. In fact, Adam Toledo had been shot to death seven hours before Chauvin's trial began.

> One day later, at a hotel in Jacksonville, Fla., officers fatally shot a 32-year-old man, who, the police say, grabbed one of their Tasers. The day after that, as an eyewitness to Mr. Floyd's death broke down in a Minneapolis courtroom while recounting what he saw, a 40-year-old mentally ill man who said he was being harassed by voices was killed in Claremont, N.H., in a shootout with the state police....
>
> On every day that followed, all the way through the close of testimony, another person was killed by the police....somewhere in the United States.... only about 1.1 percent of officers who kill civilians are charged with murder or manslaughter.
>
> The trial has forced a traumatized country to relive the gruesome death of Mr. Floyd beneath Mr. Chauvin's knee.

But even as Americans continue to process that case—and anxiously waited for a verdict—new cases of people killed by the police mount unabated. That was at least 64 people in 19 days. More than half were Black or Latino (Eligon & Hubler, 2021).

In Alameda, California, near San Francisco, one day before Derek Chauvin was convicted, an anonymous caller complained that a man was loitering in a park. Mario Arenales Gonzalez was subsequently seized, handcuffed, and pressed into the dusty ground face first as officers used their knees, elbows, and forearms to crush Gonzalez's back. Gonzalez pleaded "Don't do this to me" as the officers increased their pressure on his back for two minutes and 50 seconds (Hubler & Hill, 2021, p. A-19). After about 5 minutes, Gonzalez lost consciousness, went limp, and died. Body camera footage then showed the officers commiserating about the state of Gonzales. The three officers (Eric McKinley, Cameron Leahy, and James Fisher, were put on administrative leave while their actions were investigated. Once again, a very unremarkable offense had been turned into a police murder, although he appeared to be doing nothing illegal except probably being drunk in public.

Hard-earned Justice

At 4 p.m., Tuesday, April 20, the jury returned after only one day of deliberation, having found Derek Chauvin guilty on all three counts. The crowd outside cheered with raised fists. Chauvin's eyes darted back and forth at an accelerating rate as he was taken off to the Hennepin County jail in handcuffs. The verdict was announced two days before the funeral of Daunte Wright, and minutes before a 16-year-old Ohio girl was killed in a police shooting, after police had answered a call about an attempted shooting.

The same week (April 21) police in Columbus, Ohio, fatally shot a 16-year-old Black teenage girl they confronted as she lunged at two people with a knife. The shooting occurred just minutes before the verdict was read in the Derek Chauvin case, when Floyd's family said "We can breathe again," and two days before a funeral for Daunte Wright, who had been fatally shot by police for lacking license tags on his car during the Chauvin Trial about 10 miles away.

Police video showed the girl who was later shot lunging at two other girls with a kitchen-style knife. The first girl to be attacked fell backward, avoiding the knife. The second girl fell backward into a parked car, also avoiding the knife. The woman with the knife was beginning to strike her again when police arrived, responding to a 9-1-1 call. The woman was raising the knife as if to strike the second unarmed girl when police shot her to death. Family identified her as Ma'khia Bryant (McKay & Gorman, 2021). Within an hour, a small group had gathered, shouting Bryant's name, *one day* after the Chauvin verdict.

On April 22, as Daunte Wright's funeral was being held, his mother, crying, said: "They ought to be burying *me*." Relatives of Emmett Till, who had been lynched by White vigilantes in 1955 for looking at a White girl, also attended. Philonise Floyd, George's brother, acknowledged their attendance and called Till "The first George Floyd" (Bogel-Burroughs, 2021, p. A-17).

Yet another shooting death was being faced with pain by relatives and family of Andrew Brown, Jr., who was killed by a police bullet to the back of the head in Elizabeth, N.C., a majority-Black city of about 18,000 people as the police were serving a search warrant for felony drug charges at his Elizabeth, North Carolina home, about an hour's drive south of Norfolk, VA, April 21.

Police assert that he had sold meth, crack, etc. Several members of his family said he did not carry a gun.

A pickup truck carrying four or five officers arrived at Brown's home dressed in SWAT gear, with heavy weapons. Others arrived by car. Police surrounded Brown outside his home. As he tried to flee in his car, police with Glocks and assault weapons riddled Brown's body with at least five bullets. Five of the bullets hit Brown. The one that killed him, according to an autopsy, tore into Brown's skull at the back of his head. Brown's family asserted that he was executed. If he had been White, they say, he would have been taken alive and tried. Instead, he was shot in the back like a wild animal. As of April 26, family's request to see bodycam footage has been met with only 20 seconds. The family and Black leaders demanded to see all of it. The state's governor, other elected leaders. and community activists also supported them. Four officers were placed on administrative duty, two resigned, and one retired. The FBI arrived on the scene on April 26. Black residents objected to the militarized nature of the raid and the shooting death, thus the description of it as an execution. In a White community, police might have disabled Brown's vehicle by shooting out its tires. The defendant then would have been arrested and tried. By contrast, Wayne Kendall, also an attorney presenting the Brown family, said that the killing of Brown was "nothing but a straight-up execution" (Fausset, 2021b, p. A-14).

A judge blocked the release of the entire bodycam video for at least 30 days on April 28. Lawyer Ben Crump, who represented the families of George Floyd and others whose kin had been fatally shot by police, referred to "the militarized police force rushing to kill Andrew Brown....This has become a constant sight across America; the evolution of policing that's now terrorizing communities of color" (Fausset, 2021b, p. A-14). An average of three people each day were being killed in the United States from police violence. At the same time, U.S. Attorney General Merrick B. Garland announced an intensive investigation of the Louisville, Kentucky police department and county government, following the shooting death of Breonna Taylor (see above), over use of force, service of warrants, and accountability. This call came a week after Garland announced another investigation of the Minneapolis Police Department.

Brown's funeral was held on Monday, May 3, when the Rev. Al Sharpton's eulogy keynoting the subject: "How many funerals do we have to have?"—a subject on everyone's mind (Sharpton, 2021). Eight days later, after several days of demonstrations, the judge allowed Brown's family to see about 20 more minutes of the 118 minutes of bodycam footage. The family said afterward that nothing they had seen changed their minds: Andrew had not come into contact with the officers, they said. He was trying to get *away* from them. The police argued the opposite. However, the fact that Brown was killed by a shot to the back of his head indicated who was doing what to whom.

Who was doing what to whom seemed obvious to state prosecutor R. Andrew Womble in Elizabeth City. Acting on 40 seconds of police body-cam footage newly released May 18, Womble said he was convinced that Brown had been using his car as a "deadly weapon," to inflict harm on the police officers who were trying to arrest him. What the videocam showed many other observers was a car backing up and trying to *avoid* the officers, one of whom jumped away. The real deadly weapons, police service revolvers, shot at Brown 14 times, including once in the back of the head moments later. On grounds that Brown used his car as a so-called deadly weapon, the state prosecutor declined to bring charges against any of the officers who had shot at and killed him. The shooting was said to have been "justified." To Brown's family and others, the 40 seconds showed the officers engaged in an unjustified shooting. Perhaps without intending to implicate the officers' intent, Sheriff Tommy Wooten, Jr. of Pasquotank County said that while the three officers who shot at Brown would keep their jobs, they also would be disciplined and retrained. The nature of their discipline was not disclosed at the time.

An analysis by *The New York Times* on May 18 largely supported the family's interpretation of the newly released 40 seconds of bodycam footage:

> As he appears to be directing the car away from the deputy in front of him—who briefly places his left hand on the hood of the car—an officer fires the first shot, according to the *Times* review. The car does not appear to be moving particularly fast in the moments before the three Pasquotank County's sheriff's deputies fire a total of 145 shots in his [Brown's] direction. (Fausset, 2021b, p. A-18)

In the meantime time, in Minneapolis, the case against Chauvin continued to evolve, as a grand jury brought a new set of charges against the former MPD officer, asserting that he had violated Floyd's civil rights, willfully depriving Floyd of the Constitutional right to be protected from illegal search and seizure, which includes the right to be free from unreasonable force by a police officer. Chauvin also faced a new charge from a prior incident, that he had held a 14-year-old boy by his throat as Chauvin beat him repeatedly in the head with a large police-issued flashlight. Chauvin also pressed his knee into the teenager's neck and back he lay handcuffed, according to the DOJ's court records.

Three ex-officers (J. Alexander Kueng, Thomas Lane, and Tou Thao) also faced state charges of aiding and abetting in Floyd's death. The indictment accused Tao and Kueng "of depriving Floyd of the same rights by failing to intervene." It accused all four officers of depriving Floyd of liberty by not providing him medical attention. It said that all four "saw George Floyd lying on the ground in clear need of medical care, and willfully failed to aid Floyd, thereby acting with deliberate indifference to a substantial risk of harm to Floyd" (Donaghue, 2021a). This was a very rare instance of the DOJ stepping into a state process before its proceedings have been completed, and an indication of how seriously the federal government takes this case.

The Rev. Al Sharpton and the National Action Network said the indictments show that "We have a Justice Department that deals with police criminality" and does not excuse it....For many years we have tried to get the federal government to make it clear that these crimes are not only state crimes but violate civil rights on a federal level when police engage in this kind of behavior," the statement said. "What we couldn't get them to do in the case of Eric Garner, Michael Brown in Ferguson, and countless others, we are finally seeing them do today and this is a significant development for those of us who have been engaged in the struggle and police reform movement" (Donaghue, 2021b).

On May 25, 2021, supporters, friends, and family of George Floyd gathered to observe the first annual anniversary after ex-officer Derek Chauvin had used one of his knees as a murder weapon to deprive Floyd's brain of enough oxygen to kill him. President Joe Biden and Vice President Kamala Harris invited Floyd's family to the White House, where they discussed the proposed George Floyd Policing Act, which would outlaw chokeholds and other police tactics that can injure or kill suspects. As they met, the bill remained stalled in the U.S. Senate. More than 1000 Black people had been killed by police in the United States.

Philonise Floyd, George Floyd's brother, said; "If you can make federal laws to protect the bird, which is the bald eagle, you can make federal laws to protect people of color," said Philonise Floyd, George's brother. (Hammond, 2021).

The circumstances of the Blacks' deaths sometimes display a horrid similarity. Five weeks after Chauvin was convicted of murdering Floyd, three Washington state officers were charged, on May 27, 2010, in the death of Manuel Ellis, whom the Associated Press called "another Black man who pleaded for breath under an officer's knee," as he was punched, strangled and physically restrained before suffocating to death on a Tacoma street in March 2020.

Christopher Burbank and Matthew Collins, both White, were charged by Washington Attorney General Bob Ferguson with second-degree murder after witnesses said that they had "attacked Ellis without provocation" (Associated Press, 2021). They pleaded not guilty on May 28. Timothy Rankine, who is Asian, faced a charge of first-degree manslaughter, in Pierce County Superior Court, south of Seattle, of "kneeling on Ellis' back and shoulder as he died from a lack of oxygen."

Ellis, 33 years of age, died on March 3, 2020, having been tasered, handcuffed, and hog-tied, as his face was shrouded in a spit hood, 13 weeks before George Floyd's death sparked huge demonstrations against police brutality. Ellis name was hardly heard outside the Puget Sound area during the cacophony over the murder of Floyd, despite its eerie similarities: "The Pierce County medical examiner called Ellis' death a homicide due to a lack of oxygen caused by restraint, with an enlarged heart and methamphetamine intoxication as contributing factors….His final words—'I can't breathe, sir!'—were captured by a home security camera, as was the retort from one of the officers: 'Shut the fuck up, man!'" (Associated Press, 2021). Within minutes, Ellis did indeed shut up, from lack of oxygen.

The charging documents said that Ellis had been attacked by Burbank and Collins without provocation, as he returned home from church and entered a convenience store to buy some powdered, raspberry-filled donuts. The police asserted that "Ellis had [been] trying to get into occupied cars at a red light," and then tried to punch out the driver's side window of their cruiser. The more investigators sought witness accounts, the stranger the officers' stories became. By the time charges were filed, "The case mark[ed] the first time the attorney general's office has charged police officers with unlawful use of deadly force" (Associated Press, 2021). Two witnesses came forward with identical stories that the officers had attacked Ellis.

Ellis had a history of mental illness (schizophrenia) and addiction. According to the AP account: "In September 2019, he was found naked after trying to rob a fast-food restaurant. A sheriff's deputy subdued him with a Taser after Ellis refused to remain on the ground and charged toward officers."

A week before the officers were charged, Washington Gov. Jay Inslee had announced ways to guarantee independent reviews of police use of deadly force. Inslee signed one of the United States' strictest slates of police accountability legislation, including bans on police use of chokeholds, neck restraints, and no-knock warrants. The legislation also makes it easier to decertify police—and creates an independent office to review deadly force cases, carrying penalties of up to life in prison.

Perhaps Governor Inslee's efforts may have some effect in Washington State. In Minneapolis, Minnesota, however, where the murder of George Floyd had set off the largest wave of protests against police violence in U.S. history, and about six weeks after Derek Chauvin had been convicted of that murder, Winston Boogie Smith, age 32, yet another Black man, was shot dead by deputies of a U.S. Marshall's Fugitive Task Force. According to a CBS News report, "Authorities said Friday [June 4] that Smith, father of three, had often been harassed by police. This time, he was wanted on a weapons violation [being a felon possessing a gun] and had fired a gun before two deputies shot him." Two nights of rioting followed in the city's Uptown Neighborhood in which protestors lit several dumpster fires. Smith's family asked anyone with video evidence to come forward to compare it with police reports. Some businesses were looted and nine people arrested (Protests Erupt, 2021).

It has become clear that solving such problems is going to require more than a change of words in a legal code.

On June 25, Chauvin was sentenced to 22½ years in prison—a long time, but about half of the 40 he could have received. The prosecution had wanted 30 years; the defense had held out for immediate release. However long Chauvin finds himself behind bars, his stay is likely to be miserable. Prison is notoriously nasty for ex-police officers—especially so for White ones convicted of killing a Black man under conditions so cruel (as Floyd cried out more than 20 times, in a voice increasingly feeble that "I can't breathe"). As pointed out above, the U.S. prison system is more than half Black.

Chauvin in the meantime continued to crush the life out of Floyd—literally—as the images ricocheted around the Earth on millions of smartphones, making Chauvin world-infamous, Judge Peter Cahill emphasized: "the particular cruelty of the crime" (Forliti & Karnowski, 2021). As Amy Forliti and Steve Karnowski of the Associated Press wrote (2021, p. A-1) the day that Chauvin was sentenced: "Floyd, whose dying gasps under Chauvin's knee led to the biggest outcry against racial injustice in the United States in generations."

References

Agents will pull out of Portland, a Governor says. (2020, July 30). *New York Times*, p. A-1.

'Antithetical' to the teachings of Jesus: D.C. Bishop 'Outraged' by Trump address and use of Church as 'Prop'. (2020, June 1). *Washington Examiner*. https://www.

washingtonexaminer.com/news/antithetical-to-the-teachings-of-jesus-dc-bishop-outraged-by-trump-address-and-use-of-church-as-prop

Arango, T., & Benner, K. (2021, February 24). New federal grand jury for case against officer in death of George Floyd. *New York Times*, p. A-15.

Asher, J., Horwitz, B., & Monkovic, T. (2021, February 15). Why does Louisiana lead the nation in murders? *New York Times*. https://www.nytimes.com/2021/02/15/upshot/why-does-louisiana-consistently-lead-the-nation-in-murders.html

Associated Press. (2020, September 2). https://apnews.com/861957b3727a6bd444627454981332ca?utm_source=piano&utm_medium=email&utm_campaign=morningwire&pnespid=kOpu9KVIGhyNR2cti_j9SdJB7WZUw0LK6XEDMJ1H

Associated Press. (2021, May 28). Three officers face arraignment in Black man's restraint death. https://apnews.com/article/wa-state-wire-george-floyd-death-of-george-floyd-police-reform-6c9fc0fdcf36fe519eac9b0a30ddff2c

At least 100 Seattle police officers clearing CHOP. (2020, July 1). *"Morning Brief" Seattle Times*. https://outlook.office.com

Aviv, R. (2020, June 22). Punishment by pandemic. *The New Yorker*, pp. 56–65.

Baker, M. (2020a, June 23). No-police experiment goes awry in Seattle. *New York Times*, p. A-17.

Baker, M. (2020b, October 13). Latest statues to fall: Lincoln and Roosevelt. *New York Times*, p. A-21.

Baker, P. (2020c, September 7). Trump makes White grievance a pillar of his campaign. *New York Times*, p. A-13.

Baker, P., & Cooper, H. (2020, June 11). Pentagon weighs erasing confederate names from bases. Trump scoffs. *New York Times*, p. A-22.

Baker, M., & Kanno-Youngs, Z. (2020, July 30). Federal agencies agree to withdraw from Portland. *New York Times*, pp. A-1, A-17.

Baker, P., Kanno-Youngs, Z., & Davey, M. (2020, July 21). Trump threatens to use force in major cities. *New York Times*, pp. A-1, A-17.

Ball, E. (2020). *Life of a Klansman*. Farrar, Straus, and Giroux.

Bhambra, G. K. (2020, June 12). Good riddance to a Slaver's statue. *New York Times*, p. A-25.

Blow, C. (2020, June 19). Yes, even George Washington. *New York Times*, p. A-21.

Blow, C. M. (2021, April 5). Lessons from lynchings. *New York Times*, p. A-19.

Bogel-Burroughs, N. (2020, December 30). Louisville plans to fire two officers over botched raid that killed Taylor. *New York Times*, p. A-17.

Bogel-Burroughs, N. (2021, April 23). In Minneapolis, a day to mourn the 'Prince of Brooklyn Center'. *New York Times*, p. A-19.

Bosman, J. (2020, August 26). Anger rises as Kenosha grapples with response to police shooting. *New York Times*, p. A-23.

Bosman, J., & Mervosh, S. (2020, August 27). Further troops sent to Kenosha as unrest grows. *New York Times*, pp. A-1, A-18.

Boyette, C. (2017, August 17). Actually, Robert E. Lee was against erecting confederate memorials. *CNN (Cable News Network)*. https://www.cnn.com/2017/08/16/us/robert-e-lee-statues-letters-trnd/index.html

Bragg, N. Y., Hauck, G., McCoy, K., Abdollah, T., & Ferkenoff, E. (2021, April 2). Police supervisor tells court that officers 'could have ended' restraint of George Floyd. *USA Today*. https://www.usatoday.com/story/news/nation/2021/04/01/chauvin-trial-live-day-4-body-camera-video-george-floyd/7019204002/

Brenner, K., & Bogel-Burroughs, N. (2021, May 7). Former police officers indicted on civil rights charges in George Floyd's death. *New York Times*. https://www.nytimes.com/2021/05/07/us/politics/george-floyd-death-minneapolis-officers-civil-rights-charges.html

Brown, D. L. (2021, June). Tulsa race massacre. *National Geographic*, pp. 62–81.

Browne, M., Singhvi, A., Reneau, N., & Jordan, D. (2020, December 31). How the police killed Breonna Taylor. *New York Times*, pp. A-11,-A-13.

Brumback, K. (2021, June 15). Echoes of Breonna Taylor in shooting of Black man in Georgia. *Associated Press*. https://apnews.com/article/breonna-taylor-george-floyd-georgia-shootings-2b47ffa9db88b3848799e97b94417086?utm_source=Sailthru&utm_medium=email&utm_campaign=June15_MorningWire&utm_

Buchanan, L., Bul, Q., & Patel, J. K. (2020, July 8). Black lives matter puts another stamp on history. *New York Times*.

Burch, A. D. S., & Eligon, J. (2020, May 27). Video and police reports differ in string of deadly encounters. *New York Times*, pp. A-1, A-23.

Charles, S. (2020, December 16). 'I want accountability,' says woman seen in video of botched CPD raid. *Chicago Sun-Times*. https://chicago.suntimes.com/politics/2020/12/16/22178628/chicago-police-raid-video-social-worker-anjanette-young-black-caucus-calls-investigation

Cohen, S. (2020, July 2). As FedEx requests the Redskins to change their name, will Dan Snyder cave to critics? *Forbes*. https://www.forbes.com/sites/sethcohen/2020/07/02/the-racist-redskins-why-critics-say-its-time-to-boycott-the-nfl-team/#df0e04ce35a1

Cole, K. (2020, May 29). Omaha protest of Floyd's death draws 40. *Omaha World-Herald*, p. A-3.

Cooper, L. (2020, June 3). George Floyd: Thousands of protesters join Sydney Black lives matter protest. *Channel 9 News* (Sydney, Australia). https://www.9news.com.au/national/george-floyd-black-lives-matter-protest-rally-sydney-cbd-1000-people-streets-nsw-police/ab840cd1-9d56-4aec-88f0-49f2a9e083f2

Cordes, H. (2020, July 18). Mutual [of Omaha] drops logo with Native American Chief. *Omaha World-Herald*, pp. A-1, A-2.

Cotter, H. (2020, June 26). Seeing monuments in a new day's light. *New York Times*, pp. C-1, C-11.

Crowley, M. (2020, September 18). Trump seeks program to provide children a 'patriotic' education. *New York Times*, p. A-19.

Cummings, W. (2020, June 11). 'Go back to your bunker': Seattle Mayor, Washington Governor fire back at Trump threat to handle protests. *USA Today.* https://www.usatoday.com/story/news/politics/2020/06/11/trump-demands-gov-jay-inslee-mayor-jenny-durkans-take-back-seattle/5340870002/

Donaghue, E. (2021a, March 30). Off-duty firefighter says she was desperate to help George Floyd. *CBS News.* https://www.cbsnews.com/live-updates/derek-chauvin-trial-george-floyd-death-day-2-2021-03-30/

Donaghue, E. (2021b, May 7). Federal civil rights charges against ex-cops in George Floyd's death. *CBS News.* https://www.cbsnews.com/news/george-floyd-death-derek-chauvin-minneapolis-officers-civil-rights-violations/

Eligon, J. (2020, September 4). In Kenosha, effort to turn outrage into votes hits resistance. *New York Times*, p. A-11.

Eligon, J., & Hubler, S. (2021, April 17). Throughout trial over George Floyd's death, killings by police mount. *New York Times.* https://www.nytimes.com/2021/04/17/us/police-shootings-killings.html?

Eligon, J., Arango, T., & Bogel-Burrouoghs, N. (2021a, March 31). Teen recalls seeing Floyd 'terrified' and 'suffering.' *New York Times*, pp. A-1, A-17.

Eligon, J., Arango, T., Dewan, S., & Bogel-Burroughs, N. (2021b, March 30). As Floyd murder trial starts, 9-minute video is focus for both sides. *New York Times*, pp. A-1, A-16.

Fausset, R. (2021a, March 12). A year later, mourning the killing of a Black jogger in Georgia. *New York Times*, p. A-12.

Fausset, R. (2021b, April 28). Deputies shot North Carolina man five times, private autopsy shows. *New York Times*, p. A-14.

Fausset, R. (2021c, May 19). North Carolina officers will not face charges in killing of Black man. *New York Times*, p. A-16.

Finnegan, W. (2020, August 3 and 10). The Blue wall. *The New Yorker*, pp. 48–57.

Floyd's girlfriend recalls addiction. (2021, April 2). Associated Press in *Omaha World-Herald*, p. A-5.

Forliti, A., & Karnowski, S. (2021, June 26). Chauvin is sentenced to 22½ years in prison. Associated Press in *Omaha World-Herald*, p. A-1.

Furber, M., Eligon, J., & Burch, A. D. S. (2020, May 29). National guard deployed as Minneapolis erupts. *New York Times*, pp. A-1, A-23.

Goldmacher, S. (2020, June 15). Inspired by a moment, donors flood coffers to fund a movement. *New York Times*, p. A-14.

Haberman, M. (2020, September 7). Cohen book describes Trump as a mobster. *New York Times*, p. A-13.

Haberman, M., & Martin, J. (2020, June 24). New push to divide Americans by race, via tweets, videos, and rhetoric. *New York Times*, p. A-21.

Hammond, E. (2021, May 25). If the U.S. protects the bald eagle, it can make laws to protect people of color. *Cable News Network (CNN).* https://www.cnn.com/us/live-news/george-floyd-remembered-05-25-21/h_63d46a773fe4b2cf074efd7b3dbf6be4

Harper's Index. (2020, December). *Harper's Magazine*, p. 11.

Healy, J., & Barker, K. (2020, June 8). Other movements have faded. This one 'feels like home'. *New York Times*, pp. A-1, A-21.

Hubler, S., & Hill, E. (2021, April 29). In video, California officer[s] pin down man, who dies. *New York Times*, p. A-19.

Johansen, B. E. (2020). *Seattle's El Centro de la Raza: Dr. King'a living laboratory*. Lexington Books.

Jones, A. (2019, June 18). Cruel and unusual punishment: When states don't provide air conditioning in prison; 13 states in the hottest parts of the country lack universal A/C in their prisons. We explain the consequences. *Prison Policy Initiative*. https://www.prisonpolicy.org/blog/2019/06/18/air-conditioning/

Kanno-Youngs., Zoland, B., Peter, B., & Monica, D. (2020, July 21). "Trump Threatens to Use Force in Major Cities." New York Times, A-1, A-17.

Karnowsky, S., & Forliti, A. (2021a, March 31). Cold stare recounted at trial. Associated Press in *Omaha World-Herald*, p. A-4.

Karnowsky, S., & Forliti, A. (2021b, March 30). Witness describes seeing Floyd 'slowly fade away'. *Associated Press*. https://apnews.com/article/us-news-minneapolis-death-of-george-floyd-racial-injustice-bba19d0f75c2cd71c135eed69f5e8200?utm_source=Sailthru&utm

Kimball, R. (2020, July 2). "Rename Yale now." (advertisement) Center for American greatness. *New York Times*, p. A-5.

Kristof, N. (2020, July 25). In Portland's so-called war zone, it's the troops who provide the menace. *New York Times*. https://www.nytimes.com/2020/07/25/opinion/sunday/portland-protest-federal-troops.html

Krugman, P. (2020, June 12). Reactionaries are having a bad month. *New York Times*, p. A-24.

Kunzru, H. (2020). "Another World is Possible." Harper's Magazine, March, 2021. https://harpers.org/archive/2021/03/another-world-is-possible-criminal-justice-reform/.

Lee, R. E. IV. (2020, June 7). Robert E. Lee is my ancestor; take down his statue. *Washington Post*. https://www.washingtonpost.com

Leonard, D., & Serkev, Y. (2020, July 5). The U.S. is lagging behind many rich countries; these charts show why. *New York Times*.

Lepore, J. (2020, June 22). The riot report. *The New Yorker*, pp. 24–41.

Ley, A., Martin S., & Jones, M. (2020, June 11). Norfolk, VA. *Virginian Pilot*. https://www.pilotonline.com/news/vp-nw-portsmouth-confederate-monument-20200610-65p7wr3nkvcrneaotwycjygcqu-story.html

A look at what's next for Seattle protesters' 'autonomous zone'. (2020, June 13). Associated Press in *Omaha World-Herald*, p. 5-A.

Lucas, J. (2020, June). New books. *Harper's Magazine*, pp. 73–74.

MacFarquhar, N. (2020a, August 28). Teen suspect glorified police and weapons. *New York Times*, pp. A-1, A-19.

MacFarquhar, N. (2020b, July 8). Two injured by driver in the latest car attack that targeted protesters. *New York Times*, p. A-15.

Maslin-Nir, S. (2021, March 5). Furor in Rochester after police pepper-spray mother with toddler. *New York Times*. https://www.nytimes.com/2021/03/05/nyregion/rochester-police-woman-pepper-sprayed.html

McKay, R., & Gorman, S. (2021, April 21). Sixteen year-old fatally shot in Columbus, Ohio. *Reuters*. https://www.yahoo.com/news/ohio-police-kill-teenaged-black-032254909.html

Memorials, and a lawsuit mark anniversary of Arbery's shooting. (2021, February 24). *Associated Press*. https://outlook.office.com/mail/inbox/id/AAMkADVmNGE2MGU2LWQ0MDItNDkyNS04YTg2LTY4YmUzZDAwZDA3YwBGAAAAAA%2FRhKKKmMvQYnCF4rsc4kTBwC5ivxYey%2BbS4%2F0UJnRtHAFAAAA8tYkAADdlfbKMp2hTbjKlxLFP60vAAcSnvpkAAA%3D

Miller, R. W. (2020, July 20). 'Wall of moms' at Portland protest formed to protect demonstrators. *USA Today*. https://www.usatoday.com/story/news/nation/2020/07/20/portland-protests-wall-moms-formed-protect-demonstrators/5470348002/

Morales, C. (2021, May 14). Andre Hill's family reaches $10 million settlement with city of Columbus. *New York Times*. https://www.nytimes.com/2021/05/14/us/andre-hill-columbus-settlement.html

Mustian, J. (2021a, February 27). AP: Trooper kicked, dragged Black man who died in custody. *Associated Press*.

Mustian, J. (2021b, June 9). AP: Louisiana police unit probed over Black driver arrests. *Associated Press*. https://apnews.com/article/la-state-wire-louisiana-death-of-ronald-greene-arrests-4a47c5e0ef720019d15818cf32eb2a2a?utm_

Officer who killed Black man in Atlanta faces murder charge. (2020, June 18). Associated Press in *Omaha World-Herald*, p. 7-A.

Olmos, S., Baker, M., & Kanno-Youngs, Z. (2020a, July 18). Federal agents unleash militarized crackdown on Portland. *New York Times*, p. A-1.

Olmos, S., Rojas, R., & Baker, M. (2020b, July 20). 'We're not leaving:' Protesters keep going. *New York Times*, p. A-19.

Olsen, H. (2020, June 22). The anti-statue movement has taken a turn into absurdity. *Washington Post*. https://www.washingtonpost.com/opinions/2020/06/22/anti-statue-movement-has-taken-turn-into-absurdity/

Oppel, R. A. (2020, August 24). Portland's new D.A. lets off 300 protesters as police fume. *New York Times*, pp. A-1, A-13.

Oppel, R. A., & Barker, K. (2020, July 8). 'They'll kill me,' Floyd pleaded, records reveal. *New York Times*, pp. A-1, A18.

Oppel, R. A., Jr., & Gamio, L. (2020, June 4). In Minneapolis, police numbers tell a stark story. *New York Times*, p. A-14.

Osaka withdraws in protest; Tennis event on hold. (2020, August 27). Associated Press in *Omaha World-Herald*, p. 2-B.

Phillips, M. (2020, June 23). Trump Jr. suggests torn-down statues [to] be replaced with 'sturdy statue' of his father. Fox & Friends, *FOX News*.

Players from four leagues make statement with boycott. (2020, August 27). Associated Press in *Omaha World-Herald*, pp. 1-B, 2-B.

Pogrebin, R. (2020, June 22). New York museum to remove Roosevelt statue. *New York Times*, pp. A-1, A-19.

Prison Policy Project. (2018). https://www.prisonpolicy.org/global/2018.html

Pronczuk, M., & Zaveri, M. (2020, June 10). Statue of king is defaced, then removed, as Belgium confronts horrors of colonial rule. *New York Times*, p. A-16.

Protest erupts after Wisconsin as police shoot man from behind. (2020, August 24). *Associated Press*. https://apnews.com/0cbc14762c89304f9f052fd33a1f4445?utm_source=piano&utm_medium=email&utm_campaign=morningwire&pnespid=iuQ0s.lZWFeNnlHikUyzqPXVRR2oJvHs_vZqtK46

Protests erupt in Minneapolis over the shooting death of Winston Boogie Smith, Jr. (2021, June 5). *CBS News*. https://www.nbcnews.com/news/us-news/protest-erupts-minneapolis-over-shooting-death-winston-boogie-smith-jr-n1269729

A real life, modern day, 'Mad Max' scenario. (2020, June 15). *Blabber Buzz*, n.p.

Reinhart, E. (2020, July 6). Stop needless arrests to slow the coronavirus. *New York Times*, p. A-19.

Remnick, D. (2020, July 21). Redeeming America. *The New Yorker*, p. 8.

Responses to the COVID-19 pandemic. (2020a, May 22). *Prison Policy Initiative*. https://www.prisonpolicy.org/blog/2014/05/28/3briefings/

Responses to the COVID-19 pandemic. (2020b, July). *Prison Policy Project*. https://www.prisonpolicy.org/virus/virusresponse.html#releases

Robertson, C. (2021, June 10). 27 coffins found in Tulsa race massacre search. *New York Times*, p. A-18.

Robinson, C. L. (2020, June 9). White supremacy is a societal cancer. *Omaha World-Herald*, p. 5-B.

Rojas, R. (2020, June 29). Mississippi lawmakers vote to retire state flag rooted in the confederacy. *New York Times*, p. A-17.

Romero, S. (2020, June 16). New Mexico removes statue of conquistador known for atrocities. *New York Times*, p. A-18.

Romero, S., Nieto del Rio, G. M., & Bogel-Burroughs, N. (2020, June 26). Another video, another death; Tucson Latinos aren't surprised. *New York Times*, pp. A-1, A-21.

Sakala, L. (2010a). Breaking down mass incarceration in the 2010 census: State-by-State incarceration rates by race/ethnicity. *Prison Policy Initiative*. https://www.prisonpolicy.org/blog/2014/05/28/3briefings/

Sakala, L. (2010b). Some medical conditions make people especially vulnerable to high temperatures. *Prison Policy Initiative*, n.p.

Salman, J., Le Coz, E., & Johnson, E. (2016, December 12). Florida's broken sentencing system: Designed for fairness, it fails to account for prejudice. *Sarasota Herald-Tribune.* http://projects.heraldtribune.com/bias/sentencing/

Sanchez, R., & Cooper, A. (2021, April 2). Top homicide detective says Derek Chauvin kneeling on George Floyd was 'totally unnecessary'. *Cable News Network.* https://www.cnn.com/2021/04/02/us/george-floyd-derek-chauvin-trial-day-5/index.html

Schmitt, E., Cooper, H., Gibbons-Neff, T., & Haberman, M. (2020, June 4). Esper at odds with President on army's use. *New York Times,* pp. A-1, A-20.

Senior, J. (2020, June 8). Dare I say it? Is this the Trump tipping point? *New York Times,* p. A-25.

Sharpton, A. (2021, May 3). *NBC Evening News.*

South Omaha mob wars on Greeks. (1909, February 21). *New York Times,* n.p.

Sticker Shock. (2020, July). Bringing you the latest in empirical research about mass incarceration. *Prison Policy Initiative.* https://outlook.office.com/mail/inbox/id/AAMkADVmNGE2MGU2LWQ0MDItNDkyNS04YTg2LTY4YmUzZDAwZDA3YwBGAAAAAAA%2FRhKKKmMvQYnCF4rsc4kTBwC5ivxYey%2BbS4%2F0UJnRtHAFAAAA8tYkAADdlfbKMp2hTbjKlxLFP60vAAaWfBSyAAA%3D

Stillman, S. (2020, May 25). Compassionate release: Will the pandemic make us rethink mass incarceration? *The New Yorker,* pp. 16–20.

Sweeney, D. (2020, June 28). Rename John Wayne airport because of actor's racist comments, California democrats say. *Sacramento Bee.* https://www.sacbee.com/news/california/article243855452.html

Trump says that 'thugs' are taking airplanes. (2020, September 3). Associated Press in *Omaha World-Herald,* p. A-6.

Truscott, L. K. IV. (2020, July 7). Take down the Jefferson memorial. *New York Times,* p. A-19.

Twitter puts a warning on another Trump tweet. (2020, June 24). *New York Times,* p. B-2.

Wade, J. (2020, November 21). Police say man was reaching for a gun. *Omaha World-Herald,* pp. B-1, B-2.

Wade, J., & Machan, C. (2020, November 20). Omaha police shoot man in traffic stop. *Omaha World-Herald,* pp. B-1, B-2.

Wagner, P., & Sakala, L. (2014, May 28). Three massive new briefings from the responses to the COVID-19 pandemic. *Prison Policy Initiative.* https://www.prisonpolicy.org/blog/2014/05/28/3briefings/

Walinchus, L., & Oppel, R. A. (2020, December 14). Conflicting accounts swirl on shooting of Black man in Ohio, inciting protests. *New York Times,* p. A-16.

Where two weeks of protests swept the nation. (2020, June 16). *New York Times,* pp. F-4-F-5.

Why does the U.S. military celebrate White supremacy? It is time to rename bases for American heroes—Not racist traitors. (2020, May 23). *New York Times.* https://

www.nytimes.com/2020/05/23/opinion/sunday/army-base-names-confederacy-racism.html

Will, W., Dewan, S., Bogel-Burroughs, N., & Eligon, J. (2021, April 6). Key moments of day 6 of the Derek Chauvin trial. *New York Times*.

Williams, J. (2020, June 29). Calls to rename John Wayne Airport resurface [with] his remarks on white supremacy. *Newsweek*. https://www.newsweek.com/john-wayne-racist-airport-statue-1514152

Williams, C. E., Chief Judge. (n.d.). Bias on the bench? *The Florida Bar News*, Vol. 44:12, n.p.

2

The Perils of Populism, Racism, and Sexism: The Trump Lesson Plan for African Americans and Women

Mamie E. Locke

"We believe that unless representative government does absolutely represent the people, it is not representative government at all." These words were spoken by President Theodore Roosevelt in 1912 as he embarked upon securing the nomination for President. He set in motion a brand of frenzied populism that was echoed in 2016 by Donald J. Trump, including racial overtones. The indifference shown to women and African Americans is part and parcel of the Trump lesson plan as he preyed on the anxieties of his base to make anyone who disagreed with him enemies of the American people. Through populism and the politics of insecurity and insult, Donald Trump mobilized his base to undermine the political and socioeconomic voices of African Americans and women, especially women of color. Donald Trump used populist rhetoric, insults, and language to create a frenzy with his base to instigate backlash against those he considered enemies of the people. His campaign demonstrated a continuation of a populist appeal that began as far back as the mid-nineteenth century in various iterations, which continued with Theodore Roosevelt in 1912 and resurfaced with former presidential candidate and Alabama Governor George Wallace in the 1960s and 1970s. An underlying theme of this populism is the designation of a common enemy that must be castigated in order to uplift the purveyor of the populist message. The

M. E. Locke (✉)
Hampton University, Hampton, VA, USA
e-mail: mamie.locke@hamptonu.edu

difference is Roosevelt and Wallace were not able to solidify the populist appeal in such a way to propel themselves to the White House (although Roosevelt had previously served two terms as President as a Republican). Donald Trump, with no political experience, found himself on the stage in Cleveland, Ohio accepting the Republican nomination for President in 2016.

Although Donald Trump probably does not know or understand the concept of populism, he draws from the same playbook of past populist rhetoric which has created dissension within the Republican Party, the Democratic Party, and the nation. This chapter explores Trump's populist messaging, not only during his 2016 campaign, but within his overall history, his administration, and his politics of changing the narrative rather than engaging in public policy. Given that Trump has mastered this lesson plan of the populist message of insult and criticism, he has reshaped the Republican Party, leaders, and members such that his is the voice that dominates and controls. Despite two impeachments and Senate acquittal of charges of abusing his powers of the presidency and obstruction of Congress, Donald Trump continues a path that is designed to divide the American public. Trump's faux-populist politics of division and indifference has created a firewall that has negative implications and exclusion for African Americans and women.

Historical Perspective on Populism

This section of the paper will provide a review of populism as a movement in the United States. This will not be a detailed analysis, but an examination of how the idea of populism has ebbed and flowed at various periods of American political history. Of significance are the left and right elements that populist movements can take depending on the origins of the undertaking or individual leader. As a movement, populism is used to mobilize the masses against a perceived enemy. Populists claim to speak for ordinary and regular people, using rhetoric that is inflammatory, stirring anger, conspiracy theories, nationalist sentiments, and demonizing those considered outsiders (Kellner, 2019). Populism has been used by liberals, moderates, and conservatives to tap into the anger of those who feel disenchanted and isolated from the American political system. From the beginning, the populist movement has been racist with groups like the Know Nothings, the Populist Party of the late nineteenth century, former Alabama Governor and presidential candidate George Wallace, and groups like the Tea Party.

Populism has its roots in the American Party of 1849, better known as the Know Nothing movement. Founders and members preyed on popular passions and paranoia of the time given that it was a period of increased immigration. The Know Nothings supported the deportation of foreign beggars, and criminals and the elimination of all Catholics from public office. They also called for a naturalization period of 21 years for immigrants. The group tended to operate outside normal partisan channels, relying heavily on its members' populist appeal. They had a vision of what America should be and that was an American nationality and strong work ethic (Landis, 2019; Boissoneault, 2017).

The Know Nothings used populism to appeal to ethnic hatreds to win elections. By doing so, candidates knew that would be a distraction and they would not have to address harder issues such as class divisions. On the national level, they even launched an abortive White House run. Millard Fillmore had been Vice President under President Zachary Taylor, became President when Taylor died in office. He was a member of the Whig Party. Not very popular, Fillmore was not nominated by the Whigs for President in 1852. But the former President was a lifelong racist and nativist (anti-immigrant) and was chosen by the American Party as its presidential nominee. He campaigned under the banner "Americans Must Rule America." Speaking to an audience in Rome, New York, he warned: "You should be thankful that you live in this free and happy land. Guard well your institutions and be ever watchful against any attempt to divide or destroy your country." To the American Party leader, he made it very clear: "I have for a long time looked with dread and apprehension, at the corrupting influence which the contest for the foreign vote is exciting upon our election." (Landis, 2019). Despite these populist appeals, he lost the election.

The Know Nothings were unapologetically nativists, especially against Catholics. They also were sexist, not only objecting to women's suffrage but asserting that it was unnatural. They made nativism a political strategy and used immigrants as political targets, a tactic that has persisted. After the failed presidential run of Fillmore, the Know Nothings began to decline. Slavery became a more pressing issue than immigration. However, many of the populist ideas generated by the Know Nothings such as nativism remain and were later picked up by candidate Donald Trump in 2016 (Landis, 2019; Boissoneault, 2017).

The populist theme was retrieved during the presidential campaign of Theodore Roosevelt in 1912. As the Progressive Party candidate, Roosevelt, who had served two successful terms as a Republican President, launched a systematic attack on political parties and the critical role these organizations had played in American elections and government. Through the party, he championed instead a fully elaborated "modern" presidency as the leading instrument of popular rule. He believed that public opinion was stifled by inept Presidents and party bosses, but that through the new paradigm of the Progressives the people would reach their fulfillment with the formation of an independent executive power, freed from the provincial and corrupt influence of political parties. Roosevelt argued that the President, not Congress or the states, must become the "steward of the public welfare" (Milkis & Ong, 2012).

Roosevelt's populism was based upon progressive reform and the role political parties played in American elections and government. His focus was on shifting power from the local and state level of government to the national level. He argued that he was fighting against graft and corruption in favor of the people. So, his goal was to shift his message directly to the people and away from the party bosses. However, there was an element to Roosevelt's populism that had traces of the Know Nothings and that would be an undercurrent in later populist messages.

Roosevelt was dedicated to developing and executing a square deal under the banner of the newly formed Progressive Party. A key demographic excluded from the table of the Party was African Americans. Historian Eric Yellin noted that Roosevelt calculatingly alienated African American voters in the South because he assumed they were voting for his opponent, Republican William Howard Taft. As a result of this assumption, Roosevelt set out to create a shadow Republican Party made up of whites only. Consequently, a not-welcome sign for African Americans was hung out at the Progressive Party convention (Clark, 2016).

African Americans began to denounce Roosevelt. "To the Colored men who can find it possible, after denouncing President Theodore Roosevelt as a despot, demagogue, lyncher and betrayer of the confiding Colored race, to now support him even when he leaves his own party and help him to be the founder of a new party, we say that the white world is looking on with a contemptuous smile" (Clark, 2016). Yet another column chided: "the position of Mr. Roosevelt, disfranchising the Negroes of the South in his party is a virtual indorsement [sic] of the unconstitutional disfranchising laws of the South, and we believe that he has forfeited all right of respect or support from Afro-Americans." Dr. Reverdy Ransom was a minister in the African Methodist Episcopal Church and supporter of Roosevelt but left the Progressive Party and criticized Roosevelt's policy on African Americans and turned to the Republican Party, urging better treatment of Black people (Clark, 2016). Roosevelt did not secure the nomination, nor did Taft. Woodrow Wilson, the Democrat, won the election that year.

George Wallace's brand of populism extricated nostalgic feelings among many for a culture that seemed headed for extinction. He had become famous for his strong segregationist positions and galvanized those who believed what he believed. He decided to take that message nationally and make a presidential run at a time when the country was at a critical juncture in its history. With social and political crises at home and abroad; when hippies, pseudointellectuals, and atheists were following the limousine liberals, Wallace was a triggering figure who started a rage against all of those. The phrase "limousine liberal" was used to describe New York mayor John Lindsay by his opponent Mario Procaccino in the 1969 mayoral race. Procaccino described Lindsay as a "limousine liberal" which was defined as a meddler who wanted to improve the conditions of the poor and Blacks on the backs of hardworking White people. It was a charge that right-wing populists used; that is, that the rich and powerful escaped responsibility for their own conduct by shifting blame for whatever went wrong (Fraser, 2012). Ironically, it was the right-wing politicians such as George Wallace, who were noted for being anti-elitist, racist, populist, and chauvinistic, who used the White working class. He saluted the tenets of family values and hard work to appeal to this base for political purposes (Fraser, 2012). Wallace capitalized on the attacks against the so-called limousine liberals and pointed to them as the cause of the problems for hardworking Americans and he would be the solution.

According to Levitsky and Ziblatt (2018) in their book *How Democracies Die* there has been a sub-current in American political culture with populists like Huey Long, Joseph McCarthy, and George Wallace garnering votes and support throughout the twentieth century. Along with individuals like Trump, they have been able to always obtain around 30% of the electorate to support them although they seem to have a questionable commitment to democratic norms. With zero political experience, Trump would take some of the populist elements espoused by earlier right-wing populists and incorporate them into his message during his 2016 campaign and into his presidential administration.

The Rise of Trump's Populism

Much of populism has been immersed in racism, nativism, xenophobia, and conspiracy theories about the world. Donald Trump's world was Queens, New York, the borough of New York City where he was born and raised when it was the second whitest borough in the city. That was his world where he was encapsulated until the Immigration Act of 1965 which led to a transformation of Queens into a more diverse area. For Donald Trump, the transformation and diversification of Queens contributed to a more nativist ideological way of thinking, a xenophobic fear that has been heightened with the continued diversification of the country (Shorenstein Center, 2018). Trump's worldview has been shaped by a life of privilege and societal advantage that created an egomaniacal and narcissistic personality that never admits to being wrong and continually finding fault in others.

Trump's populism assumes that the only people who count are his own, the ones he molds into a political body, then engages, and easily casts off with once done. He in turn can use the support of "his people" as a weapon against opposition leaders and legitimate processes ensuring accountability, whether business, reality television shows, or in government. Within the Republican Party, which Trump has gone in and out of on several occasions, this tactic has in a sense fused with a much longer running Republican addiction to counter-majoritarian tactics. Trumpist populism and the Republican party minority rule tactics both comprise a response to perceived slow-rolling demographic emergencies, but in different ways. Those tactics include extreme partisan gerrymandering, voter suppression and census-gaming, and norm-shredding. An example was when Majority Leader Mitch McConnell held up of a Supreme Court seat which Trump got to fill after he was elected and inaugurated. Two of these tactics Trump has endorsed with enthusiasm, namely voter suppression and census gaming (*Washington Post*, October 30, 2019). Trump used census gaming when he attempted and failed to have the question of citizenship placed as a question on the census questionnaire.

In the minoritarian populist worldview, if the opposition is seen as illegitimate, then any and all tactics employed against it can be reverse-justified as a reassertion of the fictitious "people's will" arrayed behind the populist leader, even if that opposition does indeed represent a majority voice and makes sense (*Washington Post*, October 30, 2019). In the Trump populist world, the "people's will" was whatever he deems it to be and whatever he convinced his base it is. Any contrary view is unacceptable. It is through this lens that Donald Trump views women and African Americans.

Trump Attitude toward African Americans and Women: Populism or Hatred 2.0?

When it comes to African Americans and women, Donald Trump has developed a one-track mind. This is an attitude grounded in his Queens, New York background of White privilege. His public attitude and behavior toward African Americans and women date to the 1970s, when the Justice Department filed charges against him for discrimination and racial bias. Although he claimed on the campaign trail in 2016 that he was the least racist person that anyone would encounter, Donald Trump's life of bigotry for more than 40 years tells another story.

The 1973 lawsuit against the Trump Management Company alleged that employees in his 39 properties were directed to rent only to Jews and executives and tell African American applicants that there were no vacancies. Donald Trump and his father, Fred Trump, were named on the lawsuit. The Trumps did not admit to any wrongdoing but had to settle and sign a consent decree. They breached the decree and were back in court in 1978 and did not settle again until 1982 (Graham et al., 2019).

Trump is also known for having taken out full-page ads in New York newspapers in the aftermath of accusations of the so-called Central Park Five, teenage boys accused of raping a White woman in 1989. He called for the execution of the boys. Even after they were exonerated following the discovery of DNA evidence and the confession of the real perpetrator, Trump took out another ad calling the settlement awarded to them a disgrace. Even during his 2016 presidential run with continuous calls for law and order, he referenced the guilt of the Central Park Five. As Yusef Salaam, one of the five, pointed out: "Donald Trump's ad ran on May 1, 1989. The crime had happened April 19, 1989. We hadn't even started trial! That was just a few weeks after we were accused. He put nails in our coffin…" (Graham et al., 2019). C. Vernon Mason, Salaam's attorney, points out that during the 2016 campaign, well over two and a half decades after the crime and 14 years following the fact that the boys had been proven innocent, Donald Trump was still saying they were guilty (Graham et al., 2019).

It is interesting to note that Timothy O'Brien, author of *Trump Nation: The Art of Being the Donald*, stated that Trump inserted himself into the Central Park Five matter as a means of drawing attention to himself and as a way of becoming the spokesman for the stereotypical racist Archie Bunker New Yorker. "He trusts his gut on issues surrounding race, because he's got a simplistic, deterministic, and racist perspective on who people are…He's got a very Aryan view of people and race" (Graham et al., 2019).

Donald Trump was the architect and proponent of the birther movement. His birther discourse went beyond rationality and reinforced a White racial state. It activated anxieties over what he and his developing base saw as an increasingly multiracial and global society. The birther movement became a political conspiracy against Barack Obama that would signal to White people that he was ineligible to be President because he was not born in the United

States. This chatter began after Obama's speech at the 2004 Democratic National Convention (Kelley-Romano, 2019).

Thanks to Donald Trump, the birther conspiracy continued despite factual evidence to the contrary. Birtherism advanced the rhetoric of White supremacy. Further, in early 2012, when he anticipated challenging Barack Obama for president, Trump used the issue as a means of drawing attention to himself and mobilizing White voters. He began to not only question the legitimacy of President Obama's birth certificate, but he also engaged in dog-whistle and racist undertones that questioned the President's intellectual ability and honesty. He stated that President Obama was a Muslim who took advantage of the system to gain entry into Columbia and Harvard. Trump also questioned Obama's ability to have written a book, rendering him incapable of accomplishing what a true White American could do (Kelley-Romano, 2019).

Populists in the Donald Trump tradition have a "Manichean" worldview. That is, they break politics into a binary view of good or evil. To them, there are the pure people versus a corrupt elite. His rhetoric prompts believers to frame the world as a battle of good versus evil; of real Americans versus "other." In Trump's mind, pursuing the birther movement, he projected President Obama as "other." Although he supposedly ended the conspiracy in 2016, Trump continued to impugn the character of the President. When asked if he thought he had taken the birther issue too far, Trump's response was "no" because it made him very popular and he knew what he was doing. The Reverend Jesse Jackson, on the other hand, stated that Trump's language was "coded and covert rhetoric for stirring up racial fears" (Kelley-Romano, 2019).

Populism as a movement ebbs and flows from the individuals and organizations that tout it. Donald Trump took many aspects of populism as it framed his own beliefs and began to craft a pathway that would propel him to the presidency. The birther movement was only the beginning of his plan. It provided him with exposure as he made his rounds of morning, mid-day, and late-night talk shows. His was a greater plan being laid out to focus on the latent fears of many in America, using those fears to craft a populist platform to bring to the surface racism and nativism reminiscent of the nineteenth-century Know Nothings, tinged with the views of Roosevelt and Wallace. Significant to Trump's platform was an outward misogyny that was exacerbated by the nomination of the first woman by a major political party for president, Hillary Clinton.

During the 2016 presidential election cycle, Donald Trump promised to "make America great again." His plan was to do so by "draining the swamp," and defending "the people" from Washington insiders who in his view were corrupt, incompetent, and self-interested. Populist politics in 2016 was articulated by both a right-wing Republican and a left-wing Democratic candidate. On the right, Trump was considered the purveyor of populist politics while Senator Bernie Sanders of Vermont was his left-wing counterpart Trump described himself as a political outsider. However, he used dog-whistle politics, nationalism, and crude attacks on anyone who opposed him. Like many right-wing populists, Trump excluded anyone who was not considered to be his people, or "the people." This included ethnic minorities and immigrants. Only virtuous people could be included in his group. Left-wing populists tend to take a broader and more inclusive view of who is counted as "the people." Sanders saw himself as a strong advocate for working people within his concept of being a democratic socialist, taking on Wall Street and corrupt campaign financing (*Washington Post*, April 28, 2016). As the right-wing populist, what exactly did Trump mean when in saying he would make America great "again"?

Donald Trump's run for president was unusual and unprecedented. But it can be said to be the culmination of decades of developments within the conservative movement and the Republican Party. The movement itself was directing the party toward the kind of right-wing populism and insult politics that shaped the Trump campaign and ultimately the Trump administration itself as it continued to frame a certain level of political discourse.

Trump cultivated a political culture that brought into the base support from the little guy as he defined it. He also brought anger and insults. As he entered the Republican primary season, his campaign was characterized by insults to political rivals, celebrities, the media, institutions, and private citizens. Despite his shunning political customs and basic decency, even condemnation, Trump became Teflon, and as the more media gave attention to lack of convention and decorum, the more divisive and polarizing he became. Trump's political rivals did not take him seriously, but as he began to win more primaries and caucuses and appeal to voters with his outsider image and "anti-everything" voice, the messaging began to resonate with a segment of the population that had felt forgotten and left out, including many who had voted for Democrats for years.

The theme of "make America great again" (MAGA) was considered by some as dog whistle, coded language, a subtle message clearly understood by his base. What was meant in the subtlety was to "make America white again." For example, a Tennessee Congressional candidate took the slogan and put it on a billboard, declaring what many thought was the reality: "Make America White Again." When the candidate, Rick Tyler, was asked what he meant, he explained that he spoke to the reality of taking America back to a time when life was better, specifically, the 1950s, when television idealized the image of the perfect, happy White family. "It was an America where there were no…Islamic Mosques or radical Jihadist sleeper cells." (Melton, 2017). Although the billboard was taken down, the message had been broadcast and the sentiment understood.

In his acceptance of the Republican nomination for president, Donald Trump laid the blame for America's problems at the feet of Barack Obama and Hillary Clinton. He claimed that America was in crisis at home and abroad and in his words "Nobody knows the system better than me, which is why I alone can fix it" (Trump Speech, July 21, 2016). He claimed that his election to the presidency would mean better economic times, more jobs, industry, and a stronger military. He targeted his market: White men in the blue-collar sector, those with the most to lose when minorities and women started gaining more civil rights and more earning power in the past decades. He appealed to people who felt they were losing status as other groups became more empowered. Using words like "great" and "again" sounded positive but lacked specific meaning. However, it began to resonate with individuals who felt disenchanted with the political system.

The MAGA slogan also attracted extreme right-wing outliers. For some Trump supporters like the neo-Nazis, the Ku Klux Klan (KKK), and other White supremacists, they were able to feel good about Trump because "great" became interchangeable with White, heterosexual, male, hate, oppress, and deport. For these groups, America had once been great but no longer was but could be. In Donald Trump, they had someone who could bring back a better time. One African American questioned when was "again"? Was it before equality? Was it when African Americans could not eat in restaurants or had to drink from separate water fountains? (Melton, 2017). The idea of "again" had different meanings for those on the right and for African Americans and women.

President Bill Clinton was accused of being a hypocrite for calling MAGA racist because he had used same phrase during his presidential campaign in the early 1990s. Clinton said of MAGA: "I'm old enough to remember the good old days, and they weren't all that good in many ways… that message where I'll give you America great again is if you're [a] white Southerner, you know exactly what it means…" However, at an event in Little Rock while running for president in 1992, Clinton stated, "Together we can make America great again." (FoxNews.com). Was this a double standard? One can quibble over the use of the phrase and its translation by Trump and Clinton. However, the operative word for Clinton was "together" and to whom Clinton meant when he said "together." He was speaking to a very diverse audience and his intent was to be inclusive. In using "again" for Trump, is it to be inclusive or to sound a dog whistle?

For the populist Trump, one must point a finger at the cause of problems for "the people." He had outlined many of those during his campaign, in his Republican nomination acceptance speech, in his inaugural address and on numerous Twitter rants: mass migration/immigration, recession/job loss, the perceived failure of the political establishment, to name a few. Previous administrations, especially Barack Obama's, failed to handle any of the problems. Right-wing populists argue that political elites have failed to get a handle on the kind of immigration that threatens jobs, wages, and social cohesion. Immigrants have been coming into the United States and taking jobs away from hardworking, taxpayers. Candidate Donald Trump often focused on this aspect of public sentiments. He stated that "People want to take back control of their countries and they want to take back control of their lives and the lives of their family" (*The Guardian*, December 3, 2018). Once elected, Trump continued the narrative.

Whites without college degrees, both men and women, made up a third of the 2016 electorate. Trump won them by 39 percentage points, according to exit polls, far surpassing 2012 Republican nominee Mitt Romney's 25% margin. They were the foundation of his victories across the Rust Belt, including a blowout win in Ohio and stunning upsets in Pennsylvania and Wisconsin. In polling, these voters expressed deep racial and cultural anxieties. In exit polls, they were more likely than the country as a whole to say that illegal immigrants should be deported. But those polls also suggested economic concerns and hostility toward leaders in Washington were much more important factors driving them to Trump. At the same time, these working-class whites believed that they had lost the opportunity to achieve American prosperity as others had gotten wealthier. As non-college whites saw their jobs and businesses leave their rural communities, towns, and small cities where they were most likely to live, generally in the Rust Belt, cities like Washington, Boston, and San Francisco grew wealthier and saw more job growth (*The Washington Post*, November 9, 2016). The populist appeal of Donald Trump with promises of a better future found listening audiences with this population.

In past decades, many of the downtrodden areas lost factory jobs as expanding trade and advancing technology pushed the economy away from production work and into service areas. Many areas began to suffer as coal mines closed. Others experienced accelerated growth in high-paying energy extraction and support jobs as hydraulic fracturing grew, but when oil prices fell those jobs disappeared as fast as they came. Trump courted the working class by promising to restore the old industrial economy, cut taxes and deport immigrants. This appealed to those voters who were concerned about job loss and high unemployment and Trump provided them with someone to blame.

Trump's message generally did not resonate with African American or Latino workers, who are likely to earn less at every education level than whites do. Those workers lean Democratic by various degrees but appeared especially repelled by Trump's attacks on immigrants and his stoking of racial resentments. Although he amassed large numbers among blue-collar whites, it would not have been enough for him to win the Presidency. What helped him was his advantage among whites with college degrees. As a group, those workers were the winners of the new economy, blessed with cheaper imported consumer goods and a persistent wage advantage over their non-college counterparts (*Washington Post*, November 9, 2016). They saw Trump as an opportunity to maintain their advantage. Trump was able to pull together a coalition based on false promises. Would he be able to deliver any real results?

The 2016 presidential campaign was marked by Trump's insulting and mocking rhetoric politics. He crossed a lot of red lines through insults and inflammatory speech, labeling Mexicans criminals, insulting John McCain because he had been a POW who had been captured, which Trump didn't appreciate. Trump also mocked a disabled journalist. Trump established a right-wing populist tradition with his anti-elite bona fides by breaking norms and insulting what frequently was described as the establishment. Trump and his brand of insult politics fit into the long tradition of U. S. right-wing populism (Winberg, 2017). The media covered his ascendancy into the political stage as well as his many insults and attacks. Yet, there was limited pushback to his actions.

Insult politics captures a certain campaign rhetoric that is centered not on criticism itself but disparaging attacks against individuals or groups. Insult politics are naturally controversial and became intrinsic to Trump's strategy. Insult politics go beyond the traditional negative ad. To demonstrate that he was indeed fighting against the elite and to solidify his role as a right-wing populist, Trump had to differentiate himself from the customs and traditions of the political status quo (Winberg, 2017). He had to demonstrate to his base, those in the swing states of Michigan, Ohio, Pennsylvania, and Wisconsin, that he was their savior from the liberal establishment that was set on destroying America. They were part of the swamp in Washington that he would drain once he got there. More and more began to buy into his populist brand of making America great again.

To the surprise of many, Donald Trump was elected President of the United States on November 9, 2016. He was inaugurated on January 20, 2017. On January 21, 2017, women took to the streets in more than 20 countries in protest on the first day of his presidency. From the start, unlike most presidents, Trump began his administration with a 44% approval rating, the lowest ever of any president coming into office since polling on this question had begun. To put his numbers into perspective, Bill Clinton was at 77% in December 1992 and Barack Obama at 71% in January 2009. George W. Bush's first poll was taken shortly after he entered office with an approval rating of 57% in March 2001 (*NBC News*, 2017).

Trump's election was greeted by every racist group as a victory for themselves. A KKK newspaper noted that the Trump campaign slogan "make America great again" reflected the notion that "what made America great in the first place" was the fact that the country was founded as a "white Christian republic" and that voting against Trump was a betrayal of whites' heritage (de la Fuente, 2017). In the midst of Nazi "Hail Trump" salutes, the National Policy Institute, a White supremacist organization, organized a meeting to celebrate the Trump election. The Southern Poverty Law Center noted that in the first ten days following Trump's election there were 900 separate incidents of bias and violence against immigrants, African Americans, women, LGBTQ people, Muslims, Jews, Latinos (de la Fuente, 2017). At no time did Donald Trump denounce these endorsements or acknowledgments.

The new president was labeled a bigot by many. He openly used misogynist, racist and xenophobic language during the campaign. He used denigrating language to characterize "the Blacks" (how he referenced African Americans), Hispanics, and Muslims. All this behavior reveals a deeply biased and prejudiced individual who does not regard all humans as equals. He classifies people into groups of different worth (de la Fuente, 2017).

None of these issues were problematic for Trump, who took his victory as a sign that his behavior was acceptable, and he could continue to say and do as he had campaigned. He was ready to begin his presidential administration.

When People Show You Who They Are

Writer Maya Angelou once said that when a person shows you who they are, believe them the first time. Donald Trump's record regarding women and African Americans can be summed up in this way: he denigrates them with brazenly racist and sexist comments and observations. He does not disguise his racism, sexism, homophobia, or xenophobic attitudes, either in prepared remarks, or spontaneous statements. His early life demonstrated his contempt for African Americans in his business dealings, calling for the death penalty for the Central Park Five and prolonging the fallacious birther myth. His obsession with Twitter and making unsubstantiated remarks as factual undergird his hatred for those deemed "other." Following is a review of some of Trump's more strident racist and sexist polemics.

An early test in his administration occurred when members of the alt-right descended on Charlottesville, Virginia to protest the removal of a confederate statue. Those protesters were met by counter-protesters in the city who objected to their presence. The encounter erupted into violence and an alt-right protester drove his car into a crowd, killing a young woman. When asked about the incident, Donald Trump equivocated over White supremacist violence in Charlottesville, claiming there was there were very bad people, not just in the Nazi group, "but you also had people that were very fine people on both sides" (*Politifact*, 2019).

Trump telegraphs whiteness as Americanness. It is his populism, his messaging of racism, sexism, and misogyny that has targeted African Americans and women that generated fear in a segment of the population that saw in him a savior who would make America great again. It is this message that had Trump changing the narrative on former San Francisco quarterback Colin Kaepernick who made a political statement about law enforcement and violence against Black men by kneeling during the playing of the national anthem at the start of NFL games. Trump made the issue about patriotism and love for America. He told Kaepernick, who was released from his team, that he should find a country that works better for him. A key quality for Donald Trump is changing the narrative on issues and deflecting to another topic in order to place the focus on him.

Call it moral relativism, whataboutism, or false equivalence. If an atrocity is perpetrated by someone who has nice things to say about him, to Donald Trump it is not really an atrocity (Levin, 2017). According to Müller (2016), Trump is an "archpopulist," and in many ways a threat to democracy. He criticizes populism for being an antidemocratic discourse that follows its own logic. The archpopulists find themselves challenging reprehensible elites to restore the country back to its homogenous, authentic self (make America great "again"). Anyone who falls outside of that authenticity are enemies of the people and the goal of the archpopulists is to defeat the enemy (Müller, 2016). The populism created by Donald Trump aligns within the descriptors outlined by Müller, especially as he engages with women and African Americans.

Donald Trump has had an endless and varied supply of insults and playground taunts to hurl at opponents but appears to have a one-track mind when it comes to African Americans and women. He particularly likes hurling words like "dumb" and "dummy" (Smith, 2018). A clear pattern has emerged in the Trump administration's scandal defense playbook: go after Black women. A toxic combination of misogyny and racism helped Trump win the presidency; dog whistles and code with Trump proudly displaying his contempt for women and minorities. He vilifies Black women. His demonization of African American women in the media and political sphere varies depending on who he decides to target. He has challenged African American women's intelligence, looks, and hairstyles. He has called women losers and nasty. All of this, of course, is most often via Twitter rants. Of specific note are Trump's attacks and demonization of African American women journalists (Stan, 2017).

Trump denigrated Congresswoman Maxine Waters and television journalist Don Lemon, questioning their intelligence. He levied a sustained attack on Waters during his campaign rallies in 2018, referring to her as "low IQ" seven times and "dumb" quite frequently. He called journalist Don Lemon the dumbest man on television. These attacks on the intellectual capacity of minorities and women are extensions of Trump's long history of racial and gender bias. He has been able to connect with his base who widely accepts his staunch and deleterious language (Smith, *The Guardian*, 2018).

An examination of specific incidents is as follows. Trump called journalist April Ryan a loser and claimed that she didn't know what she was doing. He also said that "she's very nasty" and "she's a loser." As the president of the United States, Trump attacked an African American woman reporter for doing her job—that is, asking him a question he did not like. Previously when she had asked him a question at a press conference, he told her to "sit down" and stated that the media was hostile (*Newsweek*, 2018). A second incident occurred when Trump said to journalist Abby Phillips of CNN that she asked a lot of stupid questions. This was after she had queried him about whether his Acting Attorney General was going to bring in special counsel Robert Mueller, to which he told her that was a stupid question. He also accused PBS NewsHour White House correspondent Yamiche Alcindor of asking a "racist question" when she asked him if his reference to himself as a "nationalist" rather than a globalist was in support of White nationalists. He followed this statement with additional information, calling himself popular among African Americans by asking why he had some of the highest poll numbers with African Americans (*Newsweek*, 2018). This is typical of Donald Trump when engaging in Twitter rants or in press conferences. He deflects with untruths or distortions about how well-liked he is among a certain demographic. Data discussed later dismisses this claim.

The National Association of Black Journalists (NABJ) took Trump to task for his racist and continual attacks on African American women, especially fellow journalists. In 2018, NABJ President Sarah Glover stated that not only did Trump insult the media, but he reached an all-time low with his attacks on female journalists. "His dismissive comments toward journalists April Ryan, Abby Phillips, and Yamiche Alcindor are appalling, irresponsible, and should be denounced" (NABJ, November 9, 2018). Of course, no apology was forthcoming.

It is well known that the use of the phrase "you people" is racially coded and offensive to many African Americans. In an exchange with journalist Yamiche Alcindor, Trump not only used the phrase but berated and bullied her at more than one press conference. On March 13, 2020, when she asked him, that given the coronavirus outbreak, did he not take responsibility for disbanding the pandemic response team on the National Security Council. Trump's response was that it was a nasty question and he did not take responsibility for it because he knew nothing about it. He then deflected to a member of his team. He also said to Alcindor that things changed just like she no longer worked for *The New York Times* (cnn.com). At another press conference when Alcindor asked him about remarks he had made on a news show, Trump interrupted her before she finished the question, stating, "Come on, come on. Why don't you people—why don't you act in a little more positive? It's always 'get ya, get ya, get ya.' And you know what? That's why nobody trusts the media anymore…Look, let me tell you something. Be nice. Don't be threatening. Be nice" (*Washington Post*, March 30, 2020). Alcindor's mic was then shut off and Trump moved on to another reporter although she had indicated she had a follow-up question.

Donald Trump did not just insult African American women, he reached into his playbook for sexist and misogynist comments for women in general. Before, during, and after his election to the presidency, he had a history of demeaning and trivializing women. He is known to make disparaging remarks about women. Mainstream media and his Twitter account are replete with sexist, racist, and misogynist rants and remarks about women. During the presidential campaign, there was one woman seeking the Republican nomination, Carly Fiorina. At one point, Trump said of Fiorina: "look at that face…would anybody vote for that? Can you imagine that, the face of our next president?" When asked a question by Fox News reporter Megyn Kelly he called her questions ridiculous and continued with "you could see there was blood coming out of her eyes, blood coming out of her wherever." During the campaign with Hillary Clinton, Trump remarked that she could not satisfy her husband so what made anyone think that she could satisfy America.

"Does she look presidential, fellas? Give me a break." And during one of the debates, he stated, "such a nasty woman" (Lange, 2018).

Other comments have included calling Stormy Daniels, a woman to whom he paid hush money to not expose an affair, "horseface"; saying that Senator Kirsten Gillibrand (D-New York would come by his office "begging" for campaign contributions and would do anything for them; and that one could never get to look at tennis player Steffi Graf's "because the body's so good." Of former White House aide Omarosa Manigualt-Newman, Trump called her "a crazed, crying low life" and a "dog." One of his longest battles was with television host Rosie O'Donnell. He called her very unattractive and a fat pig. He said that if he was in charge of her television show, *The View*, he would get rid of her. "I mean, I'd look at her in that fat, ugly face of hers… [and say] you're fired" (Lange, 2018).

Trump also weighed in on the #MeToo Movement: "you've got today, any day and push back on these women. If you admit to anything and any culpability, then you're dead…you've got to be strong. You've got to be aggressive. You've got to push back hard. You've got to deny anything that's said about you. Never admit" [to anything]. One must also look at the fact that Trump has used vulgar, inappropriate, and uncomplimentary language relative to women. For example, he said of television host Nancy O'Dell: "I did try and f**k her." He has also said:

> "Doesn't matter what the media write as long as you've got a young and beautiful piece of a**." Further, during the 2016 campaign, the infamous Access Hollywood tape came out when he is heard saying: "I'm automatically attracted to beautiful… I just start kissing them …and when you're a star, they let you do it. You can do anything…grab them by the pussy…you can do anything" (Lange, 2018).

Despite this known behavior, Trump's wife at the time called it "boy talk." His campaign manager and later counselor to the President, Kellyanne Conway, continued to defend the behavior. There are women who support him because they said that he has hired women and helped bring down unemployment and appointed conservative judges (*Houston Chronicle*, January 27, 2020). There are women who sidelined Trump's deplorable misogynistic behavior and lewd remarks concerning women and voted for him in 2016 anyway. Many said that they did not believe his accusers or were not bothered by his sexist remarks enough to vote for Hillary Clinton (Moore, 2016). It is easy enough not to bring oneself to vote for a woman and bring oneself to a conclusion that it is acceptable to vote for an opposing candidate, but the rationale given flies in the face of reason to support an individual who admitted to behaviors that were beyond the norm in presidential politics.

Is This Presidential?

Trump has revealed and magnified racial fractures in this country. What is worse is the collective sentiment among part of the populace that seems to think and believe that it's acceptable to act on those beliefs in a virulent, and increasingly violent ways toward those with whom Trump supporters disagree. The reason they feel that way is because permission has been granted from the highest authority in American democracy, the President of the United States.

Trump told four sitting members of Congress, all women of color, Ilhan Omar of Minnesota, Rashida Tlaib of Michigan, Alexandria Ocasio-Cortez of New York, and Ayanna Pressley of Massachusetts, to "go back" to the totally broken and crime-infested places from which they came. Except for Omar, who came to the United States at age 8 and who is a naturalized citizen, all of the women heretofore mentioned were born in the United States. Trump tweeted "'The Squad' is a very racist group of troublemakers who are young, inexperienced, and not very smart." (*Vanity Fair*, 2019). He has gone so far as to accused Congresswoman Omar, a Muslim, of supporting al-Qaida and both Congresswoman Omar and Tlaib, also a Muslim, of hating Israel and all Jewish people. Asking Prime Minister of Israel Benjamin Netanyahu to ban women from the country was another action taken by Trump to prove a point. Netanyahu agreed (*Vanity Fair*, 2019).

Omar, Tlaib, Ocasio-Cortez, and Pressley are four freshmen women of Congress who formed a bond as progressive lawmakers who found common ground on issues of racial injustice, climate change, and the mistreatment of immigrant children being held at the border. But each has her own agenda. They are not a monolithic group, but individual members representing varied constituencies (*Vanity Fair*, 2019). Donald Trump lumped them together because he did not see them as anything but "other" and as he described them in his tweet. But his attack to divide and isolate them merely strengthen their resolve to come back at him in their joint press conference where they criticized the President for his racism and effort at distracting from the real policy issues of concern to the American people.

After attacking these four women of Congress, African American female journalists, Trump also attacked Congressman Elijah Cummings,[1] Chairman of the House Oversight Committee as a "brutal bully" and said his congressional district was both "a disgusting, rat and rodent infested mess" and "the worst run and most dangerous [district] anywhere in the United States". Trump said Cummings should "help clean up this very dangerous and filthy place." Some observers linked his tweets to widely condemned remarks he reportedly made in the Oval Office last year, calling El Salvador, Haiti, and some African nations "shithole countries." The president later doubled down on his attacks, accusing Cummings of doing "nothing but milk Baltimore dry" (*The Guardian*, July 27, 2019).

In the aftermath, Trump claimed that many African Americans called and thanked him for his remarks. He also said that African Americans are happy with his performance as president. He stated that "What I have done for African Americans, no president, I would say has done. Now, I'll say this; they are so happy because I get the calls." Trump claimed that African Americans were happy with the fact that he had achieved the lowest unemployment rates in history, opportunity zones, benefits for the inner city, criminal justice reform and happy that he pointed out the corrupt politics of Baltimore, and the filthy, dirty, horrible place that it is. "And they are happy as hell" (CNN, July 20, 2019).

Within the realm of being an archpopulist, Donald Trump has a history of inventing nonexistent phone calls and making dubious claims about people expressing gratitude to him for all the great things he has done, although he never did them. However, if one examines the facts African Americans are not pleased with Trump's performance as it relates to delivering on what they had to lose with him in the White House. Polls consistently show this; exit polls in 2016 Trump received 8% of votes cast by African Americans and opinion polls since his election show that he remains unpopular among African Americans. In a Fox poll, 11% of registered voters approved of Trump and how he handled race relations; 83% disapproved. When asked if Trump respects racial minorities, 78% of Black registered voters said no (CNN, July 20, 2019).

Trump touts the unemployment rate, but there was a greater decline under President Obama.

The unemployment rate among African Americans fell from 12.7% to 7.9%. For Trump who started with 7.9%, it fell to 6%. He bragged that the unemployment rate for African Americans has fallen to a record low of 6%,

---

[1] Congressman Elijah Cummings died on October 17, 2019.

but he did not give the complete picture. Trump could only claim a 1.9% drop, whereas President Obama experienced a 4.8% drop in Blacks' unemployment rate. African Americans were not happy with Trump on the economy; 64% were unhappy with his handling of most issues. There was not a single issue for which he received a positive rating (CNN July 20, 2019).

Rock-bottom Ratings from Black Women

Trump has shown himself to be an unapologetic racist, from his limited policies to his bombastic rhetoric. If anyone got the memo, it was African American women. His approval rating among Black women was 3% at one point. Trump consistently lied about the impact of his administration's policies on the Black community. Census Bureau data show that Black family median income in 2017 was $40,258, down from its 2000 peak of $42,348 and not statistically better than 2016, when President Obama left office (*NewsOne*, Sept 11, 2019).

African American women have sought to be agents of change in their opposition to Donald Trump's vitriol. The most meaningful response has been at the ballot box. African American women supported Democratic candidates in large numbers to get them elected. Senator Doug Jones of Alabama received 96% of the Black vote, but 98% of Black women voted for him. In 2017, in Virginia, Ralph Northam became Governor of Virginia with 87% of the Black vote, but with 91% of the Black female vote. And without the help of 92% of Black women voting for Democrats in 2018, Democrats would not be in charge of the House of Representatives as they are now. Black women have placed confidence in the Democratic Party as there is very limited support for Donald Trump.

Eighty-three percent of Black women give Trump a failing grade (F) with another 9 percent giving him a D. For Black women major concerns are in the areas of criminal justice reform and issues of law enforcement. Health care is also a major issue. However, when asked about major threats to them and their families, Black women clearly point to racism and the increase in hate crimes, the high cost of housing, and gun violence (*The Washington Post*, September 10, 2019). Although Donald Trump asked African Americans during the 2016 campaign "what do you have to lose," African American women feel there is a lot to lose and do not have confidence in his ability to address the needs of the community in any meaningful way.

Trump had a job approval rating among African Americans of only 9% (CNN). His approval rating, or lack thereof with African American women according to a CNN poll is at 3% (CNN). Trump has claimed that Black median incomes have risen under his administration which has not been demonstrated to be true. Statistically in 2017 African American household income was $40,258, below the 42,348 of 2016. Statistically, this is not better than it was in the last year of Barack Obama's presidency (*NewsOne*, 2019).

Responses by women to Trump and his vitriolic insults tended to remain above the fray. When he called Hillary Clinton a "nasty woman," she did not respond with similar attacks. She referenced his policies, his career, or statements made rather than comment on his appearance or personality. Without even mentioning Donald Trump by name, former First Lady Michelle Obama stated at the 2016 Democratic National Convention took aim at him with these words:

> …how we urge [our daughters] to ignore those who question their father's citizenship or faith. How we insist that the hateful language that they hear from public figures on TV does not represent the true spirit of this country. How we explain that when someone is cruel or acts like a bully, you don't stoop to their level. No, our motto is: "When they go low, we go high"… (Winberg, 2017)

There is a divide among women about their feelings on Donald Trump, depending on who's asked. Women in a progressive group in Houston, the Houston Women's Group, stated that they had hoped that Trump would grow into the job and become a good leader. However, it is a sad and critical time for the country and Trump is responsible due to his divisiveness. In the era of Republican women feel that Trump is doing a good job. They are not convinced that he is guilty of any wrongdoing. Others have done some of the same things and they are okay with that. Some see Trump more as a pragmatist with business acumen that has served him well, and, thus, the nation well (Zelinski). This, even though he has had multiple bankruptcies, has had failed businesses along with Trump University, and refuses to release his taxes as other elected officials have done. These women argue that Democrats have had an agenda against Trump since 2016, despite the fact Republicans controlled both chambers of Congress and the White House for 2 years.

The Houston Women's Group would like to see Trump held in check and that the impeachment process does that and validates their outrage. Women feel that Trump is the epitome of patriarchy and oppression of women. In their view, the entire Republican Party needs a cleansing. Trump has failed to earn their respect. He has supported through word and deed policies that negatively affect women, African Americans, other minorities, and the poor

Lesson Learned?

Not only did Donald Trump enter office with a low approval rating, but also under a cloud of suspicion regarding Russian interference with the 2016 election. With his appointed Attorney General Jeff Sessions recusing himself from any investigations, a special prosecutor was appointed to proceed with looking into whether Russia interfered with the 2016 election. In the middle of all this, Trump fired the FBI Director James Comey and many of his West Wing staff members resigned due to clouds of indictments and conspiracies. Eventually, the trail would lead to Trump himself.

In the latter part of 2019 and into 2020, Donald Trump was under the specter of impeachment. He was impeached by the House of Representatives on two charges: abuse of power and obstruction of Congress. The impeachment was essentially a party-line vote. Speaker of the House Nancy Pelosi appointed several House managers to present the House's position to the Senate. One of those individuals was a non-lawyer, but an individual who was quite capable of presenting the argument against the President. Representative Val Demings from Florida is a former social worker, police officer, and police chief of Orlando. Along with her fellow managers, Deming pointed out that the President's abuse of power and violation of the law threatened the national security of the United States and further jeopardized the integrity of free and fair elections (Owens, 2020). It is ironic that Trump's castigating of African Americans and women, would have his impeachment handled by a woman Speaker of the House and among the House Management Team, two African Americans, Deming and Congressman Hakeem Jeffries of New York. Despite evidence to the contrary of wrongdoing, Donald Trump was acquitted of articles of impeachment by the Senate.

The day prior to the vote, Trump gave his third State of the Union message. After snubbing a proffered hand from Speaker Pelosi, he proceeded to present a speech peppered with innuendos, half-truths, and outright lies. His dislike of President Barack Obama was evident throughout the speech. Trump spoke of the economic greatness of America and how he was responsible for it. In his three short years as president, the American economy had made dramatic changes, and the decay in which he had found it was over. He, of course, failed to mention the free-fall recession that President Obama inherited and had to address during his first term, nor the robust economy he had inherited and the economic recovery started with Barack Obama. It has been noted by fact-checkers that prior to the 2016 election over 8 million jobs had been added to the economy. In 2019, however, job growth slowed. Despite his prognostications to the contrary, Trump's economy did not grow the 3% that he had projected with business growth slumping in 2019 after a short rise following the tax cuts and the president's trade wars (npr.org). So, his claim that the economy is the best that it has ever been was sheer hyperbole.

Trump claimed that the unemployment rate is the lowest it has ever been, and it was due to measures he had taken after assuming office in 2017, the lowest in the history of the country. Again, this was hyperbole. The unemployment rate was 3.5% in December 2019. But during the great recession, the unemployment rate rose as high as 10%, but by the end of the Obama administration had dropped to 4.7% (npr.org). Technically, the Trump administration came into office with that unemployment rate having dipped to 3.5%.

Trump spoke about low unemployment rates for African Americans, Hispanics, and women as well as a reduction in poverty rates. He touted a reduction in the number of Americans coming off food stamps and welfare. This was an exaggerated fact. It is true that the number of Americans receiving food stamps was down by over 11 million in a 6-year period (from 47.6 million in 2013 to 36.3 in October 2019). In 2016, prior to Trump taking office, the number was down to 44 million. The number of people on food stamps had grown significantly during the recession but had begun to decline thanks to an economy that had begun to improve under the Obama Administration. It was the Trump Administration that had begun to encourage states to add work requirements and make it more difficult for individuals to qualify for food stamps (npr.org). So, Trump's message in his State of the Union was not quite factual.

Repeatedly, Trump highlighted African Americans, pointing to African Americans he had brought to the gallery as guests as well as touching on policies he felt directly appealed to the African American community. He referenced school vouchers and support for historically black colleges and universities. His vouchers proposal is not likely to get a hearing in a House committee and his African American vote count were not likely to increase beyond the 8% he received in 2016, despite launching a Black Voices for Trump campaign (npr.org).

In yet another State of the Union speech, Donald Trump exaggerated, stretched the truth, and lied. Even more disturbing, the President of the United States used the National Prayer Breakfast, usually an apolitical event, as his own platform to lash out at his personal enemies. Those "enemies of the people" included Speaker Pelosi, whom he criticized for praying for him because in his view she was not genuine, and Senator Mitt Romney because he used his religion as a justification for voting to convict Trump of wrongdoing. Rather than take the opportunity as a moment of healing for the nation, Trump once again proved himself to be polarizing and unapologetically sexist, myopic, and divisive.

Conclusion

In acquitting Donald Trump on impeachment charges, Senator Susan Collins of Maine said that in voting for his acquittal she hoped that he had learned from the case. "I believe that he will be much more cautious in the future" (cnn.com). Donald Trump saw his acquittal differently. When asked what he had learned from the impeachment process, Trump responded that "Democrats are crooked…they're vicious…they shouldn't have brought impeachment." He then tweeted: "DRAIN THE SWAMP! We want bad people out of our government!" (*The Hill*, February 15, 2020).

With all Republican Senators, excluding Mitt Romney, voting for acquittal, Donald Trump went into the 2020 election season as the only President to have been impeached while running for re-election. After the election, which he lost to Joe Biden, Trump also became the first U.S. president to be impeached twice. He also was acquitted of that one. Trump felt emboldened, had no remorse, and was strengthened in his resolve to ignore the rule of law. He retaliated against individuals who testified against him during the House hearings by dismissing Gordon Sondland as U. S. Ambassador to the European Union and Lt. Colonel Alexander Vindman from the National Security Council. Trump was following up on his notion that Article II of the Constitution entitles him to do whatever he wants to do. Trump's behavior underscores the tendencies of authoritarian political behavior outlined by authors Stephen Levitsky and Daniel Ziblatt in their book *How Democracies Die*. Following his impeachment, he tweeted the Ralph Waldo Emerson quote that "When you strike at the King…you must kill him." He likened the impeachment and trial to striking at a king, but he emerged triumphant, exonerated from what he called a great witch hunt. Congress was not able to take him down. He took his case to *his* American people on the campaign trail to speak his grievances and resentments and how he was persecuted for no reason. He can now make the case for not only making America great but keeping America (and Donald Trump) great.

The tragedy in this phase of American democracy is that many who walk the halls of Congress, notably Republicans, are so fearful of Trump's Twitter rants and what he might do that they remain silent in the wake of his many misdeeds and attacks on the Constitution, democracy and the rule of law.

Levitsky and Ziblatt state that there are four key indicators of authoritarian behavior. Republicans who remain silent should ruminate on these indicators as well as reflect on the case made by the House managers for impeachment:

1. Is there a rejection of or weak commitment to democratic rules of the game?
2. Is there a denial of the legitimacy of political opponents?
3. Is there toleration or encouragement of violence?
4. Is there readiness to curtail the civil liberties of opponents, including the media?

With the "I am a King" analogy, "Article II gives me the authority to do whatever I want," "there were good people on both sides," "…knock the crap out of them…", and "fake news media," among other statements, Donald Trump comes perilously close to autocratic behavior. Anyone who opposes him, such as the late Congressman Elijah Cummings, or the four Congresswomen known as "the Squad" continue to do, he repeatedly criticized with Twitter rants and questioned their legitimacy. His continuous alienation of American allies in favor of adversaries (Russia, Turkey, Saudi Arabia, and North Korea) should raise questions about his commitment to constitutional democracy.

Based upon a racist history, campaign rhetoric from 2016, and the more than 3 years of tweeting racism, sexism, nativism, and undermining the laws of the United States, Donald Trump has created an environment that is more divided, less tolerant, and more openly hostile. It is unfortunate that Trumpian behavior has become so normalized in American society, that his archpopulism has become acceptable to many in such a way that crowds are quick to say, "send her back" or "lock her up." Normalizing Trump's attitude and behavior toward those he deems "other" lays the foundation for the authoritarian government that Levitsky and Ziblatt reference. This is completely antithetical to the purpose of a representative democracy with three co-equal branches of government. President Donald Trump has used his position and populist approach to engender hate and fear in the American political system by pandering to the most extreme degree. The collateral damage is African Americans, other communities of color, and women.

References

Black Women really hate Trump, according to latest poll. (2019, September 11). *NewsOne*. https://newsone.com/3886539/black-women-trump-poll/

Boissoneault, L. (2017, January 26). How the 19th century know nothing party reshaped American politics. *Smithsonian Magazine*.

Clark, J. (2016, September 8). Theodore Roosevelt and the 1912 campaign: A complicated candidacy. https://blog.newspapers.library.in.gov/theodore-roosevelt-and-the-1912-campaign-a-complicated-candidacy/

Cobb, J. (2018, April 18). On race, populism, and politics. Harvard Kennedy School. *Shorenstein Center on Media, Politics and Public Policy*. https://shorensteincenter.org/jelani-cobb-race-populism-politics/

Dale, D. (2019, July 20). Fact check: No, African Americans are not happy with Trump. *CNN*. https://www.cnn.com/2019/07/30/politicsfact-check-african-americans-trump-approval/index.html

De la Fuente, A. (2017). The Whites' house. *Transition., 122*, 1–4. https://www.jstor.org/stable/10.2979/stransiton.122.1.01

Fact check: Trump delivers state of the union to tense, Partisan Congress. (2020, February 4). https://www.npr.org/2020/02/04/800983688/fact-check-president-trump-delivers-his-3rd-state-of-the-union-address

Fraser, S. (2012). *The limousine liberal: How an incendiary image united the right and fractured America*. Basic Books.

Graham, D. A., Green, A., Murphy, C., & Richards, P. (2019, June). An oral history of Trump's bigotry. *The Atlantic*. https://www.theatlantic.com/magazine/archive/2019/06/trump-racism-comments/588067/

How Trump speaks to Black American says a lot about his vision for this country. (2019, September 10). *CNN*. https://www.cnn.com/2019/09/10/politics/donald-trump-hbcus-african-americans/index.html

How Trump Won: The revenge of working-class whites. (2016, November 9). *The Washington Post*. https://www.washingtonpost.com/news/wonk/wp/2016/11/09/how-trump-won-the-revenge-of-working-class-whites/

In context: Donald Trump's very fine people on both sides' remarks. (2019, April 26). *Politifact*. https://www.politifact.com/article/2019/apr/26/context-trumps-very-fine-people-both-sides-remarks/

Kelley-Romano, S. (February 2019). Make America hate again: Donald Trump and the birther conspiracy. *Journal of Hate Studies, 14*, 33–52.

Kellner, D. (2019, August 6). Donald Trump as authoritarian populist: A Fromian analysis. In History.com (Eds.), *Populism in the United States: A timeline*. https://www.history.com/topics/us-politics/populism-united-states-timeline

Landis, M. T. (2019, January 22). The know-nothings: Populism using nativism as political strategy in the mid-19th century. https://brewminate.com/the-know-nothings-populism-using-nativism-as-political-strategy-in-the-mid-19th-century/

Lange, J. (2018, October 16). 61 things Donald Trump has said about women. *The Week*. https://theweek.com/articles/655770/61-things-donald-trump-said-about-women

Levin, J. (2017, August 12). The real meaning of "On Many Sides." https://slate.com/news-and-politics/2017/08/in-his-speech-on-charlottesville-donald-trump-told-the-nation-exactly-what-he-stands-for.html

Levitsky, S., & Ziblatt, D. (2018). *How democracies die: What history reveals about our future*. Viking.

Melton, M. (2017, August 31). Is 'Make America Great Again' Racist? *VOA News*. https://www.voanews.com/usa/make-america-great-again-racist

Milkis, S., & Ong, C. (2012). *Transforming American Democracy: TR and the Bull Moose Campaign of 1912*. Miller Center, University of Virginia. https://miller-center.org/transforming-American-democracy-tr-and-bull-moose-campaign-1912

Moore, S. (2016, November 16). Why did women vote for Trump? because misogyny is not a male only attribute. *The Guardian*.

Müller, J.-W. (2016). *What is Populism?* Philadelphia: University of Pennsylvania Press.

Owens, D. M. (2020, January 30). Black women take center stage in trump impeachment trial. *Essence*.

'Question'and 'Stupid Question'. (2018, November 9). *Newsweek*. https://www.newsweek.com/donald-trump-attacked-black-women-racist-question-1209872

Rice-Oxley, M., & Kalia, A. (2018, December 3). How to spot a populist. *The Guardian*. https://www.the guardian.com/news/2018/dec/03/what-is-populism-trump-farage-orban-bolsonaro

Samuels, B., & Chalfant, M. (2020, February 15). Trump unleashed: President moves with a free hand post-impeachment. *The Hill*. https://thehill.com/homenews/administration/483163-trump-unleashed-president-moves-with-a-free-hand-post-impeachment

Sargeant, G. (2019, October 30). Trump and the problem of 'minoritarian populism'. *The Washington Post*. https://www.washingtonpost.com/opinions/2019/10/30/trump-problem-minoritarian-populism/

Smith, D. (2018, August 10). Trump's tactic to attack Black people and women: Insult their intelligence. *The Guardian*. https://www.theguardian.com/us-news/2018/aug/10/trump-attacks-twitter-black-people-women

Stan, A. M. (2017, April 15). Trump & friends' war on African American women. *The American Prospect*. https://prospect.org/power/trump-friends-war-african-american-women/

Susan Collins says her vote to acquit Trump wasn't about predicting his behavior after saying he 'learned' from impeachment. (2020, February). *CNN.com*.

Tracey, A. (2019, August 16). 'They're as different as people come': The complex truth about the "Squad," Trump's favorite foil. *Vanity Fair*.

Trump 'Rat-infested' attack on Elijah Cummings was racist, Pelosi says. https://www.theguardian.com/us-news/2019/jul/27/donald-trump-elijah-cummings-democrat-house-oversight-bully-rat-rodent

Trump and Sanders aren't blazing new trails. Populism has run through U. S. politics for a very long time. (2016, April 28). *The Washington Post*.

Trump asked about disbanding pandemic office. https://www.cnn.com/videos/politics/2020/03/13/trump-coronavirus-press-conference-pbs-yamiche-alcindor-question-sot-vpx.cnn

Trump berates 'PBS NewsHour' reporter for 'threatening' question, hits 'nice' question out of park. (2020, March 30). *The Washington Post.* https://www.washingtonpost.com/nation/2020/03/30/coronavirus-yamiche-alcindor-trump/

Trump enters office with historically low approval rating. (2017, January 17). *NBC News.* https://www.nbcnews.com/politics/first-read/trump-enters-office-historically-low-rating-n708071

What do Black women voters want? (2019, September 19). *The Washington Post.* https://www.washingtonpost.com/opinion/2019/09/what-do-black-women-voters%2D%2Dwant/

Winberg, O. (Summer 2017). Insult politics: Donald Trump, right wing populism and incendiary language. *European Journal of American Studies, 12.* https://doi.org/10.4000/ejas.12132

Zelinski, A. (2020, January 27). So divided we can't think straight, how 26 Texas women view Trump's impeachment. *Houston Chronicle.*

3

Penal Populism: The End of Reason

John Pratt and Michelle Miao

Introduction

The phenomenon of penal populism was first identified as a characteristic of English-speaking Western democracies around the end of the twentieth century—specifically, the United States of America, the United Kingdom, New Zealand, Australia and Canada (see Roberts et al., 2003; Pratt, 2007). Since that time, however, various strands of it—the exact form that it takes and the impact it has varies from society to society—have been identified in a diverse range of countries. Generally, it demands a much more punitive approach to law breaking. This has been manifested in the form of dramatically rising imprisonment rates, as in the Anglophone world; but it has also led to clamourings for a more vigorous use of the death penalty in some Asian societies, particularly Japan (Johnson, 2006), or chemical castration of child sex offenders, as in South Korea (Koo et al., 2014) and the Czech Republic (Haney, 2016).

With each society it touches, it is as if penal populism undermines the very kernel on which modern punishment had been built: the way in which, from

J. Pratt (✉)
Victoria University of Wellington, Wellington, New Zealand
e-mail: john.pratt@vuw.ac.nz

M. Miao
The Chinese University of Hong Kong, Hong Kong, China
e-mail: michellemiao@cuhk.edu.hk

the time of the Enlightenment, science, rationality and expert knowledge were expected to outweigh emotive, uninformed common-sense, thereby ensuring that reason outweighed anti-reason in the development of penal policy. Now, though, slamming the door in the face of reason, penal populism drives up imprisonment rates when the detrimental effects—social and economic—of imprisonment are well known; or it reaffirms the place of capital punishment in modern penal systems when it is well known that there is no conclusive evidence about its deterrent effect; or it targets the bodies of offenders, in a reversion to punishment of the pre-modern era, rather than compelling them to forfeit time or money in line with the expectations of punishment in the modern world.

Most analyses of these developments have treated penal populism as a kind of localized event within the social body, as an aberration from the direction of punishment in modern society, as an infection that can be diagnosed, provided with treatment and exorcized: at which point, it is thought, the voice of reason will once again be allowed to drive modern penal arrangements in a progressive, humane direction and away from such excesses (Roberts et al., 2003; Pratt, 2008; Neto, 2009; Müller, 2012). There is, however, a myopia to these approaches. It is as if populism has burrowed into this sector of modern society alone and is then somehow confined there. It may wreak havoc in that location, but it cannot escape from it. This article, however, argues that the emergence of penal populism is neither the endpoint of nor the limits to populism and its consequences in modern society. Rather, it marks only the beginnings of its more general resurgence in the early twenty-first century. In these respects, *penal populism* should be understood as only a convenient incubating phase in which populist forces found vigour and strength before flowing much deeper into mainstream society from that gestation. And penal populism was only a warning of the much greater chaos that was to come when populism was fully unleashed. If it might be thought that penal populism represents an attack on the long-established link between reason and modern punishment, this has been only the prelude to the way in which a much more free-flowing *political populism* now threatens to bring an end to Reason itself, the foundation stone of modernity.

This article begins with an examination of the way in which, about the early 1990s, populism initially surfaced in the penal systems of the main English-speaking countries. It then argues that the shift from penal to political populism has been precipitated by two interconnected factors. First, the impact of the 2008 global fiscal crisis greatly exacerbated the way in which globalization had eroded economic security. Large sections of modern society have since been left resentful and marooned in their own helplessness before such forces, while governments seem unmoved by or oblivious to their concerns. Second, threats to both individual and national identity brought about by the mass movement of peoples across the globe—from East to West, North to South and South to North. As this has occurred, crime is no longer the main signifier of threats to well-being and the breakdown of order and authority. Rather, crime concerns have become conflated with concerns about "difference" and "otherness"—of which being a stranger, a foreigner, or an immigrant, legal or otherwise, have become one of the most potent symbols.

Beyond the controls of the penal system itself, there are thus demands that borders have to be defended, new boundaries need to be put in place—walls, electric fences, surveillance mechanisms have to be built or installed, terrorists must be "eliminated" and registers have to be kept of those with suspect religions or ethnicities to meet these more diffuse, amorphous threats. Individuals and organizations that stand in the way of what seem to be these necessary defences to individual and national health—on civil liberties or humanitarian grounds usually—are cast as traitors and "enemies of the people", people now prepared to look beyond existing democratic structures and modes of governance for solutions to restore security. In so doing, they are prepared to abandon Reason and put their trust in populist politicians to take them along a path—their leaders have no need of roadmaps or itineraries to guide them, they just tell their followers to have trust and belief in them—that will make them safe from such existential threats.

Punishment, Reason and Anti-reason

The Age of Reason arrived with the dawn of modern society. A world without reason, John Locke (1690/2016, p. 89) had written, gives rise to "despotical power … which neither nature gives, for it has made no such distinction between one man and another; nor compact can convey: for man not having such an arbitrary power over his own life, cannot give another man such a power over it; but it is the effect only of forfeiture, which the aggressor makes of his own life, when he puts himself into the state of war with another: for having quitted reason, which God hath given to be the rule betwixt man and man, and the common bond whereby human kind is united into one fellowship and society; and having renounced the way of peace which that teaches, and made use of the force of war, to compass his unjust ends upon another, where he has no right; and so revolting from his own kind to that of beasts, by making force".

Reason, it was thought by Locke and subsequent Enlightenment scholars, would thus bring an end to the tyranny, absolutism and arbitrariness in the exercise of sovereign power in the pre-modern world, the world without Reason: "the freedom then of man, and liberty of acting according to his own will, is grounded on his having reason, which is able to instruct him in that law he is to govern himself by and make him know how far he is left to the freedom of his own will' (Locke, 1690/2016, p. 35). For Thomas Paine (1794, p. 1), "the most formidable weapon against errors, of every kind, is reason. I have never used any other, and I trust I never shall". Similarly, Montesquieu (1914/2011, p. 6): "law in general is human reason, inasmuch as it governs all the inhabitants of the earth: the political and civil laws of each nation ought to be only the particular cases in which human reason is applied".

But if reason was to bring justice for all, it must also bring an end to the inconsistencies and uncertainties of the criminal justice order that reinforced the pre-modern exercise of sovereign power through brutal, public punishments to the human body: "we must overturn the barriers that reason never erecte" Diderot (1751/1967, p. 93) argued. To do so, legal theory had to disengage itself from the previous associations it had made between Divine Law and the absolute monarchs who had ruled the pre-modern world. From being some mysterious, incalculable and unpredictable force, decipherable only to those who ruled, law became, instead, man-made. It represented a contract between all citizens in a society rather than the dictates of a despot: "laws which surely are, or ought to be, compacts of free men, have been, for the most part, a mere tool of the passions of some, or have arisen from an accidental and temporary need. Never have they been dictated by a dispassionate student of human nature" (Beccaria, 1764, p. 12). The quest of legal theory then became one of showing what law *ought* to be, rather than what the Sovereign decreed it to be. It ought to provide security and order for all rather than merely the sovereign; and it ought to provide fundamental rights protected in inviolable ideas of justice that no ruler or government would be able to take away in the future. Beccaria (1764, p. 24) thus argued that law had to be made certain and knowable to all and applicable to all, in the form of criminal codes: "when a fixed code of laws, which must be observed to the letter, leaves no further care to the judge than to examine the acts of citizens and to decide whether or not they conform to the law as written: when the standard of the just or the unjust, which is to be the norm of conduct for all; then only are citizens not subject to the petty tyrannies of the many which are the more cruel as the distance between the oppressed and the oppressor is less, and which are far more fatal than that of a single man, for the despotism of many can only be corrected by the despotism of one; the cruelty of a single despot is proportional, not to his might, but to the obstacles he encounters".

In drafting these codes, science and rationality began to be applied to criminal justice. Rather than making law on the basis of the religiosity of priests or the sycophancy of courtiers, Diderot (1753/1966, p. 30) wrote that, in the Age of Reason, "there are three principal means of acquiring knowledge … observation of nature, reflection, and experimentation. Observation collects facts; reflection combines them; experimentation verifies the result of that combination". Beccaria (1764/1872, p. 46) thus urged that punishment should be efficient rather than spectacular. It should be proportionate to the crime committed rather than unnecessarily brutal: "the intent of punishments is not to torment a sensible being, nor to undo a crime already committed … Can the groans of a tortured wretch recall the time past, or reverse the crime he has committed?" Rather than simply being a demonstration of sovereign power, "the end of punishment, therefore, is to prevent others from committing the like offence" (ibid., p. 47). This meant that the amount of punishment should be proportionate to the crime committed: "if an equal punishment be ordained for two crimes that injure society in different degrees, there is nothing to deter men from committing the greater" (ibid., p. 32).

Kant (1797/1887, p. 195) then reinforced what the limits to modern punishment should be: "[it] can never be administered merely as a means for promoting another Good, either with regard to the Criminal himself or to Civil Society, but must in all cases be imposed only because the individual on whom it is inflicted has committed a crime". It was not only that there should be no punishment of the innocent; in addition, punishment of the guilty had to be an end in itself: punishment inflicted for other purposes might only lead to the excesses and iniquities redolent of the pre-modern era: "what, then, is to be said of such a proposal as to keep a Criminal alive who had been condemned to death, on his being given to understand that if he agreed to certain dangerous experiments being performed on him, he would be allowed to survive if he came happily through them?" (ibid., p. 196). Normative prescriptions for the operation of criminal law and punishment in modern society were initially set down and developed through the work of such scholars. From there, matters of law enforcement and punishment would be determined by secular experts, able to draw on collections of government statistics from the early nineteenth century to make scientific judgments when determining policy and its likely effects.

This did not then mean, of course, that Reason-driven policy and this alone made a straightforward linear progression throughout the modern period. It faced numerous impediments and took numerous detours. The emotive force and symbolic power of punishments to the human body (Hay, 1976) meant that the death penalty was not removed from the penal agendas of the main English-speaking societies until the 1970s. The emphasis on fixed and certain punishments did not preclude the introduction of indeterminate sentencing laws around the beginning of the twentieth century (Pratt, 1997). The initial emphasis on punishment as retribution gave way to a focus on treatment and rehabilitation for much of the twentieth century, often leading to the injustices that Kant had warned of when extra-punitive purposes are attached to punishment (von Hirsch, 1976).

Nonetheless, after the post-1945 revelations of Nazi atrocities, the need to protect individual human rights in criminal and penal law was given a renewed emphasis. The UN General Assembly Universal Declaration of Human Rights 1948 stipulated that "everyone has the right to liberty and security of the person. No-one shall be deprived of his liberty [except by] the lawful detention of a person after conviction by a competent court" (Article 5); and "no-one shall be held guilty of any criminal offence on account of any act or omission which did not constitute a criminal offence under national or international law at the time when it was committed" (Article 7). In 1960, the European Court of Human Rights heard its first case, "a leap forward in the history of human rights" (Howard & Morris, 1964, p. 153). The protection of individual rights was also reflected at a jurisdictional level. In the United States, prosecution because of status rather than crime was declared unconstitutional by the Supreme Court.[1] In O'Connor v. Donaldson (1975),[2] it was held that involuntary commitment of non-dangerous individuals capable of looking after themselves constituted "a massive curtailment of liberty" and was unconstitutional.

Even those areas of penal development that had resisted or departed from the expectations of Reason gradually succumbed to its demands. It had always been assumed anyway that indeterminate prison sentences (at least in the English-speaking countries) would be kept at the periphery of the penal system and rarely used. In England, Sir Evelyn Ruggles-Brise (1921, p. 58, our emphasis), Head of the English Prison Commission, was at pains to point out that such provisions "do not touch that large army of habitual vagrants, drunkards, or offenders against bylaws who figure so prominently in the prison population. *[These are] weapons to be used only where there is a danger to the community from a professed doer of anti-social acts being at large,* and reverting cynically on discharge from prison to a repetition of predatory

---

[1] Robinson v California 370 US 660 (1962).
[2] 422 US 563.

action or violent conduct". Thereafter, the US sexual psychopath laws, providing as they did for a fixed term of imprisonment for the original crime after those so diagnosed were first "cured" in a mental institution, were periodically struck down as unconstitutional or fell into disuse (Tappan, 1957). Other forms of indefinite, preventive sentencing experienced a similar fate (Bottoms, 1977). Their arbitrary and inconsistent use made their retention seem unjustifiable and their abolition seem inevitable (see the New Zealand Report of the Penal Policy Review Committee, 1981, 1982).

As for the death penalty, Reason and its attributes—science, rationality, humanitarianism—eventually triumphed over the emotive, punitive excess it had come to represent to policy makers in the post-war period. It was eventually abolished in these Anglophone societies during the 1960s and 1970s. Government was prepared, at that time, to rid itself of punishments that were thought to have no rightful place in modern democratic society: "[the death penalty] is the one remaining relic in our penal world of the old system of complete repression which was tried against criminals and so badly failed … these instruments have no proper place in the institutions of a free democracy … repressive punishments belong to the systems of totalitarian states and not democracies. It was no accident that the chief exponents of violence and severity in the treatment of criminals in other times were the Nazi and Fascist states" (UK Hansard 449, 14 April 1948, col. 1014–1015). In imposing a (temporary) moratorium on the death penalty in the USA, the Supreme Court in Furman v Georgia (1972)[3] affirmed that "one role of the constitution is to help the nation become 'more civilized'. A society with the aspirations that ours so often asserts cannot consistently with its goals take the lie of any human being, no matter how reprehensible his past behaviour".

About 1980, Reason had reached its high-water mark in the development of punishment in modern society. Imprisonment had come to be regarded very much as a "last resort penal option:" too expensive, inhumane and inefficient (Home Office, 1988). For much of the twentieth century, barriers had been steadily erected in front of it to keep out a broadening range of offenders for whom it was thought that such a sentence was too harsh and would do more harm than good: first offenders, young offenders, child offenders, those who suffered from some sort of mental instability, drunks, vagrants and ultimately virtually all non-violent offenders. Not only this, but the "back to justice" movement (von Hirsch, 1976), with its emphasis on consistent, limited and proportionate punishments reaffirmed the continuity of the penal expectations from the Age of Reason. These were still the yardstick against

---

[3] 408 US 238, 296–297.

which a society's alignment or otherwise with the presumptions and expectations of modernity could be judged.

In shaping these developments, an establishment elite, made up of senior civil servants, judges, university professors, and authoritative sections of the media such as the BBC and *The Times* newspaper as it then was, was greatly influential on government, and able to make pronouncements on the way forward for punishment with little fear or the prospect of these being contested. The Home Office (1959, p. 13) White Paper *Penal Practice in a Changing Society*—the leading statement of the aims of British penal policy in the post-war period—thus determined that punishment should take the form of "more humane and constructive methods". Furthermore, the axis of penal power that the elite had formed with governments not only excluded any representatives of those who claimed to speak on behalf of the general public, but took the view that governments should move ahead of public opinion. Abolition of the death penalty had become an illustration of a strong government, prepared to act as it saw fit and irrespective of the wishes of public opinion to the contrary. As one speaker in the British parliament explained: "I doubt very much whether at any time during the last one hundred years a plebiscite would have carried any of the great penal reforms that have been made. The appeal in the time of [Sir Samuel] Romilly was always the belief that public opinion would not stand it, but there are occasions when this House is right even if public opinion may not at that moment agree" (UK Hansard 536, 10 February 1955, col. 2083). Seemingly closing any further discussion, *The Times* editorial (13 March 1975, p. 5, our italics), opined that "it has been said that parliament is a good deal ahead of public opinion … this is to a large extent true …*it is certainly not our business to wait for public opinion on such an important issue*".

From this time, though, many of these trends and characteristics have been reversed: as if a resurgent anti-Reason now drives modern penal development. The growth of imprisonment, in some of the Anglophone countries especially, is perhaps the most obvious illustration of this. In the US, the rate of imprisonment has increased some 700% from 1975 to 2012 (from 110 per 100,000 of population to 762).[4] It has come close to doubling in the UK (from a rate of 80 per 100,000 in 1990 to 147 in 2016); and has more than doubled in New Zealand (from 85 per 100,000 in 1985 to 208 in 2015). Furthermore, indeterminate prison sentences have been refurbished and reactivated. In New Zealand, the number of prisoners serving the indefinite term of

---

[4] The World Prison Brief has been used as the source for all prison statistics. Here, the US rate represents a decline from its high of 755 in 2008.

preventive detention has increased from 12 in 1985 to 284 in 2015. One in five English prisoners in 2012 were serving indefinite sentences, dramatically undermining the previous emphasis on proportionality and consistency.

There have also been innovative penal measures that strike at the very core of what had become inviolable values of punishment in modern society. Three strikes laws, sometimes two strikes, punish prior record in addition to the crime committed. Retrospective legislation—punishing behaviour that was not criminal at its commission—is justified on the grounds that the need for public protection supersedes individual rights. The principle of no double punishments is contravened by "civil detention" provisions (that is, indefinite imprisonment) for some sex offenders at the end of a finite prison term, as is the principle that only the guilty can be punished: they are being detained because not because they have committed more crimes but because they are thought to be at risk of committing crime in the future. These moves to controlling risk at one end of the penal system have been matched at the other by controls on movement in public space of a variety of those who live their lives on the street (gang members, vagrants, beggars, etc.) in the form of supervision and surveillance to prevent future crime—but before they have actually committed one.

In addition, the language of punishment is now much more redolent of the voice of Anti-reason rather than Reason. "Three strikes", "life means life", "no parole" and so on put into legislation raw, vengeful common-sense rather than humane objectivity and rationality. At the same time, the authority of the central state has weakened (Garland, 1996). Now, rather than being prepared to move ahead of public opinion, it is ready to implement some of its wildest demands. Even so, this has not been sufficient to hold back some sections of the public from vigilante activities that challenge the state's previous monopolistic power to punish (Pratt, 2000).

Explaining the Rise of Penal Populism

One explanation of these transformations attributes them to the rise of penal populism. This needs to be distinguished, first, from "authoritarian populism" (Hall, 1979). The latter was seen as involving the imposition of "a new regime of social discipline and leadership *from above* in a society increasingly experienced as rudderless and out of control" (Hall, 1988, p. 84, our italics). But such an account does not involve any recognition of the way in which populist social movements have broken up the existing axis of penal power and formed a new one with a government that, having expelled establishment elites from influence, now puts its own illiberal stamp on punishment. Second, it also needs to be distinguished from "populist punitiveness" (Bottoms, 1995). This involves politicians "tapping into" the public's seemingly punitive stance on crime for their own electoral advantage, by manipulating this with extravagant promises about what more punishment will achieve. Here again, though, the dominant political class is still seen as being in control of events, rather than responding to the demands of outsider law and order activists and so on.

In contrast, penal populism specifically addresses the role and influence of these hitherto outsider individuals, groups and organizations on contemporary penal development. Developing the work of political scientists such as Shils (1956) and Canovan (1981) on populism, it is as if crime and punishment issues act as magnets that draw together those who see themselves as disenfranchised by governments thought to have allowed the unworthy and undeserving to prosper at their expense. In the criminal justice field, it was as if the establishment had been pulling the strings of government, prescribing generous treatment and lenient sentences for law-breakers while ignoring the well-being of crime victims and law-abiding citizens. From the 1980s, these concerns turned into howls of rage from newly emerging social movements that now claimed the right to speak on behalf of those whom the government had forgotten. Their primary demands included terminating the baneful influences of the establishment and replacing them with their own representatives. In the new axis of penal power that began to be forged, crime control policy should take the form of protecting the public from crime risks and punishing those who pose them, rather than safeguarding the individual rights of offenders and potential offenders.

Initially taken to be an almost exclusive characteristic of the main Anglophone societies, penal populism emerged out of the tensions and dynamics created by the neo-liberal restructuring that took place in these societies from the early 1980s (Pratt, 2007). It was seen as having five underlying causes:

The Decline of Deference
This helps to explain disenchantment with establishment power structures. It means that the values and opinions of elites that had previously been accepted without question are now not only respected but can provoke outrage and derision. Nevitte (1996) argued that the decline of deference is a natural consequence of post-1945 social reforms that raised the living standards of the whole population. Before the 1980s, it was assumed that establishment

figures—in the universities, the civil service and so on—formed a natural class of government on the basis of their lineage, education and wealth and the positions of power that these characteristics then guaranteed for them. Thereafter, however, those in government or government bureaucracies would no longer be viewed as the social superiors as the rest of society, having the exclusive right to pronounce on issues of the day, and would accordingly be challenged by those outside these Establishment circles.

However, the extent to which this supposed equalization has occurred in some societies (Britain, for example) would seem debatable. What seems more pertinent to the decline of deference is the way in which the criminal justice establishment failed to address issues of rising crime from the 1950s and in so doing seemed remote and detached from the concerns of "ordinary people" (Margaret Thatcher's successful use of "law and order" in the 1979 British election was one of the first illustrations of the political potency of this issue). The subsequent decline in crime from the early 1990s across most of Western society (for example, Zimring, 2012; Farrell et al., 2014) could not displace the way in which rising crime had by then become a taken for granted "social fact"—to which the establishment had no answer. Attempts by its members to explain that it was in decline rather than rising simply became proof of their own irrelevance and duplicity. By the same token, the developing area of risk control through penal measures has come to symbolize the way in which governments were prepared to jettison previous ties to the Establishment, with its now derided concerns about ensuring individual rights rather than protecting community rights. Introducing the British anti-social behaviour legislation, the Home Secretary stated that this "represent[ed] a triumph of community politics over detached metropolitan elites" (UK Hansard 310, 8 April 1998, col 370).

The Decline of Trust in Politicians and Existing Democratic Processes
Electorates grow increasingly cynical of politicians' promises and guarantees of better futures when these regularly fail to materialize (especially when this is compounded by evidence of their own scandalous conduct, as with the revelations of extensive fraudulent expenses claims by British MPs in 2009). Indeed, rather than bringing better futures, government policies may bring disaster to those citizens who loyally adhere to them. In the aftermath of economic restructuring, worthy citizens who had followed government advice and invested, often for the first time, in the stock market (making fortunes in this way was advertised as no longer being the prerogative of the already rich),

were likely to have been the ones hurt most when the first of the great post-restructuring crashes occurred in October 1987.

Using the experience of New Zealand as an illustration, this had been one of the countries at the forefront of the restructuring. The crash then contributed to a dramatic decline of trust in both its Left and Right mainstream political parties that had been committed to it—support falling to nine and 12% of the electorate, respectively, in opinion polling in the early 1990s (see Pratt & Clark, 2005). This decline of trust simultaneously led to a surge of support for the right-wing and populist New Zealand First party. It promises to place "control of New Zealand's resources in the hands of New Zealanders, by restoring faith in the democratic process", alongside "common-sense decision-making in the best interests of all" (New Zealand First, 2014). The decline also brought a change to the electoral system that has virtually guaranteed this party permanent representation in parliament. Following a referendum, the "first past the post" system was changed to proportional representation in 1996. New Zealand First will almost always be able to attract a disaffected core of the electorate sufficient to take it over the 5% threshold it now needs to gain parliamentary seats. On two occasions since, it has become "kingmaker" in coalition governments.

Much of this party's initial success came through speaking to public anxieties about crime and promising magical solutions to the problem (more police, tougher sentencing, Pratt & Clark, 2005). The major parties have been prepared to accede to these demands to win their support in parliament (Lacey, 2008). Furthermore, the popular appeal of 'law and order' that it had demonstrated encouraged the mainstream parties (as in Britain and the USA, see Jones & Newburn, 2006) to compete with each other on these terms, thereby building penal populism into government policy.

The Rise of Global Insecurities and Anxieties

From the 1980s, the modern world has become a much riskier, threatening place (Beck, 1992), in many ways a consequence of the same restructuring. If this has brought new possibilities of pleasure and fulfilment in everyday life, these are also beset with new risks—terrorism, new kinds of cancers, credit card fraud and so on. This has occurred in conjunction with the fragmentation or disappearance of many of the old and familiar symbols of security and stability. The permanence of employment and all that comes with this have disappeared for many (Standing, 2014). Family life has become much more tangential, with an increased likelihood of divorce amidst the growth of impermanent *de facto* relationships.[5]

Hence, again, the utility of crime and punishment in remedying these deficiencies in social capital. During the 1990s and early part of the twenty-first century, it seemed that crime was the most obvious and immediate source of risk and danger, the most obvious and immediate symbol of the inability of governments and their experts to do anything about making everyday life more secure. As Tyler and Boeckmann (1997) demonstrate, the more social cohesion seems to be unravelling, the more likely it is that there will then be support for severe punishments—not simply as a response to crime but as a way of providing consensus and solidarity and the restoration of authority which seems to be missing elsewhere in the social fabric. The intensity and ferocity of the new language of punishment ("three strikes" etc.) reflects the enhanced and extended role punishment has had to play in these societies in this regard

The Influence of the Mass Media

Life in modern society has come to be characterized by "the sequestration of experience" (Giddens, 1991, p. 244): "the separation of day-to-day life from contact with those experiences which raise potentially disturbing existential questions—particularly experiences to do with sickness, madness, criminality, sexuality and death". As most people in modern society became uncomfortable in dealing with these aspects of everyday life, so these matters were steadily hidden behind bureaucratic screens, with the mass media vicariously informing their publics about them. Or rather, for much of the twentieth century, what information they were provided with was shaped by authoritative sections of the media, allowing the establishment to remain largely in control of public understandings of them.

---

[5] Marriage rates (i.e. number of marriages occurring among the population of a given geographical area during a given year, per 1000 mid-year total population) are as follows: Australia, 1980: 7.4, 2013, 5.1; Canada, 1981, 7.7; 2008, 4.4; New Zealand, 1980, 7.3; 2014, 4.4; UK, 1980, 7.4, 2012, 4.4; USA, 1985, 10.1; 2012, 6.8. Ratio of marriages to divorce over the same period is as follows: Australia, 1980, 2.75:1; 2013, 2.3:1; Canada, 1980, 3:1; 2008, 2:1; New Zealand, 1980, 3:1; 2014, 2.5:1; UK, 1980, 2.7:1; 2012, 2:3:1; USA, 1980, 2:1; 2012, 2.2:1. Couples in de facto relationships in Australia increased from 5% in 1982 to 15% in 2006; in Canada, 6% in 1981 to 16.7% in 2011; in the UK, from 8.9%in 1996 to 16.4% in 2014. One-parent families increased in Australia from 8.6% in 1981 to 15% in 2011; in Canada, from 11.3% in 1981 to 16.3% in 2011; in New Zealand from 12% in 1981 to 17.8% in 2013in the UK, 13.9% in 1981 to 25% in 2014; in the USA, from 19.5% in 1980 to 29.5% in 2008. Meanwhile, average household size declined across all these societies: in Australia, from 2.8 in 1986 to 2.6 in 2006; in Canada, from 3.3 in 1981 to 2.9 in 2011; in New Zealand from 3.0 in 1981 to 2.7 in 2013; in the UK, from 2.7 in in 1981 to 2.4 in 2012; in the USA, from 19.5 in 1980 to 29.5 in 2008.

However, from the 1980s, structural changes in the media meant that this was no longer possible. Changes in media technology, the advent of satellite television, and the deregulation of broadcasting had brought about a much more diverse and pluralistic set of understandings about the world—at a time when the decline of organic community life has meant that individuals have become much more reliant on the news media rather than friends, family or work colleagues to inform them about the world. These structural changes in the media then meant that the onset of the fall in crime had little public impact. It was not really newsworthy. Instead, crime continued to be defined as the most obvious and immediate source of risk and danger. Deregulation of state broadcasting amidst the advent of new media technology meant that news reporting had become more simplified, more competitive, more readily available and more sensationalized: more than ever before, a sensational story about crime—its menace not its decline—would beat off competitors, attract the public and thereby attract more advertising revenue (Jewkes, 2004). Amidst this restructuring, the criminal justice establishment found itself unable to control the parameters of public debate and knowledge about such matters.

The Symbolic Importance of Crime Victims
The importance of crime news in the new framework of knowledge also gave much greater emphasis to victims' accounts of their experiences, rather than the detached, objective analysis of experts. In this respect, crime victims were given a new kind of authenticity and authority. Their personal experiences outweighed the statistical realities of crime. In most cases, these experiences were presented as something that could easily happen to anyone: going to school, journeying home from work and so on became the starting point for a catalogue of horrors that were then inflicted on these unsuspecting victims. When such catastrophes could befall respectable, ordinary citizens in the banality of their everyday life, it was as if what had happened to them became a universal experience and a universal danger.

Hearing, reading, watching their traumas led to demands for more emotive and expressive punishments that sufficiently reflected public anger and revulsion at such crimes; and demands, as well, for more opportunities for victims to express their own anger at their suffering, as opposed to the carefully measures tones of courtroom professionals. In a number of jurisdictions, such demands have necessitated a spatial and emotional reorganization of criminal justice proceedings, with victims at their centre, rather than their offenders, going through the detail of their victim impact statements. But when judges seem more swayed by reason rather than the pain victims when passing sentence (in reality their hands are likely to be tied by legal constraints anyway on what they can do), this further divides the criminal justice establishment from victims and potential victims and their expectations of justice. It becomes more evidence of how out of touch such elites are from everyday life.

Legitimacy Deficits and the Rise of Populist Politics

While these were the forces that combined to drive penal populism, other modern societies were seen as having built-in defences against such intrusions: a much greater deference to the criminal justice establishment and trust in government in Finland, for example, had prevented its emergence in that country (Pratt, 2007). But since the publication of Pratt's *Penal Populism*, it is clear that populism no longer confines its influence to the penal sector of the Anglophone countries. Instead, it cuts across much of political life in modern society as a whole, transforming wide-ranging areas of governance. Historically, populist movements have been found on both the left and right of the political spectrum (Betz, 1994). In Greece, for example, it brought the left-wing Syriza party to power, in opposition to EU and IMF demands for economic restructuring and massive reductions in government expenditure. It is usually the case, though, that when populism surfaces in a particular society, it moves the political agenda well to the right (see Haney, 2016 on the Czech Republic, Hungary and Poland). Even so, there are important nuances and differences within right-wing populism. In some cases, it professes to be an anti-big state (as in the UK); in others (as in Sweden and Finland), it wants to preserve extensive state services—but only for its own authentic nationals—new arrivals will not be welcome. In addition, contemporary populism has brought into being a new era of anti-democratic "strong man" politics (as in the Philippines, Turkey and Russia).

What is it, though, that has brought about the rise of this populist politics? Again, the specific mix of its causes varies. In China, for example, penal populism became a testament to the Party-state's determination to protect its citizens from evil crimes and uncertain risks associated with the profound transformation of the Chinese society to a market economy from the late 1970s (Miao, 2013). Nonetheless, what remains at the core of populism is the sense of disenchantment and disillusionment amongst large sections of society with the way in which political power has been exercised by governments, seemingly in collusion with establishment elites—favouring the unworthy and the undeserving at their expense. Initially, the penal system had been a useful receptacle for this 'legitimacy deficit'—the tension and anxiety that is generated amongst those who feel powerless, ignored or left behind by the way in which the dominant class exercises power (Beetham, 1991). In a bid to compensate and restore their legitimacy, governments were happy to direct that antagonism towards criminals and prisoners—unpopular outsiders who played the role of useful scapegoats. Thereafter, though, the much greater potency of political populism has been the product of the way in which two of the elements necessary for penal populism have become much more deeply entrenched in the fabric of modern society. These not only give a distinctive texture to the already existing cauldron of mistrust and anger on which populism feeds but ensure that it spills out of the penal sector altogether.

First, *economic insecurity and uncertainty*. The global fiscal crisis of 2008 has deepened already existing inequalities in modern society brought about by the globalization of trade and capital from the 1980s—between the winners in the casino economies that were created and its losers (Reiner, 2001). At one level, it had been thought that the 2008 crisis would impose greater financial rectitude on governments, thereby blocking penal populism and its financial profligacy (Pratt, 2008). If, to a degree, this has occurred,[6] the crisis itself had a much deeper impact on everyday life than this. By and large, winners continued to win. Indeed, the winnings of some of them greatly increased because they bought up cheap property or shares that came on the market in the subsequent recession. The number of losers, however, became greatly swollen due to attendant redundancies and intermittent unemployment, permanent underemployment, or reductions in employment conditions for many others, alongside cuts and restrictions on welfare expenditure.

At the same time, opportunities for employment in the public sector—a previous safe haven, offering longevity and security, generous pensions and regular wage increments—have significantly diminished as a result of the new limits imposed on government spending post-2008. The full extent of the changing nature of the labour market, from the beginning of restructuring in the 1980s to post-2008 economic stringency is reflected in the decline of public sector employment: from 27.6% of the Australian workforce in 1989 to 16.5 in 2014; from 25.9% in New Zealand in 1981, to 17.1 in 2013; from 27.4% in the UK in 1980 to 17.2 in 2015. For most, employment in the much more precarious and quixotic private sector awaits—if anything awaits them. The general expectations of inexorable progress associated with

---

[6] See note 4 regarding the decline in the US imprisonment rate. See also Goode (2013).

modernity, of betterment, of always improving living standards, have also evaporated. The Governor of the Bank of England has thus warned that 'Britain is experiencing its first "lost decade" of economic growth for 150 years [and that] real incomes had not risen in the past ten years' (quoted in *Daily Telegraph*, 6 December 2016).

This "precariousness" (Standing, 2014) has deepened the already existing distrust of establishment elites and supranational governmental organizations, such as the IMF, EU, World Bank and so on (for Donald Trump, the UN has become nothing more than "a good time club").[7] These are seen as either powerless to prevent the 2008 crash, or helplessly caught up in it, or responsible for it: but still flourishing themselves, all the same. The expertise they profess and its associations with reason, rationality and science are not even considered worthless anymore. It has a negative value instead. It damns and condemns them in the eyes of the public at large. "People in this country have had enough of experts." was the claim made by a leading campaigner for Britain to leave the EU in 2016, Michael Gove.[8]

In addition, the crash further burnt away traditional political loyalties. Even democracy is no longer seen as a precious gift of modernity, with built-in guarantees of good government. Instead, it is pictured as a quagmire by populists that drags many deserving but not prospering citizens down to its depths, while members of the Establishment can always find escape routes. Attempts to bridge the legitimacy deficit by extending democratic processes only bring disinterest and disdain. In Britain, elections to the European parliament have turnouts of less than 50%, while the first elections there in 2012 for local police commissioners saw less than a 10% turn out in some constituencies. It seems that it is only in plebiscites, referenda and, in the US, citizens' propositions that are understood and trusted as authentic expressions of public will. The 2016 British EU referendum had a voter turnout of 72%, compared to 66% in the general election of 2015, and only 59% in that of 2001. Alternatively, electorates may be prepared to give their support to aspiring politicians who claim to speak on behalf of "the people" rather than the establishment, who present themselves as independent-minded "strong men" rather than party loyalists, and who, as with Trump, promise to "drain the swamp" of central government and career politicians altogether rather than add more layers to the existing democratic process.

Second, *the emergence of a new kind of victimhood*. This is something more than being a crime victim, or fear of becoming one, which governments had

---

[7] Quoted in *Daily Mail*, 27 December 2016.
[8] Quoted in *The Financial Times*, 3 June 2016.

tried to offset by promising tougher punishments against the perpetrators. While cries for law and order have not been prominent in recent elections in those societies—the fall in crime no doubt reduces its purchase somewhat, fears of specific types of crime or criminals—fear of paedophiles and sexual predators, for example, in those Anglophone countries especially—seem stronger than ever. Such fears still inform the conduct of much of everyday life and have led to the introduction of further preventive measures that continue to erode fundamental features of criminal justice in modern society (Pratt, 2016).

Equally though, such fears have become conflated with fears of difference, fears of otherness—qualities variously demonstrated by strangers, foreigners, immigrants, asylum seekers, refugees ("Disabled limping migrant who uses a crutch while begging in London is exposed as a FRAUD when he is seen strolling off to buy a takeaway", *The Sun*, 16 September 2016). Fears and suspicions such as these are periodically fuelled by terrorist outrages that give further justification to such concerns and the horrendous dangers that these outsiders might be capable of, while reminding potential victims of their helplessness on such occasions. Fears such as these continue to demand more punishment, but they also demand that more controls be put in place to protect the public: sexual predators—keep them in prison, even after their sentences finish; paedophiles—hunt them down and drive them from local communities altogether; local troublemakers—issue banning, restriction and prohibition orders; asylum seekers, refugees, unwanted foreigners and all the rest of these strangers—build barriers, walls, fortifications to keep them out; protect the borders so they cannot come in; speed up deportation processes once they are caught.

These are some of the responses to this new kind of victimhood whereby it is not only the well-being and security of individuals that are endangered but also that of the nation-state itself as mass immigration is seen as corroding its values, security and identity. In Britain, these concerns have been prompted primarily by Eastern European migrants, now allowed to move to Britain without restriction since their countries joined the EU in 2004. In the East European countries themselves, it is fear of asylum seekers and refugees from the Middle East. In the US, it is fear of Mexican "rapists and murderers" crossing the border in the south and Muslim (which for many Americans is synonymous with terrorism) immigration in general. And so, it would be possible to continue collating this inventory of fear and suspicion, moving from one modern society to another.

As well as demanding protective and innovative para-penal measures, this new kind of victimization continues to erode trust in supranational organizations and establishment elites. Having positioned themselves, once again, above the everyday chaos and insecurity that they had helped to create, these are seen as weakening the nation-state by imposing foreign, alien, unwanted values and practices on it. Haney (2016) writes of East European fears of losing control over national interests as a consequence of joining the EU. Similarly in the UK, the European Court of Human Rights has become one of the most prominent signifiers of the imposition of unwanted European differences on British values and understandings. It seemingly has the power to insist that Britain should be "Europeanized" as it sees fit, with its intervention in criminal justice matters symbolizing such dangerous intrusion. Notably, the Court's declaration that the British "blanket ban" on all convicted prisoners' voting rights, regardless of the gravity and circumstances of their offenses, violates Article 3 of the European Convention on Human Rights (Hirst v UK [no 2] 2005). Similarly, with regard to "whole life sentences" (Vinter and Others v UK [2013] ECHR), a decision that reflected, it was claimed, a European "rights madness", as opposed to British commonsense (Hastings, 2013).

The consequences of deregulation and technological advancement enhance the power of the media to highlight such unwanted interventions and the social distance that exists between these ineffectual, dilettante elites and "the people", as if the will of such a body is now the only authentic expression of authority. The response of the British *Daily Mail* (4 November 2016) to Court of Appeal judges who ruled that the vote to leave the EU following 2016 had to be ratified by parliament, was to label them "Enemies of the People" and "out of touch judges" who "had declared war on democracy". As this example shows, news-making and reporting have broken out of the paradigm of reason, rationality and truth in which it had been expected to operate in modern, democratic societies, however elasticated this concept might previously have been. It has no limits, no ethical standards, no set direction to constrain it or that it has to follow. Demands that truth be told, as some journalists tried to insist during the 2016 US election, were dismissed with rejoinders by the Trump campaign that this was simply evidence of "bias" against them in the mainstream "fake" media. Indeed, for Trump himself, the journalists at CNN and the *New York Times*, who stood by truth, were "the lowest form of humanity".[9] The entire corpus of political debate in the United States thus has become progressively more Orwellian—Trump's "alt facts" become truth, as verifiable scientific "facts" are held to have become conspiracies of a "deep state".

---

[9] Quoted by *New York Times*, 12 August 2016.

But when truth is abandoned, then everything can be a lie: there is no means of distinguishing between fact and fiction, nor any point in trying to do so. The purveyors of "post-truth news" simply call on their critics to prove that what they are saying is not true. Until then, lies and conspiracies "remain a story". Lie, lie, lie. Lie again and again. "Lord, lord, how this world is given to lying".[10] Throw away truth, and then evidence and facts only become another set of lies. Rather than using truth to win votes, conjure up demons and devils—these can all be fabrications themselves—that need to be confronted by a strong man: then demand that voters put their trust in that man to rid the world of such pestilence, rather than career politicians and effete bureaucrats—what do they know of the insecurities that lie behind such dark fantasies? As it is, the rise of Facebook (2004) and Twitter (2006) since the 2008 crash has meant that individuals can not only create their own news and report it as they see fit but publish it before vast audiences. Again, this new kind of news can be entirely fabricated ("alt news") and usually speaks to some vast web of conspiracy that is supposed to exist, working to entrap the unsuspecting and the vulnerable in its lair. As one of the most prominent anti-EU campaigners in Britain stated, "The more outrageous we are, the more attention we'll get. The more attention we get, the more outrageous we'll be" (quoted by Rawnsley, 2016a).

Through strategies such as these, populist politicians have come to prominence. While they may well have tougher punishments on their agendas, this is likely to be only one component of a program that, they claim, will magically transform an entire society: rid it of corruption and inefficiency, bring a brighter future through a reassertion of authority and nationhood. This was seen most vividly in the campaign themes of the two most spectacular populist electoral successes in 2016. First, the British EU referendum. "Leave" campaigners used the logo "Take Back Control", as if by voting to leave, it would be possible to retrieve all that had been lost or stolen—presumably as a result of EU membership; it would be possible to restore national identity and rid the country of corrupting and "un-British" foreign influence; and it would be a gesture of defiance against the EU—favouring establishment. A vision of a completely mythical and irretrievable past of security and cohesion was conjured, when British people were masters of their own destiny. When was this supposed to have been—who knows? Just before Britain joined the EU in 1973? But that was a period of massive industrial conflict, rising inflation and growing racial tensions (Hall et al., 1978)—this was a time when government had *lost* control—it cannot have been then. Maybe when there

---

[10] William Shakespeare, Henry IV, Part I, Act 5, sc 4, p. 7.

was an Empire, or maybe when there was a powerful White Commonwealth, or maybe when Britain (and the colonies) fought alone against Nazi Germany—rather than subject to EU rules, laws and regulations. The route to this Nirvana involved walking away from Europe, although, in reality, not in to a glorious past but a troubled and darkly uncertain future.

Similarly, "Make America Great Again". Trump's logo in the U.S. election. Here too, the theme conveys the sense of loss and betrayal—variously blamed on corruption in central government, international financiers, Muslims, Mexicans, globalization and the infamy of wicked individuals (such as "Crooked Hillary Clinton"). Hence the need to "drain the swamp", "build a wall", "lock her [Clinton] up" and so on. This kind of purification process was necessary, it seemed, if the glorious past was to be recaptured—although exactly when remained unspecified. Nonetheless, a society could be rebuilt around dominant White men, where jobs that used to exist before globalization made them redundant would somehow reappear, and where dangerous foreigners would be kept out. In such ways, the implied promise of both "Take Back Control" and "Make America Great Again" was that not only would the nation be secure against insidious threats to its well-being that the establishment had allowed to fester, individuals would also be given back what they think has been taken from them: familiarity, certainty, security.

"An Abrupt and Ugly End"

These two electoral successes came as a profound, distressing and disturbing shock to many. They had been so unexpected—as if at the last, Reason would prove resolute in the face of whatever the anti-reason lies, distortions and made-up news were thrown at it. President Obama had attempted to counter such challenges with an "ode to reason, rationality, humility and delayed gratification" (quoted by Packer, 2016, p. 84), an argument for the renewal and continuity of "American progress". In the aftermath of defeat, however, and amidst a great surge of hate crime, racial abuse and racial intolerance that had been unleashed in its wake, the liberal intelligentsia suddenly found themselves staring at a cataclysm. Andrew Rawnsley (2016b), for example, on the vote for Britain to leave the EU, wrote that it represented "a journey into the unknown for a country never before so divided … between doing-well Britain and left-behind Britain, between the Britain that is essentially comfortable with globalization and diversity and the Britain that feels its anxieties and anger about identity loss have not been listened to". On the election of Trump, Richard Wolffe (2016) wrote that "we may as well call this what it is: a revolution … nothing else comes close to capturing the political revolt—and the chaos that surely follows … an era that stretches back to Franklin D. Roosevelt just came to an abrupt and ugly end".

In fact, the profundity of these events has an even deeper significance. Each signalled that the long journey that modernity itself had taken from the time of the Enlightenment had come to a shattering end. The defeat of Reason—of rationality, science, truth, objectivity, consistency—and its ability to structure and inform the parameters of governance in the modern world—means that only the unknown awaits. This will not be the end of uncertainty and insecurity promised by populists, but only the start of new uncertainties and insecurities, alongside the exacerbation of those already in existence. That said, the two events themselves do not constitute any *sudden* end to Reason; rather, they should be seen as marking the final moments of a process that had made such an end inevitable, a process that had systematically undermined all that had been intended to provide the certainty and stability, the cohesion and solidarity that would otherwise have been strong enough to resist the shamans of populism.

When did this process begin? When was it that all that we had come to assume was permanent would, in reality, have no permanence at all, have no more substance than a sandcastle built to stem an incoming tide? In *The Four Quartets*, T.S. Eliot (1943, p. 23) wrote "In my beginning is my end. In succession. houses rise and fall, crumble, are extended, are removed, destroyed, restored". In the beginning is the end. Where do we look for that beginning that led to the end of Reason? The starting point is likely to have been Reason's post-1945 reassertion, its response to the aberrations from its path in the ravages of the Depression years of the 1920s and 1930s, followed by the rise of anti-democratic strong men in Europe who brought catastrophe—carnage, destruction, misery and genocide. Hence the phrase that dominated political discourse in the democracies after 1945: "never again". Never again. It became the task of post-war governments to ensure that there could be no return to that previous dark time of anti-reason—never again. As Eric Hobsbawm (1994, p. 271) explained, "The inter-war experience, and especially the Great Slump, had been so catastrophic that nobody could possibly dream … of returning as soon as possible to the time before the air-raid sirens had begun to sound. All the men who sketched out what they hoped would be the post-war principles of the world economy and the future of the global economic order had lived through the Great Slump".

How was Reason to be secured against any subsequent aberrations? Planning, state intervention and control were the initial answers: "there was a great faith in the ability (and not just the duty) of government to solve large-scale problems by mobilizing and directing people and resources to collectively useful ends" (Judt 2007, p. 69). Roosevelt's New Deal had promised greater government management of the economy, poor relief and increased public expenditure. New Zealanders had been promised "cradle to the grave" security in their Social Security Act of 1938. The United Kingdom's Beveridge Report (1942, p. 170) promised to control risk and insecurity by eradicating "five giant evils: Want, Disease, Ignorance, Squalor, Idleness". Similar intents were expressed in the Canadian Marsh Report (1943) and the Australian White Paper on Full Employment (1945), as well as the U.S. Social Security and Unemployment Compensation laws enacted under Franklin D. Roosevelt. Rigorous planning by the state was the way to make certain these promises of a good future, one that gave hope to all. In 1943 Beveridge (quoted by Kynaston, 2007, p. 31) had anticipated that when peace came, "the very first thing to win is the Battle of Planning. We shall need to have planning on a national scale, boldly overstepping the traditional boundaries of urban council, rural council, county council". Similarly, the Marsh Report (1943, p. 7) explained that "the pre-war background has not been forgotten by many Canadians … and it must not be forgotten in the post-war period, in planning in advance what measures should be taken … to give reality to the aspirations and hopes which the peoples of the world are more and more clearly voicing".

Hence the physical, material and ideological shape of post-war society. The modern city would become a haven where all had a rightful place, would become a testament to the virtues of planning, of rationality, a testament to the virtues of Reason itself, its celebration of public space a necessary feature of harmonious community life. Ebenezer Howard's (1946, p. 44) vision of "the social city", for example, was based around wide, tree-shrouded avenues, homes, public gardens and a central park: "large public buildings would be at [its] centre: town hall, library, museum, concert and lecture hall, the hospital. Here, the highest values of the community are brought together—culture, philanthropy, health and united cooperation". Family life, too, had an importance beyond that of the individuals concerned. Now, it would be ordered and structured by government and its new organizations of assistance to ensure that the well-being of individuals contributed to the well-being of society as whole: "parenthood itself must become a central interest and duty; and the family and the primary group of workfellows and neighbours must become a vital core in every wider association" (Mumford, 1945, p. 214). In 1950, there were around 100 marriage guidance clinics in existence in Britain to provide the guidance and direction necessary for those struggling to meet these expectations (Clark, 1991).

What mattered most in the provision of this extensive apparatus of support and instruction, wrote leading British sociologist of the period T.H. Marshall (1950, p. 56), "is that there is a general enrichment of the concrete substance of civilized life, a general reduction of risk and insecurity, an equalization between the more or less unfortunate at all levels". Indeed, the vastly expanded public sector workforce that would be necessary to achieve all such objectives in itself went some way to achieving this by providing guarantees of employment security and status (in the UK, for example, civil servants increased from 340,000 to 720,000 between 1931 and 1955, Marwick, 1971, p. 137). These guarantees were not presaged around an especially ambitious life, to be sure, not a life that would be lived in the fast lane, frenetically grabbing at pleasures and indulgencies as they came along; but a good life, all the same, a life that now had comfort rather than hardship as an expectation, a life to be cherished rather than abandoned to whatever fate came its way. And the future seemed assured at this time. In Britain, a *Daily Telegraph* (27 December 1961) opinion poll of 16 to 18 year olds found that only 9% disagreed with the opinion that "the world would be a better place [in which] to live in ten years time". In a world of stability and security, what is particularly striking in the other responses of those polled is the regularity of their working habits. After three years, more than half were still on the same career path as when they had started. Furthermore, one in three were regular church attendees. Only one in ten was not looking forward to getting married; 85% disagreed with the assertion that it did not much matter whether or not the marriage worked out well.

Yet, the very successes of this post-war solidarity project (Garland, 1996) began to eat away at its base. Certainty and stability of personal life and relationships were the first to crumble, under demands for much greater expression of personal choice regarding sexual preferences and identities. It resulted in what had previously been taken for granted in family life and all the networks woven around it becoming much more tangential, as noted. What possible role could all the marriage guidance clinics now have in the light of the subsequent reality of family life? As Ulrich Beck (quoted in Bauman, 2000, p. 6) has written, "Ask yourself what actually is a family nowadays? What does it mean? Of course, there are children, my children, our children. But even parenthood, the core of family life, is beginning to disintegrate under conditions of divorce ... [G]randmothers and grandfathers get included and excluded without any means of participating in the decisions of their sons and daughters". Many others fall through what have become these flimsy networks altogether and find themselves living alone, one of the most significant features of current demography in modern society.[11] Whatever personal histories lie behind this—choice or misfortune, accident or cruel fate—the growing presence of this cohort more than any other represents the atomization of everyday life in modern society and the importance of structures of support and guidance beyond the family to provide interdependencies and bonds to the rest of society. In an era when we all now have to "operate at the outer edge of the ordered world, on the barbaric final frontier of modern technology" (Giddens, 1999, p. 2), when we are all involved with complex social economic and technological systems we do not understand, so many have been left on their own to try and digest and resolve the existential dilemmas and conflicts that these produce on their own.

This is because, in addition to the changing nature of family life, extra-familial structures also began to collapse from the 1980s, as Robert Putnam (2000) observed in *Bowling Alone*. The post-war solidarity project, it was now claimed, had been both inefficient and sapped the energy of individuals to make their own way in the world, make their own fortunes and spend them as they wished, rather than having the state tell them what they might do—although, of course, they would also have to manage their own risks—for good or bad. Thereafter, amidst declines in church attendance, volunteering, trade union membership and the performance of civic obligations, deregulation and globalization not only made employment prospects less predictable and permanent and more uncertain and contingent, but the attendant redevelopment of communities and movement of labour also began to dissolve local cohesion, ties and responsibilities: "enterprise culture proved to be a solvent of bonds of trust and community and a source of insecurity to many. The mobility demanded by a dynamic market economy is not easily reconciled with a settled common life. The end result was the weakening or dissolution of the ties of the community and the generation of a society of strangers" (Gray, 1993, p. 54).

Most public and political attention though—in the main English-speaking countries especially that were in the forefront of these changes—was given to celebrating the fame and fortune that greeted the winners that this economic restructuring had made possible. The losers—all those left behind or those who could not keep up with the changes—found themselves largely written out of the script. These growing divisions, the growing tension between those

---

[11] The percentage of people living alone has increased from 18.8% of the Australian population in 1986 to 23% in 2013; from 11.4% in Canada in 1981 to 27.6% in 2011; from 16% in New Zealand in 1980 to 23.5% in 2013; from 22% in the UK in 1981 to 28% in 2014; from 22.7% in the US in 1980 to 27.4% in 2012.

perpetually on the move,[12] heading up an ever-extending escalator that exponentially provided more wealth and success at each new floor and those left out, perpetually trapped in modern society's bargain basement, feeling aggrieved at governments who seemed to have so little interest in helping them to get to even the next level, informed the development of penal populism.

By introducing innovative sanctions and controls, as well as more extensive and intensive punishments on those who seemed to be the most obvious and direct threat to individual well-being, here was a simple, common-sensical, if expensive (necessitating reductions in expenditure for other social and welfare measures) way for governments to show that they had not forgotten the worthy but left-out constituency. Indeed, they were now prepared to speak its language of punishment, rather than that of their erstwhile experts, in the new axis of penal power that began to put these measures into effect. Here was the way, temporarily at least, to unify the population, to heal divisions and to restore social cohesion. If this was at the expense of many of the principles on which criminal justice in modern society had been built, then this could easily be explained away ("rebalancing the criminal justice system"), the new controls were "only for the worst of the worst", only out of touch "liberal elites" will care (see Pratt, 2016).

As we have seen, though, penal populism proved to be only a staging post towards the much more extensive populist march through modern society. The increased potency of the threats to individual and national wellbeing meant that populism was able to burst out of the constraints of the penal zone and pervade the whole social body. This does not mean that it has now finished with its transformation of the possibilities of punishment. As anxiety, uncertainty and insecurity increase, as criminality is conflated with otherness, so criminal law and punishment themselves become more diverse and amorphous, increasingly seeking to control risk rather than merely punishing crime. In so doing, the boundaries that had previously separated punishment in modern society from punishment in non-democratic, totalitarian societies are further eroded.

This, however, is a matter of little consequence for populism and its forces. What drives it is not any legacy of Reason and the Enlightenment, but anger and resentment and the construction of a magical politics around these emotive forces that promise to eliminate at a stroke all the demons and devils it identifies. In "taking back control" in "making a nation great again", who then

---

[12] Cf Bauman (2001, p. 62) "Individuals who are untied to place, who can travel light and move fast, win all the competitions that matter and count".

needs Obama's commitment to "tolerance, compromise and our common humanity … the values of liberal democracy" (Packer, 2016) to accomplish this? Who needs evidence, rationality, facts and science and all the other attributes on which modernity itself had been built, to do so? Yet, as Jonathan Freedland (2016) writes, "evidence, facts, and reason are the building blocks of civilization. Without them we plunge into darkness". And as this darkness falls, so it brings with it the end of Reason and all its light.

References

Bauman, Z. (2000). *Liquid modernity*. Polity Press.
Bauman, Z. (2001). Violence in the age of uncertainty. In A. Crawford (Ed.), *Crime and insecurity* (pp. 52–74). Routledge.
Beccaria, C. (1872/1764). *On crimes and punishments*. W.C. Little & Co. (Original work published in 1764).
Beck, U. (1992). *Risk society: Towards a new modernity*. Sage.
Beetham, D. (1991). *The legitimation of power*. Macmillan.
Betz, H. G. (1994). *Radical right-wing populism in Western Europe*. Macmillan.
Beveridge, W. H. (1942). *Social insurance and allied services: Report [The Beveridge report]*. HMSO.
Bottoms, A. E. (1977). Reflections on the renaissance of dangerousness. *Howard Journal of Criminal Justice, 16*, 70–96.
Bottoms, A. E. (1995). The philosophy and politics of punishment and sentencing. In C. Clarkson & R. Morgan (Eds.), *The politics of sentencing reform* (pp. 17–49). Clarendon Press.
Canovan, M. (1981). *Populism*. Harcourt Brace Jovanovich.
Clark, D. (1991). Guidance, counselling, therapy: Responses to "marital problems" 1950–90. *The Sociological Review, 39*(4), 765–798.
Commonwealth of Australia. (1945). *Full employment in Australia*. Australian Government Printer.
Diderot, D. (1753/1966). On the interpretation of nature, No. 15. In L. Crocker (Ed.), *Diderot's selected writings*. Macmillan. (Original work published 1753).
Diderot, D. (1967). *Denis diderot's the encyclopedia: Selections*. (S. J. Gendzier, Ed. & Trans.). Harper Torchbooks. (Original work published 1751).
Eliot, T. S. (1943). *Four quartets*. Harcourt, Brace & Co..
Farrell, G., Tilley, N., & Tseloni, A. (2014). Why the crime drop? *Crime and Justice, 43*(1), 421–490.
Freedland, J. (2016, November 9). The U.S. has elected its most dangerous leader: We all have plenty to fear. *The Guardian*. https://www.theguardian.com/commentisfree/2016/nov/09/donald-trump-us-president-nightmare

Garland, D. (1996). The limits of the Sovereign state: Strategies of crime control in contemporary society. *British Journal of Criminology, 36,* 445–471.

Giddens, A. (1991). *Modernity and self-identity: Self and society in the late modern age.* Polity Press.

Giddens, A. (1999). Risk and responsibility. *Modern Law Review, 62*(1), 1–10.

Goode, E. (2013, July 25). U.S. prison populations decline, reflecting new approaches to crime. *The New York Times.* http://www.nytimes.com/2013/07/26/us/us-prison-populations-decline-reflecting-new-approach-to-crime.html

Gray, J. (1993). *Beyond the new right: Markets, government and the common environment.* Routledge.

Hall, S. (1979). *Drifting into a law and order society.* Cobden Trust.

Hall, S. (1988). *The hard road to renewal: Thatcherism and the crisis of the left.* Verso.

Hall, S., Critcher, C., Jefferson, T., Clarke, J., & Roberts, B. (1978). *Policing the crisis. Mugging, the state and law and order.* Palgrave Macmillan.

Haney, L. (2016). Prisons of the past: Penal nationalism and the politics of punishment in Central Europe. *Punishment & Society, 18*(3), 346–368.

Hastings, M. (2013, July 10). The danger is we've become immune to human rights lunacy. It's vital we stay angry, =says Max Hastings. *Daily Mail.* http://www.dailymail.co.uk/debate/article-2359048/The-danger-weve-immune-Human-Rights-lunacy-Its-vital-stay-angry-says-MAX-HASTINGS.html

Hay, D. (1976). Property, authority, and the criminal law. In D. Hay, P. Linebaugh, & E. P. Thompson (Eds.), *Albion's fatal tree: Crime and society in 18th century England* (pp. 17–63). Allen Lane.

Hobsbawm, E. (1994). *The age of extremes.* Abacus.

Home Office. (1959). *Penal practice in a changing society.* HMSO. [Cmnd. 645].

Home Office. (1988). *Punishment, custody and the community.* HMSO. [Cm 424].

Howard, C., & Morris, N. (1964). *Studies in criminal law.* Oxford University Press.

Howard, E. (1946). *Garden cities of to-morrow.* Faber & Faber.

Jewkes, Y. (2004). *Media and crime.* Sage.

Johnson, D. T. (2006). Japan's secretive death penalty policy: Contours, origin, justifications, and meanings. *Asia-Pacific Law & Policy Journal, 7,* 62–124.

Jones, T., & Newburn, T. (2006). *Policy transfer and criminal justice.* Open University Press.

Judt, T. (2007). *Postwar: A history of Europe since 1945.* Pimlico.

Kant, I. (1797/1887). *The philosophy of law: An exposition of the fundamental principles of jurisprudence.* (W. Hastie, Trans.). T & T Clark.

Koo, K. C., Ahn, J. H., Hong, S. J., Lee, J. W., & Chung, B. H. (2014). Effects of chemical castration on sex offenders in relation to the kinetics of serum testosterone recovery: Implications for dosing schedule. *Journal of Sexual Medicine, 11*(5), 1316–1324.

Kynaston, D. (2007). *Austerity Britain, 1945–51.* Bloomsbury.

Lacey, N. (2008). *The prisoners' dilemma: Political economy and punishment in contemporary democracies.* Cambridge University Press.

Locke, J. (1690/2016). *Second treatise of government*. Enhanced Media.
Marsh, L. (1943). *Report on social security for Canada [The Marsh report]*. King's Printer.
Marshall, T. H. (1950). *Citizenship and social class*. Cambridge University Press.
Marwick, A. (1971). *The explosion of British society, 1914–1970*. Macmillan.
Miao, M. (2013). Capital punishment in China: A populist instrument of social governance. *Theoretical Criminology, 17*(2), 233–250.
Montesquieu, C. (1914/2011). *The spirit of laws* (T. Nugent, Trans.). Cosimo Classics.
Müller, M.-M. (2012). The rise of the penal state in Latin America. *Contemporary Justice Review, 15*(1), 57–76.
Mumford, L. (1945). *City development: Studies in disintegration and renewal*. Harcourt, Brace & Co.
Neto, L. (2009). El Populismo Punitivo En Espana: del Estado. [The penal populism in Spain: From welfare state to punishment state]. http://www2.pucpr.br/ssscla/papers/SessaoC_A33_pp219-245.pdf
Nevitte, N. (1996). *The decline of difference: Canadian value change in cross national perspective*. Broadview Press.
New Zealand First. (2014). *Manifesto*. Government Printer.
Packer, G. (2016, October 31). Hillary Clinton and the populist revolt. *The New Yorker*. http://www.newyorker.com/magazine/2016/10/31/hillary-clinton-and-the-populist-revolt
Paine, T. (1794). *The age of reason: Being an investigation of true and fabulous theology*. Barrois.
Pratt, J. (1997). *Governing the dangerous*. Federation Press.
Pratt, J. (2000). Emotive and ostentatious punishment. *Punishment & Society, 2*(4), 417–439.
Pratt, J. (2007). *Penal populism*. Routledge.
Pratt, J. (2008). When penal populism stops: Legitimacy, scandal and the power to punish in New Zealand. *Australian and New Zealand Journal of Criminology, 41*, 364–383.
Pratt, J. (2016). Risk control, rights and legitimacy in the limited liability state. *British Journal of Criminology, 57*, 1322–1339. https://doi.org/10.1093/bjc/azw065
Pratt, J., & Clark, M. (2005). Penal populism in New Zealand. *Punishment and Society, 7*, 303–322.
Putnam, R. (2000). *Bowling alone: The collapse and revival of American community*. Simon and Schuster.
Rawnsley, A. (2016a, November 20). The shock lessons for liberals from Brexit and the Trumpquake. *The Observer*. https://www.theguardian.com/commentisfree/2016/nov/20/lessons-liberals-brexit-trumpquake-demagogues-rules-electoral-politics
Rawnsley, A. (2016b, June 26). Brexit: A journey into the unknown for a country never before so divided. *The Observer*. https://www.theguardian.com/commentisfree/2016/jun/26/brexit-eu-referendum-disunited-kingdom

Reiner, R. (2001). The rise of virtual vigilantism: Crime reporting since World War II. *Criminal Justice Matters, 43*, 4–5.

Report of the Penal Policy Review Committee, 1981. (1982). Government Printer.

Roberts, J. V., Stalans, L., Indermaur, D., & Hough, M. (2003). *Penal populism and public opinion.* Oxford University Press.

Ruggles-Brise, S. E. (1921). *The English prison system.* Macmillan.

Shils, E. (1956). *The torment of secrecy.* Heinemann.

Standing, G. (2014). *The precariat. The new dangerous class.* Bloomsbury.

Tappan, P. (1957). Sexual offences and the treatment of sexual offenders in the United States. In L. Radzinowicz (Ed.), *Sexual offences. A report of the Cambridge department of criminal science* (pp. 500–516). Macmillan.

Tyler, T., & Boeckmann, R. (1997). Three strikes and you are out, but why? The psychology of public support for punishing rule breakers. *Law and Society Review, 31*, 237–265.

von Hirsch, A. (1976). *Doing justice.* Hill & Wang.

Wolffe, R. (2016, November 9). Trump's Victory is nothing short of a revolution. *The Guardian.* https://www.theguardian.com/commentisfree/2016/nov/09/donald-trump-victory-us-election-result-revolution

Zimring, F. E. (2012). *The city that became safe: New York's lessons for urban crime and its control.* Oxford University Press.

4

White Supremacy and the Politics of Race

Ronald E. Goodwin

Introduction

Race has been a controversial aspect of United States politics from its inception. Slavery was never consistent with the stated goals of the American Revolution, but it was already deeply imbedded into the fabric of colonial society. The Founding Fathers openly grappled not only with the issue of slavery but the legal status of Blacks. It was not until 1857 that this controversy was seemingly put to rest. The Supreme Court declared Blacks were not American citizens and possessed no legal rights that American social or political institutions were obligated to respect. Sadly, the ensuing four years of war did little to change the minds of those completely entrenched in the ideology of White supremacy. Since the legal eradication of slavery, White supremacists have tried to manipulate the democratic process (politics) to enforce what in their minds is the proper social order where whites held the superior position and people of color were subordinate. This essay examines four instances in which the politics of race were paramount in the American discourse. The outcomes of these events have had little effect on those who believe the United States of America was made by whites, for the benefit of whites.

R. E. Goodwin (✉)
Prairie View A&M University, Prairie View, TX, USA
e-mail: regoodwin@pvamu.edu

Barack Obama's Election in 2008 Did Not Lift the United States from Its Racist Past

Many in U.S. society believed Barack Obama's election in 2008 was a sign that this country had finally evolved beyond its racist past. This was not the case, however. White supremacists continue to use racially influenced political policies to maintain their particular view of society in which people of color are relegated to the margins. As a result, racial politics continue to undermine the theoretical principles of democracy by advancing the goals of specific groups over others.

Racial Politics in U.S. History

There are numerous instances of racial politics in U.S. history. What follows is a discussion of four examples of racially influenced politics illustrating the continued presence of White supremacy in our society. Four hundred years after captured Africans arrived on the banks of the James River and more than 230 years after the Founding Fathers conceded to the so-called "three-fifths compromise," which, for purposes of political representation, counted blacks as three-fifths of a person. Some still regard the black community as inferior and endorse policies that reinforce these absurd notions of race.

Forty years after the Civil War, a new generation of southern academics, led by scholars such as UB Phillips, William Dunning, Charles Ramsdell, and Claude Bowers, began a systematic review of the conflict and its immediate aftermath. They tried to convince a new generation that slave owners were not the immediate cause of the Civil War. That distinction belonged to President Abraham Lincoln. Furthermore, they argued, Reconstruction failed to achieve its goals because of vengeful Republicans and illiterate and incompetent black politicians. From their revisionist perspective, slave owners/southern White supremacists were merely protecting their way of life and their Constitutional right to own personal property. After all, these southern scholars believed, slave owners were more than benevolent to individuals whom God created to be less than themselves on the evolutionary ladder. They also produced convincing research minimizing the role slavery played in the onset of war and focused on what they perceived was the more gallant justification of two distinctive economic systems on an inevitable collision course, and the Northern jealousy of Southern political acumen.

History presents abundant evidence that many Republican carpetbaggers took advantage of the chaos for their own personal economic gain. However, Black politicians did not have that kind of influence. In fact, most were well-meaning but mere puppets as the real power was held by White Republicans who wanted to punish the South for the 750,000 lives lost in combat during four years of war. Still, these Black politicians bore the brunt of White supremacists who were unwilling to concede their failed revolution. Southern scholars successfully hid their racial prejudices as they convinced a new generation at the beginning of the twentieth century that the Black population was unworthy of such political positions and certainly not worthy of equal citizenship in a democracy that their labor built.

As he was campaigning for the presidency in 1860, Abraham Lincoln never said he was going to end the vile system of slavery. He did say that he was not in favor of its expansion into the Western Territories. After a decade of turmoil and political back-and-forth, Southerners were no longer willing to compromise on what they believed was their culture and their right to own slaves. So, southern leadership threatened to secede from the Union if Lincoln became president.

This was not the first time Southerners issued such threats. During Andrew Jackson's presidency, South Carolina opposed what they considered wanton his abuse of power. Led by Jackson's vice president, John C. Calhoun, South Carolina was poised to leave the Union. However, the promise of military force led to a conciliation on both sides.

Interestingly, South Carolina was the first state to secede from the Union weeks after Lincoln's election. The South Carolina Declaration of Secession clearly stated that slavery was the principal reason that they were undertaking this action. The remaining southern states that would make up the Confederate States of America issued similar declarations. Their ensuing Constitution expressly made slavery legal as a means of supporting what they believed was the evolutionary subordinate position of peoples of color.

As the conflict began in 1861, Lincoln refused to involve Blacks. This was to the dismay of Frederick Douglass, who saw the war as an opportunity for the Black community to prove its commitment to this democracy. Certainly, he believed, equal citizenship would not be denied one who sacrificed his life in defense of his country. Sadly, Douglass was mistaken.

Nonetheless, by 1862 Lincoln eventually succumbed to the prudent wisdom of emancipating slaves. Such an action would negatively impact the southern economy and its ability to wage a continued, drawn-out conflict. Simultaneously, it would keep foreign countries from legitimizing the Confederacy. The Emancipation Proclamation not only symbolically brought an end to slavery but endured Lincoln and the Republican Party to the Black community for the next seventy-five years.[1]

Lincoln wanted a swift return to normality after the war, with minimal punitive action levied against Confederate leadership. However, his death, just days after Robert E. Lee's surrender, led to a chaotic period of social violence and political corruption. There were those in Lincoln's own political party who wanted the South to be severely punished. That did not happen. However, Republican extremists successfully impeached Andrew Johnson, passed numerous civil rights laws, and placed the South under martial law.

With the military in place, the South could be punished discreetly. While former slaves were not given the means for economic independence, they were given citizenship and Black males had the right to vote. Republican operatives filed into the South and took control of local governments by manipulating Black votes. However, the South remained as committed to the principle of White supremacy as ever. While they were no longer able to fight the military, the Black community was extremely vulnerable.

Former slaves were dependent on the occupying federal soldiers for physical protection. However, Southerners resented this occupation; most often violently. Southern whites believed the newly established post-war local governments, led by outsiders (carpetbaggers) were going to change their lives. The Republicans had already taken away their slaves with the Thirteenth Amendment and they had no idea how much their former lives would be changed.

So, to maintain some sense of what they considered the proper societal order, White Southerners passed laws, historically known as Black Codes, preventing Blacks from owning weapons and established other racist policies to keep the Black community permanently disenfranchised (DuBois, 1935; Stampp, 1965).[2]

Still, Republicans moved to address the sudden reality that millions of former slaves were now free without a plan as to what would happen next. The creation of the Freedmen's Bureau was initially seen as the answer to that

---

[1] Effective in January 1863, the Emancipation Proclamation stated that those slaves held by states in conflict against the United Strates were free. As the Confederacy had their own Constitution and government, Lincoln had no authority over them. However, he did have authority over those slave states that had not joined the Confederacy. The border states of Delaware, Kentucky, Maryland, Missouri, and West Virginia were well-known slave states. Not wanting to push them into the Confederacy, the Emancipation Proclamation failed to free slaves held in these states. As a result, Lincoln's political move switched the principle objective of the conflict from the preservation of the Union's continuity to ending slavery. However, no slaves were immediately freed. The end of the Peculiar Institution and the Confederacy occurred only after Robert E. Lee surrendered his troops on April 9, 1865.

[2] W.E.B. DuBois, *Black Reconstruction* (New York: Russell & Russell, 1935), 223; Kenneth Stampp, *The Era of Reconstruction, 1865–1877* (New York: Vantage Books, 1965), 112.

uncertainty. This federal agency succeeded in establishing schools and brought educational opportunities throughout the South.

In Texas, for example, the Freedmen's Bureau operated from September 1865 until July 1870. While their primary responsibility was overseeing the transition from slavery to freedom for the state's Black population, crucial to this transition was the establishment of a modern labor system and schools for Blacks. However, records indicate that local Freedmen's Bureau officials in Texas may not have fully supported the idea of Black equality. They never insisted that the courts apply the laws regardless of race (see Richter, 1991; Crouch, 2010; Finley, 1996, for more detail).[3]

Regrettably, by December 1868 the lack of funds and local support led to the closing of several Bureau offices and the cessation of all its programs, except for those involving education. Incidentally, education, through the establishment and operations of Black schools, was the one area in which the Freemen's Bureau excelled (see Butchart, 1980; Morris, 1981 for more detail).[4] Even though some whites in Texas tried to educate Blacks before emancipation, wholesale attempts at education did not occur until after 1865. Former slave Rosina Hoard recalled how her former master's son tried to teach slaves to read while they were out in the fields away from his father's view. However, the master's arrival in the field meant the end of that day's lessons. Hoard said, "De workers watch for massa and when dey seed him a-ridin' down de hill dey starts singin' out, 'Ole hawg 'round de bench—ole hawg 'round de bench.' Dat the signal and den everybody starts workin' like dey have something after dem." (Hoard, n.d.).[5]

Nonetheless, Blacks began receiving formal lessons after emancipation, and by the end of 1865 over one-thousand Blacks were being taught at sixteen schools throughout the state. By 1870, there were 150 schools educating over 9000 students in Texas. While many whites committed savage acts against schools and teachers, these educational programs generally accomplished their goals of educating Blacks (Bureau of Refugees, Freedmen and Abandoned Lands, n.d.).[6]

However, newly elected Black politicians could not deter the defeated racist former Confederates from believing the Freedmen's Bureau, the presence of

---

[3] See William Richter, *Overreached on All Sides: The Freedmen's Bureau Administrators in Texas, 1865–1868*; Barry Crouch, *The Freedmen's Bureau and Black Texans*; Randy Finley, *From Slavery to Uncertain Freedom: The Freedmen's Bureau in Arkansas*; Howard White, *The Freedmen's Bureau in Louisiana*.
[4] See Ronald Butchart, *Northern Schools, Southern Blacks and Reconstruction*; Robert Morris, *Reading, 'Riting, and Reconstruction*.
[5] Rosina Hoard, *Slave Narratives*, Box 4H359, University of Texas, Center for American History.
[6] Bureau of Refugees, Freedmen and Abandoned Lands, 1865–1869, National Archives M821, roll 32.

military troops and the new carpetbagger-led governments were not constant reminders of their failed revolution. As such, Black political leaders were helpless in deterring random violence against the Black community. The violence that occurred after 1865 was eerily reminiscent of slavery. Federal records indicated that Blacks were often attacked, beaten, and some killed with little regard for justice or decency. For example, a Black male was killed because he did not remove his hat. Another was stabbed outside a church because his attacker said he did not get out of the way of a White female. A Black female reported being assaulted, stripped, and given 200 lashes with a leather strap because she supposedly made insulting noises when a White female passed her on the street. Another, who was pregnant at the time of her assault, reported receiving 150 blows from the cane of her attacker for no apparent reason. A third stated that she was kicked and violently separated from the child she was carrying. Lastly, even after emancipation, a Black husband and wife were tied, beaten, and kicked because their sons left the region without permission from their former owner (Bureau of Refugees, Freedmen and Abandoned Lands, n.d.).[7]

The result was that the former slaves were given freedom in name only. The former slaves were left to rely on the U.S. military that occupied the South as a conquered nation. The Democratic Party, still a White supremacist political entity, fought fervently to end what they perceived as a military and political occupation through a program of covert actions that undermined Black civil rights for the remainder of the nineteenth century.

The development of terrorist groups like the Ku Klux Klan and Black Hawks and their prolific campaign of violence against the Black community was no accident. These groups sought to frighten the Black community into a subordinate position as during the antebellum days of slavery.

Even though their origins were not political, the Ku Klux Klan became an unofficial arm of the Democratic Party by the end of the 1860s (Fry, 2001).[8] Taking advantage of what southern whites believed to be the superstitious nature of the Black community, these racists dressed in white hoods to resemble ghosts. They opposed any action that supported the rights of the Black community and routinely disrupted any gathering of the Republican Party, terrorized potential Black voters, and threatened anyone associated with them

---

[7] Bureau of Refugees, Freedmen and Abandoned Lands, 1865–1869, National Archives M821, roll 32, Miscellaneous Records Relating to Murders and other Criminal Offenses Committed in Texas 1865–1868; Letter from ME Davis to HA Ellis, October 13, 1866, Bureau of Refugees, Freedmen and Abandoned Lands, 1865–1869, National Archives M821, roll 32.

[8] Gladys-Marie Fry, *Night Riders in Black Folk History* (Chapel Hill: University of North Carolina Press, 2001), 110.

(Gorn, 1984)[9] Sadly, the violent attacks directed toward the Black community became commonplace throughout the South (Fry, 2001).[10]

Unfortunately, even with martial law in place, Union troops proved ineffective in deterring such violent acts. The veil of secrecy surrounding Klan members prevented the Republican-led local governments from identifying them. As a result, many Blacks who insisted on voting were oftentimes run out of town under threats of death to themselves or family members (Stampp, 1965).[11] Former slave William Hamilton remembered that Klan activity was particularly horrible where he settled after Emancipation. He said they terrorized Blacks as a means of exerting their power over the newly freed slaves. "It am allus after dark when dey comes to the house and catches the men whups him for nuttin. Dey has de power and it am done for to show dey has de power." (Hamilton, n.d.).[12]

Likewise, former slave Will Adams believed the rise of the Klan in Texas was a result of the influence of northern carpetbaggers on Blacks. "I 'members when the Ku Klux business starts up. Smart niggers caused that. The carpetbaggers ruint the niggers and the white men couldn't do a thing with them, so they got up the Ku Klux and stirs up the world. Them carpetbaggers come 'round larnin' niggers to sass the white folks what done fed them." He continued to disparage northerners in Texas when he said, "Them carpetbaggers starts all the trouble at 'lections in Reconstruction. Niggers didn't know anythin' 'bout politics." (Adams, n.d.)[13]

Still, such political manipulation and coercion of Black votes led to many Blacks being elected to political offices throughout the South. Supported by the Republican Party, these Black politicians frequently found themselves caught between vengeful Republicans, resentful racist Democrats, and the needs of former slaves (Brock, May 1981).[14] Nonetheless, historians generally believe the Republican Party supported the election of two thousand Blacks to federal and state offices. Furthermore, the post-war Republican Party succeeded in creating a new political coalition that consisted of northern political

---

[9] Elliott J. Gorn, "Black Spirits: The Ghostlore of Afro-American Slaves," *American Quarterly*, 36 (1984): 549–565.

[10] Fry, *Night Riders in Black Folk History*, 146.

[11] Stampp, *The Era of Reconstruction*, 199–201; Franklin, *From Slavery to Freedom*, 275; Randolph Campbell, *Gone to Texas* (New York and Oxford: Oxford University Press, 2003), 281; Rupert Richardson, et al, *Texas: The Lone Star State* (Hoboken, New Jersey: Prentice Hall, 2004), 244.

[12] William Hamilton, *Slave Narratives*, Box 4H359, The University of Texas, Center for American History.

[13] Will Adams, *Slave Narratives*, Box 4H359, The University of Texas, Center for American History.

[14] Euline Brock, "Thomas W. Cardozo: Fallible Black Reconstruction Leader," *Journal of Southern History* XLVII, No. 2 (May 1981): 183–206 P185.

opportunists in the South, southern White Republicans, and the newly created Black electorate that ostracized the Democratic Party and their racist constituents.

History generally regarded such Black politicians as Hiram Revels, Robert Elliot, and Robert Smalls as honorable men who sincerely tried to serve the best interests of the Black community. However, nearly every effort to improve the Black community was seen as a threat to the southern White power structure.[15] Therefore, the lives of these men, and others, were often in danger.

Sadly, the corruption that defined the Reconstruction era involved some of these Black politicians as well as their White counterparts. Instead of focusing on the betterment of the Black community, some Black politicians followed their White counterparts in participating in schemes designed to increase their personal fortunes. Most schemes were unsuccessful, and in the end, it was the Black community that suffered (Brock, May 1981).[16]

The efforts to seamlessly integrate the Black community into the fabric of American society also were largely unsuccessful. There were certainly economic and political accomplishments during this period as the Black community would no longer be mere bystanders in American history. However, to secure the presidency for Rutherford B. Hayes in 1876, the North seemingly abandoned the needs of the Black community. Full integration had not yet been realized. Even though the South acquiesced to Hayes becoming president, what they received in return restricted the evolution of the Black community. The withdrawal of federal troops meant a return to home rule throughout the South—in other words, a return to White supremacy.

Certainly, the Republican Party wanted to punish the leaders and supporters of the Confederacy. However, their commitment to civil rights for the Black community was not absolute. Black politicians should not be characterized as illiterate or incompetent. They may have been politically inexperienced, but their efforts to demonstrate that Blacks were deserving of equal social and political status should be praised.[17] The shortcomings of the era should not rest on their shoulders, as southern apologists in the academy suggested. Instead, the effort to create an inclusive society was undermined by the ideology of White supremacy.

By the twentieth century, the South would further encourage the politicization of racism through movies and popular books. The *Birth of a Nation*, for

---

[15] www.arcgis.com/apps/MapJournal/index.html?appid=86e1136a04ba42aaa80ea2e626df2c47, Accessed January 15, 2020.

[16] Brock, "Thomas W. Cardozo," 206.

[17] https://www.thenation.com/article/archive/rooted-reconstruction-first-wave-black-congressmen/, accessed January 15, 2020.

example, rallied members of the United States' racist community to believe that they were the only defenders of the American way of life, which they believed was under attack by the savage lusts of Black men and the cultural ignorance of some European immigrants. These racist attitudes were so pervasive and led to the Black community becoming so vilified that the lynching of Black World War I veterans did not receive sufficient condemnation from the White House.

* * *

By 1948, the politics of race had reached a crucial crossroads. Disillusioned with the sudden inclusion of women and Black minorities in the Democratic Party, southern White supremacists decided to support their own candidate for the White House. The Dixiecrats, officially known as the States' Rights Democratic Party, were committed to White supremacy and held fast to the premise that Blacks were inferior. They also adamantly believed the proper social order rested on the separation of the races. Conflicts within the Democratic Party over Truman's emerging civil rights policies did not begin at their 1948 national convention. This schism had begun years earlier.

Republicans, Democrats, and an Unexpected Political Realignment

In the nineteenth century, the Democratic Party was synonymous with the Confederate States. After the Civil War and for the remainder of the century, the South maintained its commitment to the Democratic Party and White supremacy. Little had changed by the beginning of the twentieth century. In fact, the resurgence of the Ku Klux Klan bolstered the image of whites as the defenders of American culture and values while the Black community was stereotyped as representing savagery and social debasement.

Nonetheless, the devastation caused by the Great Depression that an unexpected political realignment. The Black community became an important ally of the Roosevelt administration and the New Deal, not necessarily because of what the New Deal did for Blacks, but because of the racism of the 1920s and the disinterested attitudes of the Republican Party.

After decades of supporting the "Party of Lincoln," many in the Black community felt they deserved better than political alienation. The rampant violence against the Black community exposed the fact that the racism that led to four years of war in the previous century had not been excised from the American psyche. The only thing more alarming for the Black community than the numerous acts of violence was the silence emanating from the Republican Party. In fact, the policies of the Republican Party seemed to provide tacit support for the social and political subordination of the Black community.[18]

By 1930, the new economic reality of rampant unemployment and homelessness exacerbated existing racial tensions. Whites were forced to seek those menial jobs previously reserved for the nation's poor minorities.[19] However, in the Black community, the economic collapse was barely noticeable because the unemployment rate in the Black community was already twice the national average. By 1933, more than two million Blacks were on relief rolls. The Fourteenth Amendment's promises of citizenship became hollow clichés as African Americans continued to languish in segregated poverty-ridden communities.[20]

Nonetheless, by the 1932 elections, the Black community faced the choice of the non-responsive policies of Hoover and the Republicans, or the proposed social programs of Roosevelt and the Democrats. Still, the initial support for Roosevelt was timid. About 25% of Black voters supported Roosevelt in that election, but four years later, that support increased to nearly 52%.[21]

When Roosevelt introduced the New Deal, he and the vaunted Brain Trust hoped it would alleviate the miserable conditions facing most Americans. The Administration initially supported the relief agencies and their plans of financial distributions or doles. In 1935, however, Roosevelt redirected the focus of the New Deal with the introduction of the Works Progress Administration (WPA) to focus on developing work relief programs. Now, instead of merely handing out money, the Administration accepted its patrician responsibility for the unemployed and provided government-sponsored jobs to those eligible individuals on the relief rolls.

---

[18] Robert Rutland, *The Republicans: From Lincoln to Bush* (Columbia and London: University of Missouri Press, 1996), 170.

[19] John Salmond, "The Civilian Conservation Corp and the Negro," *The Journal of American History* 52 (June 1965): 75–88.

[20] Charles Martin, "Negro Leaders, the Republican Party, and the Election of 1932," *Phylon* 32 (1st Quarter 1971): 85–93; James Sears, "Black Americans and the New Deal," *The History Teacher* 10, no. 1 (November 1976): 89–105.

[21] Lerone Bennett, Jr., *Before the Mayflower* (Penguin Books, 1993), 360; Nelson Lichtenstein, Susan Strasser, et al., *Who Built America?* (New York: Worth Publishers, 2000): 437; Nancy Weiss, *Farewell to the Party of Lincoln: Black Politics in the Age of FDR* (New Jersey: Princeton University Press, 1983): 180–208.

This redirection of the political and social energies of the New Deal changed the landscape of American politics. The welfare state appeared, and the black community found a new champion in the First Lady, Eleanor Roosevelt. Mrs. Roosevelt was different. She actively sought to provide opportunities for the social and political inclusion of Blacks and women, much to the dismay of the Democratic Party's southern leadership. Under her influence, a new political coalition emerged that would influence the nation's policies for decades.[22]

At about the same time, Adolf Hitler's aggressive actions in Europe led to another conflict that engulfed the world in 1939. This naturally took attention away from the social inequities facing the Black community in the United States. Nonetheless, as in World War I, the Black community closed ranks with the rest of American society against the Nazi threats to worldwide democracy.

In 1948, in what could be considered recognition for the contributions of the two million Black servicemen during World War II, Truman eliminated racial discrimination in the U.S. military with Executive Order 9981. Historically, this was the first significant domino to fall in the decades-old fight to eliminate Jim Crow laws. This recognition went far beyond abolishing segregated military units. Truman provided Black veterans the opportunity to receive the real and intangible benefits of serving this democracy. In the following decades, military service provided the social and economic foundation for what would become the Black middle class of the 1970s and 1980s; the first generation of the Black community that successfully moved out of dilapidated inner-city neighborhoods for the supposed greener suburban pastures.

The South, however, did not see these changes as social, political, or legal milestones. Instead, they viewed Truman's actions as another attack against the social order they cherished. Southern elected officials continued to view the legal separation of Blacks and Whites and the only way to preserve civil society. The sacrifices and heroism of Black servicemen such as Doris Miller and the Tuskegee Airmen did little to change their opinions.[23]

The Democratic Party held its national convention in Philadelphia in the summer of 1948, where 161 years earlier the immortal words "We the People" were put on paper. In 1787, Blacks were not considered citizens under the Constitution. But, in 1948, 85 years after the Emancipation Proclamation, the Black community was finally seeing progress toward becoming considered as equal Americans and receiving overdue recognition as positive contributors

---

[22] Richard Hofstadter, "From Calhoun to the Dixiecrats," *Social Research: An International Quarterly* 82, no. 1 (Spring 2015): 245–261.

[23] Sarah McCulloh Lemmon, "The Ideology of the Dixiecrat Movement," *Social Forces* 30, no. 2 (December 1951): 162–171.

to a developing democracy. Such a recognition was obviously more than the South could tolerate.

Reconsidering their place in the evolving ideology of the Democratic Party, White supremacist leaders, led by South Carolina's Strom Thurmond, vowed to convene their own national convention if Harry Truman was chosen to represent the Party in the upcoming presidential election. Truman was eventually nominated and supported a platform that continued to advance the civil rights of the Black community. Rejecting what they considered to be s misguided attempt to placate the Black electorate, southern politicians held true to their promise to convene their own convention to advance a racist agenda.[24] This racist political line in the sand was reminiscent of the threats made in 1860. The result was the Confederate States of America, 4 years of horrific war, 750,000 destroyed (more than in any other U.S. war), and the final eradication of the vile institution of legal slavery in the United States.

Shortly after the Democrats adjourned their convention in Philadelphia, southern politicians met twice, in Birmingham and Oklahoma City, to plan their strategy. What emerged was the States' Rights Democratic Party (Dixiecrats). These White supremacists naturally blamed Truman and his liberal supporters for the political schism within the Democratic Party. Hiding behind the old cover of states' rights, Mississippi Congressman William Colmer deftly reawakened the ghosts of the failed Confederacy when he addressed the House of Representatives weeks before the convention in Philadelphia and accused Truman of overstepping the limits of his executive authority.[25]

With a combination of beliefs in states' rights and the inherent superiority of whites as their ideological bedrock, the Dixicrats reaffirmed their belief that the federal government did not have the authority to force sovereign states to racially accept the Black community as social and political equals. Strom Thurmond eventually became the face of continued racism and bigotry.[26] Their strategy soon became obvious: confound the electoral process and reestablish their ideological dominance within the Democratic Party.[27]

Dixiecrats also considered a coalition with conservative Republicans to create a new Conservative Party. Such a coalition, as they envisioned it, would naturally emphasize states' rights, individual freedoms, and free enterprise. The obvious implication was the preservation of the existing racial status quo

---

[24] Emile B. Ader, "Why the Dixiecrats Failed," *The Journal of Politics* 15, no. 3 (August 1953): 356–369.
[25] Barton Berstein and Allen Matusow, *The Truman Administration: A Documentary History* (New York: Harper & Row, 1966): 112.
[26] Lemmon, "The Ideology of the Dixiecrat Movement," 163.
[27] Emile B. Ader, "Why the Dixiecrats Failed," *The Journal of Politics* 15, no. 3 (August 1953): 356–369.

enforced by Jim Crow segregation. However, this strategy was rejected because of the generations-old animosity toward the Party of Lincoln for the initial act of emancipating the Black community from slavery.[28]

Most political observers believed the chaos within the Democratic Party would allow the Republican Thomas Dewey, to easily claim the White House. In a stunning upset, however, Truman won the election receiving 57% of the electoral vote to Dewey's 36%. Thurmond only received seven percent of the electoral vote and almost 1.2 million in popular votes and carried the Deep South states of Alabama, Louisiana, Mississippi, and South Carolina. The failure of the Dixicrats rested on their inability to gather greater support throughout the old Confederacy as they anticipated. However, it was obvious that the Dixicrats also failed to see the slow shift in support toward social inclusion of the Black community throughout the South.

This was the one and only appearance of the States' Rights Democratic Party. With Truman leading the Democratic Party, a temporary truce was reached. But the South never abandoned its position on states' rights and White supremacy. In the ensuing decades, this faction continued to clash with the liberal agenda of John F. Kennedy and Lyndon B. Johnson, abandoning the Democratic Party in favor of Richard Nixon and the Republican Party in 1968.

Civil Rights, the Vietnam War, and Street Chaos

The previously rejected idea of a political coalition with conservative Republicans became increasingly attractive as Vietnam War protestors and Black civil rights agitators became more and more visible. This, coupled with Nixon's overt courting of Southern votes, made the Republican Party appear as a safe port in an ever-increasingly tumultuous social storm.

* * *

The 1960s were as chaotic a decade as any in American history. The new technologies that made televisions affordable brought the horrors of the Vietnam War into American living rooms daily through the evening newscasts. It also illustrated the Black community's fight for equal rights and social respectability. The images of water hoses and vicious dogs used on Black protestors have

---

[28] Lemmon, "The Ideology of the Dixiecrat Movement," 168; Hofstadter, "From Calhoun to the Dixiecrats," 255

been permanently etched in this country's history. Nonetheless, the Vietnam War and the Civil Rights movement accelerated the change in American society that began with Franklin D. Roosevelt's New Deal. However, such changes were not welcomed by everyone. An element of society longed for the "good old days."

In 1960, Richard Nixon became the standard-bearer for the Republican Party after serving 8 years as Dwight Eisenhower's vice president. His Democratic opponent was the charismatic senator from Massachusetts, John F. Kennedy. These two engaged in the first-ever televised presidential debates, foreshadowing the influence the new technology would have in shaping future societal opinions. Kennedy has generally been considered the "winner" of these debates and would go on to win a narrow victory in November 1960.

A bitter and frustrated Nixon went home to California and ran for governor in 1962. The result was the same. At this point, most political analysts of the day believed his career in politics was over. But it was then that American society began to seriously unravel.

Many Americans believed the public assassinations of John and Robert Kennedy, civil rights icon Martin Luther King, Jr., and former Nation of Islam spokesman Malcolm X, coupled with the government's ineffective management of the conflict in Vietnam to be a precursor to all-out social anarchy. Some high officers in the armed forces actively considered a coup, but never acted on the impulse. Still living under the threat of the Cold War, such chaos was perceived to be the work of foreign agents seeking to undermine American institutions for the benefit of the Soviet Union.

Richard Nixon reappeared with a strategy to empower a new political coalition of southern Democrats and conservative Republicans. Such a political relationship was initially introduced by the States' Rights Democratic Party but failed to gather positive traction. Now, with the 1968 elections approaching, Nixon gambled that the time was right.

President Johnson's Civil Rights Act (1964) and Voting Rights Act (1965) effectively brought an end to Jim Crow. Historically, this became the proverbial last straw for the southern White supremacists. Their world was changing faster than they could comprehend. This legislation coupled with the fiasco of the 1968 Democratic convention, convinced them it was time to seriously explore new political alliances.

The Democratic Party was in disarray when delegates arrived in Chicago in August 1968. The incumbent President, Lyndon B. Johnson, had withdrawn from consideration to be the Party's nominee 4 months earlier. Robert Kennedy then became the frontrunner and the anticipated standard-bearer before his wrenching assassination in Los Angeles in June after being declared the winner of the California and South Dakota primary elections. This left Johnson's vice president, Hubert Humphrey, to carry the torch.

Seeking to avoid uncontrolled public demonstrations during the convention, Chicago's mayor, Richard Daley, made the disastrous move to call up twenty-four thousand police and National Guardsmen. This action exacerbated the conflicts between authorities and protestors. And it all played out before the nation's evening newscasts.

Vietnam protestors were meant with a degree of violence never witnessed before in the streets outside the convention hall. The police arrested individuals indiscriminately and savagely. Millions on television watched in horror as the police clubbed and bashed any and everyone in sight. Nixon successfully tied this display of lawlessness around the collective necks of the Democrats and painted them as the party of chaos and disorder.

As the campaign season entered its final weeks, both the Republicans and Democrats engaged in unscrupulous tactics. The Vietnam War was unquestionably the main issue of the campaign. Before his term as President expired, Johnson worked feverishly to find a resolution to American involvement. Before he was even elected, Nixon successfully undercut any and all efforts by Johnson. Johnson still claimed that a summit to discuss peace terms was forthcoming. Such claims later were denied by the North Vietnamese leadership.

To keep American anxiety high and portray Humphrey as an incompetent pacifist, Nixon claimed the North Vietnamese were moving troops and supplies into position to attack American forces in South Vietnam. This was an untruth, but it worked to dissuade Americans from voting for Humphrey. However, Nixon did claim to have a secret plan to end the Vietnam War. Such a plan was never presented to the American people.

Another actor in the 1968 presidential drama, George Wallace, the governor of Alabama, was probably best known for his violent stance against racial integration. The image of Wallace defiantly standing in front of the University of Alabama in an attempt to prevent Black students from entering in 1962 could be considered a low point in American history for an elected official. Nonetheless, his appeal to White supremacists was undeniable and became perhaps his biggest electoral draw. Wallace received 13% of the popular vote and carried his home state of Alabama, along with Arkansas, Georgia, Louisiana, and Mississippi. Interestingly, of the original eleven southern states that comprised the Confederacy, Wallace carried five and Nixon five (Tennessee, North and South Carolina, Virginia, and Florida). Texas was the only ex-Confederate state that the Democrats carried in 1968.

Even though Nixon won only five of the eleven original Confederate states, this was significant for the future of both the Democratic and Republican parties. For the Democrats, this meant they would become identified with the commitment to political and social inclusion of minorities and women. Over the years their broad political umbrella evolved to include environmentalists, feminists, and those tolerant of gender fluidity.

For the Republican Party, the 1968 election meant that its efforts spent courting southern voters paid immense dividends. Ronald Reagan and Donald Trump would also use their own version of the infamous "Southern Strategy" to secure the White House. However, in the 1960s, this was a big gamble.

With the emergence of civil rights as a political platform in the 1930s and 1940s, the politics of race was becoming increasingly visible. The vile images of the Bull Connor-led opposition to Martin Luther King and the Civil Rights movement embarrassed the nation. King successfully manipulated the images seen on the evening news to move most Americans away from Jim Crow and into an inclusive society.

Barry Goldwater, the architect of the neo-conservative movement of the 1970s and 1980s, saw the potential of courting the South after his own failed bid for the White House. His continual use of "states' rights" became synonymous with the opposition to the Civil Rights movement.[29] However, race was never publicly presented as the core tenet of the evolving Republican platform. Instead, they loudly advocated such traditional political standards as a small government with minimal regulations allowing the individual to achieve the so-called American dream.[30]

Nixon perfected the strategy of coded ambiguous speech (later called a "dog whistle") to appeal to his supporters.[31] Such words always provided opportunities for denials when questioned about their meanings. But such coded words were typically used to signify opposition to racial programs. For example, Nixon's new calls for law and order in American cities, as well as the much-publicized war on drugs were both received along with his support of actions meant to suppress the Black community.[32]

---

[29] R.W. Apple, Jr. "G.O.P. Tries Hard to Win Black Votes, but Recent History Works Against It," *New York Times*, September 19, 1996. https://www.nytimes.com/1996/09/19/us/gop-tries-hard-to-win--black-votes-but-recent-history-works-against-it.html, Accessed April 10, 2020.

[30] Angie Maxwell, "What We Got Wrong About the Southern Strategy," *Washington Post*, July 26, 2019, https://www.washingtonpost.com/outlook/2019/07/26/what-we-get-wrong-about-southern-strategy/, Accessed April 1, 2020.

[31] Michelle Alexander, *The New Jim Crow* (New York: The New Press, 2010), 44.

[32] Ibid.

By the 1970s, affirmative action programs allowed many in the Black community to matriculate at previously segregated institutions of higher education and live in previously all-White neighborhoods. Since the 1890s, some viewed the development of suburban housing as an escape from Blacks. The 1970s were no different as suburban communities that began in the 1950s matured into social and political forces to be reckoned with. So, the Republican Party not only capitalized on racial angst but politicized the traditional roles of women and minorities as tenets of a distinct version of Christianity.

Even with the recent denials of racial intent in the development of the neoconservative movement, there was no escaping the reality that White supremacists began supporting the Grand Old Party in earnest.[33] Nixon aides acknowledged that policies supporting the "war on drugs" were designed to target and disrupt the Black community, particularly the Black family unit. So, the neoconservative movement was built on the foundation of dismantling the antiwar left movement and the social control of the Black community through a series of attacks masquerading as law and order.[34] Thus, within a century, the Republicans and Democrats had switched ideological positions on the United States' political scale. Once the "party of Lincoln," the Republicans had become apologists for Southern White supremacy, as the Democrats, once architects of a racist "southern strategy" had become allies of the Black community on civil rights, opponents of the Vietnam war, and supporters of environmental causes, women's rights, et al.

By 1972, the political exodus of White supremacists from the Democratic Party was complete. Republicans successfully used racial politics to ideologically pit whites against Blacks.[35] Nixon politically destroyed Democrat George McGovern by carrying 49 states, receiving 520 electoral votes. His presidency then unraveled 21 months later with his resignation to avoid impeachment over the Watergate affair. Nonetheless, the political relationship between conservatives and White supremacists was now intact.

* * *

---

[33] "Nixon Aides Suggest Colleague was Kidding About Drug War Being Designed to Target Black People," *Huffington Post*. https://www.huffpost.com/entry/richard-nixon-drug-war-john-ehrlichman_n_56f58be6e4b0a3721819ec61?j4cvxkk6gn39b2o6r, Accessed March 25, 2020.

[34] Hilary Hanson, "Nixon Aide reportedly Admitted Drug War Was Meant to Target Black People," https://www.huffpost.com/entry/nixon-drug-war-racist_n_56f16a0ae4b03a640a6bbda1, Accessed April 1, 2020.

[35] Alexander, *The New Jim Crow*, 47.

The Timeline to Barack Obama

On November 4, 2008, a self-professed Black man was elected president of the United States. Forty-five years (540 months) after Martin Luther King, Jr., stood in front of the Lincoln Memorial and dreamt of a day when his children would be judged by the content of their character over the color of their skin in the words of Martin Luther King, at age 39, 20 years after his assassination, as well as 145 years (1740 months) after Lincoln's Emancipation Proclamation had enacted an end to slavery in the United States. Obama also was elected 221 years (2652 months) after the founders of this Republic had agreed to consider its Black residents as three-fifths of a person for determining congressional representation. It also was 232 years (2784 months) after Thomas Jefferson had deftly articulated a belief that all men (women had to wait until 1920) are equal in the sight of God. And, 389 years (4668 months) after the first African slaves had arrived on the banks of the James River in what would become Virginia.

On that day in November 2008 and for many weeks and months thereafter, numerous individuals believed that American society had finally buried its racist past. Conversations involving a "post-racial" society seemed to be on everyone's lips. However, there were indications before, and certainly afterward, that American society was nowhere near "post-racial." The same coalition that supported Nixon as a check on the growing political and social influence of Blacks in the 1970s made a dramatic reappearance in the form of the Tea Party Caucus of the Republican Party, and later a revival of vicious White supremacy.

In what was supposed to be a speech outlining his plan to end, or at the very least curtail, American involvement in the seemingly never-ending conflict in Vietnam, Nixon made an impassioned plea to his political base. He asked for the support of the silent majority. Historians have since defined Nixon's silent majority as middle-class whites who believed they were losing political and social influence in their country to loud and disrespectful Blacks, unruly women, Mexican fruit-pickers, and ungrateful White twenty-somethings.[36]

The foundation of the infamous silent majority was predicated upon racial prejudice. However, being an overt racist is not good for one's political fortunes. Republican strategists perfected coded speech capitalizing on the fears

---

[36] Scott Laderman, "How Richard Nixon captured White Rage—and Laid the Groundwork for Donald Trump," *Washington Post*, November 3, 2019. https://www.washingtonpost.com/outlook/2019/11/03/how-richard-nixon-captured-white-rage-laid-groundwork-donald-trump/, Accessed April 15, 2020.

of Whites of a Black takeover. Still, Nixon's political capital was not enough to save the campaigns for those overtly racist southerners who represented a constituency openly hostile to desegregation and busing.[37]

The ability to politicize the racial backlash against federally ordered school desegregation and busing would define this country's political environment in the immediate aftermath of the Civil Rights movement. Historical data indicates that most whites opposed Black students learning in seats next to their children.[38] Nixon understood this and wanted to replace the Fourteenth Amendment and ordered John Mitchell, his Attorney General, not prosecute cases involving noncompliance with the Supreme Court's decision in *Brown v Board of Education* or the Civil Rights Act of 1964. As a result, to southern White supremacists, it appeared Nixon was on their side in maintaining a White-centered society.[39]

As a suburban constituency became more influential, the entire country became more conservative and issues of race seemed to take a back seat to economic realities of the 1970s and 1980s. Classism seemingly replaced racism as the societal dividing line. Certainly, the chaos of the oil crises, stagflation, and the intensity of the renewed Cold War animosities with the Soviet Union shifted attention away from the ongoing racial disparities. It would be years before the effects of the disastrous war on drugs on the Black community, particularly the core family unit, would be known; and longer still before being formally acknowledged by the federal government.

As a result, revisionist examinations of the southern strategy and the silent majority would like to believe they were never racially influential. Southern voting patterns indicate poorer southerners, both Black and White, still tended to support Democratic policies and candidates. Conversely, upper- and middle-class southerners (Black and White) embraced the conservative policies of the Republicans. By the 1990s, the shift toward conservative economic policies by all groups resulted in a new wave of Republication Congressional power led by Newt Gingrich in 1994.[40]

After gaining control of both houses of Congress, Republican leadership guided policies toward balanced federal budgets and welfare reform. Their

---

[37] Michelle Brattain, "Forgetting the South and the Southern Strategy" *Miranda*, November 29, 2011. https://journals.openedition.org/miranda/2243, Accessed April 10, 2020.

[38] Frank Brown, "Nixon's 'Southern Strategy' and the Forces against Brown" *The Journal of Negro Education* 73, no. 3 (Summer, 2004): 191–208.

[39] Under the Civil Rights Act (1964) the Attorney General had the authority to prosecute school districts which either violated or did not act in good faith in complying with the Supreme Court's order to desegregate schools.

[40] Clay Risen, "The Myth of 'the Southern Strategy," *New York Times*, December 10, 2006, https://www.nytimes.com/2006/12/10/magazine/10Section2b.t-4.html, Accessed March 15, 2020.

successes thwarted the liberal agenda of universal health insurance.[41] However, the modification of welfare laws seriously impacted millions of families. These actions were perceived as a culmination of a decades-long attack to undermine the New Deal/Great Society policies to help poor families.

However, the Republican Party was unable to maintain the excitement of 1994. In the ensuing midterm elections, they lost five congressional seats. They successfully impeached Bill Clinton in 1998 but were unable to remove him from office. The unpopularity of the impeachment eventually led Speaker of the House, Newt Gingrich, to step down from his vaunted position.

George W. Bush, 9-11, Obama, and the Centuries-Old Struggle for Racial Equality

George W. Bush became president in 2000. Historians will have to hypothesize what his presidency would have become if the terror attacks of September 11, 2001, had never happened. Sadly, it did happen and transformed not only George W. Bush's presidency, but this culture and politics as well. For a time, American politics seemed to unify behind the defense of the country. However, some of the information that formed the basis of our military's policy have since proven to be inaccurate.

In February 2007, Barack Obama declared his intention to run for the presidency. He made this announcement in Springfield, Illinois. This certainly was no accident that such an announcement was made in the hometown of the Great Emancipator, Abraham Lincoln. Like Martin Luther King, Jr., who delivered his most oft-quoted speech in the shadows of the same. Obama consciously, or unconsciously, immediately introduced race into his campaign. However, Obama's campaign purposefully diminished discussions of racial issues. Instead, they emphasized similarities and minimized differences.[42]

While the intent may have been on minimizing racial issues, the issue of race has been a part of the electorate since the passage of the Voting Rights Act in 1965. A CNN poll revealed that nearly one-fifth of the electorate said race was a factor, to some degree, in how they voted in 2008. Since 1965, the Republican Party has directed its policies toward older White voters and

---

[41] President Bill Clinton put the First Lady, Hillary Clinton, in charge of guiding the heath care plan through Congress. In hindsight, there is intense debate as to whether the health care plan failed because of opposition to the First Lady, or the merits of the plan itself.

[42] Thomas Edge, "Southern Strategy 2.0: Conservatives, White Voters, and the Election of Barack Obama" *Journal of Black Studies* 40, no. 3 (January 2010): 426–444.

scarcely paid any political attention to the Black community. The appearance of the link between the southern strategy, racism, states' rights, and the Republican Party has been hard to overcome. So, almost by default, race played in role in Obama's election.[43]

Again, even if the Obama campaign tried to downplay race, his political opponents used every opportunity to bring it up. Even his challenger during the Democratic primaries, the former First Lady and Senator from New York, Hillary Clinton, consistently took racial jabs. A Clinton advisor often referred to Obama as the affirmative action candidate. Similarly, conservative commentators made disparaging remakes about his parentage (his mother was a White woman from Kansas and his father was a Black man from the African country of Kenya).[44]

After November 2008, conservative commentators were the first to proclaim a post-racial society and proclaimed Obama's victory was because of White support. As a result, they argued, the dream of a color-blind society was now a reality and we should immediately dismantle any remaining vestiges of affirmative action programs and gerrymandering policies. Not only were policies designed to even the so-called playing field no longer necessary, as conservatives viewed the world, but any discussion of race would also now be meaningless. A Black man was president, so anything was now possible.[45]

Racist Rhetoric Against Obama in High Gear

However, those possibilities were not necessarily welcomed by those who still believed that their country was being taken away from them. By the time Obama was sworn on January 20, 2009, the racist rhetoric against Obama was already moving into high gear. Officials from the Southern Poverty Law Center commented that there were increases in the incidence of racial hostilities as a result of the November elections. These incidents involved vandalism, racial threats, and physical attacks. Furthermore, these incidents were initiated by whites who believed that the country their forefathers built had been taken away from them. A White resident from Georgia said, "I believe our nation is ruined and has been for several decades and the election of Obama

---

[43] Ibid., 431–432.
[44] Ibid., 435.
[45] Ibid., 436–438.

is merely the culmination of the change. If you had real change it would involve all the members of [Obama's] church being deported."[46]

It is evident by such comments that some whites still consider the citizenship of Blacks to not be on equal standing as theirs. Therefore, to be a "real" Americans refers to being White.[47] And why do they have a right of ownership to an entire country. *Everyone* here came from *somewhere*, whether by choice or by force. *E Pluribus Unum*—"Out of Many, One." It is more than an extremely short lesson in Latin.

Former President Jimmy Carter addressed the question of whether levels of racial animosity increased because of Obama's election. He responded in the affirmative. After South Carolina Congressman Joe Wilson interrupted Obama's speech to Congress by shouting "You lie," Carter said such comments and other actions were racially motivated. He also said the racism in this country that was previously hidden had now bubbled to the surface as whites still believed Blacks were not qualified to occupy the White House.[48]

Politically, Obama became the new face of the Democratic Party. Seeing a Black man as the major influence in a national political party was a reality that was unbearable for some, in both parties. Race has always been an issue of contention separating and dividing the two political entities, but the tensions seemed to definitely intensify after Obama's rise to power. Furthermore, within this divide, Republican candidates developed and perfecting coded language in the post-civil rights era to solidify and incite rage among supporters.[49]

To oppose the agenda of Obama and the Obama-led Democratic Party, disgruntled conservatives organized their dissatisfaction and called it the Tea Party movement. Such a label is an obvious reference to the Revolutionary era and the destruction of British-owned tea in Boston's harbor in 1773.[50] It is interesting that these twenty-first-century conservatives chose to model their movement after an event that they would most surely oppose today. The

---

[46] *Associated Press*, November 15, 2008. http://www.nbcnews.com/id/27738018/ns/us_news-life/t/obama-election-spurs-race-threats-crimes/#.XqsOKGhKhPY, Accessed March 21, 2020.

[47] Philip S. S. Howard, "Turning Out the Center: Racial Politics and African Agency in the Obama Era" *Journal of Black Studies* 40, no. 3 (January 2010): 380–394.

[48] Ewen MacAskill, "Jimmy Carter: Animosity Towards Barack Obama is Due to Racism" *The Guardian*, September 16, 2009, https://www.theguardian.com/world/2009/sep/16/jimmy-carter-racism-barack-obama, Accessed April 15, 2020.

[49] Michael Tesler, "The Return of Old-Fashioned Racism to White Americans' partisan Preferences in the early Obama Era," *The Journal of Politics* 75, no. 1 (December 21, 2012): 110–123.

[50] This event was directly responsible for King George's tightening his grip on the colonies that in turn led to the First Continental Congress. Before the Second Continental Congress could convene in 1775, the confrontation at Lexington and Concord had already erupted. The American Revolution had begun. The activities of a few radical locals resulted in the dismantling of an empire and the birth of a new republic.

destruction of someone else's property (in very large amounts) could be classified as an act of grand theft. In today's money, the 92,000 pounds of dumped tea (enough for about 18,500 tea bags) was worth about $1 million. If the tea had been government-owned (it was owned by the British East India Company) the charge might have been terrorism. In fact, the ships carrying the tea had been built and were owned by Americans.

Nonetheless, today's ardent conservatives chose as their main issues small government and opposition to universal healthcare. By the 2010 midterm elections, the Tea Party had become a force within the Republican Party. Some observers found evidence that racial animosity certainly influences the perceptions of Tea Party rhetoric when discussing government social policies. However, they stop short of calling the Tea Party racist, believing race is not the primary ideological motive.[51] The ability to spew racist rhetoric and not be racist is in itself a contradiction. It implies the speaking of ones' truth without having the courage to deal with its ramifications.

Academics have long struggled with instruments used to ascertain public opinions. There are limitations to surveys and oral interviews. The main problem is the truthfulness of the respondent. As such, the validity of responses can certainly be called into question. Nonetheless, determining the motives of this modern incarnation of Nixon's silent majority is a huge hurdle. Racial resentment can be nearly impossible to measure when the respondent has been immersed in the politics of coded language and innuendo.

Those who identified themselves as members or supporters of the Tea Party were typically White middle-class males, politically Republican and ideologically conservative. Being conservative not only meant they believed in limited government and lower taxes, but they opposed abortion of any kind and gay marriage was seen as an offense to God. The abortion and gay marriage issues successfully engulfed the conservative religious community. Their inclusion under the Tea Party tent allowed some to claim a moral position that allowed them to hide their White supremacy behind the *Bible*.

Nonetheless, a study evaluating the Tea Party's motives in the policies and candidates they endorsed found general opposition to government welfare-type programs. While such opposition was only "modestly" influenced by racial resentment, it was acknowledged that racial resentment existed and was a consideration.[52]

---

[51] Kevin Arceneaux and Stephen P. Nicholson, "Who Wants to Have a Tea Party? The Who, What, and Why of the Tea Party Movement" *Political Science and Politics* 45, no. 4 (October 2012): 700–710.
[52] Ibid., 708.

The Tea Party and White Extinction Anxiety

As the Obama administration began preparing for the reelection campaign, the Tea Party began to consolidate under the ideology of 1950s conservatism. While the gains of the post-World War II decade powered a growing economy and gave birth to the "American dream" it was also a period of intense racism and social unrest. It was this decade that led to the social unrest characterized by urban upheavals and violent antiwar demonstrations. The underlying angst among Tea Party members focused on government programs, especially the Affordable Care Act, which benefitted those they considered undeserving. Not only were these groups undeserving, in the Tea Party's view, but they also were changing society demographically so that it was becoming increasingly nonwhite. For Tea Party members, this was unacceptable.[53]

Interestingly, racial resentment among the Tea Party was not restricted to simply Obama or the Black community. Immigration and rhetoric of securing the border implies a resentment of Latinos as well. In surveys of self-identified Tea Party supporters, lax immigration laws contribute to the nation's levels of undesirables and undeserving poor. Such concerns also are found within the broader Republican Party but are more extreme within Tea Partiers.[54]

Obama's reelection in 2012 (with 51% of the popular vote) coupled with key senatorial losses of Tea Party-endorsed candidates led to their future as influencing agents being questioned.[55] However, their ability to stir impassioned support for the defeat of Obama and his agenda could not be ignored. The continued internal wrangling for control of the Republican Party's future platform left the future of the Tea Party on shaky ground.[56]

For many, the obvious claims of a relationship between Tea Partiers and White supremacists harkened back to assertions that Richard Nixon's "silent majority" also were cloaked racists. While such claims in the twenty-first century are still hard to adequately prove, what is acceptable is the limited memory of politics and politicians.[57] Historians are well aware of revisionism. As

---

[53] Vanessa Williamson, Theda Skocpol, and John Coggin, "The Tea Party and the Remaking of Republican Conservatism," *Perspectives on Politics* 9, no. 1 (March 2011): 25–43.
[54] Ibid., 34.
[55] Andrew D. McNitt, "The Tea Party Movement and the 2012 House Election" *Political Science and Politics* 47, no. 4 (October 2014): 799–805.
[56] Michael Ray, "Tea Party Movement," https://www.britannica.com/topic/Tea-Party-movement, Accessed March 5, 2020.
[57] Brattain, "Forgetting the South and the Southern Strategy."

new information is discovered, declassified, or admitted to in deathbed confessions, the need to revisit previous events should occur.[58]

The need for revisionism is not only encouraged because of new information, but also the need to hide uncomfortable truths. Just as Civil War and Reconstruction revisionists downplayed the role of slavery, decades after the Civil Rights movement, some are minimizing the many instances of overt racism. Whereas once upon a time "states' rights" was easily understood to be a phrase indicating opposition to integration. But during the rise of the Tea Party, the meaning of "states' rights" has become much more in doubt.[59] Racism, or being called a racist, is not politically correct in an ever-changing society where groups that previously existed in the margins have rapidly entered the mainstream.

While the claims of a post-racial society were welcomed to justify Obama's initial election in 2008,[60] by his second term, the Tea Party, the influence of racism, even if hidden behind the principles of conservatism were obvious, at least to those without "rose-colored" glasses.

White supremacists initially showed their displeasure by abandoning the inner cities for newly created suburban communities and school districts. The Republican Party understood this and created a platform that harnessed their angst over the new influence of the Black community in national politics. Therefore, there is little question that when Nixon made his initial pleas for support from the silent majority, he and the Republican leadership understood they were appealing to those who were angry because of the social and political gains made by the Black community because of the Civil Rights movement.[61]

After 2012, the undercurrent of angst over Obama's continuing societal and political influence was intensifying. Mitt Romney tried, but failed, to completely capitalize on that angst. Surely not everyone who supported the

---

[58] An example of new information requiring historical revision involves Richard Nixon and the Watergate fiasco. For more than 30 years the identity of the individual who supplied information to Bob Woodward and Carl Bernstein was simply known as Deep Throat. Woodward and Bernstein's coverage of the break-in at the Watergate building in Washington DC was directly responsible for Nixon's resignation in August 1974. The identity of Deep Throat was one of the most closely guarded secrets in U.S. history. In the spring of 2005, 91-year-old William Felt, who served as an FBI Associate Director during Nixon's presidency, admitted that he had been the informant. Woodward and Bernstein confirmed that Felt was indeed Deep Throat. This revelation reopened the entire Watergate saga to new historical interpretation and analysis.

[59] Brattain, "Forgetting the South and the Southern Strategy."

[60] John McWhorter, "Racism in America is Over" *Forbes*, December 30, 2008, https://www.forbes.com/2008/12/30/end-of-racism-oped-cx_jm_1230mcwhorter.html#6e80063349f8, Accessed April 1, 2020.

[61] Eoin Higgins, "The Silent Majority Stands with Trump" https://eoinhiggins.com/the-silent-majority-stands-with-trump-e17f3afbd4e, Accessed March 31, 2020.

Republican standard-bearer in 2012 was a racist. But when a secret video of a Romney fundraising event surfaced, it brought every conservative under some scrutiny. Romney was recorded as saying:

> There are forty-seven percent of the people who will vote for the president no matter what. All right, there are 47 percent who are with him, who are dependent upon government, who believe that they are victims, who believe the government has a responsibility to care for them, who believe that they are entitled to health care, to food, to housing, to you-name-it. That that's an entitlement. And the government should give it to them. And they will vote for this president no matter what…These are people who pay no income tax.[62]

Romney's plea obviously played on the stereotypes of the black community as lazy and dependent upon the government. With an audience of fellow White millionaires, he did not directly attack Obama, but continually disparaged Obama's supporters.[63]

Four years later, Donald Trump performed surprisingly well in the Republican primaries. He succeeded where Romney had not. Trump was able to tap into the same racial angst that Nixon had mined 48 years earlier. Originally, many in the silent majority opposed the Civil Rights movement; the new version seemed violently disturbed that "their" country would elect a Black man as president.[64]

Trump purposefully spoke to this group like two old friends over a game of dominoes. He was seeking to expose that part of conservatism that could easily be confused with racism.[65] Even though the Republican leadership saw Trump as merely a political neophyte, his acumen at riling audiences during his rallies could not be ignored, nor could his appeal to White nationalists. Trump's White nationalistic rhetoric intensified along with his primary victories. Soon, "silent majority" signs were appearing prominently at rally after rally.[66] Students of irony may have noted that they were not at all *silent*, and usually not a *majority*.

---

[62] David Corn, "Romney Tells Millionaire Donors What He REALLY Thinks of Obama Voters" *Mother Jones*, September 17, 2012, https://www.motherjones.com/politics/2012/09/secret-video-romney-private-fundraiser/, Accessed April 5, 2020.
[63] Ibid.
[64] Higgins, "The Silent majority Stands with Trump."
[65] Ibid.
[66] Jeet Heer, "How the southern strategy made Donald Trump possible" *The New Republic*, February 18, 2016, https://newrepublic.com/article/130039/southern-strategy-made-donald-trump-possible, Accessed March 15, 2020.

Historically, White nationalists often have been synonymous with White supremacists. Trump succeeded in speaking to this group with specific language—not necessarily the coded language of hidden racism, but specific race-based inclinations, nonetheless. Instead of the racial stereotypes of lazy but violent Black men, Trump's twenty-first-century southern strategy emphasized rhetoric that disparaged Muslims and Latino immigrants. His claims that Mexico would pay for a wall along the Mexico—U.S. border sent his rallies in an uncontrollable frenzy.[67] Racial politics was suddenly front and center again.

* * *

By definition, a post-racial society is one in which the racism that once defined it no longer exists. Racist policies to benefit one group over another have been eradicated. Symbols of hate no longer appear in public. And, as Martin Luther King, Jr. once said, a post-racial society is one where everyone would be judged by the content of their character and not the color of their skin.

Many thought this society had evolved to that point in November 2008. Sadly, this would not be the case. The politics of race that many thought no longer existed returned with a vengeance. As previously noted, 221 years (2652 months) after the Founders compromised with their slave-holding contemporaries to limit a member of the Black community to a status of less than a White human being (in the three-fifths compromise), a Black man was elected to the presidency of the United States. The political backlash of this event was vicious. As a result, the politics of race continue to be a defining feature of this republic.

References

Adams, W. (n.d.). *Slave narratives*. The University of Texas, Center for American History.

Brock, E. (1981). Thomas W. Cardozo: Fallible black reconstruction leader. *Journal of Southern History, XLVII*(2), 183–206.

Bureau of Refugees, Freedmen and Abandoned Lands. (n.d.). 1865–1869, National Archives M821, roll 32.

Butchart, R. (1980). *Northern schools, Southern Blacks and reconstruction*. Praeger.

Crouch, B. (2010). *The Freedmen's Bureau and Black Texans*. University of Texas Press.

---

[67] Ibid.

DuBois, W. E. B. (1935). *Black reconstruction* (p. 223). Russell & Russell.
Finley, R. (1996). *From slavery to uncertain freedom: The Freedmen's Bureau in Arkansas*. University of Arkansas.
Fry, G.-M. (2001). *Night riders in black folk history* (p. 110). University of North Carolina Press.
Gorn, E. J. (1984). Black spirits: The ghostlore of Afro-American slaves. *American Quarterly, 36*, 549–565.
Hamilton, W. (n.d.). *Slave narratives*. The University of Texas, Center for American History.
Hoard, R. (n.d.). *Slave narratives*. University of Texas, Center for American History.
Morris, R. (1981). *Reading, 'riting, and reconstruction*. University of Chicago.
Richter, W. (1991). *Overreached on all sides: The Freedmen's Bureau Administrators in Texas, 1865–1868*. Texas A&M University Press.
Stampp, K. (1965). *The era of reconstruction, 1865–1877* (p. 112). Vantage Books.

5

The Civil Rights Movement in Urban Microcosm: Omaha, Nebraska

Bruce E. Johansen

Omaha's Enduring Black Community

The first known Black man to spend a night on the site that would become Omaha, who was named York, arrived as a slave with the Lewis and Clark expedition in 1804. By September 1814, Major Stephen H. Long, writing from what is today North Omaha, recorded the presence of several Blacks, probably slaves, on farmsteads. The first free Black person, Sally Bayne, was recorded on Omaha's site when the city was founded in 1854. A proposed Constitution for a state of Nebraska, drafted in 1854, limited voting to "free white males." It never was enacted (Nebraska did not become a state until 1867). The 1860 U.S. Census recorded 81 "Negroes" in Nebraska Territory, ten of whom were identified as slaves.

Some of Omaha's earliest Black residents arrived via the Underground Railroad, fleeing slavery in the South. Many of them passed through a cabin built in Nebraska City, in the very southeastern corner of the state, by Allen Mayhew during 1855, which has been preserved as a small museum. By 1867, escaped slaves and other Blacks had organized the first church in North Omaha (which was becoming the state's first enduring Black community, St.

B. E. Johansen (✉)
Communication and Native American Studies, University of Nebraska at Omaha, Omaha, NE, USA
e-mail: bjohansen@unomaha.edu

© The Author(s), under exclusive license to Springer Nature Switzerland AG 2022
B. E. Johansen, A. Akande (eds.), *Get Your Knee Off Our Necks*,
https://doi.org/10.1007/978-3-030-85155-2_5

John's African Methodist Episcopal). By the early 1880s, about 500 Blacks lived in North Omaha, supporting several businesses and churches. In 1894, Blacks in Omaha organized the first African American fair in the United States.

In 1910, the Census reported that Omaha's Black community's size was surpassed in western states only by Los Angeles and Denver. The first Black-owned early motion picture company (Lincoln Pictures) was founded in Omaha during 1920, part of a vibrant music and entertainment culture in North Omaha. (After only a year in Omaha, however, Lincoln Pictures moved to Los Angeles.) Later, North Omaha clubs hosted Count Basie, Duke Ellington, Louis Armstrong, the original Nat King Cole Trio, as well as other jazz greats, often in The Ritz Theater, with seating for 548 people. The Ritz closed during the 1950s and later was demolished. Ironically, the vibrancy of North Omaha's entertainment scene was reinforced by strict, southern-style segregation in other neighborhoods.

By 1910, this community had grown to 4,426 people, many of whom were recruited from Southern states to work in the meatpacking industry. The community supported more than a hundred locally owned businesses, including attorneys, dentists, and physicians, as well as preachers in several churches, mainly Baptist and Methodist.

Eruptions of Racial Violence

Omaha's history has been marred by occasional eruptions of racial violence. In 1890, several hundred European Americans formed a mob that seized Joe Coe, a Black worker, from a jail cell after he had been accused of kidnapping a 5-year-old White child. He was killed and lynched. Mobs of whites lacking jobs attacked Greeks as well as Blacks. During February of 1919, a mob of 3,000 whites gathered outside a city jail where a Greek immigrant who had been accused of having sex with a White woman was being held. When police refused to surrender the man, the mob attacked Greektown, an ethnic enclave, chasing residents away from their homes and demolishing 30 homes and businesses.

Between 1910 and 1920, the African-American population of Omaha more than doubled, from 4,426 to 10,315, about 5% of the city's population. Some of the immigrants were recruited as strikebreakers, contributing to racial tensions. The railroads (notably Union Pacific, with a head office in Omaha) had imported Black strikebreakers as early as 1877.

In 1919, a White mob, perhaps 3,000 or more, lynched Will Brown, 41, a Black worker, whose body was mutilated and burned, This riot also resulted in the deaths of two White men and the attempted lynching of Omaha mayor Edward Parsons Smith. The White mob set fire to the Douglas County Courthouse. It was one of more than 20 riots in major U.S. industrial cities during the "Red Summer" of 1919. Judging from the size of the U.S. Army response sent to quell the riot of September 28–29 (70 officers and 1,222 enlisted men), the Omaha riot was probably the largest in the United States that year. A federal report had observed three weeks before the riot that racial tensions were primed to explode largely from racial animosity between workers in the Omaha stockyards, as competition for jobs became intense. During periodic strikes, Blacks had been recruited to replace White workers, aggravating tension.

Adding to the mix, an Omaha police "morals squad" had killed a Black bellhop on September 11, feeding sensational newspaper coverage describing, in livid detail, his alleged rape of 19-year-old Agnes Loebeck on September 25, 1919. This coverage lit the fuse for yet more racial violence, all based on unfounded rumors. Loebeck had identified Brown as the rapist, but later investigation cast doubt on the veracity of this claim.) The Omaha *Bee,* which routinely stoked racial fears against Blacks as well as American Indians (advising whites to "Hunt them down!") had carried accounts purportedly describing several attacks by Black men against young White women.

Before the Omaha Star (which continues to publish today) was founded in 1938, by Mildred D. Brown and her husband S. E. Gilbert, North Omaha had hosted several other Black newspapers, including *The Progress* (begun in 1889), *The Afro-American Sentinel* (started in 1892), *The Omaha Monitor* (1915–1929), and *The Guide* (which begun in 1927), which reached a circulation of more than 25,000, for a time the largest African-American newspaper west of the Missouri River.

Segregation Becomes More Severe Following Riots

Segregation in Omaha became more severe after the 1919 riot. Covenants were placed on properties for sale or rent to restrict Black movement outside of North Omaha. In 1940, however, the federal government ruled them illegal.

By the 1930s, the United Meatpacking Workers of America strove to integrate that industry, which had a major impact in Omaha. The same union supported integration of public facilities during the 1950s, as well as the civil rights movement of the 1960s. At the same time, meatpacking jobs were moving out of Omaha, with employment there declining. By the 1990s, Omaha's Black community was afflicted with acute poverty at the fifth-highest rate among the United States' 100 largest urban areas. More than one-third of Omaha's Blacks (and 60% of its Black children) were living in poverty.

Into this atmosphere, Malcolm X was born in Omaha, as Malcolm Little, a son of the Rev. Earl Little, "a big six-foot-four, very Black man" (Malcolm & Haley, 1964, p. 1), who had drawn the attention of whites as a public advocate of Marcus Garvey's ideas, most notably that Blacks should return to Africa (some did, founding Liberia). Rev. Little was out of town, preaching in Milwaukee, when hooded members of the Ku Klux Klan surrounded his family's North Omaha home, at 3448 Evans St., on horseback, shouting threats, and breaking windows with their rifle butts. His wife was pregnant with Malcolm at the time, their seventh child. They resolved to move away as soon as possible after Malcolm was born, May 19, 1925. Today the site is observed with a state historical marker and listed on the National Register of Historic Places. The house was demolished before its significance was widely recognized. It was not until the 1980s that concentrated efforts were made to restore it.

Civil-rights and Economic Issues Spark Tensions after World War II

Civil rights issues sparked tensions after World War II, as Omaha lost several thousand meatpacking and railroad jobs, crimping the economy. Omaha experienced some of the United States' earliest restaurant sit-ins as early as 1948, several years before similar protests over the refusal of service began in the Southern states. Omaha also experienced a bus boycott during the late 1950s.

In 1947, the DePorres Club was founded at Creighton University to resist racial discrimination in Omaha. A year later, 30 members of the club organized a sit-in at a downtown Omaha restaurant. The restaurant, in the Douglas County Courthouse, agreed to desegregate, but the DePorres Club was expelled from Creighton. Its members were invited to meet at the offices of the Omaha Star by Mildred Brown, the *Star's* founder and publisher. Several other Omaha restaurants continued to exclude Blacks through the 1950s, posting signs that read: "We Don't Serve Any Colored Race." The DePorres Club, again assisted by Mildred Brown, organized bus boycotts in Omaha to compel the hiring of Black drivers. The boycott spread to Council Bluffs (east of the Missouri River as well). As the bus line lost money for the loss of riders, Blacks were hired.

At the same time, meatpacking jobs still were moving out of Omaha, with employment there declining. By the 1990s, Omaha's Black community was afflicted with acute poverty at the fifth-highest rate among the United States' 100 largest urban areas. More than one-third of Omaha's Blacks (including 60% of Black children) were living in poverty.

During the middle 1960s, several large cities across the United States experienced large riots during several long, hot summers. On July 4, 1966, with the temperature in Omaha at 103 degrees F., a large crowd assembled at 24th and Lake streets in the center of North Omaha. Police ordered the group to disband, and its members refused, instead of inflicting several million dollars in damage as buildings along North 24th Street were burned and looted. Four weeks later, on August 1, 1966, violence erupted again after a 19-year-old Black man was fatally shot by a member of the police (who was off-duty at the time). Several buildings were burned before almost 200 riot police enforced order.

On March 4, 1968, protesters at a presidential campaign rally for segregationist Alabama Gov. George Wallace at Omaha's Civic Auditorium were beaten by police. One African American man was fatally shot. A riot ensued. A day later, Ernie Chambers, until then known as a loquacious local barber, helped prevent a riot at Horace Mann Junior High School. Chambers' reputation as a community leader spread and two years later, after he completed a law degree, he was elected to represent North Omaha in Nebraska's Unicameral, the state legislature. Chambers was not the first Black member of the Unicameral, however. In 1892, Dr. Matthew Ricketts had been elected.

Riots occurred again on April 5, 1968, following the assassination of Martin Luther King, Jr. On June 24, 1969, riots re-ignited following the killing of Vivian Strong, a Black teenager, by police officers at the Logan Fontenelle low-income housing project. Several businesses along North 24th Street were firebombed and looted over the next several days.

State Senator Ernie Chambers' Unique Role in Nebraska State Politics

Representing North Omaha (the 11th District) in Nebraska's Unicameral (a one-house state senate), Ernest William "Ernie" Chambers has become a consistent lightning rod for controversy. He has led a storied career of more than 40 years in the statehouse during which he was turned out by term limits in 2008—and then re-elected again, after a 4-year hiatus, in 2012. Although the term-limits law seemed aimed at Chambers, half of Nebraska's 49 state senators were forced to retire after it took effect in 2008. As of 2016, Chambers was still a state senator, having served longer than anyone else in its more than 150-year history.

Chambers was born July 10, 1937, in the same North Omaha neighborhood that he would later represent in the Unicameral, to Lillian and Malcolm Chambers, a minister. His father's family stems from Mississippi and his mother's from Louisiana. Ernie's six siblings all were born in Omaha, where he graduated from Technical High School. He graduated from Creighton University in 1959 with a bachelor's degree in history and minors in philosophy and Spanish. He began a degree program in law at Creighton in the early 1960s and completed it in 1979, but refused to join the state bar association, which precluded his practice of law (except that, as a state senator, he can write and advocate bills that may become law). Chambers began reading about the Black Muslims in the late 1950s, as he went to work at the U.S. Post Office in Omaha, from which he was fired after he protested against supervisors' practice of calling male Black employees "boys."

Chambers became a community spokesman during three riots in the summer of 1966, as he negotiated peace between members of the Omaha Black community, the police, and Mayor A.V. Sorenson. Chambers led community groups to channel complaints about police behavior to the city through a Police-Community Relations Council and to acquire funding for several projects that would assist young people. He also played a prominent role in a film documentary, "A Time for Burning," filmed in 1966, that was nominated for an Academy Award (Oscar).

In Chambers' first foray into politics, he filed for a position on the Omaha School Board and was defeated. In 1970, however, he was elected to the Nebraska Unicameral to replace George W. Althouse, a short-term senator who had been appointed to replace Edward Danner after the latter had died.

During his first term, Chambers' profile was raised by his defense of David Rice and Edward Poindexter, who were charged in connection with the death of an Omaha Police officer, who had been killed by a bomb in a vacant North Omaha house. Chambers built a case that Poindexter and Rice, both Black Panthers, had been set up by federal agents as part of the COINTELPRO campaign that was being used at the time to break up militant minority groups such as the Panthers, American Indian Movement, and Brown Berets. The justice of this case was still being debated decades later as Poindexter and Rice were repeatedly denied parole. Amnesty International considers Poindexter and Rice to be political prisoners.

Chambers is known for wearing muscle shirts and blue jeans on the Unicameral floor and sometimes brings his dog to work. During the early 1980s, Chambers pushed through a state law terminating investment in South Africa nearly single-handedly, making Nebraska one of five states to do so at the time (The others were Massachusetts, Michigan, Maryland, and Connecticut).

Senator Chambers at one time described himself as a Black Muslim, and later as an atheist. He favors imposing property taxes on churches. He filed a lawsuit (*Marsh v. Chambers*) to terminate the Unicameral's practice of opening its sessions with a prayer, a suit that some opponents characterized as "suing God." A district court ruled that the prayers did not violate church-state separation, but the Eighth Circuit Court of Appeals upheld Chambers' argument. The U.S. Supreme Court in 1983 held 6 to 3 that the practice passed constitutional muster because of the "unique history" of the United States.

Nebraska's Unicameral meets within a short walk of the University of Nebraska's Memorial Stadium, which on many fall Saturday afternoons fills with more than 95,000 Nebraska Cornhusker fans, comprising one of the United States' most profitable college sports franchises. The Huskers have sold out every home game since the early 1960s. Senator Chambers proposed that the players be paid as state employees—that, without monetary compensation, they are being exploited as cheap labor. Chambers has convinced the Unicameral to pass a bill in 2003 supporting the idea that college athletes should be paid a stipend. Even with Republican Gov. Charles Thone's signature, but without NCAA support, the idea went nowhere, until it was revived on a national scale about 2020. In June 2021, when the NCAA finally enabled college athletes to monetize their skills and reputations on a national scale, few recalled whose idea this had been. Here, as well as elsewhere, Chambers has consistently been ahead of his time on Black civil-rights issues and other political advocacy.

Senator Chambers also has been a long-time opponent of the death penalty, which he believes disproportionately affects Black, Latino, and American

Indian prison inmates. He introduced bills opposing it for 36 years (including one that was passed in 1979 but was vetoed by Republican Gov. Charles Thone). In 2015, Chambers was a major force behind the passage of a ban on capital punishment that was vetoed by Republican governor Pete Ricketts. The Unicameral then voted to override the veto, with Chambers again in the lead, a most unusual action in what many people regard as a very conservative state. Voters reinstated the death penalty following a petition drive in 2016.

Chronology: Omaha's Black Community

1854: The Om'a'ho Tribe sells most of its land, about four million acres by treaty, for less than 22 cents an acre to make way for a railroad and European-American immigration into a new city bearing an Anglicized version of its name.

1854: Nebraska Territory created on condition, expressed by the U.S. Congress, that it remains "free"—that is, without slavery. However, slaves continue to be held and the earliest territorial legislature debated the practice. The Omaha City Council also debates slavery until at least 1859.

1860: A slave named Eliza escapes an Omaha business and runs to Chicago. The 1860 U.S. Census lists 81 "Negroes" in Nebraska Territory, of which 10 were said to be slaves. An early draft of a Nebraska State Constitution restricts voting rights to "free white males." (Nebraska did not become a U.S. state until 1867.)

1879: The Standing Bear trial (*Standing Bear v. Crook*) in U.S. District Court, Omaha, establishes for the first time that American Indians are defined as persons under United States federal law.

1891: Joe Coe, a Black worker, is lynched by a White mob in Omaha on suspicion that he raped a White woman. No one was charged with the murder of Coe.

1892: Dr. Matthew Ricketts, a North Omaha medical doctor, becomes the first Black to be elected to the Nebraska Unicameral (Legislature).

1913: A tornado on Easter Sunday devastates North Omaha, leveling several blocks, killing at least 100 people.

1919: Will Brown, a Black man, was lynched by a mob of several thousand White men after having been accused of raping a young White woman. This riot is one of several across the United States sparked by competition for jobs.

1921: Malcolm X's father, Earl Little, begins an Omaha chapter of the Universal Negro Improvement Association, headed by Marcus Garvey, and comes to the attention of the Ku Klux Klan, which opens its first Nebraska klavern in Omaha at about the same time.

1925: Malcolm Little (later Malcolm X) is born in Omaha; shortly thereafter, his family leaves the city under threat by the KKK.

1938: Mildred Brown and her husband founded the *Omaha Star*, the longest-lived of Omaha's many Black newspapers. She was the first Black woman to start a newspaper in the United States. It has continued to publish since its establishment as a consistent voice for civil rights, while many competitors have come and gone.

1947: The DePorres Club is founded at Creighton University to resist racial discrimination in Omaha. A year later, 30 members of the club organize a sit-in at a downtown Omaha restaurant.

1952–1954: The DePorres Club, assisted by Mildred Brown, organizes bus boycotts in Omaha to compel the hiring of Black drivers. The boycott spreads to Council Bluffs as well, until Blacks are hired.

1955: Protests were organized at Peony Park after the amusement venue excluded Blacks from a swimming meet. The case reaches the Nebraska Supreme Court, which ruled a violation of state desegregation laws, and fined park management $50.

1958: Dr. Martin Luther King, Jr. speaks in Omaha at Salem Baptist Church.

1963: Black ministers in North Omaha form the Citizens Committee for Civil Liberties (also known as 4CL—"For Civil Liberties"). Several protest marches are held, one of which draws more than 10,000 people. Youth activists protest the color barrier at Peony Park, and it falls, following protests at admissions gates for more than a month.

1964: Malcolm X returned to Omaha for a speech in front of large groups of demonstrators supporting and opposing his presence.

1966: Two days of riots in North Omaha stopped only after the occupation of North Omaha by the National Guard. A locally produced film, "A Time for Burning," is nominated for an Oscar. Riots flared again in 1968 after the assassination of Dr. King, after Omaha Police kill Vivian Strong.

1969: A sit-in at the University of Nebraska at Omaha led to the initiation of a Black Studies Department in 1971.

1970: Ernie Chambers is elected to the Unicameral (state legislature) for the first time.

1971: David Rice and Ed Poindexter, both Black Panthers, are arrested and convicted under questionable circumstances in connection with a bombing that kills a police officer. The case remained controversial for decades as parole was repeatedly denied.

1976: Omaha Public Schools began two decades of court-ordered integration via busing.

1997: Brenda Warren-Council, of North Omaha, loses (by 700 votes) a bid to become Omaha's first Black mayor. Six years later, Thomas Warren, her brother, becomes the city's first Black police chief.

2009: Senator Chambers forced out of office due to a term limits law created to stop him from serving beyond his 38 years in the Nebraska Unicameral. After a one-term hiatus under the law, he is re-elected, becoming the longest-serving state senator in the history of Nebraska.

Statistical Overview of Omaha's Black Community and Related Subjects

Before they were removed by the U.S. government as Omaha and surrounding areas were filled by immigrants on the railroads, the area around the city's future site was home to several Native American peoples, including the Ioway, Ponca, Pawnee, bands of Lakota (Sioux), and O'ma'ho, after whom the city was named ("Omaha" is Anglicized).

Minority populations in Nebraska have generally been less than the United States historical averages, but have grown rapidly in recent years, according to the U.S. Census. Hispanic (a.k.a Latino/a) population grew from 94,425 (5.5%) in 2000 to 133,832 (7.5%) in 2007, a 41.7% increase in seven years. The population of African-Americans grew from 70,043 in 2000 (4.1%) to 78,581 (4.4%) during the same period, a 12.2% increase. American Indians rose from 15,634 (0.9%) to 17,576, up 12.4%, and Asians, at 22,528 in 2000 (1.3%) rose to 30,317 in 2007, up 34.7%. The first Chinese arrived in Omaha during the last half of the nineteenth century to work on the railroads; many of the earliest Japanese were recruited to work in the stockyards and in meatpacking.

By 2010, the proportion of Latinos (called "Hispanics" in Census reports) had risen to 9.2% of Nebraska's population. Latinos by 2010 had become half of the state's minority population. In one decade (2000 to 2010) Nebraska's racial/ethnic minority population (defined as Blacks, Hispanics, Asians, and American Indians) grew from 216,769 to 326,588. During the same period, the Census category comprising "non-Hispanic Whites" grew by 0.4%. One should note that "Hispanic" usually applies to Latin Americans with Spanish—"Hispanic"—roots. "Latino" is more inclusive, describing Spanish or Portuguese heritage, plus African, and indigenous Americans, and even Anglo-American immigrants with Latino blood.

'The Hispanic/Latino population in Nebraska increased from 36,969 in 1990 to 94,425 in 2000, and 167,405 in 2010, a 353% rise in 20 years, including a 155.4% increase from 1990 to 2000 and a rise of 77.3% between 2000 and 2010. In 1990, Latinos comprised 2.3% of Nebraska's population of 1,578,385. In 2010, the state's population was 1,826,341, 9.2% of whom were Hispanic/Latino. These were official counts, which did not record a substantial number of people without immigration documents. During the last quarter-century, much of southern Omaha has become majority Latino, as have several rural towns out-state with large farming and meatpacking activities.

The foreign-born population of Nebraska also indicates the rapid influx from Latin America. According to the U.S. Census Bureau's American Community Survey, the largest share (51.5%) was from Central America, 24.6% from Asia, 9.9% from Europe, 8.7% were from Africa. A state report indicated that the top five countries of birth of the foreign born in Nebraska were Mexico, India, El Salvador, Vietnam, and China. In 2010, Mexico accounted for 41% of all foreign-born Nebraska residents. India was the birthplace of the next largest with 5.1%, followed by El Salvador with 5%, Vietnam with 3.8%, and China with 2.8% (Profile, 2015).

The overwhelming number of Latinos came to the state for employment, which is generally abundant. Nebraska's unemployment rate of 3 to 4% during the last 25 years has been consistently among the lowest in the United States. Although Latino workers generally have been welcomed in the state, the rapid increase in Latinos has met some resistance. The small city of Fremont, northwest of Omaha, enacted an ordinance requiring proof of citizenship to rent or buy housing. The city's business activity suffered when many Latinos moved to surrounding communities. In Omaha, a young Salvadoran immigrant killed a White woman, spurring much local commentary and a role, for a time, during 2016, in the anti-immigrant screeds of Donald J. Trump's presidential campaign.

Many of Omaha's earliest Mexican residents were recruited to work in the stockyards, which were in the midst of South Omaha, now a predominantly Latino/a community. The stockyards have since been closed, as their operations were moved to smaller towns out of state. Omaha's stockyards, second in size only to those of Chicago, attracted workers not only from southern states but several other countries as well. By 1907, three-quarters of the stockyards' workers were immigrants, or had immigrant fathers. According to the Dillingham Commission of the United States Senate, communities such as

Lexington, west of Lincoln, today host large immigrant populations of several ethnicities. Lexington, with a population of about 15,000, has public schools that in 2016 taught immigrants speaking 32 languages.

Today, Omaha has become an immigrant destination for Africans from several countries, including Sudan, Nigeria, Kenya, Togo, Ghana, and Cameroon. The Sudanese, with 8,500 living in Omaha as of 2015, are one of the largest such settlements in the United States, many of whom have fled factional conflict in their country. By 2015, Metropolitan Omaha's population of about 800,000 was about 14% African or African American, 15% Latino, and 5% Asian, with rapid rates of increase that reflect the state as a whole.

During the middle 1960s, several large cities across the United States experienced large riots during several long, hot summers. On July 4, 1966, with the temperature in Omaha at 103 degrees F., a large crowd assembled at 24th and Lake streets in the center of North Omaha's Black Community. Police ordered the group to disband, and its members refused, instead of inflicting several million dollars in damage as buildings along North 24th Street was burned and looted. Four weeks later, on August 1, 1966, violence erupted again after a 19-year-old Black man was fatally shot by a member of the police (who was off-duty at the time). Several buildings were burned before almost 200 riot police enforced order.

On March 4, 1968, protesters at a presidential campaign rally for segregationist Alabama Gov. George Wallace at Omaha's Civic Auditorium were beaten by police. One African American man was fatally shot. A riot ensued. A day later, Ernie Chambers, then known as a loquacious local barber, helped prevent a riot at Horace Mann Junior High School. Chambers' reputation as a community leader spread and two years later, after he completed a law degree, Chambers was elected to represent North Omaha in Nebraska's Unicameral, the state legislature. Chambers was not the first Black member of the Unicameral, however. In 1892, Dr. Matthew Ricketts had been elected.

Riots occurred again on April 5, 1968, following the assassination of Martin Luther King, Jr. On June 24, 1969, riots re-ignited following the killing of Vivian Strong, a Black teenager, by police officers at the Logan Fontenelle low-income housing project. Several businesses along North 24th Street were firebombed and looted over the next several days.

Standing Bear: My Blood Runs Red, Just Like Yours

One of the most important historical events stemming from early contact of Native peoples in the city now called Omaha involves the Ponca Standing Bear, who fought demands by the United States that he and about 30 other Poncas move from a homeland near Omaha to a tract of bare land in Oklahoma, then called "Indian Country." Standing Bear, et al. walked about 500 miles (or about 830 kilometers) as U.S. Army General George Crook and the O'mo'ho (Omaha band) of Native people offered assistance.

The result was a trial (*Standing Bear, et al. v. Crook, 1879*) in U.S. District Court, Omaha, which established for the first time that American Indians are defined as "persons" under United States federal law. As part of the trial, Standing Bear stood before the judge, cut one of his arms, and declared that Native people (himself in this case) bled red, just like every White person in the courtroom. Technically, the ruling favoring Standing Bear and his people had a limited effect, since it was restricted to the people who, so said the Army, had violated its regulation that had confined the Poncas to that tract of land in "Indian Country." In fact, after the ruling, Standing Bear tested it by visiting his relative Big Snake with plans to escort him to Omaha. Both were arrested on the spot.

Today, Standing Bear is a revered historical figure in Omaha and in academic venues across the United States. In Omaha, schools and lakes are named after him, academic conferences are held, and books have been written. In the late 1870s, however, they were forced to leave a community built with their own hands on their homeland along the Niobrara River, now close to the border between South Dakota and Nebraska (which were not yet states).

The error that sent the Poncas onto their own "Trail of Tears" was an exercise in sloppy map-making by U.S. cartographers which unknowingly gave most of the Ponca homeland to the Great Sioux Nation, their long-time enemies when the United States signed the Treaty of Fort Laramie in 1868. During the winter of 1877, Edward C. Kemble, an Indian inspector, ordered the Poncas to leave their homes for Indian Territory. The Poncas were outraged because over several years they had worked to become yeoman farmers in the Jefferson mold, just as the immigrants had demanded of them. They constructed log houses, in the immigrants' style, as they also took up Christianity. They also gave up parts of the land that the treaty said would be theirs forever when the Great White Father said the United States needed it. No sacrifice seemed to satisfy the whites.

After the Poncas were forced out of the Niobrara valley, troops tore down all of their 236 log houses, plus barns, a gristmill, sawmill, and blacksmith shop, church, and schoolhouse. The only building left standing was the government's Indian agency.

Standing Bear protested that his people were being removed from their homeland illegally: "This land is ours," he said. "We have never sold it. We have our houses…here. Our fathers and some of our children are buried here. Here we wish to live and die. We have harmed no man. We have kept our treaty. We have learned to work. We can make a good living here. We do not wish to sell our land, and we think no man has a right to take it from us. Here we will live, and here we will die" (Tibbles, 1880, p. 6). That was what the Poncas wanted to do, but not what they the Army allowed. Standing Bear and nine other Ponca chiefs were forced, again at gunpoint, to visit Indian Territory to "inspect" the land that the U.S. government had decided to give them. None of them wanted to stay in such a barren, insect-infested place.

The chiefs who were young enough to walk home decided to do so; the rest stayed in Oklahoma, under protest. Standing Bear and the other chiefs walked to Sioux City, from which they stated their objections in a telegraph to President Rutherford B. Hayes. A few months later, paying no heed to the Poncas' objections, federal troops removed 723 of them at bayonet-point from three villages along the Niobrara River to Indian Territory, "just as one would drive a herd of ponies," said the Poncas' paramount chief White Eagle (Dando-Collins, 2004, p. 34).

Standing Bear later described the scene as federal troops escorted the Poncas southward:

> They took our reapers, mowers, hand-rakes, spades, ploughs, bedsteads, stoves, cupboards, everything we had on our farms, and put them in one large building. Then they put into the wagons such thing as they could carry. We told them that we would rather die than leave our lands; but we could not help ourselves. They took us down. Many died on the road. Two of my children died. After we reached the new land, all my horses died. The water was very bad. All our cattle died. Not one was left. I stayed until one hundred fifty eight of my people had died. Then I ran away with 30 of my people, men, women, and children. Some of the children were orphans. We were three months on the road. We were weak and sick and starved…Half of us were sick. (Jackson, 1888, pp. 203–204)

It was a cold spring as the first group of Poncas undertook a march southward, which lasted 51 days under the direction of Indian Agent James Lawrence. The next group departed in May, under the aegis of agent E.A. Howard. This march endured heavy rain, and a tornado, as several more Poncas died. Having reached Indian Territory, malaria killed many more Poncas who had survived the forced marches.

A year after the third group had been removal, at least a third of the Poncas had died, including two of Standing Bear's children, a daughter, Prairie Flower (who died of pneumonia on the march), and a son, Bear Shield. Following Bear Shield's death, Standing Bear resolved to bury the bones of his in their ancestors' lands, so he escaped northward, with about 30 other Poncas.

Standing Bear's group walked for 50 days during the worst of winter, eating raw corn, and sleeping in haystacks under thin, torn blankets. Finally, with all other food sources exhausted, they ate their moccasins, as they continued their journey in the snow. "When their moccasins ran out, wrote one observer, they walked barefoot in the snow. Barely able to stand on their bloodied feet, the Poncas stumbled into the Otoe Indian Agency in southern Nebraska," (Mathes, 1989, p. 45). Their accounts, which were given to newspaper reporters in Omaha and also distributed nationally by telegraph, indicated that friendly whites gave the Poncas food, water, and shelter, against the explicit orders of the Army. Their consciences would not let the Indians die. The Poncas arrived at the Omaha Agency, where they were offered food, lodging, and seed, for use if they wished to stay.

In March of 1879, troops under General Crook arrested Standing Bear and his party and conveyed them to Fort Omaha. General Crook arriving at the fort, called Omaha newspaperman Thomas Henry Tibbles of the Omaha *Herald*. He walked to Fort Omaha. "As Tibbles returned, running part of the way, he stopped at every church he could find, asking pastors if he could address their congregations about the travail of the Poncas. At a Congregational Church, the pastor, Rev. Mr. Sherill, allowed him to speak "between the opening hymns" (Tibbles, 1880, p. 27). Newspapers east of Omaha gathered help after telegraphed dispatches had spread the news of the Poncas' travail. Legal help also was enlisted as General Crook said that he would speak for the Indians in court.

Tibbles, who became devoted to the Poncas' cause, provided pages of coverage and provocative front-page headlines, such as "Criminal Cruelty—The History of the Ponca Prisoners Now at the Barracks," and "A Tale of Cruelty That Has Never Surpassed." Tibbles' dispatches were wired to major East Coast newspapers, and a large number of protest letters to Congress on the Poncas' behalf resulted. General Crook already had announced his disgust at how Standing Bear's party were being treated and became a major conduit of a legal case (*Standing Bear et al v. Crook*) that he had every intention of losing. Following a trial during the spring of 1879 which included a speech by Standing Bear that provoked tears from the bench, Federal District Court Judge Elmer Dundy ruled during 1879 that Indians were people within the meaning of the law, and no law gave the Army authority to forcibly remove them from their lands.

By the time the case went to court in May of 1879, Standing Bear and the rest of the Poncas drew a large audience to Judge Dundy's courtroom, many of whom ignored Judge Dundy's instructions not to applaud the chief's remarks.

> [Standing Bear] claimed that, although his skin was of a different hue, yet he was a man, and that God made him. He said he was not a savage, and related how he had saved the life of a soldier whom he had found on the Plains, starved, and almost frozen to death, and of a man who had lost his way on the trackless prairie, whom he had fed and guided to his destination. In spite of the orders of the court and the efforts of the bailiffs, he was greeted with continual rounds of applause (Tibbles, 1880, p. 93).

Following Dundy's legal ruling and popular pressure provoked by national press coverage, in 1890 Standing Bear and his people finally were allowed to return home to the Niobrara River after Congress investigated the conditions under which they had been evicted. Standing Bear's efforts produced a victory, but nearly his entire family had died.

His victory has been notable ever since. A bronze statue of Standing Bear was installed in 2019 at the U.S. Capitol, above a stand and plaque reading "NEBRASKA." During the first week of July 2021, in a move with great symbolic meaning to the Poncas, especially to his family, Standing Bear's ceremonial pipe tomahawk was returned to his homeland by Harvard's Peabody Museum. Many people and organizations requested the transfer, including the Nebraska State Legislature, by a 42-0 vote.

Whiteclay, Nebraska: The Economics of Keeping American Indians Drunk

Forty years after the American Indian Movement (AIM) protested beer sales to drunken Oglala Sioux at Whiteclay, Nebraska, in 2012, the Oglala Lakota tribal council at Pine Ridge filed suit against the major beer companies that distribute their wares in that tiny border town, seeking $500 million in damages for ruined Native lives. The companies have sought to have the suit dismissed on grounds of discrimination, arguing that they have a right to profit, and Indians have a right to get drunk.

The American Indian Movement (AIM) has maintained a long-standing campaign to limit alcoholic beverage sales to American Indians in Whiteclay, south of the Pine Ridge Oglala Lakota reservation, population 12, where the only major business in town is catering to Native American drunkenness. From four metal shacks along Whiteclay's main road, 13,000 cans of beer and malt liquor sell on an average day (an annual sale of more than 5 million cans for more than roughly $4 million), nearly all of it to Oglala Sioux from the Pine Ridge Indian Reservation, which had banned alcohol sales during the 1970s.

The tribe hired Tom White, an Omaha attorney, and authorized him to sue the town's alcohol merchants as well as their suppliers. The lawsuit named Whiteclay's four beer stores, four distributors in Western Nebraska, and several large, name-brand brewers. The Oglala Sioux Tribe also filed an amended complaint in Lincoln, Nebraska U.S. District Court seeking an injunction that would limit beer sales in Whiteclay "to an amount that can reasonably be consumed" in a village of fewer than 12 people with no public drinking establishments (Duggan, 2012a, p. 6-B).

White, announcing the lawsuit on February 9, 2012, at a press conference on the steps of the State Capitol in Lincoln, asserted that the beer sales are illegal because nearly all of it is consumed on the Pine Ridge reservation, where alcoholic beverages are banned. "They are helping people violate the law," White said. "This lawsuit is about holding them responsible and stopping the devastation of an entire people and culture" (Duggan, 2012b, p. 1-A).

The lawsuit demanded $500 million in monetary damages. Pine Ridge tribal president John Yellow Bird Steele, said that 90% of criminal cases in the reservation court system and an equal proportion of illnesses there were caused or aggravated by alcohol. "We believe we can't get ahead, or function, without Whiteclay being addressed," he said (Williams, 2012b, p. A-15). Pine Ridge tribal police made 20,000 alcohol-related arrests during 2011. Twenty-five percent of babies at Pine Ridge were born with fetal alcohol syndrome or fetal alcohol spectrum disorder. White said that 85% of families at Pine Ridge are affected by alcoholism. According to an account by Timothy Williams in the *New York Times*,

> After the lawsuit was filed, Whiteclay's two-lane road, Highway 87, bustled with traffic driving to and from the beer stores. Dozens of people in various states of

inebriation wandered along the road. Other men and women were passed out in front of abandoned buildings. A [recording of] Hank Williams Jr's [song], "I'd Rather Be Gone," was among the detritus along the road, as well as empty liquor bottles, a copy of "Tabernacle Hymns No. 3," soiled clothing and a dead puppy (Williams, 2012a).

Victor Clarke, who had lived in Whiteclay 19 years in 2012 and owns Arrowhead Foods (which did not sell alcohol) said that residents of nearby towns wanted Whiteclay's problems contained there. "People don't want Whiteclay to go away," he said. "The state of Nebraska doesn't want Whiteclay to go away because it allows problems to be isolated in this one little place. You hear people in the towns around here, saying, 'We don't want these guys in our town'" (Williams, 2012a).

The beer companies agreed with Larson. On April 27, 2012, they filed a motion to dismiss the Oglalas' case, arguing that a ruling restricting beer sales at Whiteclay would force them to discriminate against residents of Pine Ridge. As the beer distributors defended the right of the Lakota to buy their products at Whiteclay on freedom-of-speech grounds, AIM activist Frank LaMere, a member of the Winnebago Tribe of Nebraska, said the state of Nebraska had "blood on their hands." Any action short of shutting down Whiteclay "and crippling the enterprise that peddles alcoholism among the Lakota people is unacceptable," he said. LaMere continued:

> The death toll exacted on the Lakota people by Anheuser Busch and its partners continues to rise, and the sooner the Sheridan County hell-hole can be leveled, the better off Nebraska will be. County, state and liquor industry officials have long known of the lawlessness and illegal activities that go on there, but they have been allowed to run from their responsibilities as public trustees by reducing the sad reality to a discussion about personal responsibility and market demand (LaMere, 2012).

The Oglala Lakotas' $500 million suit against Whiteclay's beer dealers and distributors was dismissed in a federal court in Nebraska during the first week of October 2012. After the dismissal, the Pine Ridge tribal government discussed another way to hobble the beer sales at Whiteclay: legalizing alcohol consumption on the reservation. That might reduce traffic accidents caused by drunken drivers in the Whiteclay area and allow the tribe to tax alcohol sales (Williams, 2012b).

After much publicity and legal actions, beer sales at Whiteclay were shut down, reopened, then stopped for good between 2015 and 2020. Hard-core alcoholics moved their beer purchases to other border venues, as the Oglala tribe did its best to deal with an overwhelming case-load of alcohol-related diseases among its peoples.

Mosques on the Prairie

In 2020, as most meatpacking had departed Omaha's minority communities for much smaller cities out-state, the industry remained a magnet for immigration, as well as a racial flashpoint. Witness Lexington, a city of 10,000 people where 32 languages are spoken in its public schools, where residents have been debating the location of a mosque. Lexington has been a draw for immigrants (Latinos and Vietnamese, as well as Somalis) since the packing plant opened in 1990. By 2016, Lexington's population was 60% Latino (Hammel, 2016). The U.S. Census put the Somali population at 769 in 2016, but local people said that the actual figure might be closer to 1,500, 15% of the population (Hammel, 2016).

The controversy began when workers from Somalia spread their prayer rugs across the floors of the old Longhorn Laundry, which they had purchased and renamed the Islamic Center of Lexington, as they held Muslim services five times a day. City officials complained that they were violating zoning ordinances requiring building permits and certification under the fire code. The Somalis said the city, caught up in "Islamophobia," was violating their rights to religious freedom after ignoring smaller prayer venues for 8 years.

When the Islamic Center opened at its new location, city officials required 139 added stalls of off-street parking, which mosque owners could not afford to buy, nor pave. The city rated the mosque's capacity at 400, but its owners said that no more than 80 people used the space at any one time, and plenty of public parking was available nearby. The mosque was being harassed, they said. The city planning board rejected a permit for the mosque.

The American Civil Liberties Union agreed with the Somalis. "They're just trying to push us out," said Mohamed Alinor, a 28-year-old Somali who works at a Tyson Foods plant, which employs 2,700 workers (Hammel, 2016). The Somalis sought protection from the U.S. Justice Department under the Religious Land Use and Institutionalized Persons Act of 2000, which prohibits zoning ordinances that restrict freedom of religion. Lexington's main street already hosts a number of Somali, Latino, and Asian-owned businesses, as well as two mosques.

Paul Hammel of the Omaha *World-Herald* (2016) described other conflicts over Islam on the prairie: "There have been cultural clashes before for Muslims in Nebraska. In 2008, dozens of workers at Grand Island's JBS Swift & Co. meatpacking plant walked out in protest over a lack of accommodations for prayer times during Ramadan, the Muslim holy month. After the plant proposed a schedule shift, non-Muslims staged counter-protests over the special treatment. Eventually, some 90 Muslim workers lost their jobs." Omaha by 2016 had four mosques. In January 2016, someone wrapped bacon around the handle of the front door at one of them. Such instances of vandalism increased as Donald Trump proposed a ban on Muslim immigration during his campaign for U.S. president, labeling them as terrorists.

"It's a label put on all Muslims now," said Abdul Raheem Yaseer, then assistant director of the Center for Afghanistan Studies at the University of Nebraska at Omaha, even though mainstream Muslims condemn the violence by a small group of extremists. The word "Islam," he said, means "peace." "Don't generalize," Yaseer said. "Try to expand your understanding of what mainstream is and what extremism is. There are extremists in every faith" (Hammel, 2016).

References

Dando-Collins, S. (2004). *Standing bear is a person: The true story of a native American's quest for justice*. Da Capo Press.
Duggan, J. (2012a, February 23). Amid lawsuit, tribe seeks limit on beer sales in town. *Omaha World-Herald*, 6-B.
Duggan, J. (2012b, February 20). Tribe goes to source in lawsuit over alcohol sales: The Oglala Sioux target the whiteclay, Neb. Supply chain from stores to Brewers. *Omaha World-Herald*, 1-A, 2-A.
Hammel, P. (2016, March 1). In immigrant Nebraska town, muslims clash with city over downtown mosque. *Omaha World-Herald*. http://www.omaha.com/news/nebraska/in-immigrant-nebraska-town-muslims-clash-with-city-over-downtown/article_401b623b-ac5d-5efd-ac62-6c56c0d4e5fe.html
Jackson, H. H. (1888). *A century of dishonor: A sketch of the United States government's dealings with some of the Indian tribes*. Boston: Roberts Bros., reprinted 1972 St. Clair Shores, Mich.: Scholarly Press.
LaMere, F. (2012, May 16). Blood on their hands. *New York Times*. http://www.nytimes.com/roomfordebate/2012/05/16/how-to-address-alcoholism-on-indian-reservations/nebraska-and-anheuser-busch-caused-the-disaster-at-pine-ridge-and-whiteclay.
Malcolm X., & Haley, A. (1964). *The Autobiography of Malcolm X*. Grove Press.
Mathes, V. S. (1989). Helen Hunt Jackson and the Ponca controversy. *Montana: The Magazine of Western History, 39*(1), 42–53.

Profile of the minority population in Nebraska. Nebraska Department of Health and Human Services. (2015, May). http://dhhs.ne.gov/publichealth/Documents/Profile%20of%20the%20Minority%20Population%20in%20Nebraska.pdf

Tibbles, T. H. (1972). *The Ponca chiefs: An account of the trial of standing bear* [1880]. University of Nebraska Press.

Williams, T. (2012a, March 6). At tribe's door, a hub of beer and heartache. *New York Times*. http://www.nytimes.com/2012/03/06/us/next-to-tribe-with-alcohol-ban-a-hub-of-beer.html.

Williams, T. (2012b, October 5). Tribe considers lifting alcohol ban in South Dakota. *New York Times*, A-15.

6

Blackfacing, White Shaming, and Yellow Journalism: A Jaundiced View of How Contemporary PC Erodes First Amendment Principles

Kenneth Lasson

The mask which the actor wears is apt to become his face.
—Plato

In a world of rapidly changing norms, standards, and sensitivities, it has become increasingly difficult to state one's opinions without fear of repercussion. The idea that what happened years ago can so easily come back to haunt current status and career ambitions is troubling on a number of levels, not the least of which is the danger it poses for traditional American notions of due process and civil liberties.

The twenty-first century has presented new challenges to the traditional ways that free speech in America has been encouraged and protected. This is particularly so on college and university campuses, the very places that pride themselves as being open marketplaces of ideas. Numerous campus speech codes substantially limit First Amendment rights. They come with new catchphrases like "trigger warnings" and "safe spaces" and "cultural appropriation"—all calculated in one way or another to shelter students and others from the honest give-and-take of discussion and debate about topics that might be controversial. Those with opinions that might challenge campus

---

K. Lasson (✉)
University of Baltimore School of Law, Baltimore, MD, USA
e-mail: klasson@ubalt.edu

orthodoxies are rarely invited, and often disinvited after having been scheduled, or shouted down, or otherwise disrupted. When protestors disrupt campus events, administrators often choose to look the other way, and students rarely face disciplinary actions.[1]

The latter-day dilution of free speech has been generated at least in part by the rise of postmodernism—generally defined as skepticism, irony, or distrust toward traditional narratives, ideologies, Enlightenment rationality, perceptions of human nature, morality, social progress, objective reality, absolute truth—in short, the whole concept of reasoned discourse.

On the other hand, postmodernism itself is difficult to define because to do so would violate its proponents' premise that there are no definite terms, boundaries, or absolute truths.

Over the past few years, scholars have come to espouse distinctly opposing views regarding the rights and responsibilities of colleges and universities toward their students regarding freedom of speech on campus. "Nationalism" has become a byword that divides.[2] So has the term "identity politics," which has come to signify a wide range of political activity and theory based on the shared perceptions of injustice toward members of certain social groups.[3]

Of the many examples that can be cited to illustrate the somewhat bizarre manifestations of liberal angst are the phenomena of "blackfacing" and "white shaming."

However offensive wearing blackface is today, and however insensitive those who did so years ago may have been at the time, is it fair to hold them accountable for acts committed in their youth, and perhaps condemn them to a future life of shame? Similarly, the idea of "white shaming" has become a cultural phenomenon. Talking about race with an all-White group of peers, the argument goes, is to reveal their own White ignorance. Should non-whites use white-shaming as a means to publicize their grievances?

---

[1] Speech codes are ubiquitous and often cavalierly invoked. For civil libertarians the good news is that not one of the few such codes that have been tested in court has been found constitutional; the bad news is that few have been tested. Lasson, K., The Decline of Free Speech on the Postmodern Campus: The Troubling Evolution of the Heckler's Veto (2019), *Quinnipiac Law Review 37*, 1.

[2] Nationalism is loosely defined as "identification with one's own nation and support for its interests, especially to the exclusion or detriment of the interests of other nations." The term is often conflated with separatism, secessionism, partitionism, isolationism, and sectarianism. Merriam-Webster Dictionary, https://www.merriam-webster.com/dictionary/nationalism

[3] Rather than organizing solely around belief systems, programmatic manifestos, or party affiliation, identity political formations typically aim to secure the political freedom of a specific constituency marginalized within its larger context. Members of that constituency assert or reclaim ways of understanding their distinctiveness that challenge dominant oppressive characterizations, with the goal of greater self-determination. Merriam-Webster Dictionary, https://www.merriam-webster.com/dictionary/identity%20politics

Meanwhile, the news media have come to play unprecedented roles both in the recording of fast-moving events (which nowadays are virtually instantaneous) and in influencing the occurrence and evolution of those events themselves. Thus, has it become more essential than ever to require that the media be encouraged toward professional responsibility, while at the same time being held accountable for ethical failures. The Society of Professional Journalists Code of Ethics for professional journalists requires that they support "the open and civil exchange of views, even views they find repugnant."[4]

In today's world that tenet is far more frequently disregarded than honored by the mainstream press, which often feeds upon the burgeoning world of social media—where objectivity is virtually non-existent. Journalists are subject to human biases, and to expect perfect objectivity from them is an illusory if not impossible goal. All media should abide by the ethical standards they themselves have adopted, however. As George Orwell admonished in his 1946 essay, "Politics and the English Language": "[P]olitical language—and with variations this is true of all political parties, from Conservatives to Anarchists—is designed to make lies sound truthful and murder respectable, and to give an appearance of solidity to pure wind."[5]

These are topics that too few scholars feel comfortable addressing. This article will examine the issues presented from both philosophical and practical perspectives, explore the abandonment of common sense, and offer a realistic approach for how best to retrieve it in the modern world.

* * *

The causes of the precipitous decline in traditional First Amendment principles can be traced to a number of factors, most of them having to do with a changing world order: the sharp rise of terrorism and violence, overweening attention to personal sensitivities, and the gross misapplication of the notion of political correctness. The effects have been noticeable in polarized and biased media, reflected in turn by disturbing incidents of intolerance in both society at large and on campus in particular. Administrative and legislative responses have been slow and often inadequate.

The idea of "safe spaces" in the 1970s as both places of physical safety and "consciousness-raising," have long since changed into places where the "victimized" who feel "marginalized" can take shelter. So-called "trigger warnings"

---

[4] Code of Ethics, Society of Professional Journalists, https://www.spj.org/ethicscode.asp
[5] Orwell, G. Politics and the English Language, http://www.orwell.ru/library/essays/politics/english/e_polit

follow a similar philosophy. In the early days of the Internet, they took the form of blog posts to alert survivors of traumatic experiences about content that might upset them (such as sexual violence, crime, or torture). Then they began to appear in course syllabi as gestures of sensitivity to students' personal pasts. It wasn't long before the scope of their warnings stretched to racism, classism, sexism, and other instances of privilege and oppression.[6]

But such efforts to cleanse campuses of ideas that might cause discomfort runs counter to the primary function of higher education. In today's politically correct climate students and faculty feel inhibited about stating (much less advocating) their personal views. Although trigger warnings and safe spaces ostensibly create an environment where everyone can feel free to state their opinions, they also feed into paranoia.

The ironies abound. The underlying politically correct spirit of tolerance can also stifle dialogue about controversial topics, particularly about issues regarding race, gender, and religious beliefs. On many campuses that freedom does not exist unless students' opinions are in harmony with what are commonly understood as progressive political values.[7]

A recent study found that in today's environment a majority of U.S. college students feel inhibited from saying what they believe because others might find it offensive. The basic notion of all academic inquiry has become alien for students deemed too vulnerable to deal with ideas past and present serves to hinder the free discussion of sensitive material that should be appropriate to an open educational environment. It flies in the face of the famous Woodward Report, issued by Yale in 1975, which declared that "the paramount obligation of the university is to protect [the] right to free expression."[8]

Among the symptoms of the current liberal malaise is the concept of "cultural appropriation" (sometimes called "cultural misappropriation")[9]—the

---

[6] Brown, S., A Brief Guide to the Battle Over Trigger Warnings (2016), *Chronicle of Higher Education*, https://www.chronicle.com/article/A-Brief-Guide-to-the-Battle/237600

[7] *See, e.g.*, Gonzalez, C.A., Yes, the Wars Over Campus Politics Matter (2918), *National Review*, https://www.nationalreview.com/2018/07/war-over-campus-politics-matters/

[8] Some stand-up comedians avoid college campuses because they find that satire does not sit well in the current PC environment. Under pressure from faculty and students, schools have canceled speakers like Condoleezza Rice, George Will, and Michelle Malkin. But their words were not matched by their actions. Miltimore, J., University of Chicago Pushes Back on Trigger Warnings, Safe Spaces (2016), *Intellectual Takeout*, https://www.intellectualtakeout.org/blog/univ-chicago-pushes-back-trigger-warnings-safe-spaces. In June of 2016 Israeli Deputy Foreign Minister Tzipi Hotovely was scheduled to speak at Princeton, but was disinvited at the last minute. Keidar, N., Why was Deputy Foreign Minister's Lecture Canceled? (2017), *Arutz Sheva*, http://www.israelnationalnews.com/News/News.aspx/237733. *See also* May, C.D., Letting Freedom Fade (2017), *Washington Times*, http://www.defenddemocracy.org/media-hit/may-clifford-d-letting-freedom-fade/

[9] *See, e.g.*, Cultural Appropriation and Misappropriation, http://www.religionandtheology.org/cultural_appropriation.html

claim that members of a dominant culture borrow too freely from disadvantaged minorities' language, symbols, religious traditions, fashion, music, cuisine, and folklore. This kind of "borrowing" is said to exploit minority groups of the credit they deserve, as well as reinforcing stereotypes about minority groups. To what extent does cultural appropriation inhibit language and free speech?[10]

A common example of cultural appropriation is the adoption of the iconography of another culture, which is then used for purposes that may be offensive to that culture's mores. The leaders of ancient Israel, for example, strongly condemned the adoption of Egyptian and Canaanite practices, especially cutting the hair short or shaving the beard. At the same time, the Old Testament distinguishes the religious circumcision of the Hebrews from cultures such as that of the Egyptians, for whom the practice had esthetic or practical purposes.[11]

The phenomenon of White people adopting elements of Black culture has been prevalent at least since slavery was abolished in the Western world.[12] The term is slang for a White person who adopts the mannerisms, language, and fashions normally associated with Blacks.[13] "Stolen blackness" has been recognized in the success of American entertainers from Stephen Foster to Al Jolson, from Benny Goodman to Elvis Presley and the Rolling Stones. The misuse and misrepresentation of indigenous culture are seen as an exploitative form of colonialism, and one step in the destruction of indigenous cultures.[14] Some critics have gone so far as to liken the trend to blackface.[15]

Such left-wing touchiness has gained traction in a surprising number of ways. The United Nations Declaration on the Rights of Indigenous Peoples states that:

---

[10] Nittle, N. K., A Guide to Understanding and Avoiding Cultural Appropriation (2019), ThoughtCo, https://www.thoughtco.com/cultural-appropriation-and-why-iits-wrong-2834561

[11] Leviticus 19:27–28. Why Couldn't the Jews Trim Their Beards or Their Hair or Get Tattoos?, *Evidence Unseen*, http://www.evidenceunseen.com/bible-difficulties-2/ot-difficulties/genesis-deuteronomy/lev-1927-28-why-couldnt-the-jews-trim-their-beards-or-their-hair-or-get-tattoos/. During the early sixteenth century, European men imitated the short haircuts and beards found on newly discovered ancient Greek and Roman statues.

[12] An early form of this was the "white negro" in jazz and swing music during the 1920s and 1930s. It was later seen in the *zoot suiter* of the 1930s and 1940s, the hippie of the 1940s, the beatnik of the 1950s–1960s, the blue-eyed soul of the 1970s, and the hip hop of the 1980s and 1990s. Mailer, N. The White Negro (1957).

[13] Merriam-Webster Dictionary, https://www.merriam-webster.com/dictionary/wigger

[14] Facing History and Ourselves, Stolen Lives: The Indigenous Peoples of Canada and the Indian Residential Schools / History in Search of a Name, https://www.facinghistory.org/stolen-lives-indigenous-peoples-canada-and-indian-residential-schools/chapter-7/cultural-genocid

[15] *See* discussion of blackfacing *infra* at pp.

Indigenous peoples have the right to maintain, control, protect and develop their cultural heritage, traditional knowledge and traditional cultural expressions, as well as the manifestations of their sciences, technologies and cultures, including human and genetic resources, seeds, medicines, knowledge of the properties of fauna and flora, oral traditions, literatures, designs, sports and traditional games and visual and performing arts. They also have the right to maintain, control, protect and develop their intellectual property over such cultural heritage, traditional knowledge, and traditional cultural expressions.[16]

In 2015, a group of Native American academics and writers issued a statement against the Rainbow Family, members whose acts of "cultural exploitation … dehumanize us as an indigenous Nation because they imply our culture and humanity, like our land, is anyone's for the taking."[17]

Similarly, there is debate about whether designers in the fashion industry commercialize and thereby cheapen the ancient heritage of indigenous cultures.[18] In 2003, after Prince Harry of the British royal family used indigenous Australian art motifs in a painting for a school project, one Aboriginal group protested a "misappropriation of our culture," declaring that the motifs have symbolic meanings "indicative of our spiritualism."[19] In 2012, Victoria's Secret model Karlie Kloss wore a Native American-style feathered headdress and high-heeled moccasins—which were said to be offensive to Native Americans; Victoria's Secret pulled it from the broadcast and apologized for

---

[16] United Nations Declaration on the Rights of Indigenous Peoples, Article 31:1, https://www.un.org/development/desa/indigenouspeoples/declaration-on-the-rights-of-indigenous-peoples.html

[17] Is Cultural Appropriation A Concept Outside Of The US?, *Quora*, https://www.quora.com/Is-cultural-appropriation-a-concept-outside-of-the-US. The Native American Rights Fund (NARF) emphasizes that indigenous intellectual property rights should be held collectively, not by individuals: "The long-term goal is to actually have a legal system, and certainly a treaty could do that, that acknowledges two things. Number one, it acknowledges that indigenous peoples are peoples with a right to self-determination that includes governance rights over all property belonging to the indigenous people. And, number two, it acknowledges that indigenous cultural expressions are a form of intellectual property and that traditional knowledge is a form of intellectual property, but they are collective resources—so not any one individual can give away the rights to those resources. The tribal nations actually own them collectively." Native American Rights Fund, narf.org

[18] During the seventeenth century, the forerunner to the three piece suit was appropriated from the traditional dress of diverse Eastern European and Islamic countries. Necktie or cravat was derived from a scarf worn by Croatian mercenaries fighting for Louis XIII, and the British aristocracy appropriated traditional Scottish clan tartans. In America, plaid flannel had become workwear by the time of Westward expansion, and was widely worn by Old West pioneers and cowboys—as were Mexican sombreros. By the nineteenth century, the fashion fascination had shifted to Asian culture: slim fitting pantaloons, turbans, and smoking caps. In the modern era, both Brits and Yanks adopted the rough tweed cloth clothing of the Irish, English, and Scottish peasantry, including the flat cap and Irish hat were appropriated by the upper classes as the British country clothing worn for sports such as hunting or fishing. Ross, R., Clothing: a Global History (2013), ISBN #9780745657530.

[19] A Right Royal Ripoff (2003), *The Age*, https://www.theage.com.au/world/a-right-royal-rip-off-20030820-gdw7zd.html

its use; Kloss tweeted that she was "deeply sorry if what I wore during the VS Show offended anyone."[20]

In response to such criticism, fashion designers assert that this phenomenon is in fact "culture appreciation" rather than appropriation; they characterize the use of unique cultural symbols as recognition and homage.[21]

The world of sports has likewise become embroiled in the cultural-war paradigm. The history of colonization and marginalization may not be unique to the Americas, but the practice of naming sports teams and mascots after indigenous peoples is.[22] In 2005, recognizing what it called the responsibility of higher education to eliminate behaviors that create a hostile environment for education, the National Collegiate Athletic Association (NCAA) adopted a policy against "hostile and abusive" names and mascots.[23]

Cultural appropriation has likewise been noted in dance,[24] the film and television industries, and Halloween costuming.[25]

But the bigger threat to civil liberties emanates from the new attitudes toward speech and expression. A prime example is a substantial effort undertaken by Muslim religious groups to characterize anti-Islamic rhetoric as hate

---

[20] Cowles, C., Karlie Kloss, Victoria's Secret Really Sorry About That Headdress (2012), *The Cut*, https://www.thecut.com/2012/11/karlie-kloss-really-sorry-about-that-headdress.html

[21] Pham, M. T., Fashion's Cultural Appropriation Debate: Pointless (2014), *The Atlantic*, https://www.theatlantic.com/entertainment/archive/2014/05/cultural-appropriation-in-fashion-stop-talking-about-it/370826/https://www.theatlantic.com/entertainment/archive/2014/05/cultural-appropriation-in-fashion-stop-talking-about-it/370826/

[22] Pewewardy, C., From Enemy to Mascot: The Deculturation of Indian Mascots in Sports Culture, *Canadian Journal of Native Education* 23(2), https://eric.ed.gov/?id=EJ605517 *(citing indigenous* mascots as an example of "dysconscious" racism which, by placing images of Native American or First Nations people into an invented media context, continues to maintain the superiority of the dominant culture. Such practices, it is argued, maintain the power relationship between the dominant culture and the indigenous culture, and can be seen as a form of cultural imperialism.

[23] NCAA Executive Committee Issues Guidelines for Use of Native American Mascots at Championship Events (2005), http://fs.ncaa.org/Docs/PressArchive/2005/Announcements/NCAA+Executive+Committee+Issues+Guidelines+for+Use+of+Native+American+Mascots+at+Championship+Events.html. The NCAA's policy on mascots has sometimes been problematic. For example, the Florida State Seminoles use the iconography of the Seminole tribe; their mascots are Osceola and Renegade—representing the Seminole chief Osceola and his Appaloosa horse. After the NCAA resolution the Seminole Tribe of Florida offered its support for FSU's use of Seminole culture. But in 2013, the Seminole Nation of Oklahoma expressed disapproval of "the use of all American Indian sports-team mascots in the public school system, by college and university level and by professional sports teams." Wulf, S., Why Native American Nicknames Stir Controversy Sports (2014), *ESPN Sports*, https://www.espn.com/espn/otl/story/_/id/11426021/why-native-american-nicknames-stir-controversy-sports

[24] Constable, A., Hopis Say Boy Scout Performances Make Mockery of Tradition, Religion (2016), *Santa Fe New Mexican*, https://www.santafenewmexican.com/news/local_news/hopis-say-boy-scout-performances-make-mockery-of-tradition-religion/article_d548665e-5767-5132-93e9-5d041b935d42.html

[25] Mueller, J., Unmasking Racism: Halloween Costuming and Engagement of the Racial Other (2007), *Qualitative Sociology*, https://danielledirks.files.wordpress.com/2011/10/mueller-dirks-houts-2007-qs.pdf

speech—which in much of the world, especially Europe, is considered outside the realm of protected expression. In many cases, the victims of violence are held up as justification for restricting whatever ideology motivated the killer or killers to act.[26]

Although hate speech in the United States has been largely protected by the First Amendment, events in the twenty-first century have fueled debate as to whether that should continue to be the case. In 2006, after a series of violent attacks carried out by Muslims, former U.S. speaker of the U.S. House of Representatives Newt Gingrich argued that "free speech should not be an acceptable cover for people who are planning to kill other people … [T]he fact is not all speech is permitted under the Constitution." The White nationalist violence that occurred in Charlottesville in the summer of 2017 prompted further discussion about the merits of preserving the right to express hateful rhetoric. Both polling data and anecdotal evidence indicate an erosion in the belief in free speech among younger Americans, including those who identify as liberals or leftists.[27]

Indeed, left-wing views have also been caught up in the new attitude toward hate speech. In May of 2016, Canada's then-conservative government threatened likewise to use hate-speech regulations to prosecute Israel boycott advocates on the ground that such activism is "the new face of anti-Semitism." A group of bipartisan U.S. legislators is currently sponsoring legislation to make it illegal for businesses to participate in any international boycott of Israel, a bill that the American Civil Liberties Union says can be used to criminalize advocacy of boycotts. In the United Kingdom, hate speech has come to include anyone expressing virulent criticism of United Kingdom soldiers fighting in war.[28]

American history has shown that the power to restrict the advocacy of violence can serve as an invitation to punish political dissent: witness the excesses of A. Mitchell Palmer, J. Edgar Hoover, and Joseph McCarthy, all of whom used the advocacy of violence to justify punishment of people who associated with Communists, socialists, or advocates of civil rights.[29]

---

[26] Greenwald, G., In Europe, Hate Speech Laws are Often Used to Suppress and Punish Left-Wing Viewpoints(2017), *Common Dreams*, https://www.commondreams.org/views/2017/08/30/europe-hate-speech-laws-are-often-used-suppress-and-punish-left-wing-viewpoints

[27] *Id.*

[28] *Id.*

[29] The American Civil Liberties Union was born after President Woodrow Wilson tried to criminalize dissent from his policy of involving the U.S. in World War I. *Id.*

In 2017, Canada passed a criminal statute that penalizes the use of "incorrect gender pronouns."[30] The Canadian bill is not a far cry from the current law in New York City, where citizens can be fined up to $250,000 for the crime of "mis-gendering"—which allows the city's Commission on Human Rights to punish anyone who refuses "to use an individual's preferred name, pronoun, or title because they do not conform to gender stereotypes" (for example, calling a woman "Mr." because of her masculine appearance).[31]

As with virtually everything nowadays, there's lash and there's backlash.

Many commentators consider the very idea of cultural appropriation—the seizure of the collective intellectual property rights of the originating, minority, and notably indigenous cultures living under colonial rule—to be ridiculous. They point out that the term not only lacks conceptual coherence but that its ostensible purpose does not at all constitute a social harm.[32] Others argue that the term sets arbitrary limits on intellectual freedom and artists' self-expression, reinforces group divisions, and itself promotes a feeling of enmity or grievance, rather than liberation.[33]

As to the New York and Canadian initiatives, the laws are shortsighted attempts to legislate civility—whose motivation may have been well-meant, but whose intentions clearly run afoul of the First Amendment. One can also argue that their legislative purpose is based on a totally unrealistic if not absurd assertion: that some people "prefer to use pronouns other than he/him/his or she/her/hers, such as they/them/theirs or ze/hir." In fact, there are several dozen gender identities recognized as acceptable, including "two-spirit," "non-binary transgender," and "person of transgender experience."[34]

---

[30] Bill C-16, which received royal assent and is now law, amends the Canadian Human Rights Act to include "gender identity and gender expression to the list of prohibited grounds of discrimination." Shimshock, R., *The Stream*, June 20, 2017, https://stream.org/canada-passes-law-criminalizing-use-of-wrong-gender-pronouns/. In December 2016, the Canadian Parliament passed a motion that condemned Islamophobia. Qazcini, M, War Against Free Speech: Canada Close To Passing 'Islamophobia' Law, aka Islamic Blasphemy Law (2017), *The Daily Wire*, https://www.dailywire.com/news/12957/war-against-free-speechcanada-close-passing-michael-qazvini

[31] New York City Commission on Human Rights Issues Guidance on Gender and Transgender Discrimination, https://www.thenycalliance.org/assets/documents/informationitems/L__E_Alert_-_January_2016_-_NYC_Hospitality_Alliance_-_New_York_City_Commission_On_Human_Rights_Issues_Guidance_On_Gender_And_Transgender_Discrimination-C1.pdf

[32] Avins, J., The Dos and Don'ts of Cultural Appropriation (2015), *The Atlantic*, https://www.theatlantic.com/entertainment/archive/2015/10/the-dos-and-donts-of-cultural-appropriation/411292/

[33] Young, C., To the New Culture Cops, Everything Is Appropriation (2015), *Washington Post*, https://www.washingtonpost.com/posteverything/wp/2015/08/21/to-the-new-culture-cops-everything-is-appropriation/?utm_term=.e4121b5229d4

[34] *See, e.g.*, Non-Binary Gender Identities Fact Sheet, https://www.apadivisions.org/division-44/resources/advocacy/non-binary-facts.pdf

Critics of the new laws view them as assaults on free speech—forcing people to use a particular set of approved words that they may choose not to include in their vocabularies, pointing out that there is a clear difference between restrictive speech laws borne out of public safety and laws that mandate the use of politically correct phrases.

As succinctly put by Jordan Peterson, a clinical psychologist at the University of Toronto: "The idea of cultural appropriation is nonsense.... There's no difference between cultural appropriation and learning from each other. They're the same thing. Now, that doesn't mean that there's no theft between people; there is. And it doesn't mean that once you encounter someone else's ideas, you have an absolute right to those ideas as if they're your own. But the idea that manifesting some element of another culture in your own behavior is immoral is insane."[35]

"Blackfacing" and Its Progeny

At one time blackface was a style of entertainment, often employed by White men in minstrel shows wearing burnt cork or black grease paint as makeup. The stock characters played a significant role in disseminating racist images, attitudes and perceptions worldwide. Every immigrant group was stereotyped on the music hall stage during the nineteenth century, but mocking caricatures by many performers (both White and Black) helped foster the belief that Blacks were racially and socially inferior. Originating as characterizations of plantation slaves and free Blacks, the minstrel shows played a large part in confirming those stereotypes.[36]

The term *Jim Crow* originated in 1830 when a White minstrel show performer, Thomas "Daddy" Rice, blackened his face and danced a jig while singing the lyrics to the song, "Jump Jim Crow." In 1834 George Dixon appeared as *Zip Coon*—an ostentatious figure dressed in high style and speaking malapropisms—made a mockery of free Blacks. *Jim Crow* and *Zip Coon* eventually merged into a single stereotype called simply *coon*. Also popularized were the words *Mammy*, *Uncle Tom*, *Buck*, and *Pickaninny*. All were carried over into vaudeville, film, and television, and were favorites of advertisers.[37]

---

[35] Philipp, J., Jordan Peterson Exposes the Postmodernist Agenda (2018), *The Epoch Times*, https://www.theepochtimes.com/jordan-peterson-explains-how-communism-came-under-the-guise-of-identity-politics_2259668.html

[36] History of Blackface, https://www.black-face.com/index.htm

[37] *Mammy* referred to a Black woman full of earthy wisdom who is fiercely independent and brooks no backtalk; *Uncle Tom*, typically a gentle and servile character; *Buck*, a large Black man who is proud, some-

From 1840 to 1890, minstrel shows were the most popular form of entertainment in America. (Ironically, by the late 1800s one of the most popular of the blackface performances was an adaptation of "Uncle Tom's Cabin," an anti-slavery tale, which remained the most popular play in America for over a century.)[38]

By World War I the traditional American minstrel show had virtually disappeared, although some performers continued to peddle blackface stereotypes later in vaudeville, films and television. These included Black entertainers, who found that they were not accepted on stage unless they performed in blackface. In fact, they had little choice in the roles they were offered. Until well into the 1950s, Black male actors were limited to stereotypical roles: *Stepin Fetchit*, the iconic janitor in the "Amos 'n' Andy" radio and television series; Bill "Bojangles" Robinson, the best known and most highly paid African-American entertainer in the first half of the twentieth century, and Eddie "Rochester" Anderson on the "Jack Benny Show." Similarly, the only film roles for Black women were as maids and mammys—the most famous of whom was Hattie McDaniel, who won an Oscar for her role as *Mammy* in "Gone With the Wind."[39]

The success of Black comedians such as Ernest Hogan, Bert Williams, and George Walker opened the door for multiracial casts and for later Black performers to take the stage without blackface. Williams did a coon stereotype in blackface he called "the Jonah Man," and later teamed up with Walker, billing themselves as "Two Real Coons." In 1902 they wrote, produced, and starred in "In Dahomey"—the first Black musical comedy to open on Broadway. After Walker died, Williams became the first Black to headline a Ziegfeld Follies show and the first to produce and star in his own silent films.[40]

By 1900, vaudeville had become the dominant form of American mass entertainment—a variety of separate, unrelated acts, including acrobats, animals, dancers, magicians, musicians, short skits, and comedy routines. For a time, vaudeville was the most popular form of live theater, but it died out with the advent of talking pictures. Among the many performers who got their

---

times menacing; and *Pickaninny*, a Black person with bulging eyes, unkempt hair, red lips and wide mouths into which they stuff slices of watermelon. *Id.*

[38] *Id.*

[39] One of the first to perform in blackface for White audiences was William Henry Lane, also known as "Master Juba" (often credited as the man who invented tap dancing). Eventually he became famous enough to perform in his own skin. Both *Beulah* and *Aunt Jemima* were based on the "Mammy" stereotype. Beulah was a supporting character on the popular "Fibber McGee and Molly" radio series (1945–1954) before it and became a spin-off show of its own. McDaniel eventually took the role on radio and was one of four Black women to play Beulah on the later television series. *Id.*

[40] *Id.*

start in vaudeville were Eddie Cantor, Al Jolson, Charlie Chaplin, the Marx Brothers, W.C. Fields, Jack Benny, and Bob Hope.[41]

The popularity of early silent movies—particularly "The Wooing and Wedding of a Coon" (1904), "The Slave" (1905), "The Little Black Sambo Series (1909–1911), and "The Nigger" (1915)—served to propagate racial stereotypes before large audiences around the world. In D.W. Griffith's "Birth of a Nation" (1915), the inept Jim Crow stereotypes were replaced by the savage Negro, as the Ku Klux Klan rescues the South, and Southern women from Blacks who have gained power over whites with the help of Northern carpetbaggers.[42]

Northern Blacks responded to "Birth of a Nation" by producing their own race movies made for Black audiences. The most successful Black film producer of the first half of the Twentieth Century was a former railway porter and novelist named Oscar Micheaux, who from 1918–1940 produced over 44 films, the most significant of which was "Within Our Gates" (1920), an uncompromising look at racial attitudes and prejudice among both Blacks and Whites that included both a rape and a lynching.[43]

With the advent of sound film and Hollywood productions, race movies were replaced by westerns, crime dramas, and musicals, some of which featured all-Black casts. Between 1930 and 1950, animators at Warner Brothers, Walt Disney, MGM, Merrie Melodies, Looney Tunes, R.K.O., and many other independent studios, produced thousands of cartoons that perpetuated the same old racist stereotypes. Later, these same cartoons would cycle endlessly for decades on broadcast TV or cable syndication.[44]

* * *

The most popular radio program of all time was "The "Amos'n'Andy" Show." The characters were created by Freeman Gosden and Charles Correll, two White actors with blackface and vaudeville experience. NBC began broadcasting "Amos'n'Andy" in 1928 and continued to air it until 1960.[45]

Even as the "Amos'n'Andy" television series premiered in June 1951, the NAACP was in federal court trying (unsuccessfully) to get an injunction to

---

[41] *Id.*

[42] Griffith later admitted that his film was designed to "create a feeling of abhorrence in white people, especially white women, against colored men." *Id.*

[43] *Id.*

[44] *Id.*

[45] Dunning, J., ed. On the Air: The Encyclopedia of Old-Time Radio, Oxford University Press (1998), ISBN 0195076788.

prevent CBS from televising it. In 1951, "Amos'n'Andy" ranked thirteenth in the Nielsen ratings and in 1952 it won an Emmy award. The NAACP responded by initiating a boycott of its sponsor, Blatz beer. By April 1953 Blatz withdrew its sponsorship and CBS announced that it had "bowed to the change in national thinking." The program nevertheless remained in syndication for thirteen years after it was withdrawn from the network schedule.[46]

The 1970s brought a genre called "blacksploitation" films such as Melvin Van Peebles' "Sweet Sweetback's Baadasssss Song" (1971), were small, independent productions that dealt with crime and the effects of illegal drugs on the inner cities. The cause was usually portrayed as being a result of White racism and exploitation of poor Blacks. Most White cops and politicians were portrayed as corrupt, forcing Black antiheroes to take matters into their own hands.[47]

NAACP challenges also resulted in blackface scenes being cut from TV showings of films such as "Babes in Arms" and "Holiday Inn." But by the 1970s, stereotypical "coons and mammies" were again featured in shows like "Sanford and Son," "The Jeffersons," "Good Times," "What's Happening," and "Diff'rent Strokes." The most iconic television program to poke fun at both the stereotypes and political correctness was "All in the Family," whose primary character, Archie Bunker, appeared in one form or another from 1971 to 1983.[48]

Meanwhile, negative stereotypes of Blacks have become a staple of Black music videos that glorify gangsterism. The "buck" is now a hoodlum with an attitude, and the minstrel-show plantation has morphed into a music video version of gangster life. In 2018, Donald Glover (a/k/a "Childish Gambino") turned the Jim Crow stereotype on its head with his music video "This Is America"—which confronted Black minstrel stereotypes in the media, gangster rap, gun violence, and police brutality.[49]

---

[46] "Amos and Andy" still played on 50 US stations as late as 1963 Videotapes and DVDs continue to circulate among collectors. *Id.*

[47] Similar films were "Superfly," "Shaft," "Blackula," "Black Caesar," "Hell up in Harlem," "Black Gestapo," "Foxy Brown." Such films eventually generated a backlash led by Black leaders that put an end to blackspoitation films by 1980. *Id.*

[48] *Id.*

[49] The video ends with Gambino running as fast as he can through a dark hall while being chased by White shadows; no matter how fast he runs they are still closing in on him. The message: for American blacks, racism and White supremacy are inescapable. *Id.*

We may have come full circle with the program "Blackish," a sitcom that debuted in 2014 about a father of four who worries that his four children are losing touch with urban Black culture because of their affluent upbringing.[50]

* * *

Over time the use of blackface came into disrepute because it was perceived as largely based upon racist stereotypes of Black people.

Colored, an old term for African-American people, is now considered offensive, and *negro* has fallen out of favor among younger Black Americans.[51] Even the term "black" itself is sometimes regarded as politically incorrect. Ironically, perhaps, "person of color" is usually taken positively in our time, and is widely applied to anyone who is not "white," a term which, itself, can be a rather amorphous group label.

In 2010, a maelstrom of criticism was leveled at former Senate leader (and majority leader) Harry Reid when he used the word "Negro" while commenting on then-Senator Barack Obama's dialect. Although it's still used within the title of United Negro College Fund, it is not politically correct to refer to or use this as an adjective regarding Black people. Likewise, although the term "colored" is also inappropriate—even though it is on display in the title of the National Association for the Advancement of Colored People (NAACP).[52] Although it depends largely upon the individual, nowadays it is more acceptable to use Black, People of Color, or African American.[53]

In fact, the designation "Black" has been around longer than "African-American" or "People of Color." It was embraced in the 1960s during the Civil Rights movement, particularly when James Brown's 1968 song proclaimed, "Say it loud, I'm black and I'm proud." It became synonymous with Black pride and empowerment. Some Blacks rejected this designation as an attempt to marginalize them because the term lacks sufficient geographic or ancestral reference. Others objected to its focus on dark skin since Blacks are not monochromatically dark.[54]

---

[50] Stephen, B., How to Live Within a Black Body: Ta-Nehisi Coates's "Between the World and Me," https://ibw21.org/commentary/how-to-live-within-a-black-body-ta-nehisi-coatess-between-the-world-and-me-is-a-letter-to-his-son-and-a-lesson-for-us-all/

[51] What Do Black People Want To Be Called?, *Prejudice and Discrimination*, https://prejudiceanddiscrimination.com/what-do-black-people-want-to-be-called-2/

[52] Would it be more appropriate for the organization to change its name to the National Association for the Advancement of People of Color (NAAPC)?

[53] What Do Black People Want To Be Called?, *supra*.

[54] *Id.*

"People of Color" was an attempt to be inclusive of all minorities, although many Blacks reject it as their primary designation because it is not specific. Others chose the "African American" designation after Jesse Jackson urged its use in 1988, because it did not focus on a lone physical attribute nor did it refer to other ethnicities.[55] A 1989 survey by ABC and the *Washington Post* found 66% of Black respondents preferred the term black, and 22% African American.[56] In 2003, another poll by the same organizations noted a shift: African American was the preferred term (48 percent) while 35% favored black, and 17% liked both. In today's society, most Blacks find "African American," "People of Color," and "Black" acceptable.[57]

"White Shaming"

In 2014, when Jodi Linley became a professor at the University of Iowa, she declared her commitment to designing classes that "fight white privilege" by both unveiling and rejecting the notion that "neutrality and objectivity are realistic and attainable." Describing herself as a mentor "of mostly white graduate students who will become higher education leaders," she wrote that "as a "queer, able-bodied, cisgender woman" she wanted "to dismantle whiteness in my curriculum, assignments and pedagogy." She pledged to expose her students to "their own white ignorance" in a "peer-reviewed academic journal"; to do otherwise, she said, would make her complicit in perpetuating White supremacy. "For white students," she wrote, "talking about race with an all-white group of peers … [reveals] their own white ignorance."[58]

Prof. Linley suggested five strategies that other professors could use to deconstruct White privilege in their own classes, such as making sure students know that their views on race will be challenged, "interrupting oppression" that occurs in classroom settings, and segregating students by race so they can have more productive dialogues about privilege. "For white students, talking

---

[55] "It puts us in our proper historical context," Jackson said. "It also asserted pride in African ancestry. On the other hand, many blacks don't know from which of the 50 African countries their ancestors originated, so they might feel the designation is inauthentic." *Id.*

[56] Ten percent of the respondents found both acceptable; two percent expressed no opinion. *Id.*

[57] Swarns, R., "African-American" Becomes a Term for Debate (2004), *New York Times*, http://latinamericanstudies.org/slavery/term.htm

[58] Airaksinen, T., Prof Pledges To "Deconstruct Whiteness" In All Her Courses (2017), *Campus Reform*, https://www.campusreform.org/?ID=9569. "Cisgender" (sometimes "cissexual," often abbreviated to simply "cis") is a new-age term for people whose gender identity matches the sex that they were assigned at birth. *Id.*

about race with an all-White group of peers facilitates their realization that they are raced beings, thus revealing their own White ignorance."[59]

Welcome to the brave new world of "white shaming"—a phenomenon based on the assumption that, alone among all actors in history, White people should apologize for their skin color—which appears to be growing in the liberal circles of academia.[60]

Some commentators trace White shaming statements to European colonialism. For centuries White monarchs dominated the globe by way of trade and military power—evidence for some that White people are devilish and self-serving.[61]

The existence of slavery—the idea that one human being can actually, literally, and legally *own* another human being—supports this assumption. But slavery is as old as *The Bible*; it predates European colonialism by at least 3000 years. The Romans enacted mass enslavement, as did many of the Greek city-states before them. Between the years 700 and 1900 C.E., dominance over the slave industry was held by Islam. As many as 28 million Africans were bought and sold in Arab slave markets throughout the Middle East between those dates. One reason we do not see many African communities in the Middle East is that Arab traders typically castrated their slaves.[62]

The most profound source of White guilt, however, may derive from the fact that between 1500 and 1800 nearly 25 million people were brought from West Africa to the Americas during the European transatlantic slave trade. Never before had the world seen slavery on such a massive scale.[63]

Pope Gregory XVI condemned slavery outright in 1839, and by the late nineteenth century it had been largely abolished throughout Europe. With abolition came prosperity—not out of White guilt or shaming, but because of

---

[59] *Id*. These remarks were widely criticized on social media, which apparently surprised both Prof. Linley and her superiors. The University of Iowa issued this statement: "Recently, one of our faculty members was singled out for publishing a peer-review article on race issues in higher education. This faculty member was targeted, harassed, and threatened by many people from around the country through email, phone calls, and social media." *Glock Talk*, https://www.glocktalk.com/threads/white-shaming-is-new-rage-on-college-campuses.1673770/print and https://www.wnd.com/2017/08/white-shaming-is-new-rage-on-college-campuses

[60] How would such an apology be expressed? The author suggests a simple phrasing he remembers his daughter used when she was ordered to apologize for some comment she had made as a teenager: "I'm sorry, *okay*?" [inflection/emphasis supplied].

[61] *See, e.g.*, Wolf, L., Welcome to the Brave New World of White Shaming (2015), *Townhall*, https://townhall.com/columnists/leonwolf/2015/02/25/welcome-to-the-brave-new-world-of-white-shaming-n1961862

[62] Farron, S., Black Slavery in the Middle East (2017), *American Renaissance*, https://www.amren.com/features/2017/02/black-slavery-middle-east/

[63] Lewis, M. P., White-Shaming Over the European Colonial Era (2018), *National Monitor*, http://natmonitor.com/2018/12/31/white-shaming-over-the-european-colonial-era/

the advent of constitutional governance, modern financial structures, technology based on the use of electricity, oil, natural gas, and coal, and public education systems.[64]

* * *

The issue of slavery has been resurrected in the Twenty-first century by a number of political figures calling for reparations to descendants of American slaves.[65] Such views have also served to transmogrify political correctness.

In today's climate, one might legitimately ask if George Washington or Thomas Jefferson would be boycotted as commencement speakers because of their well-documented ownership of slaves. Washington first became a slave owner at the early age of eleven, when (in 1743) his father left him the 280-acre family farm near Fredericksburg, Virginia, as well as ten slaves. As a young adult, Washington purchased at least a dozen more slaves on his own. He acquired many more by virtue of his marriage to Martha Custis. By the time he died Mount Vernon's enslaved population numbered 317 people. Mount Vernon's enslaved community took opportunities, when possible, to physically escape. In April of 1781, for example, fourteen men and three women slaves fled to the British warship HMS Savage which was anchored in the Potomac off the shore of Washington's plantation.[66]

Despite having been an active slaveholder for 56 years, Washington struggled with the institution of slavery and spoke frequently of his desire to end the practice. In 1799, at the end of his life, he made the bold step to free all his slaves—the only slave-holding Founding Father to do so.[67]

Jefferson's views on slavery were likewise complex. He consistently spoke out against the practice of slavery—while he owned more than 600 slaves throughout his adult life and freed only seven. In 1767 at age 24, Jefferson inherited 5000 acres of land and the legal ownership of 52 people by his father's will. In 1768, Jefferson began construction of his Monticello

---

[64] *Id.*

[65] Democratic Hopefuls Embrace New Meaning for Slave Descendants, *NBC News*, https://www.nbcnews.com/politics/2020-election/democratic-hopefuls-embrace-new-meaning-reparations-slave-descendants-n976096

[66] Ten Facts About George Washington and Slavery, George Washington's Mount Vernon, https://www.mountvernon.org/george-washington/slavery/ten-facts-about-washington-slavery/. Slaveowners administered punishments to control their workforce; in his later years, Washington urged overseers to motivate workers with encouragement and rewards—but he approved of "correction" when those methods failed. *Id.*

[67] By law, neither George nor Martha Washington could free the 153 slaves who came by way of the Martha Custis dower. Upon Martha's death in 1802, they were divided among the Custis grandchildren. *Id.*

plantation. After his marriage to Martha Wayles in 1772, he inherited two plantations and the legal ownership of 135 men, women, and children who were to be kept as slaves. By 1776, Jefferson was one of the largest planters in Virginia; however, the value of his property (land and slaves) was increasingly offset by his growing debts, which would make it difficult for him to free the slaves without losing them as assets.[68]

In his writings on American grievances justifying the Revolution, Jefferson attacked the British for sponsoring human trafficking to the colonies. In 1778, under his leadership, slave importation was banned in Virginia, one of the first jurisdictions worldwide to do so. As president, he led the effort to criminalize the international slave trade that passed Congress and he signed in 1807, shortly before Britain passed a similar law.[69]

In 1784, Jefferson proposed federal legislation banning slavery in the New Territories of the North and South after 1800, which failed to pass Congress by one vote. In his *Notes on the State of Virginia*, published in 1785, Jefferson wrote that slavery corrupted both masters and slaves alike and supported colonization of freed slaves—but he also promoted the ideas that African Americans were inferior in intelligence and that emancipating large numbers of them would make uprisings more likely.[70]

Most historians believe that, after the death of his wife Martha, Jefferson had a long-term relationship with an enslaved woman named Sally Hemings. Jefferson allowed two of Hemings' surviving four children to "escape"; the other two he freed through his will—the only ones to gain freedom from Monticello.[71] Again, ironically, Jefferson supported mixed-race marriages in his *Notes on Virginia*; so did Patrick Henry.

In 2015 there was a heated debate among students at the University of Missouri about whether a Jefferson statue on campus should be removed because it represented "the dehumanization of black individuals whom Jefferson himself viewed as inferior." In 2017 students at the University of Virginia—which Jefferson had founded almost two centuries

---

[68] Thomas Jefferson and His Slaves: Making Sense of the Contradictions of the Founding Fathers, *Grateful American Foundation*, No date. https://gratefulamericanfoundation.com/historic-partners/10894/

[69] Cohen, W., "Thomas Jefferson and the Problem of Slavery." (1969), *Journal of American History* 56,503 https://www.worldcat.org/title/thomas-jefferson-and-the-problem-of-slavery/oclc/808022551

[70] Appleby, J. O., and Schlesinger, A. M., eds. A. M., *Thomas Jefferson*. (2003). New York: Times Books.

[71] Some historians speculate that Hemings was Martha's half-sister. In his will, Jefferson freed three older men who had been forced to work for him for decades. In 1827, the remaining 130 people who had been kept as slaves at Monticello were sold to pay the debts of Jefferson's estate. Jenkins, C. L., Slavery at Jefferson's Monticello, Smithsonian NMAAHC/Monticello, January–October 2012 (2012), https://www.washingtonpost.com/blogs/therootdc/post/slavery-at-jeffersons-monticello-slave-exhibit-opens-friday-at-smithsonians-african-american-museum/2012/01/25/gIQAk4KKTQ_blog.html

earlier—shrouded his statue in Black and covered it with signs reading "racist" and "rapist."[72]

* * *

Revisionist notions of free speech have reached the point where even the American Civil Liberties Union, the traditionally iconic defender of First Amendment values, has been shouted down as a "liberal white supremacist" organization. In October 2017, students affiliated with the Black Lives Matter movement crashed an event at the College of William & Mary, rushed the stage, and prevented the invited guest (the ACLU's Claire Gastañaga, a W & M alumna) from speaking. The topic of her talk: "Students and the First Amendment."[73]

At first, Ms. Gastañaga attempted to spin the demonstration as a welcome example of the kind of thing she had come to campus to discuss. "Good, I like this," she said as they lined up and raised their signs. "I'm going to talk to you about knowing your rights, and protests and demonstrations, which this illustrates very well. Then I'm going to respond to questions from the moderators, and then questions from the audience." But the protesters quickly drowned her out, shouting "ACLU, you protect Hitler, too," "blood on your hands," "the revolution will not uphold the Constitution," and "liberalism is white supremacy." Twenty minutes later the protest's leader delivered a prepared statement, declaring that the disruption was in response to the ACLU's defense of the Charlottesville alt-right's civil liberties. Organizers then canceled the event. When some members of the audience approached the podium in an attempt to speak with Ms. Gastañaga, the protesters surrounded Gastañaga and drove everybody else away.[74]

This was the so-called alternative right on full display, a loosely defined group of people with far-right ideologies who reject mainstream conservatism in favor of White nationalism. The term drew considerable media attention

---

[72] The University was founded in 1819. Earlier almost 500 students and professors had asked the school's president to refrain from quoting Jefferson in campus-wide emails. *Id.*

[73] Miller, J., Protesters Cover UVA's Thomas Jefferson Statue in Black Shroud (2017), *New York Post*,. See also Beam, A., If Lee Goes, Will Washington and Jefferson Follow? (2017), *Boston Globe*; Ng, D., Thomas Jefferson Statue Incites Debate at Mizzou (2015), *Los Angeles Times*, and Soave, R., Black Lives Matter Students Shut Down the ACLU's Campus Free Speech Event Because "Liberalism Is White Supremacy (2017), *Reason.Com*, http://reason.com/blog/2017/10/04/black-lives-matter-students-shut-down-th

[74] William & Mary responded with a statement to the effect that "silencing certain voices in order to advance the cause of others is not acceptable in our community." But without a promise to identify the perpetrators and make sure this never happens again, the college's statement is meaningless rhetoric. Soave, R., *supra*.

and caused controversy during and after the 2016 United States presidential election. Some say it has morphed from a movement centered on White nationalism into one that promotes overt racism, White supremacy, neo-fascism, and neo-Nazism.[75]

The notion of checking one's privilege through White shaming has triggered a predictable backlash. "Right now," writes one critic, "Americans are inundated with a variety of liberal politics that try to turn what should be political reckonings against the truly powerful into an epidemic of guilt and complicity in which a huge portion—or sometimes, nearly all of us—are to blame. That's not only not true—it's politically ineffective."[76]

The *New Republic* likewise highlighted a bizarre manifestation of the white-privilege meme: White parents instructing their schoolchildren in the evils of themselves.[77] A profile in the *New York Times* of the Friends Seminary school near Manhattan's East Village described "white affinity groups," where students and faculty members tackle issues of White privilege, often in all-White settings—a product of the idea that "whites should not rely on their black, Asian, or Latino/a peers to educate them about racism and white dominance."[78]

Yellow Journalism

"Yellow journalism" is a term associated with news media that present little or no legitimate well-researched information, including sensationalized headlines, exaggerations of events, and scandal-mongering. Its modern usage is a pejorative to decry any journalism that treats news in an unprofessional or unethical fashion. Closely related is "checkbook journalism," the controversial practice of news reporters who pay sources for their information without verifying its truth or accuracy. In the U.S. such a practice is generally considered

---

[75] The Rise of the AltRight (2016), *The Week*, https://theweek.com/articles/651929/rise-altright

[76] Kilpatrick, C., Why The Right Loves Privilege Politics (2015), *Jacobin*, https://www.jacobinmag.com/2015/05/99-1-percent-income-inequality-class/. *See also* Fitzgerald, D., White-Led White Shaming (2015), *The American Spectator*, https://spectator.org/white-led-white-shaming/

[77] Bovy, P. M., The Rise of the Privilege Epiphany (2018), *New Republic*, https://newrepublic.com/article/146522/rise-privilege-epiphany, and "The Perils of Privilege," New Republic, March 6, 2017, https://newrepublic.com/article/140985/perils-privilege-phoebe-maltz-bovy-book-excerpt

[78] Spencer, K., At New York Private Schools, Challenging White Privilege From the Inside (2015), New York Times, https://www.nytimes.com/2015/02/22/nyregion/at-new-york-private-schools-challenging-white-privilege-from-the-inside.html. *See also* Fitzgerald, *supra*.

unethical, with most mainstream newspapers and news shows having a policy forbidding it.[79]

The term was coined in the late nineteenth century to describe the mid-1890's sensationalistic reporting in a circulation war between Joseph Pulitzer's *New York World* and William Randolph Heart's *New York Journal*. Hearst read the *World* while studying at Harvard University and resolved to compete with Pulitzer. The competition was fierce. Both Pulitzer and Hearst invested substantial resources in their Sunday editions, which functioned like weekly magazines, going beyond the normal scope of daily journalism.[80]

Perhaps the most notable early critical response to the screaming headlines and lurid reporting came in an 1890 law-review article that viewed yellow journalism as an unprecedented threat to individual peace and liberty. Authored by Samuel Warren and Louis Brandeis, this was the first articulation of the right to privacy and is still considered one of the most influential essays in the history of American law. Some historians trace its impetus to a specific incident where journalists intruded on a society wedding, but it was more likely inspired by the general coverage of intimate personal lives in society columns of newspapers.[81]

Early on in their article Warren and Brandeis call attention to the advent of instantaneous photography and the widespread circulation of newspapers as contributing factors in the invasion of an individual's privacy, taking particular aim at society gossip pages:

> The press is overstepping in every direction the obvious bounds of propriety and of decency. Gossip is no longer the resource of the idle and of the vicious, but has become a trade, which is pursued with industry as well as effrontery. To satisfy a prurient taste the details of sexual relations are spread broadcast in the columns of the daily papers. To occupy the indolent, column upon column is filled with idle gossip, which can only be procured by intrusion upon the domestic circle.[82]

---

[79] Rogers, T., Why Reporters Should Avoid Checkbook Journalism (2019), *ThoughtCo.*, https://www.thoughtco.com/why-reporters-should-avoid-checkbook-journalism-2073718. *See also* Campbell, W. J., Yellow Journalism Puncturing the Myths, Defining the Legacies (2003), which lists five characteristics of yellow journalism: (1) scare headlines in huge print, often of minor news; (2) lavish use of pictures, or imaginary drawings; (3) use of faked interviews, misleading headlines, pseudoscience, and a parade of false learning from so-called experts; (4) emphasis on full-color Sunday supplements, usually with comic strips; and (5) dramatic sympathy with the "underdog" against the system.

[80] The Sunday papers featured included the first color comic strips—which might be the genesis of the term "yellow journalism." *See* Mott, F., American Journalism *(1941) at p. 539*, ISBN 9780415228947.

[81] Warren, S. and Brandeis, L., The Right to Privacy (1890), *Harvard Law Review* 4, 193. *See also* Glancy, D. J., The Invention of the Right to Privacy (1979), *Arizona Law Review* 21, 1.

[82] *Id.*

Pulitzer and Hearst are also well known for their roles in pushing the United States to enter the Spanish-American war. Having clamored for a fight for 2 years, Hearst took credit for the conflict when it came, and took off immediately for Cuba as a war correspondent. In both 1896 and 1900, Hearst endorsed and promoted Williams Jennings Bryan for president. In 1901, critics charged that it was Hearst's yellow journalism that caused the assassination of President William McKinley.[83]

News reporting does not seem to have changed much in the past century. Consider the breathless accounts of political infighting during the spring of 2019: After U.S. presidential candidate Joe Biden called North Korean leader Kim Jong Un "a tyrant," Kim labeled Biden a "fool of low IQ" and an "imbecile bereft of elementary quality as a human being."[84] A political science professor at New York University tweeted that President Donald Trump had said "Kim Jong Un is smarter and would make a better President than Sleepy Joe Biden"—and then admitted that he had fabricated the quote.[85]

Here was a case of *actual* fake news—to be differentiated from *slanted* news reporting, which displays bias, but not falsehood.

It did not take long for the Trump-Biden cacophony to escalate into overt nastiness. Trump said he hoped Biden would win the Democratic nomination because his low-level intelligence (he called Biden "a dummy") would make him easier to beat in a presidential election." He pointed to Biden's dismal finish in the 2008 presidential campaign, saying Barack Obama "took him off the trash heap.... He's even slower than he used to be."[86]

Biden responded that Trump is "literally an existential threat to America."[87]

* * *

---

[83] Campbell, *supra*.

[84] North Korea Calls Biden "Fool of Low IQ" over Kim Criticism (2019), *Politico*, https://www.politico.com/story/2019/05/22/joe-biden-north-korea-fool-1340544

[85] Trump seized on the widely-reported quote, by Prof. Ian Bremmer, as an example of journalistic malpractice and called for modification of libel laws in order to hold news media accountable. Miles, F., and DeMarche, E., Trump Seizes on NYU Professor's Tweet to Push Change of Libel Laws (2019), *Fox News*, https://www.foxnews.com/politics/trump-seizes-on-nyu-professors-tweet-to-push-change-of-libel-laws

[86] Saavedra, R., Trump Rips Biden: "Obama Took Him Off The Trash Heap," "Is A Dummy," "Weakest Mentally (2019), *The Daily Wire*, https://www.dailywire.com/news/48289/trump-rips-biden-obama-took-him-trash-heap-dummy-ryan-saavedra

[87] Joe Biden: President Donald Trump Is Literally An Existential Threat to America (2019), *NBC News*, https://electionsdirectory.com/election2018/joe-biden-president-donald-trump-is-literally-an-existential-threat-to-america/

Trump's victory in the 2016 presidential election propelled a national debate on the extent of liberal advocacy and bias in much of contemporary news reporting.

A few commentators have taken a more intelligent approach. One of them is conservative watchdog, Mark Levin. "We have to have a national discussion about this," said Levin, "not with the media, but among ourselves like our founders did, in our homes, our restaurants, in our churches, in our civic groups, at a grassroots level, about what we're going to do about it, because if we don't have a free press we cannot sustain our republic." He said much of the media have given up fairness to take out Trump by any means necessary, including fake and "pseudo" news. "What's going on today with these attacks on the president of the United States, literally trying to burden him to such an extent that he cannot function, undermines the republic."[88]

While Trump has often stated that the media are the "enemy of the people," Levin correctly noted that the president has done little beyond rhetoric to squeeze the media. In contrast, he cites historical precedents, pointing out that presidents from John Adams to Barack Obama prosecuted reporters and limited their access. "A handful of media outlets are trying to balance how they report, and most of them come under attack from the 98 per cent who demand uniformity." Many news reporters contributed to Democratic campaigns. "Every time Donald Trump says something, you say it's the end of the world. You operate in a bubble in Washington, you operate in a bubble in New York. You have no comprehension of what is going on in the country, said Levin."[89]

"The media will not only marginalize themselves," Levin concluded, "but they will continue to be the greatest threat to freedom of the press today—not President Trump or his administration, but the current practitioners of what used to be journalism."[90]

* * *

Among the leading news outlets, anti-Trump coverage is ubiquitous and measurable. During his first hundred days in office, Trump was the topic of more than 40% of all news stories—three times the amount of press coverage

---

[88] Bedard, P. Mark Levin: Media 98% Anti-Trump, "Incestuous" with Democrats, Fake News Real (2019), *Washington Examiner*, https://www.washingtonexaminer.com/washington-secrets/mark-levin-media-98-anti-trump-incestuous-with-democrats-fake-news-real. Levin's book on the subject, UNFREEDOM OF THE PRESS, quickly became a best-seller.

[89] One report found that 430 members of the media had contributed $382,000 to the Clintons. *Id.*

[90] *Id.*

received by previous presidents—and most of it was unfavorable. According to a study by Harvard University's Shorenstein Center on Media, Politics and Public Policy, the media "set … a new standard for unfavorable press coverage of a president." The report noted that coverage by CNN and NBC "was the most unrelenting—negative stories about Trump outpaced positive ones by 13-to-1 on the two networks …. not merely negative in overall terms, [but] unfavorable in every dimension."[91]

In April 2019 the *Washington Post* headlined that "Trump Has Made More Than 10,000 False or Misleading Claims."[92] That allegation was quickly challenged: the "falsehoods" allegedly included accurate statements of the number of new jobs since Trump's election, as well as executive orders that he did, in fact, sign. For example, while the United States is not the fastest growing economy in the world, as Trump has stated, it is nonetheless the fastest in the developed world, which the *Post* did not point out. Similarly, although Trump said his administration believes in "buy American, hire American," he has a long history of outsourcing a variety of his own products; but he did sign the order, and the fact his personal track record does not live up to that is irrelevant. (If anything, it supports his order, since in theory, it would force reluctant businesspeople like himself to buy and hire Americans.)[93]

Other examples of Trump quotes, the *Post*'s interpretation of them, and the facts:

> QUOTE: "These newly employed citizens are joining 5.5 million more workers who have found jobs since the election."
>
> POST: "Trump often inflates the number of jobs created under his presidency by counting from Election Day, rather than when he took the oath of office."
>
> FACTS: There have been about 4.9 million jobs created since January 2017, according to the Bureau of Labor Statistics. Job growth under Trump in the first two years was little different than Obama's last two years." In fact, Trump literally said, "since the election."[94]

---

[91] Kass, J., Harvard Study: Media Has Been Largely Negative on Trump (2017), *Chicago Tribune*, https://www.chicagotribune.com/columns/john-kass/ct-trump-media-coverage-harvard-kass-0521-20170519-column.html. The report specifically named the primary sources of the bias: the *New York Times*, *Wall Street Journal*, *Washington Post*, *CBS Evening News*, CNN's *The Situation Room*, and NBC *Nightly News*. See also Perloff, J. The Shadows of Power (1988), which exposed the Council of Foreign Relations' history of infiltrating the mainstream media.

[92] Rizzo, S. and Kelly, M., President Trump Has Made More Than 10,000 False or Misleading Claims (2019), *Washington Post*, https://www.washingtonpost.com/politics/2019/04/29/president-trump-has-made-more-than-false-or-misleading-claims/?utm_term=.817328ec4ebd

[93] Goldstein, S., Opinion: Washington Post's 10,000 Trump Untruths Is About 25% Fake News (2019), *Market Watch*, https://www.marketwatch.com/story/washington-posts-10000-trump-untruths-is-about-25-fake-news-2019-04-29

[94] *Id.*

6 Blackfacing, White Shaming, and Yellow Journalism... 215

*

QUOTE "Since we passed our historic tax cuts and reforms just over one year ago, wages are rising fast, and they're rising most quickly for the lowest-income Americans."

POST: "Wages grew at an annual rate of 3.2% in December, but wage growth was consistently higher before 2009. Still, Goldman Sachs found that for the first during an economic recovery that began in mid-2009 that the bottom half of earners are benefiting more than the top half. Whether that can be attributed to the tax cut is unclear."

FACTS: Not only are wages growing the fastest since the recession, they are fastest for lower-income workers. The cause-and-effect of tax cuts and wage growth is unclear but not definitely wrong.[95]

* * *

*

QUOTE "When I spoke to you as a candidate three years ago, America's economy was stagnant."

POST: "This is wrong. Many of the positive economic trends Trump regularly references started under the Obama administration."

FACTS: Average GDP growth rate last nine quarters has been 2.8%. Average growth rate in the prior nine quarters was 2%.[96]

* * *

*

QUOTE: "Remember, President Obama said manufacturing jobs are gone. You need a wand, a magic wand. We found the magic wand because they're coming and they're coming fast."

POST: "Trump is misquoting Obama. The 'magic wand' referred to recreating jobs of the past through negotiating 'a better deal.'"

FACTS: Manufacturing jobs growth has been stronger during Trump administration than Obama's.[97]

---

[95] *Id.*
[96] *Id.*
[97] *Id.*

*

QUOTE: "The unemployment rates for African-Americans, Hispanic-Americans and Asian-Americans have all reached their lowest levels in the history of our country."

POST: "The current African American unemployment statistic has been in existence for less than 50 years. It reached a low of 5.9% in May 2018, but rose to 6.7% in March. An older set of government data suggests Black unemployment went much lower in the 1950s. The Asian-American statistic has been around for less than 20 years. And while it reached a low of 2.0% rate in May 2018, it rose to 3.0% in March, the most recent month. Hispanic unemployment has also rebounded. Lately, Trump has been using the word "reached," perhaps to indicate the lows are in the past."

FACTS: The lowest levels in recorded history, yes. His inclusion of the word "reached" makes it accurate.[98]

* * *

*

QUOTE: "People that graduate without a high school diploma—it's a big group—lowest in the history of our country."

POST: "This dataset has only be recorded since 1992, so Trump has no basis to claim the "history of our country." The unemployment rate for high school dropouts reached a low of 5.0% in July 2018, but by the time Trump made this statement it had risen to 5.9%, a figure last reached in 2000."

FACTS: Graduate rate without a diploma is lowest in recorded history, and still better now than before the Trump administration.[99]

* * *

*

---

[98] *Id.*
[99] *Id.*

QUOTE: "So we have low-income and distressed communities, and they're getting a tremendous incentive to have a lot of money going to those communities. And it's having a very, very big effect. It's been great."

POST: "The impact of the Opportunity Zones is not yet clear, according to the Tax Foundation. This is in part because key data collection requirements that would be needed to assess the progress were stripped from the final version of the bill."

FACTS: It is difficult to tell at this stage. The White House says counties with a large presence of zones had annualized wage growth of 8% in Q2 and Q3 2018, and it says property values in zones have climbed 20%, citing Zillow data. So, it is a defendable claim even if there does need to be more examination.[100]

* * *

*

QUOTE: "The economy is roaring."

POST: "The economy appears to be slowing. The growth rate for the gross domestic product was 4.2% in the second quarter of 2018, 3.4% in the third quarter and 2.2% in the fourth quarter."

FACTS: "Roaring" is a subjective term, but with low unemployment and high GDP it is not a false claim.[101]

In mid-June of 2019, when Trump officially launched his campaign for a second term, he filled the 20,000-seat Amway Center in Orlando and many more of his base fans waited outside.[102] Fox News was the only network to carry the rally live.

* * *

It's worth noting that Mr. Trump does make statements on a daily basis that are sometimes significantly at odds with the facts. But the sheer level of negative coverage gives weight to his contention that the media are bent on destroying his presidency. His allegations about "fake news" may be becoming a self-fulfilling prophecy.

---

[100] *Id.*

[101] *Id.*

[102] Taylor, J., Trump Launches Reelection Bid with Promises of Greatness and Familiar Grievances (2019), *National Public Radio*, https://www.npr.org/2019/06/19/733904818/trump-launches-reelection-bid-with-promises-of-greatness-and-familiar-grievances https://www.npr.org/2019/06/19/733904818/trump-launches-reelection-bid-with-promises-of-greatness-and-familiar-grievances

* * *

A different kind of assault on free speech has come through the evolution of what's been deemed "political correctness"—with abuses from both the right and the left.

The American Civil Liberties Union, for example, decries the use of word the "criminals" to describe juvenile delinquents. In the spring of 2019, hundreds of young people rampaged through the downtown area in Baltimore. Some caused damage running atop the roofs of parked cars. That prompted a tweet from the Baltimore City Fraternal Order of Police that officers should "protect each other" and not "fall into the trap that they are only kids…. Some are criminals! Keep the current policies and consent decree in mind." That comment drew criticism online, calling it racial profiling.[103]

Is the term overused? Is there widespread racial profiling in American police departments? Could it be that the profiling analysis profoundly confuses cause and effect—that police develop tactics in response to the disproportionate victimization of minorities by minorities, and that it is really the *tactics* that are the problem?[104]

Even environmentalists cannot escape overweening conscientiousness. Consider Starbucks' decision to abandon plastic straws for recyclable lids. Straws are a tiny share of waste—according to one estimate they account for just 0.025% of the eight million tons of plastic that flow annually into the ocean. On the other hand, the ostensibly recyclable new lids contain more plastic than the straws, but consumers have to separate them from the cups and throw them into recycling bins. How many people are going to do that? In 2008 Starbucks set a "bold goal" to serve 25% of its beverages in reusable cups by 2015; it later revised the goal to 5%—in part because it was inefficient for bartenders to wash dirty cups while other customers waited.[105]

But there's scant evidence that these gestures benefit customers, shareholders, employees, or the environment.[106]

---

[103] Garcia, V., Mark Levin: "Have You Ever Seen A Dumber Media In Your Life? (2019), *Fox News*, https://www.foxnews.com/politics/mark-levin-have-you-ever-seen-a-dumber-media-in-your-life

[104] There's no credible evidence that racial profiling exists, yet the crusade to abolish it threatens a decade's worth of crime-fighting success. MacDonald, H., The Myth of Racial Profiling (2001), *City Journal*, https://www.city-journal.org/html/myth-racial-profiling-12022.html

[105] Even if the lids get as far as the bins they will probably end up in landfills. Made of polypropylene, they used to be sent to China for recycling—until China stopped accepting U.S. waste. Cleaning glasses and mugs also requires the use of water and paper towels, which end up in the trash. *Id*.

[106] Finley, A., Would You Like Guilt With Your Latte? (2019), *Wall Street Journal*, https://www.wsj.com/articles/would-you-like-guilt-with-your-latte-11558989233

Similarly, Dunkin' Donuts spent nearly a decade devising an alternative to foam cups. But some decomposable cups were too expensive to produce in large volumes, while others, manufactured from recycled materials, simply collapsed. The company settled on cups made from "ethically sourced paper"—which in most places cannot be recycled.[107]

The investment firm Goldman Sachs likewise tried to be environmentally sensitive by banning paper cups from its offices and asking employees to bring mugs instead. The bank also announced it would stop carrying throwaway utensils in its cafeterias and replace plastic soda bottles with aluminum cans in vending machines, because too many employees were throwing those items in the trash rather than recycling. Whether bankers would be willing to wash dishes at the office (or choose to eat out instead) remains open to question. There is no doubt, though, about the fiscal efficacy of bottles versus cans: aluminum production requires much larger amounts of energy and produces greater amounts of carbon dioxide.[108]

Corporations might perceive a branding benefit with such campaigns—showing employees, customers, and shareholders that they care about the environment—but how many investors buy shares in a company because of its "sustainable" policies? To what extent are the measures cost-ineffective: how much do office paper-cup purges aggravate employees and reduce productivity; how much do these policies actually reduce earnings and lower share prices? How many consumers care if the food they buy comes in recyclable packages? How much do higher costs from more expensive materials reduce purchases?[109]

Businesses would be better advised to set office thermostats a few degrees higher, or perhaps thinking out of the box and provide employees paid time-off for tree-planting or highway-cleaning projects.[110]

* * *

The core problem with modern journalism is that resources are spread thin. The news industry is rife with cutbacks. The emphasis is on volume and speed,

---

[107] Minter, A., Skipping Straws May Be Hip. But There Are Much Better Ways To Fight Pollution (2018), *Bloomberg Business*, https://www.bloomberg.com/opinion/articles/2018-06-07/plastic-straws-aren-t-the-problem

[108] *Id. See also* U.S. Energy Requirements for Aluminum Production, https://www1.eere.energy.gov/manufacturing/resources/aluminum/pdfs/al_theoretical.pdf

[109] *Id.*

[110] *Id.*

not accuracy. Editorial oversight is diminished. Advertisers are leaving in droves. Circulation is declining.[111]

There are, of course, situations where journalists have been terminated for reasons that have little or nothing to do with their political biases. In 2017, for example, CBS fired Charlie Rose, co-host of its popular morning newscast and widely regarded as one of the most prominent journalists in the world, after eight women accused him of sexual misconduct.[112] Rose resigned, with an apology: he said that he had been an advocate for the careers of the women with whom he had worked in the last 45 years and that he regretted his actions.[113]

Scott Pelley, a longtime anchor of the *CBS Evening News*, was likewise pushed out in the spring of 2019 because of low ratings and "friction" between him and CBS News President David Rhodes. According to others, Pelley's clear anti-Trump attitudes did not appeal to the average American.[114]

> For his part, Pelley feels that this is the best time to be a reporter, because—
> The president has given all Americans a priceless opportunity to reflect on how essential free speech and a free press are to our beloved country. There was a brief, dark, moment in our history when the government took away our freedom of expression. The Sedition Act of 1798 made it a crime for anyone to "utter" criticism of the House, Senate or the president. This was the tyranny James Madison had been determined to prevent when he wrote the First Amendment in our Bill of Rights: Congress shall make no law respecting an establishment of religion, or prohibiting the free exercise thereof, or abridging

---

[111] Dowling, D., Rejoining the Ranks of "Ex-Journalists" Isn't Just My Problem. It's Yours Too (2018), *The Shinbone Star*, https://exjournalistsunite.wordpress.com/2018/03/28/rejoining-the-ranks-of-ex-journalists-isnt-just-my-problem-its-yours-too/

[112] In 2014 *Time Magazine* named Trump one of the world's most influential people. https://time.com/collection-post/70815/charlie-rose-2014-time-100/

[113] "It is essential that these women know I hear them and that I deeply apologize for my inappropriate behavior," Rose said. "I am greatly embarrassed. I have behaved insensitively at times, and I accept responsibility for that, though I do not believe that all of these allegations are accurate," he added. "I always felt that I was pursuing shared feelings, even though I now realize I was mistaken." Longeretta, E., Charlie Rose Apologizes After Eight Women Accuse Host of "Unwanted Sexual Advances": "I Am Greatly Embarrassed" (2017), *Us Magazine*, https://www.usmagazine.com/celebrity-news/news/charlie-rose-apologizes-eight-women-accuse-host-unwanted-sexual-advances/. Rose was replaced by John Dickerson, who himself was removed after Susan Zirinsky became president of CBS News, ostensibly because of low ratings. See https://www.politico.com/story/2018/01/09/john-dickerson-replace-charlie-rose-329034 and https://thehornnews.com/youre-fired-cbs-news-gets-huge-shake-up-top-star-out/

[114] Scott Pelley is fired from CBS Evening News, Daily Mail, May 31, 2017, https://www.dailymail.co.uk/news/article-4557520/CBS-News-anchor-Scott-Pelley-pushed-job.html

the freedom of speech or of the press, or the right of the people peaceably to assemble and to petition the Government for a redress of grievances.[115]

The Sedition Act outraged Madison, who in 1800 wrote that "Congress had assumed a power that is expressly and positively forbidden by one of the [constitutional] amendments thereto: a power, which more than any other, ought to produce universal alarm; because it is leveled against that right of freely examining public characters and measures, and of free communication among the people thereon, which has ever been justly deemed the only effectual guardian of every other right.[116]

What Madison meant was that every American and his or her right to say, write, and read what they want. "Don't be misled," said Pelley. "Any constraint on 'the press' applies to every citizen's voice. 'Enemy of the American people,' in President Trump's phrase? We are the American people. Journalists bring vitality to the national conversation. We bridge differences, serve public safety, expose corruption, constrain power and give voice to the voiceless. As Madison might say today, Freedom of the Press is the right that guarantees all our other rights. No mail bomb, no president, no Congress, can alter one enduring fact of freedom—there is no democracy without journalism."[117]

In truth there is no such thing as completely unbiased news. Even if a journalist tries to report only facts, he or she must still decide which ones to include and in what order. Phrasing also differs subjectively.

Consumers of news should seek opposing points of view and draw their own conclusions. They should recognize that many of today's media outlets rely on a business model that encourages them to sensationalize news; they rely on advertising, which pays more money when they get more viewers or clicks. These types of outlets should be used only to *confirm* a source.

They should understand that the sole purpose of many sites is to amass viewership and money. And, yes, some seek to spread false information for political purposes.[118]

Journalists and editors are not unlike anyone else, but they are subject to pressures that force their narratives and reporting.

Would objective and ethical news coverage yield better results?

---

[115] Opinion: CBS' Scott Pelley on the State of Journalism Today (2018), *Stamford Advocate*, https://www.stamfordadvocate.com/opinion/article/CBS-Scott-Pelley-on-the-state-of-journalism-3435270.php
[116] Report on the Virginia Resolutions-1798. https://founders.archives.gov/documents/Madison/01-17-02-0128
[117] *See* Pelley, *supra*.
[118] Objective News Report, https://www.objectivenewsreport.com/

Politics always involves causes and comparisons of policies and personalities—but fairer coverage would mean more healthy debate—and perhaps a better outcome for the nation and its collective psyche.

References

Airaksinen, T. (2017). Prof Pledges to "Deconstruct Whiteness" in all her courses. *Campus Reform*. https://www.campusreform.org/?ID=9569

Appleby J, Schlesinger A (2003), Thomas Jefferson: The American Presidents Series: The 3rd President, 1801–1809, MacMillan, ISBN 9780805069242. https://www.amazon.com/Thomas-Jefferson-Presidents-President-1801-1809/dp/0805069240.

Avins, J. (2015). The dos and don'ts of cultural appropriation. *The Atlantic*. https://www.theatlantic.com/entertainment/archive/2015/10/the-dos-and-donts-of-cultural-appropriation/411292/

Beam, A (2020), If Lee Goes, Will Washington Follow, BOSTON GLOBE, July 8, 2020. http://www0.bostonglobe.com/opinion/columns/2017/08/20/lee-goes-will-washington-and-jefferson-follow/1NOZxRCB96888qzercMroL/story.html?p1=Article_Inline_Bottom.

Bedard, P. (2019). Mark Levin: Media 98% Anti-Trump, "Incestuous" with democrats, fake news real. *Washington Examiner*. https://www.washingtonexaminer.com/washington-secrets/mark-levin-media-98-anti-trump-incestuous-with-democrats-fake-news-real. Levin's book on the subject, UNFREEDOM OF THE PRESS, quickly became a best-seller.

Bovy, P. M. (2018). The rise of the privilege epiphany. *New Republic*. https://newrepublic.com/article/146522/rise-privilege-epiphany, and "The Perils of Privilege". *New Republic*, March 6, 2017, https://newrepublic.com/article/140985/perils-privilege-phoebe-maltz-bovy-book-excerpt

Brown, S. (2016). A brief guide to the battle over trigger warnings. *Chronicle of Higher Education*. https://www.chronicle.com/article/A-Brief-Guide-to-the-Battle/237600

Campbell, W. J. (2003). *Yellow journalism puncturing the myths, defining the legacies*.

Cohen, W. (1969). Thomas Jefferson and the problem of slavery. *Journal of American History, 56*, 503. https://www.worldcat.org/title/thomas-jefferson-and-the-problem-of-slavery/oclc/808022551

Constable, A. (2016). Hopis say Boy Scout performances make mockery of tradition, religion. *Santa Fe New Mexican*. https://www.santafenewmexican.com/news/local_news/hopis-say-boy-scout-performances-make-mockery-of-tradition-religion/article_d548665e-5767-5132-93e9-5d041b935d42.html

Cowles, C. (2012). Karlie Kloss, Victoria's secret really sorry about that headdress. *The Cut*. https://www.thecut.com/2012/11/karlie-kloss-really-sorry-about-that-headdress.html

Cultural Appropriation and Misappropriation On Your Course? SOCIETY, December 18, 2017. https://www.shadesofnoir.org.uk/cultural-appropriation-and-cultural-misappropriation-on-your-course.

Democratic hopefuls embrace new meaning for slave descendants. (n.d.). *NBC News*. https://www.nbcnews.com/politics/2020-election/democratic-hopefuls-embrace-new-meaning-reparations-slave-descendants-n976096

Dowling, D. (2018). Rejoining the ranks of "Ex-Journalists" isn't just my problem. It's yours too. *The Shinbone Star*. https://exjournalistsunite.wordpress.com/2018/03/28/rejoining-the-ranks-of-ex-journalists-isnt-just-my-problem-its-yours-too/

Dunning, J., ed. (1998). *On the air: The encyclopedia of old-time radio*. Oxford University Press. ISBN 0195076788.

Facing history and ourselves, stolen lives: The Indigenous peoples of Canada and the Indian residential schools / history in search of a name. (n.d.). https://www.facinghistory.org/stolen-lives-indigenous-peoples-canada-and-indian-residential-schools/chapter-7/cultural-genocid

Farron, S. (2017). Black slavery in the middle east. *American Renaissance*. https://www.amren.com/features/2017/02/black-slavery-middle-east/

Finley, A. (2019). Would you like guilt with your latte? *Wall Street Journal*. https://www.wsj.com/articles/would-you-like-guilt-with-your-latte-11558989233

Fitzgerald, D. (2015). White-led white shaming. *The American Spectator*. https://spectator.org/white-led-white-shaming/

Garcia, V. (2019). Mark Levin: Have you ever seen a dumber media in your life? *Fox News*. https://www.foxnews.com/politics/mark-levin-have-you-ever-seen-a-dumber-media-in-your-life

Glancy, D. J. (1979). The invention of the right to privacy. *Arizona Law Review, 21*(1), 5.

Glock Talk. (2017). White shaming is new rage on college campuses. https://www.glocktalk.com/threads/white-shaming-is-new-rage-on-college-campuses.1673770/print and https://www.wnd.com/2017/08/white-shaming-is-new-rage-on-college-campuses

Goldstein, S. (2019). Opinion: Washington Post's 10,000 Trump untruths is about 25% fake news. *Market Watch*. https://www.marketwatch.com/story/washington-posts

Gonzalez, C. A. (2018). Yes, the wars over campus politics matter. *National Review*. https://www.nationalreview.com/2018/07/war-over-campus-politics-matters/

Greenwald, G. (2017). In Europe, hate speech laws are often used to suppress and punish left-wing viewpoints. *Common Dreams*. https://www.commondreams.org/views/2017/08/30/europe-hate-speech-laws-are-often-used-suppress-and-punish-left-wing-viewpoints

History of Blackface (2021), Bloomsbury Academic, ISBN 9781501374012. https://www.black-face.com.

Is cultural appropriation a concept outside of the US? (n.d.). *Quora*. https://www.quora.com/Is-cultural-appropriation-a-concept-outside-of-the-US

Jenkins, C. L. (2012, January–October). Slavery at Jefferson's Monticello, Smithsonian NMAAHC/Monticello. https://www.washingtonpost.com/blogs/therootdc/post/slavery-at-jeffersons-monticello-slave-exhibit-opens-friday-at-smithsonians-african-american-museum/2012/01/25/gIQAk4KKTQ_blog.html

Joe Biden: President Donald Trump is literally an existential threat to America. (2019). *NBC News*. https://electionsdirectory.com/election2018/joe-biden-president-donald-trump-is-literally-an-existential-threat-to-america/

Kass, J. (2017). Harvard Study: Media has been largely negative on Trump. *Chicago Tribune*. https://www.chicagotribune.com/columns/john-kass/ct-trump-media-coverage-harvard-kass-0521-20170519-column.html

Keidar, N. (2017). Why was deputy foreign minister's lecture canceled? *Arutz Sheva*. http://www.israelnationalnews.com/News/News.aspx/237733

Kilpatrick, C. (2015). Why the right loves privilege politics. *Jacobin*. https://www.jacobinmag.com/2015/05/99-1-percent-income-inequality-class/

Lasson, K. (2019). The decline of free speech on the postmodern campus: The troubling evolution of the Heckler's Veto. *Quinnipiac Law Review, 37*, 1.

Leviticus. (n.d.). 19:27–28. Why couldn't the Jews trim their beards or their hair or get tattoos? *Evidence Unseen*. http://www.evidenceunseen.com/bible-difficulties-2/ot-difficulties/genesis-deuteronomy/lev-1927-28-why-couldnt-the-jews-trim-their-beards-or-their-hair-or-get-tattoos/

Lewis, M. P. (2018). White-shaming over the European colonial era. *National Monitor*. http://natmonitor.com/2018/12/31/white-shaming-over-the-european-colonial-era/

Longeretta, E. (2017). Charlie Rose apologizes after eight women accuse host of "Unwanted Sexual Advances": "I Am Greatly Embarrassed". *US Magazine*. https://www.usmagazine.com/celebrity-news/news/charlie-rose-apologizes-eight-women-accuse-host-unwanted-sexual-advances/

MacDonald, H. (2001). The myth of racial profiling. *City Journal*. https://www.city-journal.org/html/myth-racial-profiling-12022.html

Mailer, N. (1957). The White Negro, DISSENT. https://www.amazon.com/white-negro-Norman-Mailer/dp/B0006ED4JY.

May, C. D. (2017). Letting freedom fade. *Washington Times*. http://www.defenddemocracy.org/media-hit/may-clifford-d-letting-freedom-fade/

Miles, F., & DeMarche, E. (2019). Trump seizes on NYU professor's tweet to push change of libel laws. *Fox News*. https://www.foxnews.com/politics/trump-seizes-on-nyu-professors-tweet-to-push-change-of-libel-laws

Miller, J (2017), Protesters Cover UVA's Thomas Jefferson Statue in Black Shroud, NEW YORK POST. https://www.nypost.com/2017/09/13/protesters-cover-uvas-thomas-jefferson-statue-in-black-shroud/

Miltimore, J. (2016). University of Chicago pushes back on trigger warnings, safe spaces. *Intellectual Takeout.* https://www.intellectualtakeout.org/blog/univ-chicago-pushes-back-trigger-warnings-safe-spaces

Minter, A. (2018). Skipping straws may be hip. But there are much better ways to fight pollution. *Bloomberg Business.* https://www.bloomberg.com/opinion/articles/2018-06-07/plastic-straws-aren-t-the-problem

Mott, F (1941). American Journalism at p. 539, MacMillan, ISBN 9780415228947. https://www.amazon.com/American-Journalism-Pt2-1690-1940/dp/0415228948.

Mueller, J. (2007). Unmasking racism: Halloween costuming and engagement of the racial other. *Qualitative Sociology.* https://danielledirks.files.wordpress.com/2011/10/mueller-dirks-houts-2007-qs.pdf

NCAA. (2005). Executive committee issues guidelines for use of native American Mascots at championship events. http://fs.ncaa.org/Docs/PressArchive/2005/Announcements/NCAA+Executive+Committee+Issues+Guidelines+for+Use+of+Native+American+Mascots+at+Championship+Events.html

New York City Commission on Human Rights Issues Guidance on Gender and Transgender Discrimination. (n.d.). https://www.thenycalliance.org/assets/documents/informationitems/L__E_Alert_-_January_2016_-_NYC_Hospitality_Alliance_-_New_York_City_Commission_On_Human_Rights_Issues_Guidance_On_Gender_And_Transgender_Discrimination-C1.pdf

Ng, D. (2015). Thomas Jefferson Statue incites debate at Mizzou. *Los Angeles Times.*

Nittle, N. K. (2019). A guide to understanding and avoiding cultural appropriation. *ThoughtCo.* https://www.thoughtco.com/cultural-appropriation-and-why-iits-wrong-2834561

Non-binary gender identities fact sheet. (n.d.). https://www.apadivisions.org/division-44/resources/advocacy/non-binary-facts.pdf

North Korea calls Biden "Fool of Low IQ" over Kim criticism. (2019). *Politico.* https://www.politico.com/story/2019/05/22/joe-biden-north-korea-fool-1340544

Objective News Report. (n.d.). https://www.objectivenewsreport.com/

Opinion: CBS' Scott Pelley on the state of journalism today. (2018). *Stamford advocate.* https://www.stamfordadvocate.com/opinion/article/CBS-Scott-Pelley-on-the-state-of-journalism-3435270.php

Orwell, G. (1946). Politics and the English language. http://www.orwell.ru/library/essays/politics/english/e_polit.

Perloff, J (1988), The Shadows of Power: The Council on Foreign Relations and the American Decline, ISBN 13: 9780882791340. https://www.amazon.com/Shadows-Power-Council-Relations-American/dp/0882791346.

Pewewardy, C. (n.d.). From enemy to Mascot: The deculturation of Indian Mascots in sports culture. *Canadian Journal of Native Education, 23*(2) https://eric.ed.gov/?id=EJ605517

Pham, M. T. (2014). Fashion's cultural appropriation debate: Pointless. *The Atlantic*. https://www.theatlantic.com/entertainment/archive/2014/05/cultural-appropriation-in-fashion-stop-talking-about-it/370826/https://www.theatlantic.com/entertainment/archive/2014/05/cultural-appropriation-in-fashion-stop-talking-about-it/370826/

Philipp, J. (2018). Jordan Peterson exposes the postmodernist agenda. *The Epoch Times*. https://www.theepochtimes.com/jordan-peterson-explains-how-communism-came-under-the-guise-of-identity-politics_2259668.html

Qazcini, M. (2017). War against free speech: Canada close to passing 'Islamophobia' Law, aka Islamic Blasphemy Law". *The Daily Wire*. https://www.dailywire.com/news/12957/war-against-free-speechcanada-close-passing-michael-qazvini

Report on the Virginia Resolutions. (1798). https://founders.archives.gov/documents/Madison/01-17-02-0128

A Right Royal Ripoff. (2003). *The Age*. https://www.theage.com.au/world/a-right-royal-rip-off-20030820-gdw7zd.html

Rizzo, S., & Kelly, M. (2019). President Trump has made more than 10,000 false or misleading claims. *Washington Post*. https://www.washingtonpost.com/politics/2019/04/29/president-trump-has-made-more-than-false-or-misleading-claims/?utm_term=.817328ec4ebd

Rogers, T. (2019). Why reporters should avoid checkbook journalism. *ThoughtCo*. https://www.thoughtco.com/why-reporters-should-avoid-checkbook-journalism-2073718

Ross, R. (2013). *Clothing: A global history*. ISBN #9780745657530

Saavedra, R. (2019). Trump rips Biden: "Obama Took Him Off The Trash Heap," "Is A Dummy," "Weakest Mentally". *The Daily Wire*. https://www.dailywire.com/news/48289/trump-rips-biden-obama-took-him-trash-heap-dummy-ryan-saavedra

Scott Pelley is fired from CBS Evening News. (2017, May 31). *Daily Mail*. https://www.dailymail.co.uk/news/article-4557520/CBS-News-anchor-Scott-Pelley-pushed-job.html

Shimshock, R. (2017, June 20). *The Stream*. https://stream.org/canada-passes-law-criminalizing-use-of-wrong-gender-pronouns/. In December 2016, the Canadian Parliament passed a motion that condemned Islamophobia.

Soave, R. (2017). Black lives matter students shut down the ACLU's campus free speech event because "Liberalism Is White Supremacy". *Reason.Com*. http://reason.com/blog/2017/10/04/black-lives-matter-students-shut-down-th

Spencer, K. (2015). At New York private schools, challenging white privilege from the inside. *New York Times*. https://www.nytimes.com/2015/02/22/nyregion/at-new-york-private-schools-challenging-white-privilege-from-the-inside.html

Stephen, B. (n.d.). How to live within a black body: Ta-Nehisi Coates's "Between the World and Me". https://ibw21.org/commentary/how-to-live-within-a-black-body-ta-nehisi-coatess-between-the-world-and-me-is-a-letter-to-his-son-and-a-lesson-for-us-all/

Swarns, R., Rachell Swarns, African-American" Becomes a Term for Debate, NEW YORK TIMES, August 29, 2004; What Do Black People Want To Be Called?, Prejudice and Discrimination. https://www.prejudiceanddiscrimination.com/what-do-black-people-want-to-be-called-2.

Taylor, J. (2019). Trump launches reelection bid with promises of greatness and familiar grievances. *National Public Radio*. https://www.npr.org/2019/06/19/733904818/trump-launches-reelection-bid-with-promises-of-greatness-and-familiar-grievances

Ten facts about George Washington and slavery, George Washington's Mount Vernon. (n.d.). https://www.mountvernon.org/george-washington/slavery/ten-facts-about-washington-slavery/

The rise of the alt-right. (2016). *The Week*. https://theweek.com/articles/651929/rise-altright

Thomas Jefferson and his slaves: Making sense of the contradictions of the founding fathers. (n.d.). *Grateful American Foundation*. https://gratefulamericanfoundation.com/historic-partners/10894/

U.S. Energy Requirements for Aluminum Production. (n.d.). https://www1.eere.energy.gov/manufacturing/resources/aluminum/pdfs/al_theoretical.pdf

United Nations Declaration on the Rights of Indigenous Peoples (2007), Resolution adopted by the General Assembly. https://www.un.org/development/desa/indigenouspeoples/wp-content/uploads/sites/19/2018/11/UNDRIP_E_web.pdf.

Warren, S., & Brandeis, L. (1890). The right to privacy. *Harvard Law Review, 4*, 193.

What do black people want to be called? (n.d.). *Prejudice and discrimination*. https://prejudiceanddiscrimination.com/what-do-black-people-want-to-be-called-/

Wolf, L. (2015). Welcome to the brave new world of white shaming. *Townhall*. https://townhall.com/columnists/leonwolf/2015/02/25/welcome-to-the-brave-new-world-of-white-shaming-n1961862

Wulf, S. (2014). Why native American nicknames stir controversy sports. *ESPN Sports*. https://www.espn.com/espn/otl/story/_/id/11426021/why-native-american-nicknames-stir-controversy-sports

Young, C. (2015). To the new culture cops, everything is appropriation. *Washington Post*. https://www.washingtonpost.com/posteverything/wp/2015/08/21/to-the-new-culture-cops-everything-is-appropriation/?utm_term=.e4121b5229d4

7

In the Spirit of Queen Araweelo: An Analysis of Congresswoman Ilhan Omar's Disruption of Nativism and White Supremacy

Dorian Brown Crosby

Currently, the United States is structured to operate as a liberal democracy. It strives to uphold its ideals of freedom, equality, and justice for everyone. However, it fails miserably in many instances, especially regarding citizens pushed to the periphery of society. Previous presidents—regardless of their political ideology and their shortcomings—have always upheld the United States as a democracy. Democratic principles under President Donald Trump, however, were gravely tested. It is safe to say that for the first time in history, Americans experienced an aggressive, unapologetic move away from democracy toward authoritarian rule. A solely White racial vision of the citizenry is a component of this non-democratic direction. Trump used traditional media and social media to vilify anyone seeking elected office who opposed his political agenda. U.S. House of Representative Ilhan Omar (D-MN) was one of those people. A *Los Angeles Times* (2019) headline emphasized this point. It stated, "Rep. Ilhan Omar was a favorite Trump target. What's going on?" (Englemaryer, 2019, para. 1).

Representative Omar is a naturalized U.S. citizen. She is a Somali Muslim who arrived in the United States as an African refugee from a country the

---

D. Brown Crosby (✉)
Department of Political Science, Spelman College, Atlanta, GA, USA
e-mail: Dcrosby1@spelman.edu

© The Author(s), under exclusive license to Springer Nature Switzerland AG 2022
B. E. Johansen, A. Akande (eds.), *Get Your Knee Off Our Necks*,
https://doi.org/10.1007/978-3-030-85155-2_7

United States identifies as a terrorist State.¹ In 2018, Somalis and other citizens elected her as the first Somali to hold a U.S. Congressional seat, which made her the first woman of color to represent the state of Minnesota. She was also the first Somali elected to Minnesota's House of Representatives in 2016. She and U.S. House of Representative Rashida Tlaib (D-MI) are the first two Muslim women elected to Congress. Representative Omar is also the first Congressperson to wear a *hijab*. Culturally, as an elected official, her political participation defies traditional Somali gender roles that view politics as a male domain. Additionally, her political presence contradicts many Americans' perception of who should wield power in the United States. Representative Omar embodies everything nationalists, and White supremacists deem un-American and unworthy of citizenship (Naturalization Act, 1790). Therefore, for them, her identities also negate her right to seek elected office. Serwer (2019) states:

> No belief in American history has been more threatening to democracy, or consumed more American lives, than the certainty that only white people are fit for self-government, and the corresponding determination to exclude other citizens from the polity. (Serwer, 2019, para. 2)

The intersectionalities of Representative Omar's gender, race, religion, class, progressive liberalism, country and continent of origin, and citizenship, do not fit nativists' and White supremacists' preferred male, Anglo-Saxon, Protestant-Christian, native-born citizen description of a U.S. decision-maker (Smith, 1988, p. 234). Indeed, she is the antithesis of their perception of a U.S. citizen, member of the House of Representatives, and an American. For instance, her critics call her unpatriotic, anti-Semitic, a terrorist sympathizer, or terrorist when she vocalizes her perceived inconsistencies in U.S. foreign and domestic policy. Therefore, this analysis focuses on why Ilhan Omar's presence in U.S. politics is so unsettling to the White establishment. It also examines how former President Trump's media attacks on Representative Omar represented and perpetuated the political and social resistance toward her.

The examination begins with the feminist framework that guides the discussion on why Representative Omar's racial, gender, ideological, and

---

¹ The United Nations High Commissioner for refugees defines a refugee as a person who is forced to flee their home country because of a justifiable fear of persecution based on race, religion, ethnicity, nationality, social group membership, political engagement, and opinions (UNHCR, 2021).

For this text, State is written with a capital "S" to distinguish a sovereign entity in the international system from a state that comprises the United States of America.

religious identities agitate proponents of the status quo, while also challenging Somali cultural gender roles, like the ancient Queen Araweelo. Next, the chapter discusses the historical nativist and White supremacy public policies and social attitudes that foster resistance to Representative Omar's intersecting identities to elucidate the acceptance of President Trump's attacks on her. Finally, the similarities between Representative Omar and Queen Araweelo draw the discussion to a close. An explanation of Queen Araweelo follows.

Cultural and Feminist Context

Queen Araweelo

The legend of Queen Araweelo dates back centuries in Somali history. She is a salient cultural symbol for many Somali women. For men, she represents insubordination to a patriarchal society. For women, she is the epitome of Somali women's physical strength and intellect that a patriarchal system dismisses or restrains (Affi, 2010). There are different versions of her story. The most recounted one places her in early Somalia around the fifteenth century. As the oldest of the king's three daughters, she automatically acquired the throne. As a child, she rejected Somalia's socially constructed gender roles. She wanted the same opportunities to gain an education as Somali boys. She wanted equality for the other girls and women in Somali society as well. Therefore, when she became queen, during a time of clan conflicts, she instructed all women to abandon their roles in society and leave the domestic responsibilities to their husbands. When the women went on strike, the men had to undertake domestic duties of caring for children and the house, which created the reversal of culturally assigned gender roles. Queen Araweelo's husband objected to her positioning herself in the head of the household role and encouraging other women to do the same. She is also said to have castrated male prisoners or hung them by their private parts. These reversals of Somali traditions worked toward the matriarchal society she sought to establish.

Many Somali males favor this version of Queen Araweelo's narrative because it portrays intelligent and forceful women who demand equality as brutal and harsh. Representing the women as non-feminine and unwanted because they dared to demand equality, some could perceive as acceptable retaliation for Somali women asserting themselves. Gender equality is associated with Somali women acting outside of their socially constructed accepted behavior of quiet, tolerant, and content. Patriarchal versions of the tale depict the women as monstrous or ugly because their conduct is deemed inconsistent with such "feminine" behavior. For example, the ending of one version of Queen Araweelo's story says that her grandson killed her. In another version of her death, a member of one of the warring clans kills her. When she dies, her reign ends, and Somalia is thrust back into civil war. These endings could represent a resurgence of male dominance and the return to traditional Somali gender roles or that a woman ruling Somalia was a failure.

Older Somali women recall a different version of Queen Araweelo's life (Mohamed, 2014). It offers a narrative also centered around women's gender roles. In this account, her reign begins at the end of a bloody civil war that claimed thousands of lives due to conflict and starvation. Her husband was killed in the early years of the battle, and her only two children perished due to starvation. Her reign began when clan warfare ended. Araweelo protected the women after Somali bandits attacked them. As a result of her valor and control, the women selected her as their leader. News of the remarkable unity shown by Queen Araweelo's group of women spread across the land. Women who found themselves without male heads of households due to war and starvation joined Queen Araweelo's group of women for protection. Soon the number of women grew exponentially, and they became a powerful group of women. Their reputations for unity, protection, and strength inspired many Somali women across the country to demand gender equality in their localities.

Regardless of the different renderings of the story, Queen Araweelo remains a beacon of feminism for Somali women in the Diaspora. Likewise, she is an inspiration for Somali women like Ilhan Omar, who demand gender equality and social justice in the United States. In that spirit, Ilhan Omar confronts the malicious personal attacks on all her identities by Donald Trump and others because they disagree with her politics and reject her as belonging to the United States and Congress.

Intersectional Feminism

Intersectionality posited by Kimberlé Williams Crenshaw provides the framework for analyzing resistance toward representative Ilhan Omar and how she confronts it (Crenshaw, 1989). Crenshaw's intersectionality addresses the various sectors of discrimination African American women have endured for centuries.[2] Intersectionality explains how African American women experi-

---

[2] The term African American refers to descendants of enslaved Africans in the United States in this chapter.

ence gender, race, age, class, and other prejudices simultaneously (Jordan-Zachery, 2007). These identities represent the varied ways institutionalized biases affect African American women. Thus, African American women must overcome various hindrances to their political, economic, and social advancements. Confronting such prejudices weigh on African American women psychologically (Everett et al., 2010). Likewise, the emotional stress of combating discriminatory public policies, social attitudes, and behaviors may have physical effects.

Although Omar is not an African American, she has stated that she embraces her identities and intersectional feminism as a woman of African descent. For instance, she describes herself on her website as "Somali. Black. Muslim. Woman. Refugee. Minnesotan" (Ilhan for Congress, 2021). U.S. politics uses her African ancestry to place her in the same socially constructed racial category of "Black" with African Americans.[3] Consequently, she is susceptible to the same discrimination endured by African American women. This essay is a nascent approach to answering Julia S. Jordan-Zachery and Nikol Alexander-Floyd's question, How do Diasporic Black women engage in politics? by focusing on an African refugee woman resettled in the United States who attained the highest office for a Somali naturalized citizen (Jordan-Zachery & Alexander-Floyd, 2018, p. xvi). Therefore, intersectionality is an appropriate framework to analyze U.S. House of Representative Ilhan Omar's political presence, politics, and frankness, especially in the current eruptive, divisive political climate stoked by the Trump administration.

Somali women leaped into U.S. political history with the election of Ilhan Omar to the Minnesota State legislature. Her political rise is indicative of the influential Somali political voting bloc in Minneapolis, Minnesota, and the historical and contemporary *community informed politics* of Somali women (Brown Crosby, 2020). Her political candidacy pushed gender role boundaries within the Somali community. Therefore, Omar represents a path for women to step outside socio-cultural, patriarchally prescribed gender boundaries, and engage in a culturally designated men's domain. Her political participation represents hope for an increase in Somali women's involvement in electoral politics. Her candidacy, election, and Congressional tenure also highlight Somali women's capabilities in the public sphere (Ingiriis & Hoehne, 2013). Indeed, her participation in U.S. local, state, and national politics occurs while embracing her identities.

---

[3] "Black" in this writing denotes anyone identifying as a descendant of Africans regardless of their geographical location.

Who Is Ilhan Omar?

Representative Ilhan Omar was born in Mogadishu, the Capitol of Somalia, in 1982. She is the youngest of seven siblings. Her father and grandfather raised her after her mother died when Omar was 2 years old. Her family fled Somalia's civil war when she was 8 years old. They sought refuge in the Utange refugee camp, which is approximately 3 miles (5 kilometers) outside the port city of Mombasa in Kenya. Her father, grandfather, six siblings, and she lived in the crowded refugee camp for 4 years. After years of waiting and vetting by the United States, she and her family finally resettled in the United States in 1995. She was 12 years old.

The family first lived in Arlington, Virginia, then moved to Minneapolis, Minnesota, in 1997. After bouts with bullying in middle school in Virginia, feeling excluded by her peers, and the bickering and fights among her diverse high school classmates, Omar helped create a student diversity program at Edison High School. The program filled the need for cultural interactions among students. The exchanges provided her with early lessons in leadership, the strength in cultural diversity, coalition-building, collaboration, and identifying and addressing needs. She further nurtured her political interests by earning a degree in political science and international studies from North Dakota State University in 2011. Representative Omar continued her community involvement as a community nutrition educator with the University of Minnesota. Likewise, she was a Child Nutrition Outreach Coordinator for the Minnesota Department of Education. She also was a senior policy aide for Minneapolis City Councilman Andrew Johnson in the mid-2000s.

Minneapolis, Minnesota's Somali Community

With a Somali population of approximately 69,000, Minnesota is home to the largest Somali community in the United States (Brown, 2019). Most Somalis reside in the twin cities of Minneapolis and St. Paul that comprise the metropolitan area (Wildhie, 2021). Unfortunately, people in the United States are familiar with Minneapolis Somalis because of U.S. domestic and global anti-terrorism efforts that focus on this community. Consequently, Minnesota Somalis and Somalis in the United States remain scrutinized and labeled as terrorists. From January 2017 to 2020, former President Donald Trump's Executive Order against refugees of color consistently targeted displaced persons from Somalia, among other African and Middle Eastern countries.[4] Although U.S. Somali communities continue to face racial, religious, citizenship status, and gender discrimination, Minnesota Somalis have made tremendous political strides.

In a predominantly White district that includes Somali refugees, Somalis who have become naturalized citizens, and Somalis born in the United States, many of Representative Ilhan Omar's constituents share her culture and similar forced migration and resettlement experiences. She understands their concerns and the resources needed to reach the U.S. federally mandated goal of economic self-sufficiency for refugees. She understands Islamophobia as a Muslim woman who endures stares, questions, and criticisms. Representative Omar also receives constituent support for covering her head, arms, and legs out of respect for her religion. Not everyone, however, is a proponent for Somalis in Minneapolis, Minnesota.

Donald Trump demeaned and degraded the Minneapolis, Minnesota Somali community during his visit as a 2016 presidential candidate and as president. In a 2016 presidential candidacy rally in Minnesota, Donald Trump told his supporters,

> Here in Minnesota, you've seen first-hand the problems caused with faulty refugee vetting, with very large numbers of Somali refugees coming into your state without your knowledge, without your support or approval. Some of them [are] joining Isis and spreading their extremist views all over our country and all over the world. (Jacobs & Yuhas, 2016)

Donald Trump continued to target Minnesota Somalis after he became president in 2017. He belittled them and emboldened White supremacists to act on their prejudices against Somalis and other Muslims (Chiu, 2019). He was especially vicious toward Representative Ilhan Omar. Nevertheless, the political support she enjoyed from voters supported her current political clout in Minneapolis and with Somalis in the United States and the Diaspora. In other words, Trump's attacks against her only reinforced her connection to her constituents. For example, a BuzzFeed headline spoke to the reverse effect of his media attacks. It read, "Trump Says Minnesota Can't Stand Ilhan Omar. His Attacks Have Made Her More Popular Than Ever Back Home" (Hensley-Clancy, 2019). Therefore, Representative Omar's Progressive politics still bode well in her district. The issues she addresses affect her Somali and non-Somali voters. Resolving her constituent's concerns must occur, though, within and against the U.S.'s established discriminatory political, economic, and social system.

---

[4] The first iteration of the Executive Order banned nationals from Somalia, Sudan, Iraq, Syria, Yemen, Libya, and Iran (Trump, 2017).

Why Ilhan Omar Upsets the Status Quo

White Supremacy

White supremacy is a conjured concept of wealthy White male landowners and policy decision-makers during the formation of the United States of America. It is a historical and contemporary concept. The perception of White supremacy undergirds the political, economic, social, and psychological system that justified enslaving Africans, forcing them to reproduce, and selling their offspring to maintain a permanent, enslaved labor force.

In the 1600s, social class separated people in the colonies, not race. Things changed in 1641 when Massachusetts became the first colony to legalize the enslavement of Africans. Up to this point, indentured servants from Europe socially mingled with Africans, mostly without incident because they were all economically bound to provide labor primarily for the upper-class European settlers. In 1662, Virginia passed the hereditary slave law. It made every child born of an enslaved African woman a slave, regardless of the freedom status or ethnicity of the father (Ray, 2017; Goetz, 2009). As a result, race—based on biological appearance such as skin complexion—slowly replaced socio-economic status as the constructed category to identify colonists and European and African indentured servants. Race defined the owners and laborers in the fledgling capitalist economy. From then on, race was the determinant of who owned, controlled, and distributed resources in the colonies and the emergent United States of America.

As a social construct of wealthy, White (Anglo-Saxon), Christian (Protestant) males, poor Whites had to buy into the perception of African inferiority to justify and ensure the sustainment of a White privileged system (Allen, 2012). Non-elite White support for the status quo relied upon them believing that it was better to be White than Black. That way, poor Whites could not focus on the fact that political, economic, and social decision-making processes excluded them and their interests (Allen, 2004). Discriminatory public policies and reinforced prejudiced social attitudes continue to uphold this race-based system. W.E.B. Du Bois addressed how and why poor Whites accepted the notion in his critical 1935 essay Black Reconstruction. He wrote:

> In the South, on the other hand, the great planters formed proportionately quite as small a class but they had singularly enough at their command some five million poor whites; that is, there were actually more white people to police the slaves than there were slaves. Considering the economic rivalry of the black and white worker in the North, it would have seemed natural that the poor white

would have refused to police the slaves. But two considerations led him in the opposite direction. First of all, it gave him work and some authority as overseer, slave driver, and member of the patrol system. But above and beyond this, it fed his vanity because it associated him with the masters. Slavery bred in the poor white a dislike of Negro toil of all sorts. He never regarded himself as a laborer, or as part of any labor movement. If he had any ambition at all it was to become a planter and to own "niggers." To these Negroes he transferred all the dislike and hatred which he had for the whole slave system. The result was that the system was held stable and intact by the poor white. (Du Bois, 1935/2012, p. 9)

White male elites were in control. They owned most of the property, which meant they held economic power. White elites gave themselves sole political power, which is why legislation created by White males subjugated most of the property free Africans owned. As a result of their political and economic control, they dictated social protocol and behaviors. Also, the dominant culture reflected Western ideas, religion, government, art, governing, and other life facets. Ultimately, the socially constructed racial category of White enveloped western cultural norms. "White" became the dominant racial category, regardless of European ancestry, socioeconomic status, or religion. Although there were conflicts and hierarchies among Whites, they deemed themselves the superior race and enslaved Africans and their descendants the inferior race (Hill Fletcher, 2017). Nevertheless, despite discriminatory social, political, and economic policies, domestic terrorism by White supremacists and nativists, and psychological trauma, enslaved Africans and their descendants survived, fought, and forged a new identity as African Americans.

Ilhan Omar's, 2020 memoir with Rebeca Paley, *This Is What America Looks Like: My Journey from Refugee to Congresswoman*, discusses an example of this White entitlement African Americans defy. On page 234, she describes confronting a Minnesota legislator who objected to her Democratic Caucus election as assistant minority leader. As she is leaving his office, he states that he finally figured out what was so different about her. She says sarcastically thought it was her hijab. It was not. He said, "it's that you somehow walk into a room like you're a White man." This statement emanates from the legislator's association of Representative Omar as "Black" in addition to being a woman, Muslim, and naturalized citizen from Somalia, an African terrorist country. He viewed all her identities as inferior. Therefore, it was unacceptable to him for her to think that she could walk, think, speak or interact with a White male—the ultimate representation of power—as if she were his equal.

The verbalization of the Minnesota state legislator's worldview is confirmation that he and others like him in other state legislatures and the U.S. Congress dismiss Black women legislators (Hawkesworth, 2003). Even if they successfully pass legislation, hold leadership positions, or have seniority, Black women elected state officials still endure the message of "not belonging" (Smooth, 2001). These silent and verbal communications of an "outsider" target Black women more than Black men state lawmakers (Hedge et al., 1996). As a naturalized citizen, Representative Omar's presence as a Muslim woman of African descent elected to the Minnesota state legislature was perceived as a violation of her place in the constructed system of White privilege. Her confidence to embrace her identities and confront the lawmaker disregarded the system's assigned place of inferiority for her. Indeed, this Minnesota state legislator is a glaring example of a benefactor of a patriarchal political, economic and social system that perpetuates White privilege and views African refugees with the same contempt that White nationalists and supremacists hold for African Americans.

Once Somalis (and other African refugees) enter the United States, they are recognized based on race, not culture. As a result, Somalis are identified in the socially constructed racial category of "Black." Consequently, resettling Somali refugees into their new lives occurs within the U.S. racial system that determines the ownership, control, and distribution of resources (Brown Crosby, 2020; Delgado & Stefancic, 2017; Crenshaw et al., 1995). For example, when Somali men encounter the U.S. criminal justice system via a police stop, they face similar prejudices as African American men (Crosby & Brazelton, 2017). Therefore, to ensure their needs and interests are met, Somalis must and do engage in politics.

Addressing community concerns is how Representative Omar began her political rise in Minneapolis, Minnesota. She represents marginalized communities and those who feel excluded from U.S. politics, which helped solidify her 2020 re-election campaign base. She even re-purposed Trump's supporters' harsh July 2019 North Carolina political rally shouts of "send her back" as part of her re-election campaign slogan, which was "Send her back to Congress!" (Karnowski, 2020; McCarthy, 2019; US News, 2019). Representative Omar recalls that their shouts at the rally reaffirmed that, "They don't want me here, and my president agrees" (Omar, 2020 p. 226). Unsurprisingly, nativists disagree with her policies and advocacy on behalf of refugees, immigrants, Palestinians, and asylum seekers.[5]

---

[5] Immigrants choose to leave their home countries while refugees leave involuntarily due to war, violent conflicts, natural disasters, environmental catastrophes, or guerrilla warfare. An asylum seeker is a person from another country already in the United States requesting to remain in the United States (USCIS, 2021).

Nativism

One definition of nativism is the political protection of people indigenous to a specific territory by excluding persons identified as outsiders (Friedman, 1967). As a Somali, Muslim, refugee, woman who became a naturalized U.S. citizen, Representative Omar's identities represent everything nativists and White supremacists reject as an American.

Nativism in the United States is associated with resisting and rejecting the immigration of people from Africa, Asia, the Caribbean, the Middle East, and the Pacific Islands. However, in the United States, it is misleading to identify Whites as the first claimants to what became United States territory. As science has shown, the true nativists would be indigenous Americans. For many, the indigenous peoples in the United States and their ancestors are the only groups native to North America and thus should control the immigration debate. Yet, U.S. history records the replacement of indigenous peoples with European colonists and their descendants as the rightful owners of North American land. The colonists were also accredited with 'civilizing' the indigenous peoples. Therefore, Europeans constructed and perpetuated a U.S. history and immigration policy based on White supremacy and patriarchy. In other words, Whites made themselves the "natives."

Nativism relates to the elusive definition and description of an American. However, in the United States, the socially and politically preferred American for nativists is a person of the socially constructed White race. The term American is also associated with the ideals of liberty, justice, and equality. Since the nineteenth century, it was acceptable for European immigrants to fold into the White race if they upheld these principles. However, when it came to people of color, the fact that they abided by these principles was not enough to define them as Americans. Regardless of their subscription to the principles of liberty, equality, and justice, non-Europeans remained outside the construct of an American because they were not of the right race (Goldstein, 2017, p. 500). Thus, race became the qualifier for acceptance as an American over adherence to foundational U.S. principles.

Those in favor of restrictive immigration policies based on race seem to support former President Trump. Statements such as Donald Trump's 2016 presidential campaign slogan "Make America great again" reflected this xenophobia and isolationism. His supporters wanted to prevent more people of color from entering the United States (Young, 2017). Trump's propaganda was reminiscent of early portrayals of prejudice, stereotypes, and irrational thoughts about 'foreigners' that led to the 1882 Chinese Exclusion Act (Lee,

2002, p. 36). However, U.S. immigration policies have been biased against people of color since the country's inception. Early on, members of the U.S. Congress, who were wealthy White Protestant, Anglo-Saxon males, defined an American. That description has always favored Western and Northern Europeans (Perea, 1997, pp. 19–20). For example, ex-President Trump stated boldly his preference for immigrants from Norway instead of immigrants from Haiti and African countries in 2018 (Aizenman, 2018). Immigration and other U.S. foreign and domestic policies also excluded women. Today, Representative Ilhan Omar must combat two culturally different yet similar patriarchal systems in her advocacy for refugees, immigrants, asylum seekers, and those in temporary protective status.[6]

Double Patriarchy

Patriarchy in the United States resembles Somalia's patriarchal society. For example, socially constructed gender roles place men as head of the household. Hence, the domestic sphere is designated as the woman's domain (El-Bushra & Gardner, 2004). Women are expected to accept their roles and carry out their daily routines quietly and efficiently. Although women have made tremendous progress by raising their political voices, in the United States and Somalia, politics is still viewed as a male domain, and it is unacceptable for women to step outside of their prescribed gender roles to engage in politics (Kolshin, 2016; Jama, 1994).

Coming from a Somali patriarchal society, Representative Omar is already occupying a socio-cultural space designated for men. Her support among the youth is robust because, for them, especially young Somali women, she represents an opportunity to push past the socio-cultural boundaries that many women view as restrictive to their political progress.

Similarly, women are especially unwelcome by nativists and White supremacists in the highest U.S. government decision-making spaces. The wealthy, White, Anglo-Saxon, Protestant-Christian males who founded the United States never intended women, particularly of African descent, nor Muslims to occupy seats of power in the fledgling democratic-capitalist society. Instead, women were to remain subjects of their husband's decisions and wishes. Nevertheless, Representative Omar's political participation as a grassroots

---

[6] In the United States, Temporary Protected Status (TPS) means nationals from other countries are permitted to remain in the United States for a limited number of days designated by the federal government. Once those days have expired, those under temporary protection must return to their home country unless the United States extends their time.

candidate for elected office represents hope for increased Somali women's participation in U.S. politics.

Her candidacy and election also presented the opportunity for some Somali men to relinquish their traditional views of women's limitations and acknowledge their capabilities in the public sphere. President Trump, however, maintained a gender-biased viewpoint. His past remarks and behaviors revealed a pattern of misogyny. His tweets against Representative Omar and her progressive Democratic women colleagues of color in the U.S. House of Representatives reflected his disdain for women he perceived as stepping outside of their gendered place or are African American, Muslim, or Latin American. For instance, in Trump's disagreement with Representative Omar's fellow Democratic members of the House of Representatives Ayanna Pressley of Massachusetts, Alexandria Ocasio-Cortez of New York, and Rashida Tlaib of Michigan when they criticized Trump's border immigration policies of separating families, and his attempt to take advantage of generational and ideological splits within the Democratic party, Trump tweeted:

> So interesting to see "Progressive" Democrat Congresswomen, who originally came from countries whose governments are a complete and total catastrophe, the worst, most corrupt and inept anywhere in the world (if they even have a functioning government at all), now loudly. and viciously telling the people of the United States, the greatest and most powerful Nation on earth, how our government is to be run. Why don't they go back and help fix the totally broken and crime infested places from which they came. Then come back and show us how it is done. These places need your help badly, you can't leave fast enough. I'm sure that Nancy Pelosi would be very happy to quickly work out free travel arrangements! (Silverstein, 2019)

Representative Omar responded with this statement, "You are stoking White nationalism bc [because] you are angry that people like us are serving in Congress and fighting against your hate-filled agenda" (Omar, 2019a).

This tweet is more of a reflection of Trump's disdain for women than it is defending the United States. Although he does not mention the Congresswomen by name, the interpretation is that he was referring to the four Progressive lawmakers. More accurately, three of the Congresswomen were born in the United States, while Ilhan Omar was born in Somalia. She became a naturalized citizen at 17 years old when her father became a naturalized citizen.[7] Thus, all the Congresswomen are U.S. citizens (Rogers & Fandos,

---

[7] The legal age a permanent resident (Green Card holder) can become a naturalized citizen is 18. However, there are legal circumstances that allow for the automatic naturalization of children under 18 whose parent becomes a naturalized citizen (USCIS, 2021).

2019). The tweet mentioned above and many other Trump tweets reflected ex-President Trump's gender, race, and religious prejudices. His comments also represented the rejection of the Congresswomen because their identities were not what nativists and White supremacists preferred as an American or political leader. His objectification of women personally and publicly reinforced his political rhetoric, especially when Ilhan Omar criticized U.S. foreign policies as a U.S. House of Representatives' Foreign Affairs Committee member.

U.S.–Israeli Relations and Policies

Representative Omar is an outspoken critic of the United States' policies toward what she perceives as unconditionally supporting Israel at the expense of Palestinians. Her critique against U.S. foreign policy toward Israel highlights the historical religious undertones of U.S.–Israeli political relations and the support those policies receive from some U.S. Jewish organizations and ultra-conservatives. Former President Trump and others have even called her anti-Semitic because of her comments. For instance, in 2012, Omar tweeted, "Israel has hypnotized the world. May Allah awaken the people and help them see the evil doings of Israel" (Beaucamp, 2019). This resurfaced tweet triggered an avalanche of backlash in traditional and social media after Ilhan Omar was elected to the U.S. House of Representatives in 2018. Democratic and Republican Congresspersons issued separate bipartisan reprimands. The political and public admonishment was so intense that Omar issued an apology. She said, "It's now apparent to me that I spent lots of energy putting my 2012 tweet in context, and little energy in disavowing the anti-Semitic trope I unknowingly used, which is unfortunate and offensive" (Marcos, 2019).

In early February 2019, Representative Omar engaged in a Twitter thread responding to the backlash against comments she and Representative Rashida Tlaib made in support of the Boycott, Divestment, and Sanctions (BDS) Movement against Israel (Yglesias, 2019). House minority leader Kevin McCarthy (R-CA) tweeted his disapproval of their remarks criticizing Israel. He called for House Speaker Nancy Pelosi to reprimand the newly-elected Democratic Congresswomen for what he referred to as anti-Semitic statements. He also stated that if the Democratic leadership failed to punish the Congresswomen, he would, with a Republican legislative resolution denouncing anti-Semitism (McPherson, 2019).

In response to McCarthy's statements, Journalist Glenn Greenwald criticized McCarthy for stating that Omar and Tlaib's criticisms were worse than U.S. House of Representative Steve King's (R-Iowa) defense of White supremacy (Bresnahan, 2019). Greenwald also agreed with Omar and Tlaib's point. As a result, Omar retweeted Greenwald's post. However, her tweet also included the remark, "It's all about the Benjamins baby" (Essa, 2019).[8] When the opinion editor of *The Forward* newspaper, Batya Ungar-Sargon, asked Omar to whom her money innuendo referred in a tweet, Omar replied, "AIPAC" (Essa, 2019).[9] Omar's tweet seemed to imply that Republican lawmakers supported Israel in exchange for Jewish lobbyists' support (Nelson, 2019).

Similarly, Representative Omar's, 2019 questioning of the U.S. Jewish interest group's influence on behalf of Israel drew bipartisan contempt. Jewish communities were enraged because her comments insinuated that they were more loyal to Israel than the United States. Omar's statements drew a rebuke from Democrats and ire from Republicans, especially President Trump.

Representative Omar was once again publicly and politically chastised by many who thought her words perpetuated Jewish tropes. The backlash against the tweets was swift from Republicans and Democrats who called the tweets anti-Semitic. House Speaker Nancy Pelosi delivered a Democratic reaction urging her to apologize. Pelosi's response signaled to the Jewish community, elected officials, and Jews in Israel that Omar's comments were outside the expected supportive stance of the Democratic party toward Israel.

The next day, President Trump called for Omar to resign during a cabinet meeting. He said, "Anti-Semitism has no place in the United States Congress. And I think she should either resign from Congress or she should certainly resign from the House Foreign Affairs Committee." On Airforce One, he also said, "I think she should be ashamed of herself" (Fabian & Samuels, 2019). Trump's retort implied that Representative Omar, as a Muslim and supporter of displaced Palestinians, was against the U.S. backing of Israel. After Omar was pressured to and apologized, Trump called her apology "lame" (Siegel, 2019).

---

[8] "Benjamins" is a colloquial reference to the U.S. $100.00 dollar bill because Benjamin Franklin's face is on the note.

[9] The *Forward* is an American magazine that covers political, social, art, and other news important to Jewish-Americans. It was founded in 1897.

AIPAC stands for The American Israel Public Affairs Committee. AIPAC is a bipartisan Israeli lobbyist group. More details on the organization are on its website, which is https://www.aipac.org/about-aipac/mission

In August 2019, President Trump again displayed bias when Representative Omar and Representative Tlaib announced they were visiting Israel. President Trump responded with this tweet, "It would show great weakness if Israel allowed Rep. Omar and Rep. Tlaib to visit. They hate Israel & all Jewish people, & there is nothing that can be said or done to change their minds" (Egan, 2019).

It is unthinkable for a U.S. president to encourage a foreign country's banning of U.S. citizens from that country, especially if it is an ally. However, this irritating tweet demonstrated President Trump's affinity for global leaders who engage his racism, sexism, and Islamophobia. Politically, the tweet spoke volumes about the length he was willing to reach to ensure the continuation and support for the long-standing U.S.-Israeli alliance. Supporting Israel is crucial for Trump's evangelical constituents who perceive U.S. foreign policy toward Israel through a Biblical lens.

Conflicts between Jews and Muslims carry historical and contemporary connections to global politics. Therefore, Representative Omar's vocalization of what she viewed as discrepancies and hypocrisy in U.S. foreign policies toward Israel and Palestinians touched on highly political Middle Eastern policies in the United States. Her discussion of Jews supporting the state of Israel was problematic because supporters of U.S.–Israeli policies had a problem with the message and messenger. As a Muslim, her comments were viewed by many as anti-Semitic. That religious point of contention exists because Representative Omar practices the same religion as countries that support Palestinians and are against Israel and Jews.[10] Secondly, because she is ethnically from a country the United States identifies as one that harbors terrorists, she is labeled a terrorist. Finally, even though Representative Omar is a naturalized citizen, she came to the United States as a refugee from Somalia, making her more susceptible to suspicions regarding her patriotism and loyalty to the United States. Thus, critics rejected and scolded her and her political perspectives because she was a Muslim woman of African descent labeled a terrorist sympathizer, anti-Semite, and unpatriotic.

Islamophobia, Xenophobia and Terrorist Stereotypes

Christianity, specifically Protestantism, is the religious preference of nativists and White supremacists in the United States (Turek, 2017). U.S. terrorist groups often justify their violent actions with Biblical scriptures (Southern

---

[10] It is understood that Muslim countries practice Islam differently. The sects of Sunnis and Shi'ites are recognized as two of the most commonly known branches of Islam.

Poverty Law Center, 2017). The elite, White males who provided the political, economic, and social foundation for the United States never anticipated Muslims entering the power center. Indeed, their construction of U.S. culture excluded Islam. Thus, another point of contention between former President Trump and Representative Ilhan Omar is that she is from a country where 99% of the population practice Islam. The United States has also identified Somalia as a terrorist State. Such a declaration influences domestic and foreign policy. For example, politics and social attitudes after September 11, 2001, grew increasingly antagonistic toward Muslims. President George W. Bush's 'war on terror' provided the foundation for justifying U.S. military strikes and strategies against terrorism to bring the culprits to justice (Bush, 2001, p. 65). Consequently, Muslims in the United States were stereotyped as terrorists because of extremists in Somalia.

Muslims from Somalia and other countries in Africa and the Middle East became literal and physical casualties in the U.S.'s rightful quest to blame and punish the September 11th attackers. Somalia became the focal point for the U.S. anti-terrorism efforts in East Africa. Thus, Somali refugees were labeled as terrorists, even though U.S. vetting scrutinized for alerts that Somalis applying for resettlement were terrorists. Therefore, the resettlement for Muslim refugees was subsequently clouded with fear of Muslim terrorists entering the United States to inflict more violence. Under Trump, the guard against an internal attack on the United States forged new immigration policies that many perceived as a discriminatory travel ban against Muslims. The Trump administration disputed the accusation. Along with conservatives in the Republican party, they portrayed the Executive Order as a necessary protectant of national security. The following statement is an excerpt from President Trump's January 27, 2017, Executive Order Protecting the Nation from Foreign Terrorist Entry into the United States. It reads:

> Numerous foreign-born individuals have been convicted or implicated in terrorism-related crimes since September 11, 2001, including foreign nationals who entered the United States after receiving visitor, student, or employment visas, or who entered through the United States refugee resettlement program. Deteriorating conditions in certain countries due to war, strife, disaster, and civil unrest increase the likelihood that terrorists will use any means possible to enter the United States. The United States must be vigilant during the visa-issuance process to ensure that those approved for admission do not intend to harm Americans and that they have no ties to terrorism. (Trump, 2017, para. 3)

President Trump unleashed a barrage of images and social media content to portray Representative Omar as un-American, a terrorist sympathizer, and a Muslim to be feared. First, he claimed that Representative Omar belittled the tragic event of September 11, 2001, during a speech she delivered to the Council on American-Islamic Relations on March 23, 2019, when he tweeted that she referred to that terrible day as "some people did something." Then, to fan the flames of Islamophobia, President Trump tweeted a video with imagery of the fateful events and the words "WE WILL NEVER FORGET!" Consequently, a firestorm of media and conservative critics slammed the Congresswoman for what they viewed as proof that her loyalty was not with the United States but with Muslim terrorists. The tweet was later explained as an edited excerpt of her entire speech, which meant the wording was presented out of context. Nevertheless, Trump's erroneous tweet generated a surge in the number of death threats Omar received (Rosenberg & Epstein, 2019).

President Trump continued to make erroneous and inciting statements about Representative Omar supporting terrorists by retweeting a post showing a video of her dancing from Terrence K. Williams, a conservative comedian, and Trump supporter. The video was edited and posted as evidence of Omar celebrating the tragic September 11th events. President Trump retweeted the post accusing her of siding with terrorists by partying on the anniversary of 9/11. Representative Omar responded in a tweet that rebutted his false claim. She tweeted, "This is from a CBC event we hosted this weekend to celebrate Black women in Congress. The President of the United States is continuing to spread lies that put my life at risk" (Omar, 2019b).

The original video was posted by Adam Green, the co-founder of Progressive Change Campaign Committee, on September 13, 2019, during a Congressional Black Caucus (CBC) weekend celebration. The post and the CBC event were completely unrelated to anything concerning September 11th. Representative Omar and the CBC called for Twitter to exercise more responsibility for the death threats the retweet (and Trump's other tweets) produced by removing it (Lima, 2019; Sonmez, 2019). Nevertheless, President Trump continued to harass her and resettled Somali refugees in the United States with his dangerous tweets. Despite Trump and his supporters' (elected officials and those in the electorate) resistance to her presence in the United States and U.S. Congress, Representative Ilhan Omar perseveres in her quest for social justice. She champions women's rights, human rights, and civil rights while embracing her intersectional identities. Likewise, she continues to disrupt the notion that only White men should hold power. By walking in and speaking her truth, she continues the legacy of Queen Araweelo.

In the Spirit of Queen Araweelo

Queen Araweelo was a political figure like Ilhan Omar. Granted one is alive and one was a possible historical figure, and their positions of power and historical periods were different; their life situations were similar. Both were survivors of a war that included violence against women and a battle for women's rights. Both overcame Somali culturally defined gender roles to enter the political arena as free-thinking women. Both valued Somali traditions that anchored their existence and influenced their worldviews. Although Representative Omar's constituents include non-Somali voters, her experiences and the needs of her Somali community inform her political decisions. Queen Araweelo also used her life and the needs and interests of her people to shape her politics.

Representative Omar remains an advocate for marginalized communities and those that experience discrimination. Again, her 2020 campaign and re-election offended nativists and White supremacists because they view White males as the country's rightful leaders. As the 2016 presidential election showed, former President Trump is the leader for many White supremacists and nativists citizens. Thus, as the United States moves closer to the 2022 midterm elections and the 2024 presidential election, Trump loyalists will likely continue their political and personal attacks against her. Nonetheless, like the ancient Queen Araweelo, Representative Omar will continue to embrace her identities and transform her political and social spaces.

References

Affi, L. (2010, January 25). *Arraweelo: A role model for Somali women.* AILAMOS. https://www.somaliaonline.com/community/topic/1723-arraweelo-a-role-model-for-somaliwomen

Aizenman, N. (2018, January 12). *Trump wishes we had more immigrants from Norway. Turns out we once did.* NPR. https://www.npr.org/sections/goatsandsoda/2018/01/12/577673191/trump-wishes-we-had-more-immigrants-from-norway-turns-out-we-once-did

Allen, R. L. (2004). Whiteness and critical pedagogy. *Educational Philosophy and Theory, 36*(2), 121–136.

Allen, T. W. (2012). *The invention of the white race: volume 2: the origin of racial oppression in anglo-America* (2nd ed.). Verso Books.

Beaucamp, Z. (2019, March 6). *The Ilhan Omar anti-Semitism controversy, explained: Why her comments about "allegiance" to Israel created such a firestorm and why it all matters.* Vox. https://www.vox.com/policy-and-politics/2019/3/6/18251639/ilhan-omar-israel-anti-semitism-jews

Bresnahan, J. (2019, February 10). *Ilhan Omar ignites new anti-Semitism controversy with comments on AIPAC; The first-term Democrat suggests GOP support for Israel is fueled by campaign donations.* POLITICO. https://www.politico.com/story/2019/02/10/ilhan-omar-israel-aipac-money-1163631

Brown, H. (2019, July 23). *What is the history behind Minnesota's Somali-American community?* CBS Minnesota. https://minnesota.cbslocal.com/2019/07/23/minnesota-somali-american-population-good-question/

Brown Crosby, D. (2020). *Somalis in the neo-south: African immigration, politics, and race.* Peter Lang Publishing.

Bush, G. W. (2001). *Address to the joint session of the 107th Congress: selected speeches of George W. Bush.* The National Archives and Records Administration. https://georgewbush-whitehouse.archives.gov/infocus/bushrecord/documents/Selected_Speeches_George_W_Bush.pdf

Chiu, A. (2019, October 11). *'Stunning in ugliness & tone': Trump denounced for attacking Somali refugees in Minnesota.* The Washington Post Online.

Crenshaw, K. (1989). Demarginalizing the intersection of race and sex: A black feminist critique of antidiscrimination doctrine, feminist theory, and antiracist politics. *University of Chicago Legal Forum, 1989*(1), Article 8, 138–167.

Crenshaw, K., Gotanda, N., Peller, G., & Thomas, K. (1995). *Critical race theory. The key writings that formed the movement.* The New Press.

Crosby, D., & Brazelton, S. R. (2017). The disadvantages of African American and Somali men in the US criminal justice system. *Spectrum: A Journal on Black Men, 6*(1), 99–120.

Delgado, R., & Stefancic, J. (2017). *Critical race theory* (3rd ed.). New York University Press.

Du Bois, W. E. B. (2012). *Black Reconstruction in America: Toward a History of the Part of which Black Folk Played in the Attempt to Reconstruct Democracy in America, 1860–1880.* United Kingdom: Transaction Publishers. (Originally published in 1935 by Harcourt, Brace and Co.), p. 9.

Egan, L. (2019, August 15). Trump urges barring Omar and Tlaib, and Israel agrees. *NBC News.* https://www.nbcnews.com/politics/donald-trump/trump-urges-israel-block-omar-tlaib-visit-n1042691

El-Bushra, J., & Gardner, J. (2004). *Women and conflict: Somali women's testimonies.* Pluto Press.

Englemaryer, C. S. (2019, July 18). *Los Angeles Times.* https://www.latimes.com/politics/story/2019-07-18/trump-ilhan-omar-send-her-back

Essa, A. (2019, February 12). *Ilhan Omar's 'Benjamins' tweet storm: 'Criticising AIPAC is not anti-Semitic'.* Middle East Eye. https://www.middleeasteye.net/news/ilhan-omar-comment-israel-draw-renewed-attention-lobby-influence-washington

Everett, J., Hall, J., & Hamilton-Mason, J. (2010). Everyday conflict and daily stressors: Coping responses of black women. *Affilia, 25*(1), 30–42.

Fabian, J., & Samuels, B. (2019). *Trump calls on Omar to resign over remarks condemned as anti-Semitic*. The Hill. https://thehill.com/homenews/administration/429609-trump-calls-on-omar-to-resign-over-remarks-condemned-as-anti-semitic

Friedman, N. L. (1967). Nativism. *Phylon (1960-), 28*(4), 408–415.

Goetz, R. A. (2009). Rethinking the "unthinking decision": Old questions and new problems in the history of slavery and race in the colonial south. *The Journal of Southern History, 75*(3), 599–612.

Goldstein, J. A. (2017). Unfit for the constitution: Nativism and the constitution, from the founding fathers to Donald Trump. *U. Pa. J. Const. L., 20*, 489.

Hawkesworth, M. (2003). Congressional enactments of race-gender: Toward a theory of raced-gendered institutions. *The American Political Science Review, 97*(4), 529–550.

Hedge, D., Button, J., & Spear, M. (1996). Accounting for the quality of black legislative life: The view from the states. *American Journal of Political Science, 40*(1), 82–98.

Hensley-Clancy, M. (2019, July 25). Trump says Minnesota can't stand Ilhan Omar. His attacks have made her more popular than ever back home. *BuzzFeed News*. https://www.buzzfeednews.com/article/mollyhensleyclancy/trump-says-minnesota-cant-stand-ilhan-omar-his-attacks-have

Hill Fletcher, J. (2017). *The sin of white supremacy: Christianity, racism, & religious diversity in America*. Orbis Books.

Ilhan for Congress. (2021, June). https://ilhanomar.com/about/

Ingiriis, M. H., & Hoehne, M. V. (2013). The impact of civil war and state collapse on the roles of Somali women: A blessing in disguise. *Journal of Eastern African Studies, 7*(2), 314–333.

Jacobs, B., & Yuhas, A. (2016, November 7). Somali migrants are 'disaster' for Minnesota, says Donald Trump. *The Guardian*. https://www.theguardian.com/us-news/2016/nov/06/donald-trump-minnesota-somali-migrants-isis

Jama, Z. M. (1994). Silent voices: The role of Somali women's poetry in social and political life. *Oral Tradition, 9*(1),185, 202. https://journal.oraltradition.org/wp-content/uploads/files/articles/9i/8_jama.pdf

Jordan-Zachery, J. S. (2007). Am I a black woman or a woman who is black? A few thoughts on the meaning of intersectionality. *Politics & Gender, 3*(2), 254–263.

Jordan-Zachery, J. S., & Alexander-Floyd, N. G. (Eds.). (2018). *Black women in politics: Demanding citizenship, challenging power, and seeking justice*. SUNY Press.

Karnowski, S. (2020, January 23). *Rep. Ilhan Omar launches re-election bid with big advantages*. Associated Press. https://abcnews.go.com/Politics/wireStory/rep-ilhan-omar-launches-reelection-bid-big-advantages-68485604

Kolshin, S. A. (2016, October). 2016 elections in Somalia: The rise of Somali women's new political movements. *SIDRA Institute*. https://sidrainstitute.org/wp-content/uploads/2018/04/Somali_Womens_new_political_movements.pdf

Lee, E. (2002). The Chinese exclusion example: Race, immigration, and American gatekeeping, 1882-1924. *Journal of American Ethnic History, 21*(3), 36–62.

Lima, C. (2019, September 18). *Ilhan Omar urges Twitter to take down Trump's false tweet.* POLITICO. https://www.politico.com/story/2019/09/18/ilhan-omar-trump-twitter-9-11-1501933

Marcos, C. (2019, January 22). *Rep. Omar apologizes for tweet about Israel.* The Hill. https://thehill.com/homenews/house/426425-rep-omar-apologizes-for-tweet-about-israel

McCarthy, T. (2019, July 18). Trump rally crowd chants 'send her back' after president attacks Ilhan Omar. *The Guardian.* https://www.theguardian.com/us-news/2019/jul/17/trump-rally-send-her-back-ilhan-omar

McPherson, L. (2019, March 8). Republicans still might try to censure Omar, McCarthy suggests. *Roll Call.* https://www.rollcall.com/2019/03/08/republicans-still-might-try-to-censure-omar-mccarthy-suggests/

Mohamed, F. M. (2014). *The Somali queen: Queen Arraweelo.* Somali Media Company.

Naturalization Act of March 26. (1790). ch. 3, § 1, 1 Stat. 103 (1790) (repealed 1795). https://govtrackus.s3.amazonaws.com/legislink/pdf/stat/1/STATUTE-1-Pg103.pdf

Nelson, C. (2019, March 7). *Minnesota Congresswoman Ignites Debate On Israel And Anti-Semitism.* NPR.|MPRNews. https://www.npr.org/2019/03/07/700901834/minnesota-congresswoman-ignites-debate-on-israel-and-anti-semitism

Omar, I. [@IlhanMN] (2019a, July 14). *You are stoking white nationalism bc you are angry that people like us are serving in Congress and fighting against* [Tweet]. Twitter. https://guides.himmelfarb.gwu.edu/APA/social-media-twitter-instagram

Omar, I. [@IlhanMN] (2019b, September 14). *The President of the United States is continuing to spread lies that put my life at risk* [Tweet]. Twitter. https://twitter.com/ilhanmn/status/1174327692415705088?lang=en

Omar, I. (2020). *This is what America looks like: My journey from refugee to congresswoman.* Dey Street Books.

Perea, J. F. (Ed.). (1997). *Immigrants out!: The new nativism and the anti-immigrant impulse in the United States* NYU Press.

Ray, K. (2017). Constructing a discourse of indigenous slavery, freedom and sovereignty in Anglo-Virginia, 1600–1750. *Native South, 10,* 19–39.

Rogers, K., & Fandos, N. (2019, July 14). *Trump Tells Congresswomen to 'Go Back' to the Countries They Came From.* The New York Times. https://www.nytimes.com/2019/07/14/us/politics/trump-twitter-squad-congress.html

Rosenberg, E., & Epstein, K. (2019, April 13). *President Trump targets Rep. Ilhan Omar with a video of twin towers burning.* https://www.washingtonpost.com/politics/2019/04/13/president-trump-targets-rep-ilhan-omar-with-video-twin-towers-burning/

Serwer, A. (2019, August 5). *The Most Dangerous American Idea. The Atlantic.* https://www.theatlantic.com/ideas/archive/2019/08/reagan-nixon-trump-white-nationalism/595465/

Siegel, B. (2019, February 12). President Trump: Rep. Ilhan Omar 'should resign from Congress': lawmakers decry 'anti-Semitic comments' on Twitter. *abc News.*

https://abcnews.go.com/Politics/house-democratic-leaders-call-omar-apologize-anti-semitic/story?id=60992550

Silverstein, J. (2019, July 15). Trump tells Democratic congresswomen of color to "go back" to their countries. *CBS News*. https://www.cbsnews.com/news/donald-trump-racist-tweets-progressive-democratic-congresswomen-go-back-to-countries-nancy-pelosi-slam-president/

Smith, R. M. (1988). The "American creed" and American identity: The limits of liberal citizenship in the United States. *The Western Political Quarterly, 41*(2), 225–251.

Smooth, W. (2001, November 15-18). *African American women State legislators and the politics of legislative incorporation.* Monograph. Prepared for the Center for American Women and Politics Forum for Women State Legislators.

Sonmez, F. (2019, September 18). *Rep. Omar says Trump 'put my life at risk' after he retweeted a false claim that she 'partied' on 9/11 anniversary.* The Washington Post Online.

Southern Poverty Law Center. (2017, September 25). *Hate in God's name.* https://www.splcenter.org/20170925/hate-god%E2%80%99s-name

Trump, D. J. Executive Office of the President. (2017). *Executive order protecting the nation from foreign terrorist entry into the United States.* 13769. Federal Register.

Turek, L. F. (2017). Race and Protestantism in America. In J. Corrigan (Ed). *Oxford Research Encyclopedia of Religion.* Oxford University Press.

UNHCR: The Refugee Agency-USA, (2021 September 20). *What is a refugee?.* https://www.unhcr.org/en-us/what-is-a-refugee.html.

US Citizenship and Immigration Services. (2021a, June 30). *I am the child of a U.S. Citizen.* https://www.uscis.gov/citizenship/learn-about-citizenship/i-am-the-child-of-a-us-citizen

US Citizenship and Immigration Services. (2021b, June 28). *Refugees and asylum.* https://www.uscis.gov/humanitarian/refugees-and-asylum

US Citizenship and Immigration Services. (2021c, June 28). *Temporary protected status.* https://www.uscis.gov/humanitarian/temporary-protected-status

US News. (2019, July 18). Crowd chants 'send her back' as Trump attacks Ilhan Omar—video *Reuters & The Guardian.* https://www.theguardian.com/global/video/2019/jul/18/crowd-chants-send-her-back-as-donald-trump-attacks-ilhan-omar-video

Wildhie, A. (2021, July 15.) *HOW SOMALIS HAVE SHAPED THE STATE: Somali and Somali American Experiences in Minnesota. MNOpedia.* https://www.mnopedia.org/somali-and-somali-american-experiences-minnesota

Yglesias, M. (2019, February 11). The controversy over Ilhan Omar and AIPCAC money explained. It's only somewhat about the Benjamins. *VOX.* https://www.vox.com/2019/2/11/18220160/ilhan-omar-aipac-benjamins-kevin-mccarthy

Young, J. G. (2017). Making America 1920 again? Nativism and US immigration, past and present. *Journal on Migration and Human Security, 5*(1), 217–235.

8

Australia: Tainted Blood—Scientific Racism, Eugenics and Sanctimonious Treatments of Aboriginal Australians: 1869–2008

Greg Blyton

The Eugenics movement that emerged in England in the latter half of the nineteenth century was a continuance of European scientific racism sustained by a flotilla of political and academic ignorance that defined human credibility by hereditary traits, including colour and race. The movement may be defined as a European intellectual promotion to scientifically improve western societies through state systems that regulated human reproduction. In Australia, the foundations of the eugenics movement were heavily influenced by two former Cambridge University students, English scientists, Sir Francis Galton (1822–1911) and Charles Robert Darwin (1809–1882). It was a case of intellectual imperialism with colonial policymakers in Australia willingly adopting eugenics ideologies from their two English tutors. However, it would be unfair to blame a single man for the sanctimonious ways his concepts and theories were applied in policy and practice in relation to the treatment of Aboriginal Australians by Australian federal and state governments.

The exploitable resources here were an entire continent and its resources, as well as the human capital of its indigenous peoples. Even more tempting to the invaders were natural resources such as coal, the world's main source of climate change, and, well into the twentieth century, uranium.

There appears to be a strong tendency to downplay the influence of the eugenics movement in Australian history with a counter-claim that policy-makers were motivated by humanitarian reasons regarding the governance of

G. Blyton (✉)
Tea Gardens, NSW, Australia

Aboriginal Australians. This well-meaning cliche is also found in histories in countries outside Australia where draconian measures were used to manage indigenous and other minority group populations. According to Goering (2014), despite many negative impacts of eugenics, policymakers believed they were doing the right thing when the movement started, '…in the early part of the twentieth century by seemingly well-intended scientists and policy makers, particularly in the United States, Britain, and the Scandinavian countries'.[1] If Australian state governments meant well then the road to hell for Aboriginal Australians was paved with good intentions of insidious effect.

Like a well-kept secret, Australian eugenics histories are scarce in relation to Aboriginal Australians and appear to have slipped under the radar. The few studies conducted on the eugenics movement in Australia tend to focus on education, immigration and family planning rather than Aboriginal people. Some writers have associated eugenics with the Stolen Generation, but overall, the influence of the eugenics movement and its impact on Aboriginal Australians has been largely understated.[2] This taciturnity by historians is based on a fear to tag Australian history with the tarnished reputation eugenics gained as a result of Hitler and his extermination policies of Jewish people. According to Goering (2014), the eugenics movement attained infamy and was associated with some highly controversial actions with horrific results. She writes:

> "Eugenics" is a term loaded with historical significance and a strong negative valence. Its literal meaning—good birth—suggests a suitable goal for all prospective parents, yet its historical connotations tie it to the selective breeding programs, horrifying concentration camps, medical experiments, and mass exterminations promoted by Germany's Nazi regime in World War II.[3]

Goering's opinion is corroborated by Gilham (2001) who writes, 'What eugenics wrought in the first half of the twentieth century was far worse than anything Galton could have envisioned'. These included '60,000 court ordered sterilizations' in the United States, involuntary sterilizations in Sweden, Norway and Canada as well as 'nearly 400,000' in Germany 'to cleanse the German population of unwanted elements'.[4] So perhaps historians

---

[1] Sara Goering (2014) "Eugenics", *The Stanford Encyclopedia of Philosophy* (Fall 2014 Edition), Edward N. Zalta (ed.), URL = https://plato.stanford.edu/archives/fall2014/entries/eugenics/
[2] Ibid., p. 227.
[3] Sara Goering (2014) "Eugenics", *The Stanford Encyclopedia of Philosophy* (Fall 2014 Edition), Edward N. Zalta (ed.), URL = https://plato.stanford.edu/archives/fall2014/entries/eugenics/
[4] Nicholas Wright Gilham (2001) *A Life of Sir Francis Galton: From African Explorer to the Birth of Eugenics*, Oxford University Press, p. 2.

choose not to tarnish the Australian nation's brand name by association to the Nazi Holocausts or as Rodwell (1999) suggested, 'writing about eugenics would have meant Australian educational historians writing about themselves, and the tradition out of which they grew'.[5]

Galton is the invisible man judging by his inconspicuous absence in contemporary Australian history with zero books written about him in Australia, yet dozens of books have been crafted in the northern hemisphere remembering the life of the founder of the eugenics movement. Darwin is remembered in Australia with a city named in his honour as well as university in the Northern Territory, yet Galton seems to be the forgotten man of Australian history.[6] Galton was even knighted, by King Edward, an honour denied to Darwin by Queen Victoria following voluminous protests from religious leaders.

Yet it is Galton who has disappeared from Australian history that stands as an omission that requires attention. Galton appears to have policymakers in Australia aping his eugenic ideals that ultimately shape colonial policy and practice towards Aboriginal Australians. While Darwin's influence is indisputable, Galton also had a powerful influence in Australia and was highly regarded by colonial elites. A Melbourne newspaper reported in glowing terms of both men as well as the virtues of eugenics in 1929:

> Doubtless man will slowly progress towards the practice of Eugenics and in the meantime valuable teaching is put forward by such bodies as the Eugenics Society of London. For the last 17 years the president of this society has been Major Leonard Darwin, of the illustrious line of Erasmus and Charles Darwin, and kinsman of Francis Galton. In February last, on the occasion of the Galton dinner, Major Darwin surveyed the changes that he had noted in the field of eugenics during his long term of office.[7]

In assessing the impact of eugenics in Australia it is important to understand Darwin's influence, not only in terms of colonial thinking but also in relation to his influence on Galton. According to Taylor (2008), Darwin's book *Origin of the Species (1859)* was of monumental global significance and '…

---

[5] Grant Rodwell (1999) *Eugenics and Australian State Education 1900–1960*, PhD Submission, University of Newcastle, NSW, p. 8.
[6] Darwin is the capital city in the Northern Territory and Charles Darwin University in same city.
[7] *Science Notes by Tellurian*, The Australasian, Melbourne, 20 April 20, 1929, p. 52.

incontestably the most important biological treatise ever written; it is probably also the book that has affected most radically humanity's conception of itself'.[8]

Not only did Darwin influence Australian colonial elites, but he was also a major influence on Galton's eugenics ideals who writes 'The publication in 1859 of the *Origin of Species* by Charles Darwin made a marked epoch in my own mental development, as it did in that of human thought generally'.[9] Indeed, it would seem plausible to suggest Galton tailors an Armani suit for Darwin's monkey in *Hereditary Genius* (1869) and *Inquires into Human Faculty and its Development* (1883) by applying eugenics to natural selection and evolution.

Galton, the forgotten man of Australian history, was a person of power, influence, and wealth. He expressed his eugenics ideologies and vision of a super race in *Hereditary Genius* that was published by Macmillan in London in 1869.[10] In the following year, this book was being advertised and sold in Australian bookstores in Sydney and Melbourne.[11] He was particularly newsworthy in Melbourne, Victoria, and ongoing reports of his research were published in Australian colonial tabloids from the 1860s and throughout the twentieth century. As an explorer and adventurer, his travels in Africa were reported in Australian tabloids from a transcript of a lecture delivered by Dr. David Livingstone.[12] His work in meteorological statistics and fingerprints were also deemed noteworthy.[13] Indeed, Galton is mentioned in an alumnus of Cambridge University in the same company as Darwin and Charles Dickens.[14]

Galton's reception was only one indication of the seriousness with which eugenics was received worldwide before the 1930s, when Germany's Nazis took command of this school of thought and applied it with torturous, fatal efficiency. By the 1920s, eugenics was embraced by a range of famous figures ranging from U.S. President Woodrow Wilson to the Grand Wizards of the Ku Klux Klan.

---

[8] Taylor (2008) Andrew *Books That Changed the World: The Fifty Most Influential Books in the World*. Quercuc Publishing, London, p. 123.
[9] Galton, Francis. (1908) *Memories of My Life*, Methuen and Company London, p. 287.
[10] *Hereditary Genius: An Inquiry into its Laws and Consequences*, Mount Alexander Mail, 23 June 1870, p. 4.
[11] *Advertising*.
[12] *African Exploration*, The Sydney Morning Herald, 26 December 1864, p. 3.
[13] *The Royal Society Soiree*, The Tasmanian Times, 8 June 1870, p. 2.
[14] *England*, The McIvor Times and Rodney Advertiser, 22 September 1865, p. 2.

Galton was a pinnacle of a pseudo-scientific thinking that had been built on a premise of White supremacy which had been brewing among European social scientists throughout the eighteenth and nineteenth centuries. Indeed, eugenic ideologies were active in western societies for thousands of years prior to the eugenics movement in England in the latter part of the nineteenth century. As noted by Goering, 'philosophers have contemplated the meaning and value of eugenics at least since Plato recommended a state-run program of mating intended to strengthen the guardian class in his *Republic…*'.[15] Galton draws much of his inspiration from the ancient Athenian culture, including the term 'eugenics' which he coined in *Inquires into Human Faculty and its Development* in 1883. He writes:

> …what is termed in Greek, eugenes namely, good in stock, hereditarily endowed with noble qualities…We greatly want a brief word to express the science of improving stock, which is by no means confined to questions of judicious mating, but which, especially in the case of man, takes cognisance of all influences that tend in however remote a degree to give to the more suitable races or strains of blood a better chance of prevailing speedily over the less suitable than they otherwise would have had. The word eugenics would sufficiently express the idea…[16]

Galton refined this pseudo-science by adding an elaborate system of statistics that measured human traits and applied a quantitative methodology which became a critical component of the eugenics movement. Men such as Karl Pearson and Charles Davenport were inspired by Galton's methodology and developed the eugenics movement into the 1920s where human worth was judged by a mathematical coding of hereditary traits. Galton laid the groundwork of a statistical approach that identified positive and negative hereditary traits. He stated in *Hereditary Genius*:

> The theory of hereditary genius, though usually scouted, has been advocated by a few writers in past as well as in modern times. But I may claim to be the first to treat the subject in a statistical manner, to arrive at numerical results, and to introduce the 'law of deviation from an average' into discussions on heredity.[17]

---

[15] Sara Goering (2014) "Eugenics", *The Stanford Encyclopedia of Philosophy* (Fall 2014 Edition), Edward N. Zalta (ed.), URL = https://plato.stanford.edu/archives/fall2014/entries/eugenics/

[16] Francis Galton (1883) *Inquires into Human Faculty and its Development*, Macmillan Publishers, London, p. 17.

[17] Galton, Francis 1892. *Hereditary Genius An Inquiry into its laws and consequences*. Macmillan and Company and New York, London, p. vi.

Galton added mathematics to a narcissistic self-adulation of the White race where skin colour was a critical hereditary trait in a colour wheel of White superiority. According to theorists such as Galton, the human race was graded by a hierarchy of five colours which in descending order of importance were white, yellow, red, brown and black. Galton's obsession with colour was intense. On 13 September 1871, he penned a letter to Darwin of his laboratory work in London, which reveals colour experiments with rabbits and rats that might struggle to meet contemporary ethical standards. The following is an extract from one of those letters which highlights Galton's attempts to breed colour:

> My dear Darwin:
> Latterly, my whole heart has been in rats;—white, old English black, & wild grey, which I have had Siamesed together in pairs, chiefly white & wild grey (for my stock of black is low) in a large number of cases—perhaps 30 or 40. pair. These have been fairly successful (sic) operations so far as the well-beig (sic) & comfort of the animals is concerned but unexpected, out-of-the way accidents, are continually occurring. One pair died after 63 (about) days of union and injection into the body of the one passed into the other… Ever sincerely your's [sic] | Francis Galton[18]

It was a commonly accepted premise among European theorists that the superior race was White. French aristocrat, Count Arthur de Gobineau (1816–1882) claimed that civilized states of humanity could only be achieved by drawing upon the superior hereditary qualities of the White race. His writings wax lyrically of the virtues of the White race in *An Essay on the Inequality of Human Races (1853–1855)*:

> Such is the lesson of history. It shows us that all civilizations derive from the white race, that none can exist without its help, and that a society is great and brilliant only so far as it preserves the blood of the noble group that created it, provided that this group itself belongs to the most illustrious branch of our species.[19]

So, it can be seen Galton had predecessors such as Gobineau who promoted alleged scientific claims built on beliefs of alleged White superiority. With the advent of the eugenics movement in Australia, a sense of cultural

---

[18] *From Francis Galton 13 September 1871*, Darwin Correspondence Project, University of Cambridge accessed @ https://www.darwinproject.ac.uk/letter/DCP-LETT-7938.xml on 29022020.
[19] Arthur de Gobineau, *An Essay on the Inequality of Human Rcaes (1853–1855)*, translation Adrian Collins, Heinemann, London 1915, p. 210.

superiority was augmented by one of racial superiority. The eugenics movement also provided a scientific rationale that morally endorsed a militant conquest of Aboriginal Australians. This fatalistic view of Aboriginal Australians was further compounded when colonial elites adopted Galton's theory of a superior race.

The notion of a superior race did not originate with Galton but was found in the thinking of several European theorists, including Gobineau, who promoted concepts of a superior Aryan race as a pinnacle of human evolution. But it was Galton's eugenics movement and in particular his first publication *Hereditary Genius* (1869) that introduced the concept of a superior race in the Australian colonies. In this book, Galton expressed a notion of a superior race which he linked to 'breeding' in relation to the superiority of ancient Athenian Greek society.[20] In his opinion, the Athenians were a superior race and at least two grades above his own degenerative White society. He writes:

> Now let us attempt to compare the Athenian standard of ability with that of our own race and time. We have no men to put by the side of Socrates and Phidias, because the millions of all Europe, breeding as they have done for the subsequent 2, 000 years, have never produced their equals. They are, therefore, two or three grades above…as much as our race is above that of the African negro.[21]

Galton's intent was not only to bring social reform in England but also to promote his eugenics ideals to British colonies abroad such as Australia. He writes, 'No nation is a higher human breed more necessary than to our own, for we plant our stock all over the world and lay the foundations of the dispositions and capacities of future millions of the human race'.[22] Galton proposed improving human racial stock through state regulation could be achieved by promoting positive human hereditary traits and eliminating negative traits. In this highly subjective proposal, racial origin was either a positive or negative trait and Aboriginal Australians were classified in the latter category.

He warned social policy in *Hereditary Genius* that poor governance led to the fall of the Athenian culture and cited random marriages and influxes of migrants as the main reason 'why this marvellously gifted race declined'.[23] According to Galton, at their peak, the Athenian culture had 'purity of race'

---

[20] Francis Galton (1883) *Inquires into Human Faculty and its Development*, Macmillan Publishers, London, p. 17.
[21] Francis Galton, *Hereditary Genius*, p. 342.
[22] Francis Galton (1909) *Essays in Eugenics*, The Eugenics Society London, p. 34.
[23] Ibid., pp. 342, 434.

and 'morality' which was absent in his present English society. This was due to too frequent marriages of the criminal and feeble-minded lower classes who were multiplying at a disturbing rate, as well as emigration. Galton also proposed that race and skin colour were critical indicators of hereditary credibility and there is little doubt his pedigree ideology left a legacy in Australia which historians have chosen to forget.

However, it should be noted that scientific racism and beliefs of White superiority preceded Galton. When the First Fleet arrived at Sydney in January 1788, British colonists saw Aboriginal Australians as a primitive, savage and uncivilized people compared to their own sophisticated, enlightened and civilized culture. According to Broome (2008), 'The first Europeans in Australia were generally ethnocentric in their attitudes to the Aborigines rather than racist, since most of them claimed a cultural superiority over the Aborigines, not a racial superiority'.[24]

A sense of cultural superiority was found in the archival records of officers of the First Fleet such as Lieutenant David Collins, second in charge of the infant penal colony. He rates Aboriginal people at Sydney by a cultural standard of civilization when he writes, 'That they are ignorant savages cannot be disputed; but I hope they do not in the foregoing pages appear to be as wholly incapable of becoming one day civilized and useful members of society'.[25]

Likewise, another officer of the fleet, Captain Watkin Tench, was assessing Aboriginal Australians based on cultural, not racial qualities when he writes. 'If they be considered a nation whose general advancement and acquisitions are to be weighed, they certainly rank very low, even in the scale of savages'.[26] This subjective ethnocentric evaluation of Aboriginal people at Sydney by colonial leaders provided as rationale for occupation and possession. As noted by Broome (2008) '…the Aborigines were denigrated as "savages" and the Europeans glorified as "pioneers." In this way European colonization was justified.'[27] In the following decades, there were few changes in the opinion of British colonists who still believed they were 'civilized' compared to Aboriginal Australians who remained 'primitive savages'.

---

[24] Richaed Broome (2008) *Aboriginal Australians: Black Responses to White Dominance 1788–2001*, Allen and Unwin Pty Ltd, Crows Nest, NSW, p. 92.

[25] Collins, David: (1975) *An Account of the English Colony of New South Wales, With Remarks on the Dispositions, Customs, Manners, etc, of the Native Inhabitants of that country*, two volumes, this facsimile edited by Brian H. Fletcher MA PhD published in association with The Royal Australian Historical Society by A. H. & A. W. Reed, Sydney, p. 513.

[26] Tim Flannery (1999) *1788 Watkin Tench* Text Publishing Company Melbourne Victoria, p. 252.

[27] Richard Broome, *op cit*, p. 95.

Even those occasional colonists who were humane towards Aboriginal people such as Robert Dawson, inaugural manager of the Australian Agricultural Company at Port Stephens, NSW, still considered they were 'primitive savages'. He believed that numerous acts of violence were committed against Aboriginal People and wrote, 'The natives are a mild and harmless race of savages; and where any mischief has been done by them, the cause has generally arisen, I believe in bad treatment by their white neighbours'.[28]

Dawson observed large numbers of orphan children in Aboriginal communities impacted upon by violence on these bloody frontiers where Aboriginal Australians were '…treated in distant parts of the colony, as if they had been dogs, and shot by convict—servants, at a distance from society, for the most trifling causes'.[29] On rare occasions when Europeans were punished by colonial courts for violent crimes against Aboriginal people such as massacres or murder, it would lead to protests from sectors of the wider community.

For example, a colonial newspaper published a response to the hanging of seven colonists for massacring at least twenty Aboriginal men, women and children in 1838. This was known as the Myall Creek massacre. The following extract highlight a derogatory comment by a colonist who argues that 'white men' should not be punished for murdering Aboriginal people:

> I look on the blacks (said this enlightened and philanthropic juror) as a set of monkies, and the earlier they are exterminated from the face of the earth the better. I would never consent to hang a white man for a black one. I knew well they were guilty of the murder, but I, for one, would never see a white man suffer for shooting a black.[30]

Yet, violence was denied by Darwin when he visited Sydney in January 1836 where he claimed that the decimation of Aboriginal communities of southeastern central New South Wales was a result of Aboriginal cultural deficit rather than British violence and militant conquest. Darwin had gained a position aboard the HMS Beagle (1831–1836) as a naturalist and conducted studies throughout many parts of the world culminating in his previously mentioned *Origin of the Species* (1859).[31]

---

[28] Robert Dawson: *The Present State of Australia: Descriptions of the Country, Its Advantages and Prospects with Reference to Emigration and a particular Account of the Manner, Customs, and Condition of its Aboriginal Inhabitants*, Smith, Elder and Co, Cornhill, London, 1831, pp. 57,58.

[29] Ibid.

[30] *To the Editor of the Australian*, The Australian, 18 December 1838, p. 2.

[31] Pike, Douglas, *Australian Dictionary of Biography*, Melbourne University Press, Victoria, pp. 286, 287.

While the Beagle was anchored in Sydney Harbour (January 12 to January 30), he ventured into the surrounding districts where he observed Aboriginal people on a number of occasions admiring their spear throwing skills and pacific disposition. Nevertheless, Darwin classified Aboriginal Australians as belonging to the 'savage' races of humanity basing his assessment on cultural factors. He writes:

> They will not however cultivate the ground, or even take the trouble of keeping flocks of sheep, which have been offered to them; or build houses & remain stationary-Never the less, they appear to me to stand, some few degrees higher in civilization, or more correctly a few lower in barbarism, than the Fuegians.[32]

Having learned of the rapid declines of Aboriginal populations from communications with colonists, he attributes this demise to alcohol, disease and food deprivation. He writes, 'When the difficulty is procuring food is checked of course the population must be repressed in a manner almost instantaneous compared to what can take place in civilized life'.[33]

Darwin saw these population declines as natural processes where 'The variety of man seem to act on each other; in the same way as different species of animals—the stronger always extirpating the weaker'.[34] He does not attribute these declines as any fault of colonists such as violence, but conveniently explains the fall as a part of a natural evolution where there is a 'survival of the fittest.' To Darwin 'fittest' was synonymous with 'civilization'.

Galton never visited Australia, but still manages to have an opinion of Aboriginal Australians which was highly derogatory. He writes, 'I possess a few serviceable data about the natural capacity of the Australian, but not sufficient to induce me to invite the reader to consider them'.[35] Whereas Darwin applied his theories to species extinction, Galton applied his to race extinction and explained the destruction of Aboriginal populations as inevitable and a result of their lack of capacity to adapt efficiently to 'civilization'. He proposed that rapid population declines of Indigenous populations were the fate of the races of 'savage man' and stated:

---

[32] Nicholas, F.W. & Nicholas, J.M. (2008) *Charles Darwin in Australia*, Cambridge University Press, Melbourne, pp. 40, 41.
[33] Ibid.
[34] Ibid.
[35] Galton, Francis, 1892, *Hereditary Genius An Inquiry into its laws and consequences*, Macmillan and Company and New York, London, pp. 339, 340.

The number of the races of mankind that have been entirely destroyed under the pressure of the requirements of an incoming civilization, reads us a terrible lesson. Probably in no former period of the world has the destruction of the races of any animal whatever, been effected over such wide areas and with such startling rapidity as in the case of savage man. In the North American Continent, in the West Indian Islands, in the Cape of Good Hope, in Australia, New Zealand, and Van Diemen's Land, the human denizens of vast regions have been entirely swept away in the short space of three centuries, less by the pressure of a stronger race than through the influence of a civilization they were incapable of supporting.[36]

Frontier conflicts between Aboriginal and colonial people during the latter part of the eighteenth century and most of the nineteenth century had left Aboriginal Australians dispossessed of land and resources and in a vulnerable state of absolute poverty. This 'dying race' theory promoted by Darwin and Galton provided a placebo for any guilt felt by colonists for their murderous acts as well as a convenient alibi to explain the swift Aboriginal population declines. Colonial violence, miscegenation, dispossession, poverty and disease are diminished as secondary causes with the victims and their culture the primary cause of their own demise.

According to Broome (2008), 'Like God and Providence, Social Darwinism provided a neat "explanation" which absolved the whites from any blame for the decline of the Aborigines'.[37] By the 1930s, such beliefs were further embellished by some theorists who claimed Aboriginal Australians were a 'dying race' before British settlement which had only accelerated an inevitable extinction.[38] As summed up by popular Australian writer Ion Idriess in 1934, 'the primitive is dying out. It is absurd here to blame the white man'.[39]

Following this albeit incidental conquest the dilemma for colonial administrators was how to manage the survivors. From the 1860s the 'smoothing of the dying pillow' became a theme of so-called humanitarian sectors who governed state Aborigines Protection Boards.[40] Despite strong evidence to the contrary one school of thought maintain a view that these boards held good intentions and meant well for Aboriginal people. For example, *The Encyclopedia of Aboriginal Australia* (1994) described these boards as 'Official instrumen-

---

[36] *HEREDITARY GENIUS:AN INQUIRY INTO ITS LAWS AND CONSEQUENCES* BY Francis Galton, Mount Mail Alexander Mail, Victoria, 23 June 1870, pp. 334, 335.
[37] Richard Broome, *op cit*, p. 96.
[38] *Our Aborigines*, The Sydney Morning Herald, NSW, 5 June, 1937, p. 12.
[39] *Farewell Stone Age; The Passing of the Aboriginal*, The Western Australian, 20 August 1934, p. 19.
[40] *Aborigines Protection Society*, South Australian Register, Adelaide, 26 June, 1860, p. 3.

talities for shielding Aboriginal people and their societies from the influence of non-Aboriginal people'.[41] While it was likely some officials were philanthropic that such a claim would have more merit if the standards of care were higher rather than a paternal 'smoothing of the dying pillow'.

When the history of these boards is considered, it becomes evident their policies and subsequent amendments run a closely parallel Galton's progressive views on eugenics. Blood quantum becomes a critical component in the way policies were designed and significant terminology changes emerged based on hereditary traits, particularly skin colour. This was particularly evident in changes to the terms colonial administrators identified Aboriginal Australians in legislation which were based on hereditary traits, colour and blood quantum.

In the Victorian Aborigines Protection Act (1869), an Aboriginal person was defined in the following way: 'Every aboriginal native of Australia and every aboriginal half-caste or child of a half-caste, such half-caste or child habitually associating and living with aboriginals, shall be deemed to be an aboriginal within the meaning of this Act'.[42] An amendment to this act in 1886 proposed to exclude 'half castes' and regardless of the intent Aboriginal people are being defined by blood quantum. As noted by Boucher (2015), 'The latter piece of legislation drew a distinction between "full-bloods" and "half-castes" in ways that now seem to presage the biological, social and cultural engineering whose legacies troubled the memory politics of late twentieth-century Australia'.[43]

Language was clearly another key indicator of the influence of eugenic ideologies in Australia with descriptions of Aboriginal Australians closely aligned to Galton's measurement of hereditary traits including colour and race. Early colonial records identify a distinct change in word sets compared to the language used in the late nineteenth and first half of the twentieth century. In the early years, colonists referred to Aboriginal Australians as aborigines, Blacks, natives, savages and occasionally mulatto. But in the latter half of the nineteenth century, 'full-blood' and 'half caste' becomes the prominent adjective used when describing Aboriginal Australians, not only in legislation but also

---

[41] Ed's: Davison, G. Hirst, J., & Macintyre (1999) *The Oxford Companion to Australian History*, Oxford University Press, Melbourne, pp. 226, 227.

[42] *AN ACT To provide for the Protection and Management of the Aboriginal Natives of Victoria [11th November 1869]*, see section 8 accessed @ https://www.foundingdocs.gov.au/resources/transcripts/vic7i_doc_1869.pdf

[43] Boucher, Leigh & Russell, Lyn (2015) *The 1869 Aborigines Protection Act: Vernacular ethnography and the governance of Aboriginal subjects*, Settler Colonial Governance in Nineteenth-Century Victoria, p. 65.

in colonial tabloids throughout Australia.[44] By the early twentieth century, there were further additions to the vernacular with the emergence of 'quadroon' and 'octaroon'; human classification was being defined by blood quantum. These new terms in legislation and media indicate the influence of eugenics ideologies.

From the early twentieth century, these blood quantum definitions of Aboriginal Australians were becoming increasingly frequent in colonial tabloids. A colonial newspaper reported on 29 November 1911, that an Aboriginal man who was charged with trespass after having a disagreement with the mission manager. The report stated, '*The Quadroon Sentenced*: On Friday before the Hon. E. A. T. Perry, P.M., the adjourned case of G. Davis charged with being a quadroon and residing on an Aboriginal Reserve without a permit came up for decision'.[45] The essence of Aboriginal governance was being judged by alleged blood quantum. In 1930, a self-confessed 'octaroon' appeared in Alice Springs court with a lawsuit against the Aborigines Protection Board in the Northern Territory for wrongful arrest. It was reported on 14 October 1937:

> Alleging that she had been unlawfully detained at the half-caste Institution, Zoe Reid, of Alice Springs claimed £250 from Dr. P. J. O'Reilly, deputy Chief Protector of Aborigines, and Mr. William McCoy, superintendent of the half-caste institution, at Alice Springs court today. The plaintiff said she was an octaroon and therefore was not liable to enter the Institution, but the defendants claimed that the plaintiff was a quarter caste and therefore subject to control.[46]

This blood quantum definition of Aboriginal people reflected the influence of Galton's eugenics ideologies where hereditary traits were the public perception of Aboriginal Australians. In the political domain amendments to the nineteenth century, Aboriginal Protection Acts refined definitions of Aboriginal people like specimens in a science laboratory. For example, in 1869 the Victorian Government defined Aboriginal people in *The Act* as 'full-bloods' and 'half castes', but amended this legislation in 1915 stating, 'All quadroon, octoroon and half-caste lads over 18 on the Board Stations shall leave and shall not be allowed on the Station or reserve again except for brief

---

[44] See https://trove.nla.gov.au/newspaper/search?adv=y
[45] *The Quadroon Sentenced*, Macleay Chronicle, Kempsey, NSW, 29 November 1911, p. 8.
[46] *Unlawfully Detained Octaroon's Claim, Alice Springs, Wed.* The National Advocate, Bathurst, NSW, 14 October 1937, 2.

visits to family at the discretion of the Station manager'.[47] New terminology had emerged in tandem with the influences of eugenics such as 'quadroon' and 'octoroon', but the Aborigines Protection Board went a step further defining Aboriginal people in NSW as 'any admixture of aboriginal blood'.[48]

By the turn of the nineteenth century, Australian colonial society had become xenophobic in pursuant of a eugenics-driven vision of a superior race which crystallized as the White Australia Policy. The perceived threat to 'racial purity' was two-fold, being emigration of undesirable races and Aboriginal Australians. As noted by Thompson (2010), 'As it entered the twentieth century, Australia boasted that its stock was 98 per cent British', a 'corollary of British Australian nationhood', which aimed to preserve 'racial purity'.[49] In order to prevent other races from migrating to Australia a 'Dictation Test…in any unspecified European language' proved an '…effective means of exclusion'.[50]

The emergence of notion of 'racial purity' and a super race was not exclusive to Australia within the eugenics movement and its principle ideal of breeding a superior human race rapidly spread across the globe from England to Europe and America.[51] When Australia became a federation in 1901 the White Australia Policy emerged as a vision of a Utopian society ideally occupied by fair-skinned Caucasians and devoid of 'coloured people'. This ideal is closely aligned with Galton's theories of 'racial purity' as Australian colonial elites became were immersed in a Frankenstein world of pseudo-science.

During the early twentieth century, Australian colonial society had a vision of a White Australia inspired by the eugenics movement. 'Coloured races' were seen as an impediment in attaining this goal as the *Daily Telegraph* reported in March 1905, 'In the absolute sense of the phrase a White Australia cannot exist until all the aborigines have perished from the face of the continent. The numbers dwindled rapidly during the first century of British occupation. They are dwindling rapidly now. And in West Australia, according to Dr. Roth, their disappearance is being hastened by the treatment they have experienced at white hands'.[52]

---

[47] Repealed 1928 accessed @ https://www.humanrights.gov.au/sites/default/files/content/education/bringing_them_home/Individual%20resources%20and%20activities/8_laws_vic.pdf
[48] https://www.legislation.nsw.gov.au/acts/1909-25.pdf
[49] John Thompson (2008) *Documents That Shaped Australia: Records of a nation's Heritage*, Murdoch Books, Australia, p. 204.
[50] Ibid.
[51] Sara Goering, *op cit.*
[52] *The White Australia Policy*, The Daily Telegraph, Sydney, 1 March 1905, p. 6.

In Australia, a Commonwealth Federation of the states in 1901 was established based on the Australian Constitution that excluded Aboriginal Australians from the national population census. Furthermore, the Australian Immigration Act (1901) provided strong evidence that Galton's eugenics ideologies had gripped the mindset of Australian policymakers. Both sets of legislation created strong barriers to 'coloured races' migrating to Australia, including Asians and Pacific Islander peoples and maintained a fatalistic view of Aboriginal Australians.[53]

The Australian Constitution excluded Aboriginal Australians as citizens by effectively leaving them as wards of the states. This was one strategy in a plan, namely the White Australia Policy, to protect Australian colonial society from racial and moral turpitude through segregation and exclusion of 'inferior races'. As reported by *The Bulletin*, 'If Australia is to be a country fit for our children and their children to live in, we must KEEP THE BREED PURE. The half-caste usually inherits the vices of both races and the virtues of neither. Do you want Australia to be a community of mongrels?'[54]

In 1911 Galton's death was widely communicated by newspaper throughout Australia commemorating the passing of this 'great' English scientist. He was described as a 'noteworthy man' and 'one of the greatest scientific inquirers of his time'.[55] In the following decades, Galton's legacy was not forgotten. Sydney's first eugenics society was formed in 1912 and a Racial Hygiene Association in 1926 which named one of its main objectives as the 'Education of the community on eugenic lines'.[56] It is often assumed that the eugenics movement was dominated by men, but the Racial Hygiene Association had a number of outspoken and influential women, including Ruby Rich, Mary Montgomerie Bennett and Bessie Rischbieth.[57]

As Rodwell (1999) claimed the Eugenics movement has largely been overlooked within the Australian academic milieu possibly because it was a little too close to home. For instance, academics, including a vice-chancellor from the University of Melbourne were reported to have made up a significant number of memberships in the Eugenic Society of Victoria which was active from 1936 to 1961. Anatomy faculties were eugenicist havens with large collections of Aboriginal remains objects of critical studies which reinforced

---

[53] John Thompson (2010) *op cit*, p. 204.
[54] Richard Broome, *op cit*, p. 97.
[55] *Francis Galton*, Daily Standard, Brisbane, 11 September 1914, p. 8.
[56] Memorandum and Articles of Association of the Racial Hygiene Association of New South Wales THE COMPANIES ACT 1899, Booth and Sons Pty Printers, Sydney, p. 3.
[57] Ann Rees (2015) *'THE QUALITY AND NOT ONLY THE QUANTITY OF AUSTRALIA'S PEOPLE' Ruby Rich and the Racial Hygiene Association of NSW*, Australian National University, Canberra.

theories of the inferiority of Aboriginal people and the supremacy of White people.[58]

It is often claimed by Australian historians that the formation of Aborigines Protection Boards was motivated by an ambition to protect Aboriginal people from hostile sectors of the White community. The was inferred in the Aborigines Protection Act in Victoria in 1869 which claimed to 'provide for the Protection and Management of Aboriginal Natives of Victoria'.[59] However, such mission statements lack credibility when it was considered how they were treated or 'managed' under the auspices of these boards. According to Howie-Willis (1994), these boards restricted liberty, influenced marriages and took control of Aboriginal children:

> All the boards acquired coercive powers which they exercised to restrict the people's freedom to travel, own property and possessions, live and work where they wished [to] form marital relationships, raise their children as they pleased and use the land on the reserves.[60]

To some degree, these boards probably did ward off negative elements of White society, but the only ones who were being really protected in this arrangement were White colonists. The missions, reservations and commons removed Aboriginal people from Australian society and acted as buffers to protect White people from undesirable traits of colour and moral turpitude. Most of these open-air concentration camps served to manage the eventual extinction of the 'full-bloods'. According to one of the few Aboriginal spokespersons in NSW in the first half of the twentieth century, the extinction of Aboriginal Australians was only a matter of time if prevailing conditions continued. Jack Patten expressed these concerns when he addressed a small gathering at Town Hall, Sydney in January 1938 where he protested against the appalling conditions of Aboriginal Australians under the NSW Aborigines Protection Board. He stated:

> White people do not realize the terrible conditions of slavery under which our people live in the outer districts…women of our race are forced to work in return for rations, without other payment. Is this not slavery? We say that it is a disgrace to Australia's name that our people should be handicapped by under-

---

[58] Cervini, Erica, *A Theory out of Darkness*, Sydney Morning Herald, 13 September, 2011 (see education section).

[59] *AN ACT To provide for the Protection and Management of the Aboriginal Natives of Victoria [11th November 1869]* accessed @ https://www.foundingdocs.gov.au/resources/transcripts/vic7i_doc_1869.pdf

[60] David Horton (ed.) (1994) *The Encyclopedia of Aboriginal Australia Volume 1*, Aboriginal Studies Press, Canberra, p. 22.

nourishment and poor education, and then be blamed for being backward. We have had 150 years of the white men looking after us, and the result is, our people are being exterminated.[61]

It would appear that Patten's plea for improved conditions for Aboriginal Australians fell on deaf ears. A decade later Aboriginal Australians continue to live in poverty in many parts of Australia as the number of 'full-blooded' continues to decline. On August 28, 1947, a newspaper reported a need to improve housing for Aboriginal Australians in New South Wales (NSW). The report stated that the number of 'full-blooded' had significantly declined and Aboriginal Australians were living in an appalling state of poverty on the fringes of rural towns. It stated, 'All of the 10,616 aborigines in NSW are completely detribalised, with no inclination to return to their native state. Only 584 of that number are full-blooded. Many are living in tumble down shacks on the outskirts of country towns'.[62] Absolute poverty characterized the lives of thousands of Aboriginal Australians and was one of the primary reasons given by Aboriginal administrators to justify the removal of Aboriginal children.

During the latter part of the nineteenth century, a eugenic approach was applied to Aboriginal children who became a subject of legislation which gave state boards the power to physically remove them from their parents. In Western Australia legislation was passed which gave the board the power to remove Aboriginal children who were indentured from 6 to 21. Similar legislation was passed in other states such as NSW which collectively resulted in the removal of thousands of Aboriginal children. According to a contemporary government department:

> The Aborigines Protection Act (NSW) 1909 gives the Aborigines Protection Board power to assume full control and custody of the child of any Aborigine if a court found the child to be neglected under the Neglected Children and Juvenile Offenders Act 1905 (NSW). The Aborigines Protection Amending Act (NSW) 1915 gives power to the Aboriginal Protection Board to separate Indigenous children from their families without having to establish in court that they were neglected.[63]

---

[61] John Thompson (2010) *Documents that Shaped Australia: Records of a Nations Heritage*, Pier 9 imprint of Murdoch Books Pty Ltd Australia, p. 240.
[62] *New Home Plan for Aborigines by Beth Henderson*, The Sun, Sydney, 28 August 1947, p. 18.
[63] http://www.nma.gov.au/online_features/defining_moments/featured/aborigines_protection_act

Following the NSW Aborigines Protection Act (1909), a number of state institutions were established to house Aboriginal children removed from their parents by government authorities. These institutions were gender segregated and isolated Aboriginal children from their parents and siblings and were little more than vocational training centres producing lowly paid unskilled labour for sectors of White society. One of the most infamous of these institutions was Kinchela Boys Home which was established in 1909 and located at Smithtown on the north coast of NSW.

Its principal purpose was to train Aboriginal boys in agricultural skills like fencing, tractor driving and similar farm work. A female equivalent institution was seen at Cootamundra Domestic Training Home, which was located in south-western NSW and specialized in preparing Aboriginal girls for domestic servitude. Both of these institutions remained in operation until the late 1960s under a system that denied these children any contact with their families and guaranteed abuse and a lowly paid unskilled job. A former inmate of Cootamundra portrayed a bleak picture of life in the state-run Aboriginal girls institution when she recalled:

> As I was growing up, being abused was a natural thing in the home. I got into trouble because I tore me dress and I had to wear a potato bag dress for a week. The most abused that, in the home was mostly being whipped by—whipped with the wire, you know, the leather strap wrapped around it. They usually hit you with that. And then you'd be thrown into the box room. And then the deputy maiden, she was cruel, she used to hit me over the head a lot. I used to cop that a lot. As I was growing up. But then you know, you don't think of those sort of things as abuse. You think it's just a natural that that's life.[64]

The removal of Aboriginal children was a major part of a eugenics-driven plan to breed out Aboriginal Australians, through a selection process determined by colour and blood quantum. Galton's eugenics movement found many disciples in Australia who embraced his eugenics ideals and theories of race and hereditary traits, especially skin colour. In the 1920s, Adelaide anthropologist Herbert Basedow proposed that the 'taint'[65] of colour in Aboriginal Australians could be bred out reflecting the White Australia Policy of seeking racial purity. He stated in 1825:

> We may now understand why it is that the quarter-blooded progeny from the union of a half-blooded woman with a European father is always lighter in

---

[64] http://stolengenerationstestimonies.com/testimonies/993.html
[65] Herbert Basedow (1925) *The Australian Aboriginal*, F.W. Preece and Sons, Adelaide, p. 59.

colour than its mother, and the octoroon even lighter. Union further on the European side produce children practically White; and no case in on record where the colour in a later generation reverted back to the darker again. The latter, we know, happens only too often when there is a taint of the Negroid blood running in a family, even though the mixing of race took place generations back.[66]

Throughout the 1920s and 1930s, governments engaged these hereditary and blood quantum theories underling the ever-present influence of the eugenics movement. In the Mosely Royal Commission in Western Australia in 1935 the 'half-caste problem' was presenting challenges for Aboriginal administrators and proposals of segregation were central in the dialogue. The Royal Commission reported:

Dealing with half-castes—and this clause has chief reference to these people—Dr. Bryan has spoken strongly against the mating of half-castes with half-castes, on the ground that it will perpetuate the black and coloured elements. And still, 'without advocating the marriage of whites and half-castes, he does support the mating of a half-caste with a coloured person higher in the white scale.[67]

These so-called scales of human worth based on 'coloured elements' show that eugenic ideologies had a firm grip on the mindset of administrators of these boards who supposedly protected and managed the well-being of Aboriginal Australians. To these administrators, the road to racial purity required 'the scientific breeding-out of black blood from half-castes by marrying them to whites or persons with a greater proportion of white blood'.[68]

However, the piece DE resistance of the eugenics movement occurs when the state Aborigines Protection Boards unanimously agree at a national summit in April 1937 to launch a plan to 'breed out' the Aboriginal population in Australia. The Canberra Times reported the outcome of this meeting of church leaders, anthropologists and politicians and its eugenics agenda:

Following a resolution adopted by the conference, efforts will be made to merge half castes and quadroons with the white Australian population, and Commonwealth assistance will be sought to this end. After an exhaustive discussion the meeting decided "that this conference believes that the destiny of the

---

[66] Herbert Basedow (1925) *The Australian Aboriginal*, F.W. Preece and Sons, Adelaide, pp. 59,60.

[67] Report of the Royal Commissioner appointed to investigate, Report, and Advise upon matters in relation to the Condition and Treatment of Aborigines, Western Australia, 1935. p. 8 located @ https://aiatsis.gov.au/sites/default/files/docs/digitised_collections/remove/93309.pdf

[68] *Half-Castes: Scientific Breeding-Out*, The Central Queensland Herald, 15 April 1934, p. 15.

natives of aboriginal origin, but not of full blood, lies in their ultimate absorption by the people of the Commonwealth, and therefore recommends that all efforts be directed to that end."[69]

From this time onward, the removal of Aboriginal children increased concomitant with the growth of public and private foster care often in the form of institutional settings. This separation process was deemed a success by Western Australian Aboriginal Protectors such as A. P. Neville who stated, 'The object of the homes is to care for and train quarter-caste children and children of lighter colour who cannot be provided for elsewhere, and I regard these institutions as being of great value'.[70] Neville summed up the status of Aboriginal Australians in 1948:

> The fact that the full-blood people are apparently dying out, while the coloured people are increasing and all the time slowly approaching us in culture and colour, lessens our problem of assimilation. Though the full-bloods constitute about sixty-five per cent, and the coloreds thirty-five per cent of the total native population, the former have decreased by some ten thousand in the past decade, while the latter have grown by nearly a like figure.[71]

About 50 years later a government inquiry was launched concerning the removal of Aboriginal children during the twentieth century. The *Bringing Them Home Report (1997)* investigated this Stolen Generation and found that the removal of Aboriginal children was an official practice in all Australian states. The full impact of the Stolen Generation is unknown due to incompetent record-keeping with estimates ranging from 20,000 to 100,000. While Australian historians haggle over the numbers and ages of these children it cannot be denied that these were policies and practices strongly aligned with eugenics ideals. A Human Rights Commission reported:

> The full scale of removals is still not known because many records have been lost. The Bringing Them Home Report Commission estimated that between one-tenth and one-third of all Aboriginal and Torres Strait Islander children were removed from their homes during the years in which forcible removal laws operated. Subsequent research by Professor Robert Manne estimated the number of Aboriginal and Torres Strait Islander children removed from their families in the period 1910–1970 was closer to the figure of one in ten, or between

---

[69] *Merger with the White People*, The Canberra Times, 23 April 1937, p. 4.
[70] Moseley Royal Commission 1935, p. 15.
[71] A.0.Neville (1947) *Australia's Coloured Minority: Its Place in the Community*, Currawong Publishing Pty Ltd, Sydney, p. 58.

20,000 and 25,000 individuals. The policies of the Protection Act were designed to 'assimilate' or 'breed out' Indigenous people. The forced removal of Aboriginal and Torres Strait Islander children from their families was official government policy from 1909 to 1969. These children became known as the 'Stolen Generations'.[72]

On 13 February 2008, former Prime Minister Kevin Rudd made a national apology to the survivors of the Stolen Generation on behalf of the Federal Parliament which recognized the failures of past government policies and treatments regarding Aboriginal Australians. He stated:

> We apologize for the laws and policies of successive Parliaments and governments that have inflicted profound grief, suffering and loss on these our fellow Australians. We apologize especially for the removal of Aboriginal and Torres Strait Islander children from their families, their communities and their country.[73]

Rudd fell short of mentioning that these policies and practices were shaped by eugenicist ideals which manifested as a systematic attempt by government authorities to biologically dissolve Aboriginal communities through segregation and removal.[74] Galton the intellectual imperialist had left a legacy.

---

[72] https://www.humanrights.gov.au/publications/face-facts-2012/2012-face-facts-chapter-1#Heading475
[73] John Thompson (2010) *op cit*, p. 340.
[74] Thompson, John (2010) *Documents that Shaped Australia: Records of a Nations Heritage*, Pier 9 imprint of Murdoch Books Pty Ltd, Australia.

9

Brazil and Australia: Indigenous Peoples and the Fires This Time

Bruce E. Johansen

In 2019 and 2020, the signature malady of the global climate crisis became raging wildfires. They occurred with previously unknown size and ferocity in California, the Amazon Valley, and Australia (as well as many other places, from Chile, to Siberia)—and even, as an indication of things to come, along the west coast of Greenland. In each of the wildfires' major sites, environmentalists ran smack into political systems dominated by established nationalistic interests with mindsets (whether the USA's Donald Trump, Brazil's Jair Bolsonaro, or Australia's Scott Morrison) at least a century and a half old, which is to say able, with straight faces, to deny that greenhouse gases are a problem at all. In each case, this denial was fed by copious amounts of political cash from established interests that have become very good at combining oil, gas, and coal to produce copious corporate profits. If carbon dioxide had a sense of irony (or even a sense of humor) it would have been roaring with laughter. As it is, in our world, greenhouse gases have no political preferences, no emotions, no envy, and no sense of guilt about ruining the Planet Earth. All they do is hold heat.

Similarly, when the worldwide virus crisis exploded in March, Bolsonaro extended his adamant sense of absolute denial to it, comparing the disease that had killed tens of thousands of people by that time to the common cold.

B. E. Johansen (✉)
Communication and Native American Studies, University of Nebraska at Omaha, Omaha, NE, USA
e-mail: bjohansen@unomaha.edu

He said that Brazilians had a unique ability to resist such things. Soak them in sewage, and they survive, he said. "God is Brazilian," he told supporters. "The cure is right there" (Londoño, et al., 2020a, A-5). Brazilians rose *en masse*, pounding pots and pans in the streets to oppose what they regarded as insane statements by Bolsonaro. An impeachment movement grew apace. Several state governors instituted stay-at-home orders. Twitter, Facebook, and Instagram deleted Bolsonaro's rants against social distancing as a threat to public health. In the *favelas* (slums) of Rio de Janeiro, drug gangs and community leaders imposed nighttime curfews and urged residents to restrict outdoor movements to essential tasks. Bolsonaro accused the news media of inciting panic to undermine his influence. By May, the undertakers could not commission burial places fast enough to accommodate the dead, who were collapsing in the hundreds per hour.

Brazil's Wild Northwest

Aside from Bolsanaro's utter lack of knowledge about the natural sciences (COVID vaccines would turn people into crocodiles, he said), his environmental knowledge walked the thin edge between slim and none. His brain seemed stuck in neutral at about 1850. He seemed to be stuck in the era of cowboys and Indians, Manifest Brazilian destiny, versus indigenous peoples. Nationalism in Brazil has been aimed at the Amazon Valley, of the same sort of self-congratulation that propelled the United States across North America in the nineteenth century during the era of "manifest destiny," a belief that God had granted the United States a mandate to conquer the "wild west." The same sort of belief was the guiding animus of Brazil's new far right, under strongman leader, Jair Bolsonaro. It is a nationalism that fells trees, builds cities in the jungle, and seizes the lands of indigenous peoples, styled in 1830 by US President Andrew Jackson as the lamp that lights the lights of civilization in the wilderness.

Bolsonaro has asserted that vaccines will turn people into crocodiles, while accelerating logging of their lands by outside trespassers. Members of the tribes believe that he wants to exterminate them, by any means necessary. At the same time, beginning early in 2020, the virus began to ravage their villages. Mining and large-scale farming also are on his list, as Bolsonaro makes no secret of the fact that he is re-enacting the United States' westward movement almost two centuries ago. "Where there is Indigenous land," he has said, "there is wealth underneath it" (Londaño & Casado, 2020).

Bolsonaro thus is wiping out protections of Native peoples outlined in Brazil's Constitution, as he cripples funding of the federal National Indian Foundation, an agency charged with upholding the laws protecting indigenous peoples in Brazil. As with Donald Trump, Bolsonaro ignores clauses of the Constitution that run contrary to his desires. He has declared that indigenous peoples who wish to live on their own lands practicing their own cultures impede development of a modern economy, a line that easily could have been lifted from US President Andrew Jackson's beliefs in 1830, except that Bolsonaro's language has a raw edge that Jackson lacked. Indians who wish to remain on their own lands are "prehistoric creatures," he has declared. In 1998, when he was a lawyer, Bolsonaro said it was a "shame that the Brazilian cavalry hadn't been as efficient as the American one, which exterminated the Indians" (Londaño & Casado, 2020). (He did not mention that European colonists tried to exterminate Brazil's indigenous peoples early in the sixteenth century.) The original peoples, who numbered 5 to 10 million before the Portuguese arrived, were reduced to 70,000 by war, enslavement, and disease by the 1950s.

To all of these imported threats to indigenous peoples' survival, in 2020 was added the coronavirus (COVID-19), which ravaged their territories as it inflected hundreds of thousands of people in the rest of Brazil. One of the foremost vectors of this disease was more than 1000 workers for the federal Indigenous health service (Sesai) who tested positive for the virus. The employees of this agency are charged with *protecting* indigenous peoples' lives. "the tell-tale symptoms began in late May [2020], wrote Manuela Andreoni, Ernesto Londoño, and Letícia Casado of the *New York Times*. "about a week after government medical workers made a routine visit to the Kanamari Indigenous community in a remote part of the Amazon [Valley] elderly members of the group were struggling to breathe" (Andreoni et al., 2020, A-15). Testing supplies became very scarce, so asymptomatic carriers of COVID-19 may have been infecting indigenous peoples without knowing it.

Coronavirus has been only the latest wave of imported maladies to ravage the indigenous peoples of Brazil and Australia. Urbanization and industrialization continue in the Amazon Valley, large parts of which are no longer rain forest. It has become Brazil's wild northwest, the fastest-growing region, in terms of human presence, in South America, the "world's last great settlement frontier" in the words of Brian J. Godfrey, a geography professor at Vassar College and co-author of *Rainforest Cities* (Romero, 2012). All of this has implications for the world's carbon cycle, as both climate change and human agency convert a long-time carbon dioxide "sink" into a net source of greenhouse gases. Deforestation in the Amazon Valley, once regarded as the "lungs of the world," by 2015 had become one of Earth's largest sources of greenhouse gas emissions.

Forest cover in Brazil continued to decline at record rates in 2016 and 2017, according to satellite data compiled by Global Forest Watch, despite efforts by the government (at that time) to curtail illegal logging, and as corporations such as Cargill with large operations there pledged to farm in a more sustainable manner. Despite all of these efforts, smaller farmers continued to clear land, and large tracts were burned because of recurrent drought. "The big concern is that we are starting to see a new normal, where fires, deforestation, and climate change are all interacting to make the Amazon more flammable," said Mikaela Weisse, a research analysis with Global Forest Watch (Plumer, 2018). The fact that the Amazon watershed is no longer the "world's lungs," as a matter of dire concern to the entire Earth, beset as it is by steady warming of the atmosphere also caused by human emissions.

Survival International reported on December 1, 2015 that "Wildfires are raging through the Brazilian Amazon, destroying vast areas of forest on the eastern fringes of the 'earth's lungs,' [which until recently absorbed carbon dioxide and produced oxygen]. The fires are reportedly being started by illegal loggers, in retaliation for tribal peoples' [the Awá tribe's] efforts to defend their territories and keep the invaders out. They threaten one of the few remaining areas of pre-Amazon forest in Brazil, the last environment of its type in the world". More than half of the Awá's indigenous peoples' land had been destroyed by fire by 2019.

Deforestation Slows, then Accelerates Again

In recent years, until 2019, Brazil had slowly been reducing forest loss, but in an uneven fashion. Between 1995 and 2005, forest loss in the Brazilian Amazon averaged 19,500 square kilometers per year—roughly the area of Israel. By 2013, that rate had been cut by 70%, even as beef and soya production continued to grow. A combination of measures was applied: corporate commitments coupled with strong laws, satellite surveillance, and robust enforcement, restrictions on access to credit for farms and ranches in counties with high deforestation, the creation of protected areas and indigenous reserves, and improvements in land tenure and governance. Brazil's federal government worked closely with the beef and soya industries, and nongovernmental organizations, as well as their international partners. In 2008, for example, Norway committed US$1 billion to Brazil because it wanted to demonstrate practical new ways to protect forests globally. "Even so," according to one report., "Brazil's progress is fragile—deforestation in the Amazon has increased over the past 18 months [2014–2015]".

After a decade during which Amazon deforestation stalled, by 2016 it was accelerating again. Growing worldwide demand for several crops (most notably soybeans) was increasing the size of farms, and burning of jungle habitats. According to the *New York Times* (Tabuchi et al., 2017): "In the Brazilian Amazon, the world's largest rain forest, deforestation rose in 2015 for the first time in nearly a decade, to nearly 2 million acres from August 2015 to July 2016. That is a jump from about 1.5 million acres a year earlier and just over 1.2 million acres the year before that, according to estimates by Brazil's National Institute for Space Research….In Bolivia… deforestation appears to be accelerating as well." About 865,000 acres of land have been deforested, on average, annually for agriculture since 2011, an area nearly the size of Rhode Island, according to estimates from the nongovernmental Bolivia Documentation and Information Center.

Deforestation in the Amazon Valley shot up abruptly between July, 2018, and July, 2019, most of it during the beginning of Jair Bolsonaro's term as president. The net loss of forest, 3769 square miles (12 times the size of New York City) represented a 30% increase from the previous year, and the largest annual net loss since 2009 (Londoño & Casado, 2019, A-4). By the end of 2019, Brazil's deforestation, most of it clear-cutting for farming or the timber harvest, reached a third of all the forest loss in the world. Global Forest Watch estimated that Brazil's forest loss in 2019 released more than 2 billion tons of carbon dioxide into the atmosphere per year, more than the emissions from all of the vehicles on United States roads and highways in the same period. Bolivia lost 720,000 acres during 2019, double the loss in 2019 (Fountain, 2020b, A-14).

Much of the increase in deforestation during 2018 and 2019 was illegal, although such "unlawful economy" harvests have very rarely been prosecuted. Gilberto Camara, secretariat (director) of the Group on Earth Directions (a public and private policy analysis' group), said "From the point of view of future generations the loss of biodiversity and the rise of [carbon dioxide] emissions are huge setbacks that will have enormous consequences over the next 10, 15 years, and beyond" (Londoño & Casado, 2019, A-4).

In Brazil, fires sprung up in unexpected places. On March 8, 2020, a NASA satellite took images of two large fires in Pantanal, in southwestern Brazil, usually a wetland. The fires also occurred during the rainy season. Drought had dried up many of the area's swamps, and killed some of the wide variety of wild fauna in a national park. Heretofore, occasional small fires set by farmers or lightning had been snuffed by a wet environment, but as a witness to the climate crisis, that has now changed (Fire, NASA, 2020).

"We're facing the risk of runaway deforestation in the Amazon," eight former environment ministers in Brazil wrote in a joint letter during May, 2019, arguing that Brazil needed to strengthen its environmental protection measures, not weaken them (Casado & Londoño, 2019). Bolsonaro, who was sworn in as Brazil's president on a development platform in 2019, called figures on deforestation compiled by agencies of his government "lies," a tactic that US President Donald Trump used when information with which he disagrees is denounced as "fake news." Bolsonaro argued that non-Brazilians (especially environmentalists) should shut up about the demise of the Amazon rainforest. To him, their concern is "environmental psychosis" (Casado & Londoño, 2019). Bolsonaro tried to shut down the federal government's Environment Ministry, which compiles deforestation statistics, but Brazilian farmers, who were concerned about an international boycott of Brazilian products, urged him to back down. Instead, he cut the Environment Ministry's budget by 24% a year, along with similar cuts in other agencies. At one point, Bolsonaro blamed the actor Leonardo DeCaprio for the fires with no evidence other than his advocacy of environmental causes.

By 2019, fires were on the march again, as record amounts of former forest were being consumed. On paper, Brazil has many environmental regulations, most involving fines. Even before Bolsonaro came to power, many environmental fines were ignored; all but 5% were contested in court, a process that can take several years, as deforestation continues. Bolsonaro and his environment secretary, Ricardo Salles, wanted to suspend environmental enforcement by reducing or eliminating the fines entirely.

Deforestation of the Amazon Valley had been decreasing before Bolsonaro was sworn in as Brazil's president on January 1, 2019. In fact, it had been "at the heart of Brazil's environmental policy for much of the past two decades" (Casado & Londoño, 2019). Brazil had slowed and nearly stopped logging in the Amazon, earning international accolades because of its role in producing more than 20% of the world's oxygen and mitigating global warming. Bolsonaro cut environmental regulation of logging and other forms of commercial exploitation. Before August of 2019, when fires swept large areas of the Amazon Valley, deforestation had increased 39% in 1 year. By June of 2019, deforestation increased 80% over June 2018 (Casado & Londoño, 2019). Bolsonaro's government encourages logging, instead of imposing fines and destroying logging equipment used in what used to be protected areas. Bolsonaro believes that any attempt to curb exploitation in the Amazon is part of an international conspiracy to hamper his country's economic growth.

"The horrific fires in the Amazon are a result of the pro-business, anti-environmental policies and racist rhetoric of Brazil's President, Jair Bolsonaro," Sonia Guajajara, an indigenous leader from Brazil, told Survival International. "The predatory behavior of loggers, miners and ranchers has been getting much worse under the anti-indigenous government of Jair Bolsonaro, who normalizes, incites and empowers violence against the environment and against us. The sheer scale of Bolsonaro's violence against humanity and nature means we have to redouble our efforts to defeat the terrifying threat his administration poses, not only to the indigenous peoples of Brazil, but to our entire planet." (Brazil, 2019). All of this was associated with Bolsonaro's attempts to reduce the impact of FUNAI, Brazil's indigenous affairs department, which also enables expansion of agribusiness and extractive industries' to exploitation of natural resources on indigenous territories.

Soon after fires spread across the Amazon Valley, Bolsonaro asserted without evidence that environmentalists were lighting them so that they could blame his policies for allowing more burning for farming and urban development.

> The Brazilian president, Jair Bolsonaro, has accused environmental groups of setting fires in the Amazon as he tries to deflect growing international criticism of his failure to protect the world's biggest rainforest. A surge of fires in several Amazonian states this month followed reports that farmers were feeling emboldened to clear land for crop fields and cattle ranches because the new Brazilian government was keen to open up the region to economic activity.

Alt facts, anyone? Actually, Brazil's president was engaging in a cover-up. In Brazil, cutting down trees at the current rate could lead to runaway deforestation, President Bolsonaro has been sticking to his promise to cut enforcement, which will lead to more fires.

Wildfires and Greenhouse Gases

Brazil's Amazon was not the only large region facing direct assault by fire during the last half of 2019, nor is Bolsonaro the only national chief executive seeking political points by fanning the flames. Donald Trump behaved not unlike Bolsonaro, both leveraging massive ignorance of climate science. Trump's quest to eliminate rules that restrict the fossil fuel industry has homed in on California as a particular target. That's in part because of California's unique role as a beacon of the nation's climate change policies. "Some signature federal climate change programs Mr. Trump seeks to dismantle originated in the state", said Jerry Brown. This situation has "brought home to many Californians the brutal reality of a changing climate and cemented the feeling that politicians far away in Washington are not just ignoring it but actively working to undermine their efforts to address it," reported the *New York Times*. "The seas are rising, diseases are spreading, fires are burning, hundreds of thousands of people are leaving their homes," Jerry Brown, the former California governor, told a hearing in Washington, D.C. "California is burning while the deniers fight the standards that can help us all....This is life-and-death stuff," he said (Fuller & Davenport, 2019). Climate change will also bring more specific threats to California. Increased drought could devastate the state's farmers, warming waters could close fisheries and spur the growth of toxic algae, and rising seas could inundate the homes of 200,000 Californians and erode two-thirds of California beaches by 2100," Brown concluded (Fuller & Davenport, 2019).

As fires raged in the Amazon Valley and many other locations around the Northern Hemisphere during the summer of 2019, scientists were becoming more concerned that such fires could accelerate global warming past a global "tipping point," when the entire Earth would be trapped in an unstoppable feedback loop that will accelerate warming to unstoppable and unbearable levels. The Amazon Valley is of particular interest because of its declining role in producing a large proportion of Earth's oxygen. The increase in wildfires is a worldwide problem, however, on all landmasses (except Antarctica). By the time the Amazon Valley fires burned out in 2019, California and other parts of the United States were scorched by raging fires spawning "firenadoes" from 80 mile-an-hour Santa Ana winds in California. The California fire season began earlier than usual in 2020 (as has become the new "normal," and by mid-August fierce flames were scorching larger areas in some areas than 2019, along with wild "firenadoes," during the fiercest blazes. Heat-driven fires rise so quickly that they form thunderheads, dropping rotating clouds. This kind of weather phenomenon had been all but unknown until recent years. Along with fast-moving wildfires came rolling electrical blackouts affecting hundreds of thousands of people.

Until recent years, wildfires were a seasonal affliction in California and elsewhere in the United States West. Nearly all notable fires did most of their damage between about mid-October and February. Following about 2010, however, the fire season began to expand. By 2021, fire in the Los Angeles basin, not many miles from the city itself, were igniting in mid-May. The anticipated severity of the fire season to come was being forecast by the measure of drought in seasons when much of Southern California had once been green and moist. During mid-May of 2021, a sizable fire ravaged parts of an up-scale neighborhood called Pacific Palisades. "We normally don't have this type of fire, this size of fire, in May, Ralph M. Terrazas, chief of the Los Angeles Fire Department, said. "I think [that] we really have to think about brush fires as a year-round challenge" (Fuller, 2021).

Forests to Ashes

As more of the Amazon's forests are felled for economic development, turning rich, oxygen-producing areas to savannah and ashes, the area on balance has become a net carbon dioxide producer rather than a net source of oxygen. In scientific language, the Amazon is becoming a source of CO_2 rather than a "sink." This change, together with similar trends in other fire-ravaged areas around the world are rapidly adding to the proportion of CO_2 in the world atmosphere at a rate equal to or greater than human emissions, which have been increasing since the dawn of the fossil fuel age two centuries ago.

Wildfires are only one dramatic illustration of the rainforest's conversion. Another cause that accelerates the conversion is the felling and burning of trees by ranchers expanding range for their cattle. Roughly 80% of Brazil's beef is consumed domestically; the rest is exported as far away as China, an enormous potential market (Kraus et al., A-8). International environmental organizations have taken notice of expanding Amazon beef operations and proposed boycotts, with little effect.

Fazenda Canaa established a 270,000-acre cattle ranch in 2013, converting jungle to savannah in a Brazilian rainforest reserve, where such enterprises are nominally forbidden. World environmental issues do not concern him. The land is fertile and produces plentiful grass for his 400 cattle. Roughly 200 million cattle were being raised in Brazil on about 173,800 acres of land—an area the size of California, Massachusetts, and New Jersey combined, according to the Yale School of Forestry. Cattle ranching in Brazil provides $6 billion a year in export revenues and 360,000 jobs (Krauss et al., 2019, A-8).

The inauguration of President Jair Bolsonaro in January, 2019, was taken by Amazon ranchers and farmers as a boon that allowed them to expand their operations. "If there was [anything to be] crystal-clear about," said Jeremy M. Martin, vice president for energy and sustainability at the Institute of the Americas, "It was that he [Bolsonaro] is 100% willing to compromise the Amazon [rainforest] for economic growth" (Krauss et al., 2019, A-9).

Deforestation rates are highly sensitive to government environmental policies in Brazil and surrounding countries. Between 2004 and 2012, for example, Brazil's deforestation rate plunged by about 80% due to restrictions by the government. After that, with Bolsonaro in charge, forest protection was dismissed by Bolsonaro, as a communist or Marxist plot. As policies changed and deforestation surged, Brazil's actions influenced those of smaller countries on its borders.

Carbon Sink to Carbon Source: Scientific Work

Just as a lush tropical rainforest augments precipitation, deforestation can enhance drought. D.V. Spracklen and colleagues wrote in *Nature* (2012: 282): "Vegetation affects precipitation patterns by mediating moisture, energy and trace-gas fluxes between the surface and atmosphere. When forests are replaced by pasture or crops, evapotranspiration of moisture from soil and vegetation is often diminished, leading to reduced atmospheric humidity and potentially suppressing precipitation. Climate models predict that large-scale tropical deforestation causes reduced regional precipitation."

When most of the land is forested, trees retain moisture, and feed it back into the atmosphere, creating more rain in a feedback cycle. Once a certain proportion of the rainforest has lost its cover, reduced rainfall increases the chances of drought, which enhances more fires in a feedback loop. Scientists have calculated that deforestation takes on a momentum of its own when roughly 20 to 25% of forest cover has been lost. By the end of August, 2019, in the Amazon Valley, this figure had reached 19.3% (Fisher, 2019, A-6). The point at which the Amazon Valley may reach "dieback," also a self-perpetuating cycle, maybe 2020 or 2021, one or two fire seasons away. The Amazon in total holds 100 billion tons of carbon dioxide. All the coal-fired power plants on Earth emitted 15 billion tons of CO_2 in 2017 (Fisher, 2019, A-6). "The Amazon is thought to be reaching a point past which it will begin driving its own destruction," wrote Max Fisher in the *New York Times* (2019: A-6).

The Amazon is very sensitive to drought, according to a 30-year study, published March 6, 2009, in *Science*, which provides the first scientific evidence that a drying environment causes increasing carbon loss in tropical forests as it kills trees (Amazon Carbon, 2009). "For years the Amazon forest has been helping to slow down climate change. But relying on this subsidy from nature is extremely dangerous," said Professor Oliver Phillips, from the University of Leeds, in the United Kingdom, who was the lead author of this research. "If the earth's carbon sinks slow or go into reverse, as our results show is possible, carbon dioxide levels will rise even faster" (Amazon Carbon, 2009).

What is more, drought in the Amazon and other rainforests combine with rapid climate change, habitat loss, and the spread of invasive species to reduce biodiversity in some of what used to be the richest habitats on land anywhere on Earth. Thiago Rangel wrote in *Science*: "These human-induced processes may have boosted the background rate of species extinction by 100 to 1,000 times. However, species do not go extinct immediately when their habitat shrinks, climate changes beyond their tolerance limit, or an invasive species spreads. It may take several generations after an initial impact before the last individual of a species is gone" (Rangel, 2012, 162).

Scientists have been measuring the Amazon's Valley's declining capacity as a carbon sink. R.J.W. Brienen and colleagues wrote in *Nature* (2015, 344) that rates of net increase in biomass have declined by one-third in roughly 20 years, from the 1990s to about 2014. Until recently, forests, most notably those of the Amazon Valley, have been absorbing a large amount of the carbon dioxide produced by human activities. Signs are that this important carbon sink may have reached its maximum capacity (295). "While this analysis confirms that Amazon forests have acted as a long-term net biomass sink," Brienen, et al. wrote, "We find a long-term decreasing trend of carbon accumulation. This is a consequence of growth rate increases leveling off recently, while biomass mortality persistently increased throughout, leading to a shortening of carbon residence times. Potential drivers for the mortality increase include greater climate variability, and feedbacks of faster growth on mortality, resulting in shortened tree longevity" (Brienen, et al., 344).

The Amazon Valley in the World Trade Web

In 2010, the Amazon Valley experienced its second "100 year drought" in 5 years. "This is what's quite alarming—that we've seen these two very unusual events," said Simon Lewis, a University of Leeds (Great Britain) forest ecologist. "And those two unusual events are consistent with those predictions that suggest that the Amazon may be severely impacted over the next few decades by these droughts" (Joyce, 2011).

Human activity is pushing the Amazon Valley toward drought in many ways, of which fossil fuel effluvia is only one. Rising sea surface temperatures in the Atlantic Ocean change circulation patterns in the atmosphere in ways that can induce drier weather in parts of the valley, as changes in climate patterns from more frequent El Niño episodes (which also may be provoked by rising temperatures) do the same. Land-use changes associated with the spread of logging, ranching, and farming also cause parts of the shrinking rainforest to dry out, as world demand surges for tropical timber, soybeans, and free-range beef, among other products.

Roads expand to link production centers in the Amazon Valley to ports on South America's Pacific coasts, allowing exports to the rapidly developing economies of China, India, and other parts of Asia. Demand for "green" ethanol meanwhile causes more Amazon forest to be cleared for sugar cane fields. In an area where 25 to 59% of rainfall is "recycled" by the forest, once roughly 30 to 40% of the rainforest disappears, the area as a whole could pass a threshold, a "tipping point," into a drier climate on a long-range basis (Malhi et al., 2008, 169). Per Cox of the Center for Ecology and Hydrology in Winfrith, UK anticipates that increased drought frequency could devastate about 65% of the Amazon's forest cover by the end of the twenty-first century (Cox et al., 2004, 137).

In 2019, smoke from the fires reached Sao Paulo, the largest city south of the equator, on winds several hundred miles from their primary sites in Bolivia and the northwestern Brazilian state of Rondonia. The city was "plunged into daylight darkness….The sky was almost pitch-black as cars crept along with their headlights on. On social media, many people tweeted—some only half-jokingly—about the impending apocalypse" (Smoked-cloaked City, 2019, 6).

On August 29, 2019, after several weeks of Bolsonaro's assertion of Brazil's sovereign right to let large swathes of the Amazon Valley burn to ashes and charred stumps, the country adopted a 60-day ban on new fires, as well as clearing new land that has been accelerating deforestation. This ban came as President Bolsonaro had been asserting that any law that curbed development in the Amazon Valley threatened Brazil's emphasis on economic expansion.

Several hundred government environmental workers in Brazil released an open letter on August 28, 2019, as widespread fires swept the Amazon, asserting that President Bolsonaro's policies had contributed to a rise in deforestation, resulting in fires that had increased by more than 40% in 1 year. The signatories of the letter, gathered in 2 days, argued that without a major policy change Brazil's environmental protection system could collapse, accelerating warming of the atmosphere worldwide. Budget cuts, staff reductions, political meddling, and elimination of environmental regulations have resulted in more fires, the environmental workers said. In 1 month (August, 2019, the workers said) at least 27,400 fires had been detected in the Amazon Valley (Londano & Casado, 2019, A-8). Officials in Ibama, the main federal environmental agency, had been unable to carry out its work in the state of Pará, where deforestation has been increasing rapidly. Those who are most active in deforestation also have been threatening environmental workers and burning their remote stations as police fail to offer aid or protection. At the same time,

Bolsonaro has refused to accept international aid to assist in quelling the fires, calling the offers a challenge to Brazil's sovereignty.

Cities Grow as the Rainforest Withers

In the meantime, Manaus, which had been a village in 2000, grew to more than two million people by 2019. In the same year, the population of the Amazon Valley as a whole had surpassed 30 million. Of 19 Brazilian cities that had doubled in population in a decade, 10 were in the Amazon. During those has changed into an urban area "with an air-conditioned shopping mall, gated communities, and a dealership selling Chevy pickup trucks" (Romero, 2012). In Manaus, the Rio Negro flows into the Amazon, a confluence "as seemingly wide and wild as the ocean," which requires an hour to cross by boat (Federal, 2020, 55).

During the late 1970s, with Brazil ruled by a dictatorship that regarded the rainforest as *terra nullius* (empty land, ripe for exploitation), an unpaved highway named BR-319 was constructed through the rainforest from Manaus, 570 miles southwest to Porto Velho, where BR-319 hooks into a paved road to Sao Paulo, the largest city in Brazil. Sawmills and lumberyards were built along the road, where several thousand workers processed wood that had been Illegally cut in the rainforest. The military government declared the area a free-trade zone, which soon became a major center for the manufacture of motorcycles and related products, like Kawasaki, Harley-Davidson, and Honda moved in (Federal, 2020, 56). In 1985, the military junta collapsed, and was replaced by a regime opposed to illegal logging and rapid development of the Amazon valley. The road was left to deteriorate. When Bolsonaro was elected, plans emerged not only to restore BR-319, but to eventually pave it as well.

Philip Fearnside, a United States ecologist with the National Institute of Amazonian Research (INPA), said that BR-319 is a vital route that "runs through the heart of the Amazon....What protects the forest best is its being inaccessible" (Federal, 2020, 59). "More population leads to more deforestation," said Fearnside (Romero, 2012). The road slices through Nascentes do Lago Jari National Park, one of the world's most bio-diverse areas, Where as many as a thousand species of trees share a square kilometer, as many as in the United States as a whole. It is also a dangerous place to ride a motorcycle because hungry panthers revel at the sight and smell of exposed human flesh (It is best to take a car or a truck, do not stop to urinate, and keep the windows rolled up).

Construction of hydroelectric dams is drawing workers to the Amazon Valley as well, as are open-pit iron ore mines near Pará, and Parauapebas, as well as other locations, meeting heavy demand in several other nations, most notably China. According to one observer, "Already the Amazon desert is emerging in Rondonia. As far as the eye can see, there is only red, cracked ground. The red dust fills the air and sky itself turns red. Ten years ago this area was jungle, then it was slashed and burned to form farmland. But the jungle soil is notoriously poor, so it was used for pasture." (Brandenburg & Paxton, 1999, 225).

The Mato Grosso region of the Amazon, formerly a rain forest, is becoming a dryland savanna. The destruction of the forest reinforces itself because rain clouds form more easily above moist forests. Deforestation also degrades soil quality because most of the Amazon's nutrients come from decaying vegetation. "By removing the forest you remove the nutrients," said Yadvinder Malhi of the University of Oxford. The deforestation of the Mato Grasso ("Great Forest" in Portuguese) is being aggravated by logging; about 17% of this region's forests already have been cleared (Brahic, 2009).

Gold Mining's Role in Deforestation

Fire, of course, is not the only human insult defiling the natural majesty of the Amazon Valley. Gold mining in Brazil and adjoining countries has been turning jungles into mud-strewn wastelands drowning in waste plastic and the effluvia of mining machinery, as well as toxic water that is killing dwindling numbers of Native peoples, whose lives revolve around two stark choices: work in the mines, or starve.

Jon Lee Anderson wrote in *The New Yorker* (2019, 45, 46):

> At the riverside, the effects of mining become impossible to ignore. The water of the Rio Branco…that runs past the [Kayapo] community [of Turedjam] was a nauseous pale yellow. In most Amazon villages, people go to the river every day, to bathe, to wash clothes, or escape the heat of the late afternoon. Here there was no one. Across the river, on ranches, the land was rumpled and gouged, with dirt piled up next to wide craters filled with the same livid colors as the Rio Branco [that] no longer resembled a river; mining had turned it into a spreading mass of craters, filled with toxic lime-white water.

Anderson talked with Jorge Silva, who had studied physics, but never had been able to find paying work in that field. He also worked as a gym teacher and electrician, but prospecting for gold offered the only living wage. Looking Anderson in the eye, he said: "All of us here realize we're fucking the environment. It's not like we want to—it's that we haven't found any alternative means to survive" (Anderson, 2019, 50).

Bolsonaro in Political Quicksand

By 2020, Bolsonaro was sinking into a vat of political quicksand for which Brazil is infamous "Battered by a torrent of investigations into him and his family, an economy in free-fall and criticism of his cavalier handling of one of the world's fastest growing coronavirus epidemics, Mr. Bolsonaro is fighting for political survival" (Londoño et al., 2020a, b). All of this was feeding an impeachment inquiry into Bolsonaro's cavalier references to a pandemic that already had killed more than 65,000 Brazilians as he refused to display empathy for any of the victims of a disease he has called "a "measly cold." (On July 7, 2020, he tested positive for the virus.) Instead, he tried to deflect blame onto the World Health Organization, which Bolsonaro said promotes homosexuality and encourages toddlers to masturbate, as he refused to tighten quarantines. His initial response to criticism that he had been reckless and callous was "so what?" (Londoño et al., 2020a, b). All of this raised speculation among senior military officers that a coup was under consideration, another Brazilian political custom.

The daft, flailing presidency of Bolsonaro has spawned reactions, such as the launch of *Samba Zine,* which "features only L.G.B.Q. Brazilian individuals, communities, and causes." *Samba Zine* was begun during the summer of 2019 with the first edition of 200 pages during September. The magazine planned to publish twice a year. It has no advertising, but places a company's products in photo spreads for a fee. This is a second magazine project for Julian Corbetta, who also founded *Made in Brazil,* which celebrates the Brazilian male physique.

Despite Bolsonaro's anti-gay rhetoric, Pedro Alvas, an actor, said "There are ad campaigns in the country [Brazil], with gay couples, trans-sexual individuals, drag queens; this would have been unthinkable years ago. Companies know the importance of 'pink' money" (Remsen, 2019, D-3). Brazil's Supremo Tribunal (Supreme Court) ruled in June, 2019, that gay and trans people should be included under laws against racism. This action was taken after Grupo Gay de Bahia, an advocacy group, reported 420 deaths of L.G.B.Q. people by homicide or suicide in Brazil during 2018. By the end of August, 2019, more than 100 gay individuals had been murdered (Remsen, 2019, D-3).

Pedro Pedreira, a photographer who contributed work to the first issue of *Samba Zine*, said, "It documents Brazilian queer culture, right now and in this moment of political calamity. I think it gives us some hope. The fashion and a hint of sexiness gives us the fantasy we need in these dark days" (Remsen, 2019, D-3). Along these lines, Corbetta said that he was inspired by "a photograph of a male model wearing only a diamond-studded thong (with a rhinestone heart applied to the model's right buttock, for flair." (Remsen, 2019, D-3).

Regardless of human folly, the fires returned in earnest at the beginning of the next dry season, during June of 2020, inflicting record damage, and sparking speculation that the new scorching season could be worse than the last. Little had changed along the frontier that President Bolsonaro had consigned to be ground under the foot of human exploitation.

Gold Miners killed two Yanomami men near the Venezuelan border as yet another brought pollution, disease, death, and greedy human beings intent to rip and run. In 1993, 16 Yanomami were killed in what became known as the Haxiumu massacre, which Brazilin courts later described as an act of genocide.

In 2020, however, the miners brought something new to the Yanomami—the agonizing death of the COVID-19 pandemic, which created new energy for their campaign to get the miners off their homeland, which also could advance the date of the Yanomamis' extinction.

Deforestation of the Amazon Valley: It Is Not Only Brazil

Large amounts of deforestation afflict not only Brazil, but every country with which it shares the Amazon basin—Venezuela, Columbia, Peru, Paraguay, and Argentina. Each of them has prepared development plans that require felling of trees: mining, agriculture, cattle ranching, logging, road building, and construction of towns and cities. Almost half of the Amazon basin lies outside of Brazil, mainly along its northern and western borders. Development in all of these areas is occurring at unprecedented rates. If a country is politically stable and can provide a workforce and utilities, developers swarm in. For example, any lull in Columbia's guerilla civil war opens "once-forbidding jungles to settlers. Illegal gold mining is fueling forest loss in Peru. Cattle ranchers in Bolivia are razing rainforest to meet beef demand in China" (Romero, 2019).

9 Brazil and Australia: Indigenous Peoples and the Fires This Time   291

"We've gone in Colombia from gunpoint conservation under the guerrillas to a massive deforestation spike," said Liliana Dávalos, a field biologist at Stony Brook University who estimated that deforestation climbed 50% from 2017 to 2018 in Colombian national parks formerly controlled by armed rebels". Some of the almost 500,000 acres of forests lost in Columbia during 2018 have gone into growth of illegal drugs. Before the guerilla movement (the Revolutionary Armed Forces of Colombia, FARC), ceased fighting in 2016, after a half-century of activity, deforestation had been restricted by FARC to defend its secret camps from air raids and drone spying. After the peace agreement, many of FARC's demobilized guerillas joined the land rush. The guerillas were aided by corruption in the government that inhibited registration of deeds, as well as other incentives, such as lower-than-usual taxes and other fees on deforested land. Colombia's government anticipates a doubling of cattle ranching.

In Peru, deforestation has jumped due to increasing production of coco (for cocaine) and illegal gold mining. More than half of that nation's land lies within the Amazon Basin. Small mines have destroyed forests totaling about 170,000 acres in 5 years. Agriculture and ranching are also producing a surge in deforestation in Bolivia, where President Evo Morales has made expanding the country's agricultural frontier a priority, sometimes by distributing land to farmers. The opening of China's beef market to Bolivian exporters is thought to be driving some of the forest loss as ranchers seek pastures for expanding herds.

Fires raged in the Amazon Valley during the summer of 2019, as "vast stretches of savannah also were aflame in central Africa" (Pierre-Louis, 2019, A-1). Arctic areas of Siberia also were experiencing record wildfires covering about 6 million acres. Even Greenland had small wildfires on its now-snowless western coast.

In 2020, fires in Siberia got off to an early start in May, propelled by record warmth in the Arctic. "Heatwave" may sound oxymoronic, but temperatures in the Arctic reached 100 degrees F. What has been surprising is the rapid increase in the scale and intensity of the fires, largely driven by a large swath of large fires in the northern Sakha Republic. Estimates showed that about half of the fires in Arctic Russia during 2020 were burning through areas pregnant with peat, decomposed organic matter that is a highly flammable large natural carbon source. Peat fires can burn longer than forest fires and release vast amounts of carbon into the atmosphere. Fires in Arctic Russia released more carbon dioxide (CO_2) in June and July 2020 alone than in any complete fire season since 2003 (when data collection began). In addition, the amount of carbon stored in northern peatlands is double the previous estimates (Another, 2020).

Indonesia also was experiencing intense peat fires. Worldwide, wildfires by 2018 and 2019 were pouring about as much carbon dioxide into the air as human emissions, and killing trees that previously had absorbed carbon dioxide and produced oxygen. John Abatzoglu, an assistant professor of geography at the University of Idaho, said that hotter, drier weather "is going to continue promoting the potential for fires....[providing] a risk of large, uncontainable fires globally" (Pierre-Louis, 2019, A-1).

Another place where few people might expect spectacular wildfires is Chile. Yet, in late December of 2019, more than 200 homes were scorched in the suburbs of Valparaíso an urban area of almost a million people on the Pacific coast near Santiago. More than 700 people were left homeless when the flames invaded the urban area on Christmas Eve. Evidence (such as the fact that several fires had been set at the same time) indicated that the fire had been set intentionally. However, weather conditions contributed to the rapid spread of the fire. A steady, dry, warm wind in the area was characteristic of the area's worst drought on record—conditions that also have plagued Brazil's Amazon Valley, Australia, Indonesia, and California at about the same time.

The causes of fires in the Amazon and Indonesia are similar: farmers burning fields and forests to expand their businesses, often for palm oil in Indonesia, a profitable cash crop that has led to massive deforestation in Sumatra and parts of Borneo that are part of Indonesia. The fires have been destroying large parts of tropical forests that heretofore have provided habitat for many endangered birds and other animal species. The fires quickly get out of hand and out-race the feeble efforts of small firefighting units that cannot extinguish them. In the meantime, the fires convert once-healthy oxygen-producing forests into smoldering ashes, carbon dioxide producing flames, and noxious smoke that has sickened several thousand people, closed schools and businesses, and canceled many airline flights to and from Indonesia as well as Singapore (Paddock & Suhartono, September 18, 2019a, A-4).

As in the Amazon Valley, fires in Indonesia were unusually intense during the summer and fall of 2019 because of severe drought. Indonesian president Joko (Jokowi) Widodo said: "We are dealing with sizable forests, vast peatlands" he said. "Therefore I ask everybody, all the people, not to burn land, both forests and peat." As Widodo said this, one report said that "Towering flames devoured trees and brush in what was once dense jungle, leaving behind a blackened wasteland of charred stumps and bushes" (Paddock & Suhartono, September 26, 2019b, A-6). Burning of forests, here and elsewhere, turns them into savannah grasslands, increasing drought and heat. No number of presidential admonitions will stop that. The fires have been characterized as "hellish," "turning the sky blood-red over central Sumatra, and creating dense clouds of smoke that have caused respiratory problems for almost a million people" (Paddock & Suhartono, September 26, 2019b, A-6). Slash-and-burn agriculture is illegal in Indonesia, but prosecutions for violations of environmental laws have been nearly non-existent.

Wildfires Envelop Australia

Australia has been experiencing large wildfires for several years during its calendar summer, usually December through March. However, in 2019, the fire season "down under" started very early (the first week of September), and bore a startling resemblance to the fires in the Amazon Valley, except that Australia's, in terms of area burned, was several times as large. Aside from Antarctica, where wildfires are not usually a problem because of ice, Australia has less precipitation than any other continent on the Earth.

In both the Amazon and Australia, the fires were among the worst in local history. Local experts ascribed both to climate change, and for the same reasons. The number of hot days in Australia has doubled in 50 years (Cave, 2019, A-8). Joelle Gergis, a climate scientist at the Australian National University, said that the fires were "a sign of things to come….It is devastating to see these usually cool and wet rainforests burn….Although these remarkable rainforests have clung on since the age of the dinosaurs, searing heat and lower rainfall is starting to see these [once] wet areas dry out for longer periods of the year, increasing brushfire risk in these precious ecosystems" (Cave, 2019, A-8). In 2019, about 65% of Queensland and practically all of New South Wales was suffering drought. As in Southern California, the fire season had become nearly year round. In Australia, iconic koalas, which usually feed on the leaves of eucalyptus trees, were threatened with extinction as flames consumed the trees, which burn very quickly, as the koalas, some of them on fire, fell from their perches.

As of January 13, 2020, the human toll of fires was lower than earlier blazes that had covered less ground. The 2009 "black Saturday" fires in Victoria State (e.g., https://www.britannica.com/event/Australia-bushfires-of-2009) killed 173 people over a smaller area than those of 2019 and 2010, but "After those fires, there was a rethinking of fire warnings and preparation. The result is that the current fires, though far more extensive than those in 2009, have led to far fewer deaths and property losses, in part due to better warnings and precautionary evacuations" (Brian Martin, personal communication, January 13, 2020).

Devastation of Plants and Animals

The devastation of animals and their habitats during Australia's wildfires has been much higher than on humans and their homes. With emphasis on koalas and kangaroos, not much attention has been paid to many very small species that are unique to Australia, For example, velvet worms resemble caterpillars, blue with a velvet-like texture (thus their popular name). They sleep as a group, and several at once are called a "cuddle." Despite the affectionate name and "nice" nature toward humans, velvet worms are predators, with claws along their bottom sides. Nozzles atop their heads squirt a sticky substance that helps to apprehend prey. They are also very collective in nature; once one catches something to eat, all velvet worms kin a cuddle gather around for a bite or two. Most of them live near Canberra, Australia's capital, which has been badly scorched by the fires. They inhabit decomposing logs that are prime fuel for fires. Velvet worms' range is limited to a small area, and only in Australia. Loss of a large percentage of their population may doom all of them to extinction. Tanya Latty, an entomologist at the University of Sydney, is one scientist who has been trying to save them with a captive breeding program, one who studies Australia's "mega-diverse" array of species. That continent "belongs to a group of countries that together are home to 70% of the world's biological diversity but make up just 10% of Earth's surface" (Sullivan, 2019). What goes for kangaroos and koalas also goes for at least 250,000 insect species, only a third of which have been named.

"Insects are best known as pollinators," Latty said, "but they play a critical role in waste management, too. We're not overrun in our own waste, because insects are doing the hard yards of cleaning that up for us," she said. "And they're doing it for free." The key to protecting them is protecting their habitat, she added" (Sullivan, 2019).

Kate Umbers, a biologist at Western Sydney University, specializes in the Australian alpine grasshopper, which changes color according to body temperature, from black at 50 degrees F. to turquoise at 77 F. " It's possible, because grasshoppers can burrow into vegetation, that they can hide in very tiny spaces, that many of them will make it through the fire," Umbers said (Sullivan, 2019). But any survivors would need to find food after a fire. The grasshoppers thrive near water, particularly around the tree line of snow-gum eucalyptus. "So they don't do well when things dry out," Umbers said. "Which is unusual again for a grasshopper. Some of them even go swimming" (Sullivan, 2019). Similarly, female trapdoor spiders, which live in burrows near Perth, enclose themselves with tops, and live in them for several years. They can survive fires, but starve afterward.

A few insect species benefit from fires, such as the fire beetles, which mate in burned areas. They can detect heat, and abandon a burned site after about 3 days. Black and Whistling kites light fires with small embers that they carry before burning prey injured by blazes. Feral cats are drawn to recently burned areas for injured reptiles. By one estimate, feral cats consume about 650 million small reptiles a year in Australia (Sullivan, 2019).

Like the fires in the Amazon Valley, those in Australia took place in some areas that once were rain forests, now transitioning into scorched savannah. The political situation has been similar, too: nationalistic, right-wing leadership interested in resource exploitation has been driving devastation of forests. In the Amazon, this took the form of logging, urban development, gold mining, and oil exploration; in Australia, coal mining usually calls the developmental tune. The coal industry exercises a great deal of power in Australia, where it is the world's largest coal exporter. The same is true of liquefied natural gas (LNG). Thus, as Australia burns in the biggest fire in living memory, the debate over climate change has degenerated into an exchange of insults between supporters of the fossil fuel industries and environmentalists. In the meantime, the atmospheric level of carbon dioxide (which has no political affiliation) soars, of course not only from the burning of coal and oil, but also from the combustion of fire.

The Politics of Smoke and Fires

By early November, 2019 (late May weather-wise in the Southern Hemisphere), intense bushfires were raging along Australia's east coast, in New South Wales and Queensland. The leader of the Rural Fire Service said that this outbreak could be "The most dangerous bushfire week this nation has ever seen," as New South Wales declared a state of emergency (Bushfires, 2019). Kendra Coufal, who moved from Omaha, Nebraska to coastal Queensland and became a medical doctor, said that her area had not been directly affected by the fires, but that, because of persistently thick smoke "Some days look like the sun didn't even rise" (Baker, 2020, 11).

In addition to the Australian coal industry's financial pipeline to major political figures, right-wing media owned by Rupert Murdoch have been underplaying the size and intensity of the fires, and blaming them on just about anything except climate change. Australia has fires all the time, Murdoch media tell its audiences. That much is true, but what goes unsaid is that halfway through the burning season, until the end of 2019, the burned area in New South Wales was equal to the several previous years combined (Cave, 2020a, B-2). It's all part of what critics see as a relentless effort led by the powerful media outlet, NewsCorp, Murdoch's corporation, to do what it has also done on the United States and Britain—shift blame onto the left, protect a conservative leader, and divert attention from climate change (Cave, 2020a, B-5). In Murdoch's world, many fires are a result of arson, even sometimes set by publicity-seeking "greenies," a derogatory label for environmentalists. While scientists see a continent that is more vulnerable to the climate crisis than any other area on Earth (except, probably, the Arctic), NewsCorp sees a publicity campaign by malign "greenies" to victimize coal and its political supporters.

Isabella Kwai of the *New York Times* described the fires (2019, A-7): "As the fire stalked the east coast of Australia…the daytime sky turned inky black, then blood red." Emergency sirens wailed, followed by the thunder of gas explosions. Thousands of residents fled their homes and huddled near the shore. There was nowhere else to go.

As the government prepared navy ships and helicopters to lift stranded people off the shores that had been besieged by racing flames and triple-digit heat, in what became part of Australia's largest evacuation since World War II, Prime Minister Scott Morrison, a staunch conservative, said that this was not the time to discuss the climate crisis, even after several weeks of Australia's worst drought, heat, and fires on record. During November and December, to January 8, 2019, 15 million acres were burned in New South Wales and other parts of Australia. Many of the fires struck areas where blazes have been infrequent, such as the northern coast. This area, heretofore mainly a tropical rainforest, has been reduced to kindling by withering heat and drought. Two weeks after that, the burned area across Australia had reached 25.7 million acres, an area the size of Indiana (McGuirk, 2020, 8-A).

An estimated six million people who live along Australia's east coast (one-fourth of the nation's population) were facing conditions similar to those in California and the Amazon Valley in what has become a nearly annual event—massive fires driven by strong winds, low humidity, and high temperatures. The fire season of 2019–2020 started earlier and quickly became more damaging than any Australia had ever seen, all as Prime Minister Morrison denied climate change and dismissed the scope of the country's suffering—even as fire agencies warned of "catastrophic" fire danger in the Greater Sydney and Greater Hunter regions, as well as many others. As the fires spread, no rain was reported anywhere in Australia. The flames invaded some of Sydney's suburbs, where 600 schools closed, at least three people died, and 150 homes were torched (Bushfires, 2019). For much of the Sydney area, a catastrophic fire warning was called for a week, which gave firefighters the power to requisition resources from all government agencies.

Heat was hitting all-time records as drought parched most of Australia, which is about the size of the lower 48 of the United States. On December 17, 2019, averaging maximum temperatures for all weather stations produced a high of 105.6 °F. A day later, the same average was 107.4 °F. One Australian told the British Broadcasting Corporation (BBC) that the ambient air "felt like opening an oven door" (Kolbert, 2020, 13). During the last week of 2019, raging wildfires threatened suburbs of Melbourne, as temperatures rose to 108 °F one day. More than 10,000 people evacuated their homes. Fires across Australia had scorched more than 20,000 square miles in 1 year by the time 2019 ended. Nine people died in the Melbourne area, as more than 1000 koalas also were seared. Search crews fought fires to rescue Australia's signature animal.

Sports events were being postponed or canceled throughout southeast Australia because of dense smoke. Tennis matches were especially vulnerable because they were held outdoors, in Australia's record summer heat, with matches going on for several hours. Even indoor sports events were canceled in Canberra on days when pollution was rated as the worst in the world. Enough acrid smoke seeped through air conditioning systems to activate smoke alarms many miles from the actual fires. The Australian Open tennis tournament, scheduled to begin in Melbourne during mid-January, was considered for termination. By the third week in January, after smoke had made some players sick, officials said that they would cancel outdoor matches if it got any worse. Fires continued to burn in some areas, but heavy rain and hail in others helped to partially cleanse the sky, even as dust storms plagued others areas. After a week of wild weather, heat and drought returned. The tennis tournament went on.

By the end of 2019, as 120 fires continued to rage throughout Australia, uncounted millions of koalas died in flames in the state of New South Wales alone. After a month of devastating conditions, the fires were widely being characterized as apocalyptic. Rainfall in 2019 was below to very much below average across most of Australia, continuing a long-term drought in the region. To "Rainfall deficiencies have affected most of the New South Wales, Queensland, and South Australian parts of the Murray–Darling Basin since the start of 2017," the Australian Bureau of Meteorology reported. "The deficiencies have been most extreme in the northern Murray–Darling Basin, especially in the northern half of New South Wales and adjacent southern Queensland, where areas of lowest-on-record rainfall extend across large parts of northeastern New South Wales…The 34 months from January 2017 to October 2019 have been the driest on record…for the state of New South Wales (35% below average)" (Bushfires, 2019).

"A Blast Furnace" and "Firenadoes"

After several weeks of wicked wildfires, as a new decade dawned, the situation got worse. Residents besieged by fire ran as their houses exploded. Tens of thousands of people came to a stop in massive traffic jams as smoke hid the sun and turned the sky ashen black.

Navy ships rescued several thousand people marooned on beaches who had become trapped between the fires on one side and the ocean on the other. Officials said that the death toll of animals was approaching half a billion (Friday, 2020). This was an estimate from counting the known number of deaths in a group of relatively small areas and multiplying by the entire area burned. It was subject to debate, as was the number of animals that survived the fires themselves, but later starved or died of dehydration and lack of food.

Officials called the weather situation, which was expected to continue for several days, a "blast furnace" (Albeck-Ripka et al., 2019, A-1). "It's a biological Armageddon, rarely seen, said Prof. Kingsley Dixon, an ecologist and botanist at Curtin University in Perth" (Albeck-Ripka, 2020, A-7). As often is the case with global warming, extreme weather conditions may occur within short distances. A few hundred miles to the northwest of Australia, in Indonesia, Jakarta, on the island of Java, beset by another stagnant weather pattern, was receiving its heaviest rainfall on record. The extremes from stagnant weather patterns all are evidence of the global climate crisis.

A NASA satellite photo captured evidence that the fires were creating a new type of cloud that spawned very large areas of violent weather that meteorologists called "pyrocumulo-nimbus," thunderstorms that are generated by intense, very hot fires. Smoke and ashes from fires rise, create thunderheads which also may draw up water, dumping downpours of viscous mud. The same thing may happen downwind in major volcanic eruptions. At the same time, "Colossal plumes of smoke [were] choking Sydney and have turned the sky above New Zealand's largest city, Auckland—some 1,300 miles away—an apocalyptic orange" ("Editor's Letter," 2020, 2).

Figure: NASA photograph from, space showing the formation of pyrocumulo-nimbus clouds during fires over New South Wales, Australia, early January, 2020. (Source: NASA Earth Observatory.)

Over New South Wales, smoke from the fires was being sucked into the stratosphere, as high as five miles, forming anvil tops like gigantic thunderstorms, as lightning danced on their undersides, and ash fell instead of rain. These ash clouds came to be called "firenadoes"—which could snake their way back to earth with enough power to overturn heavy trucks and cars. Lightning from these vortexes sometimes lit new fires. The fire season was young (equivalent roughly to June 30–July 1 in the Northern Hemisphere) but Australia already had had its worst fire season in recorded history. Australia's firefighting capabilities had been overwhelmed. Much of the burned land had been mountain retreats only weeks beforehand. During the first week in January, intense fires broke out along Australia's north coast in an area heretofore known for its verdant greenery. As in Brazil's Amazon, drought and fire over an extended period were turning formerly rich forests into parched savannah.

People with memories for these sorts of things were putting Australia's fires into meteorological context. In a single year, as pointed out elsewhere, massive, damaging fires had ravaged large areas around the world, record floods had made farming nearly impossible in the middle of North America; India had withered in temperatures as high as 126 F, and another heat wave had broken records across Europe—all of this and more in 1 year. Paul Krugman wrote in the *New York Times* (2020, A-22) that with regard to weather, apocalypse had become the new normal. "On one side, the dangers of climate change are no longer predictions about the future. We can see the damage now, although it's only a small taste of the horrors that lie ahead." At the same time, the Leader of the Free World, Mr. Alt-facts himself, was still calling it all a Chinese hoax. The lights were on late in the Ministry of Truth at 1600 Pennsylvania Avenue.

Criticism of public officials in Australia was hotter than the weather, engaging its own blast furnace. David Elliott, New South Wales' emergency services minister, departed Australia on January 2 for a vacation in England and France, and reaped a whirlwind on social media. Elliott hinted, as his plane lifted off, that he might return to Australia when and whether the fire situation demanded his attention. Prime Minister Scott Morrison already had taken a vacation in Hawaii when the crisis was in its early stages. He met with rage and ridicule from environmentalists who had long criticized his dismissal of global warming (Albeck-Ripka et al., 2019, A-8). Morrison also asserted that fire control was a state, not a federal, responsibility.

As the intensity of the fires increased, Morrison cut his vacation short, returned to Australia, and rather half-heartedly apologized. He then undertook a tour of some of the burned-out areas in full damage control, in a largely unsuccessful effort to salvage his political reputation. What he found was fury:

> The public's patience was nearly exhausted and turning rapidly to fury….Mr. Morrison visited a fire-ravaged community, Cobargo, to see the damage and express support to residents. They heckled him out of town. "You left the country to burn," one person yelled before the prime minister walked away and set off in his car (Albeck-Ripka et al., 2020, A-5).

Mogo, a small town in southeastern Australia, has an aquifer near the surface that always had kept the grass green, even when fires struck elsewhere. About January 1, 2020, a firestorm swept through town, filling Mogo's pure water springs with ash, and searing half of Mogo's main street. If a place such as this can burn, residents asked, "Is anyone safe in rural Australia?" (Kwai, 2020). Another problem, aside from climate change, is that formerly rural areas have been becoming more urban as suburbs expand. Australia's population in the bush but also near cities has risen 10% in 10 years. Add that to intense drought and you have a rapidly rising risk of fire that may harm people and their homes.

Fires Roll Through Villages A Second Time

By the second week of January, 2020, "surrounded by hills black as soot," from the first blast of fires up to 50 feet in height, winds of 50 to 60 miles per hour, and temperatures close to 100 °F. picked up again, and drove a second fire front through southeastern Australia, searing what was left of villages and forests that had already been burned once. "It's like the fire is a sentient being," said Sulari Gentill, a novelist with a husband and a son who are volunteer firefighters in Batlow. "It feels like it's coming to get us" (Cave & Akbeck-Ripka, 2020). Everyone who has watched the fires marvels at their power, unpredictability, and unwillingness to die, no matter what firefighters, who feel mercilessly overmatched, threw at them. Soon fires were merging, as lightning started new ones.

Some people whose houses had burned during the first scorching slept in horse trailers hoping to protect their dogs and farm animals. Many were living on donated food and water, without electricity amidst the ruins of houses or "a shed or cars reduced to steel skeletons, cherished mementos gone up in flames, water pipes and wires melted into tangled knots....[and] street signs melted" (Cave & Akbeck-Ripka, 2020). Many displayed the kind of shock similar to battle fatigue. "We're all on edge," said Deb Wiltshire, 52, the owner of a cafe in Batlow that is now closed because of fire damage. "You think it's over and done, then you get told it's on its way back" (Cave & Akbeck-Ripka, 2020).

Across rural New South Wales, the army troops called out by a federal government that 2 weeks earlier had denied the severity of the fires lined up bulldozers to help create containment zones. Planes and helicopters dropped fire retardant on the advancing flames. At the same time, Prime Minister Morrison announced a review (in Australia, a "royal commission") to study the fires and government response, but stalled when asked whether he would support wide-ranging measures to combat the climate crisis, such as reducing Australia's dependence on fossil fuels. For him, the fires and climate still seemed to be dissociated events. With protests against him Friday evening in Sydney and several other Australian cities, Morrison appeared on a right-wing radio show where the host told the audience that the prime minister was already doing *too much* to combat climate change.

Morrison, however, gave some indication that he was tip-toeing into an understanding of climate change's role in the fires: He said on January 12, 2020, that the fires were an indication of a "new normal" in "a changing climate that would require the country to adopt better policies for disaster management....including floods, cyclones [and other things]. Morrison's lack of association of changing weather and climate with emissions of fossil fuels led many critics to say that little had or would change on Morrison's watch. Royal commission reports have a reputation of being compiled in 12–18 months, then filed and forgotten. "It's a fob-off," said John Blaxland, a professor at the Australian University in Canberra. "They give you a good 18 months of political grace for the issue to die down politically, then shelve it when it comes out" (Tarabay, 2020, A-6).

Post-Apocalyptic Fiction Has Been Moved to Current Affairs

Richard Flanagan, an Australian novelist who has won the Man Booker Prize, reflected on the broader scope of the climate crisis in his homeland, and the fateful ignorance of its political leaders, so typical of their type worldwide: "Australia today is ground zero for the climate catastrophe. Its glorious Great

Barrier Reef is dying, its world-heritage rain forests are burning, its giant kelp forests have largely vanished, numerous towns have run out of water or are about to, and now the vast continent is burning on a scale never before seen" (Flanagan, 2020).

By January 4, 2020, with their extinguishment not yet in sight, Australia's fires had burned an area three times the size of those in California during 2018, and six times that of fires in the Amazon Valley in 2019. At the same time, Australian Deputy Prime Minister Michael McCormack blamed the fires on exploding horse manure.

A bookstore in New South Wales had posted a sign: "Post-Apocalyptic Fiction has been moved to Current Affairs" (Flanagan, 2020). And while Australia burned, its highest political leaders pledged fealty to coal mining in particular and to fossil fuels in general—"willing the country to its doom" (Flanagan, 2020). Since 1996, Australia's leaders had acted as if a climate crisis did not exist. Meanwhile, in 2019 mining magnate Clive Palmer poured Australian $60 million (US $42 million) into a national election for a massive advertising campaign that helped propel the Liberal-National Coalition to an upset victory. Palmer also announced plans to open the largest coal mine on Earth. Some local-level legislators in Australia considered measures that could condemn anyone who protested the rule of fossil fuels in Australia to as many as 21 years in prison (Flanagan, 2020). "Australia is a burning nation led by cowards," wrote a leading broadcaster, Hugh Riminton, speaking for many people. To which he might have added "idiots," wrote Flanagan. "Such are those who would open the gates of hell and lead a nation to commit climate suicide" (Flanagan, 2020).

On January 4, 2020, the Australian government, comparing the damage of the fires to atomic bombs without the radiation, announced large-scale civilian use of the military on a scale not seen since World War II (Australia had sent troops to United States wars in Korea, Vietnam, Afghanistan, and Iraq). At roughly the same time, Prime Minister Morrison was doing his best to emulate US President Donald Trump by advocating an Australian exit from the 2015 Paris Accords, meant to unite the nations of the world in an affirmative effort to reduce greenhouse gas emissions. True to his coal industry benefactors, Morrison insisted that the Paris Accords were unnecessary. A headline in the United Kingdom *Guardian* said: "Australia Took a Match to U.N. Climate Talks While Back Home the Country Burned" (Kolbert, 2020, 14). By mid-January, participants were felled by smoke at the Australian Open tennis matches, and NASA announced that the fires' smoke had been detected nearly circling the Earth by satellites.

Having briefly touched on a street diagnosis of Australian leadership's mental capacities ("Idiots,") it may be germane to venture here a *very* basic course in climate science. Carbon dioxide, methane, and other greenhouse gases do not love or hate you. They do not care whether you believe that they are dangerous, or not. They have no morals and make no distinction between people who stuff their pockets with money from coal barons and those who do not. They have no wishes or dreams. All they do is a very effective job of holding heat in the lower atmosphere. The more of it we have, the hotter the temperatures, and, eventually, hotter and damaging the weather.

The Fires Next Time

Back in Brazil, 80,000 fires had been detected during 2019 by November, when the arrival of the rainy season snuffed most of them. President Bolsonaro said that he was looking forward to the next dry season and its smoke and fires, which, to him, represent economic growth and prosperity. Brazil by 2019 was exporting more than $6 billion worth of beef, more than any other country in world history, as well as 15 million tons of soy, with China its main customer (Sandy, 2019, A-12). Bolsonaro was cutting government funding to weaken enforcement of laws meant to protect rainforests, as "waves of loggers, ranchers, and miners moved in, emboldened by the president and eager to satisfy global demand," wrote Matt Sandy in the *New York Times* (2019, A-12).

By the time the rainy season arrived, deforestation in Brazil had risen 30% in 1 year. Carlos Nobre, a climate scientist at the University of Sao Paulo, said that "The Amazon is completely lawless….The environmental criminals feel more and more emboldened" (Sandy, 2019, A-12). Bolsonaro, who had pledged that "not a single centimeter" would be reserved for indigenous peoples, savored the coming of the next drought-plagued, scorching summer: "Deforestation and fires will never end," he said—one supposes, until the last acre is charred, and inhumane heat renders the Amazon Valley and many other parts of our wounded Earth uninhabitable (Sandy, 2019, A-12).

In Australia, even as Prime Minister Morrison proposed tepid changes in existing policies, and nothing to combat climate change, climate experts across Australia have warned that weather patterns that fueled the fires of 2019 and 2020 will only intensify as greenhouse gas levels rise and temperatures warm. "This particular weather event occurs when a low-pressure system from the Southern Ocean races north and collides with a high-pressure system on the NSW [New South Wales] coast. The two systems then force hot, dry air from inland Australia…towards the coast, resulting in strong westerly winds for days, before an abrupt southerly change when the cold front sweeps past" reported Mike Foley in the *Sydney Morning Herald*. Under present projections, the risk maybe four times that of the present. This, as Morrison stood in Parliament and "scoffed at climate concerns by brandishing a lump of coal and exhorted, 'Don't be scared. [It] won't hurt you." (Australia's Wildfires, 2020, 7-A).

Australian National University Climate Change Institute Prof. Mark Howden said that global warming would make dangerous bushfire events more likely. "Many intense fires in south-east Australia are associated with strong winds channeled ahead of powerful cold fronts, with the winds drawn from the hot continental interior," Professor Howden said (Foley, 2019).

"It's like the air is being forced through a narrow pipe. Furthermore, if it is an intense and deep cold front, there may be strong, gusty winds after the front has passed, which also enhances fire spread. The frequency of these frontal systems is projected to increase by up to a factor of four by the end of this century due to climate change" Foley wrote (2019). Furthermore, a report by the Commonwealth Scientific and Industrial Research Organisation (CSIRO) and Bushfire Cooperative Research Centre (CRC), *Assessing the Impact of Climate Change on Extreme Fire Weather Events over South-Eastern Australia*, supported the scientific consensus that these weather events were increasing in frequency and could occur up to four times more often by 2100 if carbon emissions and climate change increased unchecked (Foley, 2019).

Hazard-reduction burns and land clearing promoted by the Morrison government will not reduce fire damage under present or future conditions, Australian experts assert. A 2010 study from Wollongong University, *The Effect of Fuel Age on the Spread of Fire in Sclerophyll Forest in the Sydney Region*, found there was only a 10% chance a fire would be stopped by a hazard-reduction burn. The report said that road barriers were most effective at halting fires. "This summer's fires have burnt though many areas that had hazard-reduction burning. They can help control fires in moderate weather conditions, but in severe conditions it might just help reduce the severity," he said (Foley, 2020).

As wildfires continued to ravage large areas of Australia, more foresters evidenced interest in aboriginal methods of controlling forest growth. These methods, as practiced in Northern Australia, involve setting small, carefully controlled fires in overgrown areas with a close eye on temperatures, humidity, wind conditions, and the life cycles of plants, all timed to the monsoon. Attention to size of the fires and local conditions set these fires apart from much larger hazard-reduction burns. The idea, wrote Thomas Fuller and

Matthew Abbott in the *New York Times*, "is to reduce underbrush and other fuel that accelerates hot, damaging fires" (Fuller & Abbott, 2020, A-4).

During the fourth week of January, fires continued even as scattered rains fell. In Melbourne, the rain was brown, laced with smoke, and small bits of cinder. Brown rain also discolored the Yarra River. Three firefighters from the United States were killed when their C-130 Hercules, carrying fire retardant, crashed in mountains south of Canberra. The high temperature reached 110 F. at Sydney's airport on a dry, hot wind from inland. Canberra's airport closed as fires approached the city's suburbs. Officials told drivers that they could be incinerated if flames leaped across roadways. In the surrounding region, 80 fires continued to burn, half of them out of control.

"What's unfolding right now is really just a taste of the new normal," wrote Australian climate scientist Joelle Gergis in *The Guardian*.com (quoted in *The Week* magazine). "I fear that we've reached a tipping point in human-caused climate change and that weather conditions considered extreme by today's standards will seem sedate in the future." She emphasized that everyone on Earth needs to cut greenhouse-gas emissions and adjust to a rapidly destabilizing world: "There is genuinely no more time to waste," she said. "We must act as if our home is on fire—because it is" (Australia, 2020, 13).

By February, 2020, rain had snuffed Australia's fires for the 2019–2020 Austral summer, but the country faced a new problem: torrential rains. "In just a few days," reported NASA's Earth Observatory, "parts of Queensland and New South Wales (NSW) were soaked by more rain than many areas saw in all of 2019. The deluge swelled rivers out of their banks and swamped parched lands, leading to muddy floods in many coastal regions. Australia's Bureau of Meteorology reported more than 8 inches) in 24 h and 20 to 28 inches in some areas in a week." Several storms raced inland off the Pacific Ocean between February 5 and 10, as "a coastal trough positioned parallel to the east Australian coast strengthened, maintaining widespread showers and rain" (Extreme Rain, 2010). Some of the heaviest rains flooded in and near Nowra and Bomaderry, about 100 miles southwest of Sydney, one of the areas worst hit by wildfires in a textbook example of drought and deluge that has become more frequent worldwide as the atmosphere warms.

The paradox of drought and deluge works like this: as temperatures warm, water evaporates more quickly, drying foliage, which creates conditions favoring drought, and allows wildfires to start more quickly, and burn longer. Warming air and ocean temperatures often also force stagnation of weather patterns, including desiccating high pressure over desert areas, a frequent problem in Australia even before continuous global warming. Warmer air also holds more moisture, meaning that when rains do arrive, they are often heavier than previously. This process can be aggravated by tropical cyclones that often move farther north (in the Northern Hemisphere) and south (in the Southern Hemisphere) than when the atmosphere was cooler, and retains more heat at the same time, often making rainfall heavier.

All of these factors were on full display in Australia between November, 2019, and February, 2020, by the time Cyclone Liesi snuffed the fires, bringing torrential rains that ran off dry, packed ground. At the same time, the federal government, held in thrall by powerful Australian coal interests, continued to ignore warnings from scientists. Leslie Hughes, a climate scientist at Macquarie University in Sydney, said: "We've been writing about climate change being a stress multiplier for many years. It's absolutely been foreseen that our climate is becoming more variable and more severe" (Cave, 2020b, A-4). And as the climate warms, past may be prologue—or worse.

Regardless of what Prime Minister Morrison and others in the Australian government may profess, a team of scientists found that an extremely high-risk situation had been made at least 30% worse because of human-caused global warming. "We're very sure that is a definite number that we can scientifically defend," said Geert Jan Van Oldenborgh of the Royal Netherlands Meteorological Institute, lead author of the study (Fountain, 2020a, A-6). Further study of discrepancies between climate models and observed temperatures may raise the 30% figure, he said (Fountain, 2020a, A-6).

For some time after the fires' last ash cooled, scientists found that the heat generated by Australia's fires augmented a worldwide warming trend in the atmosphere to raise water temperatures offshore, and accelerate the death spiral of the coral reef. For the third time in 5 years, including 2016 and 2017, record warmth killed coral in massive amounts, especially in the reef's northern reaches. Corals are very temperature-sensitive and grow very slowly. Temperatures above 88F for a sustained period usually turn them white, leaving a shell empty of living things.

"In terms of water temperatures around the reef, February [2020] was the warmest month on record, with readings in some places more than 5 degrees Fahrenheit above average for the time of year, [the Australian government] recently reported," The *New York Times* reported (Pérez-Peña, 2020). By 2019, according to the same agency, about 40% of the reef system was "in poor to very poor condition," and "some critical ecosystem functions have deteriorated since 2014." "Climate change," the reef authority said, "remains the single greatest challenge to the reef" (Pérez-Peña, 2020). The 2020 season was "the first time we've seen severely bleached reefs along the whole length of the reef—in particular the coastal reefs. Those are bleached everywhere," said

Professor Terry Hughes, director of the Australian Research Center of Excellence for Coral Reef Studies at James Cook University.

Thus the endgame: bleached coral and dead fish in the ocean, ashes on land. This is the future that Australia faces.

During the summer of 2021, however, the fires gave Brazil a break. What was raging during this new season of apocalypse, however, was the world COVID-19 pandemic. President Bolsonaro was finding it much tougher to laugh it off. No longer was he sounding like Donald Trump and calling the pandemic no worse than little flu. In fact, by June, 500,000 people had died in Brazil, which now was being ravaged by its own variant, known as Gamma, which was easier to catch than any of the others. By refusing to take necessary actions, such as masking and promoting vaccines, Bolsosnaro maybe dancing right into Gamma's jaws. Or so it seemed in the middle of 2021. As calls for impeachment grew, the political picture was indicating that the virus might have the president's political neck.

Not that the virus cares. All it wants is fresh, unprotected habitat, of which Brazil has been providing plenty. In June of 2021, one-third of worldwide COVID-19 deaths were occurring in Brazil (Pedroso & Koch, 2021). The daily death toll had doubled in 6 months. In 1 year, the total annual death toll has shot up from 50,000 to 500,000. Vaccine distribution has been slow, and in Brazil many people have been passing it up, led by Bolsonaro. In June of 2021, only 11.4% of Brazilians had been fully vaccinated. More than 100 countries had restricted entry by Brazilians. Brazilians had been staging large anti-Bolsonaro rallies in most large cities, for which participants have risked infection. Software developer Mariana Oliveira said she had decided to protest and take the risk of being infected because "The government is a worse threat than the virus" (Pedroso & Koch, 2021).

References

Albeck-Ripka, L. (2020, January 8). The rush to save Joeys and more amid Australia's Inferno. *New York Times,* A-7.

Albeck-Ripka, L., Tarabay, J., & Pérez-Peña, R. (2019, January 3). Fire forecast for Australia: 'Blast Furnace.' *New York Times,* A-1, A-6.

Albeck-Ripka, L., Turabay, J., & Kwai, I. (2020, January 6). 'You left the country to burn': Australia's leader dodges a nation's fury. *New York Times,* A-5.

Amazon Carbon Sink Threatened by Drought. (2009, March 5). *NASA Earth Observatory.* http://earthobservatory.nasa.gov/Newsroom/view.php?id=37493&src=eoa

Anderson, J. L. (2019, November 11). Letter from the Amazon: Blood gold. *The New Yorker*, 40–51.

Andreoni, M., Londoño, E., & Casado, L.. (2020, July 20). Brazil health workers may have spread virus to indigenous people. *New York Times*, A-15.

Another Intense Summer of Fires in Siberia. (2020, August 7). *NASA Earth Observatory*. https://earthobservatory.nasa.gov/images/147083/another-intense-summer-of-fires-in-siberia?src=eoa-iotd

Australia: A Lack of Leadership as Nation Burns. (2020, January 17). *The Week*, 13.

Australia's Wildfires Provide a Searing Preview. (2020, January 14). *USA Today*, 7-A).

Baker, K. (2020, January 14). Amid all the chaos, turn your attention to the Australian brushfire disaster. *University of Nebraska at Omaha Gateway*, 11.

Brahic, C. (2009, March 5). Parts of Amazon close to tipping point. *New Scientist*. http://www.newscientist.com/article/dn16708-parts-of-amazon-close-to-tipping-point.html

Brandenburg, J. E., & Rix Paxson, M. (1999). *Dead Mars, dying Earth*. The Crossing Press.

Brazil. (2019, August 28). Survival International. Mailer.

Brazil Bans Most Burning for 60 Days to Curb Fires. (2019, August 30). Associated Press in *Omaha World-Herald*, 7-B.

Brienen, R. J. W., Phillips, O. L., Feldpausch, T. R., Gloor, E., Baker, T. R., Lloyd, J., Lopez-Gonzalez, G., Monteagudo-Mendoza, A., Malhi, Y., Lewis, S. L., Martinez, R. V., Alexiades, M., Dávila, E. Á., Alvarez-Loayza, P., Andrade, A., Aragão, L. E. O. C., Araujo-Murakami, A., Arets, E. J. M. M., et al. (2015). Long-term decline of the Amazon carbon sink. *Nature, 519*, 344–348.

Bushfires Still Raging in New South Wales. (2019, November 9). *NASA Earth Observatory*. https://earthobservatory.nasa.gov/images/145861/bushfires-still-raging-in-new-south-wales?src=eoa-iotd

Casado, L., & Londoño, E.. (2019, July 28). Under Brazil's far right leader, Amazon protections slashed and forests fall. *New York Times*. https://www.nytimes.com/2019/07/28/world/americas/brazil-deforestation-amazon-bolsonaro.html

Cave, D. (2019, December 10). Fire season arrives early in Australia, destroying popular lodge near rainforest. *New York Times*, A-8.

Cave, D. (2020a, January 9). Murdoch manipulates debate on Australia's fires. *New York Times*, B-1, B-5.

Cave, D. (2020b, February 24). Drought, fire, deluge: Climate's multiplier effect pounds Australia. *New York Times*, A-4.

Cave, D., & Akbeck-Ripka, L. (2020, January 9). Fires threaten Australian towns that have already been burned once. *New York Times*. https://www.nytimes.com/2020/01/09/world/australia/fires.html

Cox, P. M., Betts, R. A., Collins, M., Harris, P. P., Huntingford, & Jones, C. D. (2004). Amazonian forest dieback under climate-carbon cycle projections for the twenty-first century. *Theoretical and Applied Climatology, 78*, 137–156.

Editor's Letter. (2020, January 27). *The Week*, 2.

Extreme Rain Douses Fires, Causes Floods in Australia. (2020, February 13). *NASA Earth Observatory*. https://earthobservatory.nasa.gov/images/146284/extreme-rain-douses-fires-causes-floods-in-australia?src=eoa-iotd

Federal, F. (2020, January–February). The road to ruin? *Smithsonian*, 54–65.

Fire in the Pantanal. NASA Earth Observatory. (2020, March 11). https://earthobservatory.nasa.gov/images/146409/fire-in-the-pantanal?src=eoa-iotd

Fisher, M. (2019, August 30). How the Amazon could self-destruct. *New York Times*, A-6.

Flanagan, R. (2020, January 4). Australia is committing climate suicide. *New York Times*. https://www.nytimes.com/2020/01/03/opinion/australia-fires-climate-change.html

Foley, M. (2019, December 31). Experts warn extreme bushfire weather risk growing. *Sydney Morning Herald*. https://www.smh.com.au/politics/federal/experts-warn-extreme-bushfire-weather-risk-growing-20191231-p53nw1.html

Foley, M. (2020, January 6). More hazard-reduction burns not the answer, experts warn. *Sydney Morning Herald*. https://www.smh.com.au/politics/federal/more-hazard-reduction-burns-not-the-answer-experts-warn-20200107-p53p8i.html

Fountain, H. (2020a, March 5). Warming contributed to wildfires. *New York Times*, A-6.

Fountain, H. (2020b, June 3). 'Going in the wrong direction': Tropical forests are shrinking. *New York Times*, A-14.

Friday Morning Brief, Seattle Times. (2020, January 3). https://outlook.office.com/mail/inbox/id/AAMkADVmNGE2MGU2LWQ0MDItNDkyNS04YTg2LTY4YmUzZDAwZDA3YwBGAAAAAAA%2FRhKKKmMvQYnCF4rsc4kTBwC5ivxYey%2BbS4%2F0UJnRtHAFAAAA8tYkAADdlfbKMp2hTbjKlxLFP60vAAYGVmZNAAA%3D

Fuller, T. (2021, May 17). Warning shot for California: A Los Angeles wildfire in May. *New York Times*. https://www.nytimes.com/2021/05/17/us/palisades-fire-california-drought.html

Fuller, T., & Abbott, M. (2020, January 17). Reducing, and cutting emissions, the aboriginal way. *New York Times*, A-4.

Fuller, T., & Davenport, C. (2019, November 2). California is feeling the brunt of climate change with more intense fires; the trump administration is blocking the State's efforts to fight it. *New York Times*. https://www.nytimes.com/2019/11/02/us/climate-change-california-fires-trump.html

Joyce, C. (2011, February 7). 'Alarming' Amazon droughts may have global fallout. National Public Radio in NASA Earth Observatory. http://www.npr.org/2011/02/07/133462608/alarming-amazon-droughts-may-have-global-fallout?ft=1&f=1007

Kolbert, E. (2020, January 13). Don't wait. [Talk of the Town]. *The New Yorker*, 13–14.

Krauss, C., Yaffe-Bellany, D., & Simoes, M. (2019, October 11). Why is the rainforest in Brazil still burning? *New York Times*, A-8, A-9.

Krugman, P. (2020, January 3). Apocalypse becomes the new normal. *New York Times*, A-22.

Kwai, I. (2020, January 1). To flee devastating fires, Australians seek refuge on water, 11 are dead. *New York Times*, A-7.

Londaño, E., & Casado, L. (2019, August 29). Government environmental workers criticize Bolsonaro in open letter. *New York Times*, A-8.

Londaño, E., & Casado, L. (2020, April 19). As Bolsonaro keeps Amazon vows, Brazil's indigenous fear 'ethnocide;' president Jair Bolsonaro is moving aggressively to open up the Amazon rainforest to commercial development, posing an existential threat to the tribes living there. *New York Times*. https://www.nytimes.com/2020/04/19/world/americas/bolsonaro-brazil-amazon-indigenous.html

Londoño, E., & Casado, L. (2019, November 19). In Brazil, Amazon deforestation has risen sharply on Bolsonaro's watch. *New York Times*, A-4.

Londoño, E., Andreoni, M., & Casado, L. (2020a, April 2). President of Brazil defiantly rejects calls to institute a lockdown. *New York Times*, A-5.

Londoño, E., Casado, L., & Andreoni, M. (2020b, May 1). Bolsonaro fights for survival, turning to empowered military elders. *New York Times*. https://www.nytimes.com/2020/05/01/world/americas/brazil-bolsonaro-coronavirus-crisis.html?campaign_id=2&emc=edit_th_200502&instance_id=18088&nl=todaysheadlines&regi_id=35795487&segment_id=26447&user_id=8953ac8150496623ee2c782e2065b2e1

Malhi, Y., Roberts, J. T., Betts, R. A., Killeen, T. J., Li, W., & Nobre, C. A. (2008, January 11). Climate change, deforestation, and the fate of the Amazon. *Science, 319*, 169–172).

McGuirk, R. (2020, January 21). In Australia: Dust, hail, floods. *USA Today*, 8-A.

Paddock, R. C., & Suhartono, M. (2019a, September 18). Fires in Indonesia spur fears as Amazon burns. *New York Times*, A-4.

Paddock, R. C., & Suhartono, M.. (2019b, September 26). 'Hellish' fires choke Indonesia under blood-red sky. *New York Times*, A-6.

Pedroso, R., & Koch, J.. (2021, June 19). Bolsonaro's rule is 'worse threat than coronavirus' say Brazilians as nation passes 500,000 [Deaths]. *Cable News Network*. https://www.cnn.com/2021/06/19/americas/brazil-covid-deaths-intl-cmd/index.html

Pérez-Peña, R. (2020, March 26). Australia's record heat means another blow to great barrier reef. *New York Times*. https://www.nytimes.com/2020/03/26/world/australia/bleaching-great-barrier-reef.html

Pierre-Louis, K. (2019, August 29). Complex fires gain ferocity as earth heats. *New York Times*, A-1, A-8.

Plumer, B. (2018, June 27). Tropical forests suffered near-record tree loses in 2017. *New York Times*. https://www.nytimes.com/2018/06/27/climate/tropical-trees-deforestation.com

Rangel, T. F. (2012). Amazonian extinction debts. *Science, 337*, 162–163.

Remsen, N. (2019, August 29). A Brazilian fantasy during dark days. *New York Times*, D-3.

Romero, S. (2012, November 24). Swallowing rain forest, cities surge in Amazon. *New York Times*. http://www.nytimes.com/2012/11/25/world/americas/swallowing-rain-forest-brazilian-cities-surge-in-amazon.html

Romero, S. (2019, August 30). Amazon forests vanish at breakneck speed, and it's not just Brazil. *New York Times*. https://www.nytimes.com/2019/08/30/world/americas/amazon-rainforest.html

Sandy, M. (2019, December 6). Amazon Under Bolsonaro: 'Completely Lawless'. *New York Times*, A-12.

Smoked-cloaked City: Sao Paulo. (2019, August 30). *The Week*, 6.

Spracklen, D. V., Arnold, S. R., & Taylor, C. M. (2012, September 13). Observations of increased tropical rainfall preceded by air passage over forests. *Nature, 489*, 282–285.

Sullivan, H. (2019, January 9). Some of Australia's smallest species could be lost to wildfires. *New York Times*. https://urldefense.proofpoint.com/v2/url?u=https-3Anl.nytimes.com

Tabuchi, H., Rigby, C., & Whitefeb, J.. (2017, February 24). Amazon deforestation, once tamed, comes roaring back. *New York Times*. https://www.nytimes.com/2017/02/24/business/energy-environment/deforestation-brazil-bolivia-south-america.html

Tarabay, J. (2020, January 13). In Australia, fire inquiry aims to defer carbon policy. *New York Times*, A-6.

10

Though the Heavens Should Fall: The Mansfield Decision (1772)

Barbara Alice Mann

The American Revolution has long been acclaimed as a righteous and liberating fight against taxation without representation and such tyrannous behavior as a government's forcing its citizens to house and feed its soldiers, even when those soldiers are oppressing them.[1] These arguments were pressed on the Continental Congress by William Henry Drayton in 1774 and have long been taken up as the only considerations. Although these certainly were glorious impetuses behind the American Revolution, there were other triggers, since obscured, that nevertheless deserve attention. Not the least of these was that settlers were not about to give up their African slaves.[2] Retaining slavery is a reason that the vast majority of the "heroes" of the American Revolution were large-scale slave owners like George Washington, who "owned" 400

---

[1] William Henry Drayton, "A Letter from Freeman of South Carolina, to the Deputies of North America, Assembled in High Congress at Philadelphia." In Robert Wilson Gibbs, ed., *Documentary History of the American Revolution, 1764–1776: Consisting of Letters and Papers Relating to the Contest for Liberty, Chiefly in South Carolina, from Originals in the Possession of the Editor, and Other Sources* (1774; New York: Appleton & Co., 1855) taxation, 14, 17; quartering and billeting, 25–26.

[2] Barbara Alice Mann, *President by Massacre: Indian-Killing for Political Gain* (Santa Barbara, CA: Praeger, An Imprint of ABC-CLIO, 2019) 216–19.

Barbara Alice Mann (✉)
Toledo, USA
e-mail: Barbara.mann@utoledo.edu

human beings in 1797.³ Slavery was an engine of colonial prosperity, with Wall Street existing as THE American market selling and speculating in slaves since the Dutch settlers began it in 1659.⁴

Slavery was at once repressed yet prominent. In the Freudian sense, repression is likened to an obstreperous man tossed out of the conference room for disrupting proceedings, with guards thereafter barring the door against his reentry.⁵ In just this way, slavery was omnipresent, psychologically noisy yet denied, constantly pricking conscience. Euro-settlers projected their uneasiness over slavery by presenting themselves as its victims, with slavery looming as a *Euro-settler* fate. In South Carolina, for instance, Revolutionary landholders likened any challenge to their rights as an attempt to enslave them.⁶ When the Mansfield Decision of 1772 ripped the veil of misdirection from the face of projection, it forced slavery, naked, into the open.

The Mansfield Decision on June 22, 1772, thus carried repercussions far beyond the one man set free on that day by the King's Court Bench (the rough equivalent of the US Supreme Court). To his lasting fame, the presiding judge, William Murray, the First Earl of Mansfield, Lord Chief Justice from 1756 to 1788, decided the fraught case of *Somerset* versus *Stuart*. It pitted the human rights of James Somerset ("Somersett"), an enslaved African, against the "property rights" of a Virginia "master," Charles Stuart ("Steuart," "Stewart").⁷ Somerset had already been a slave in Africa, when on March 10, 1749, British Captain John Knowles shipped him west along his usual route from Africa to Virginia and Jamaica for sale into colonial slavery. In Virginia, Somerset was sold to Stuart on August 1, 1749.⁸

---

³ Fritz Hirschfeld, *George Washington and Slavery: A Documentary Portrayal* (Columbia, MO: University of Missouri Press, 1997) 56.
⁴ Frederick Trevor Hill, *The Story of a Street: A Narrative History of Wall Street from 1644 to 1908* (New York: Harper & Brothers, 1908) viii, facing 14, 28, 33, 67, 94–95, 131; Anne Farrow, Joel Lang, and Jenifer Frank, *Complicity: How the North Promoted, Prolonged, and Profited from Slavery* (New York: Hartford Courant Company, 2005) 20, 82, 92, 125; Alan J. Singer, *New York and Slavery: Time to Teach the Truth* (Albany, NY: SUNY, Excelsior Editions, 2008) 1–2, 28, 30, 47, 51.
⁵ Sigmund Freud, *Five Lectures and Psycho-Analysis* (New York: W. W. Norton, 1961) 25.
⁶ Jack P. Greene, "'Slavery or Independence:' Some Reflections on the Relationship among Liberty, Black Bondage, and Equality in Revolutionary South Carolina," *The South Carolina Historical Magazine*, vol. 101, no. 1 (January, 2000): first published 1979, 15; comparisons to chattel slavery, 20–23, *passim*.
⁷ "The Negro Case," 12 George III, in T. B. Howell, *A Complete Collection of State Trials and Proceedings for High Treason and Other Crimes and Misdemeanors from the Earliest Period to the Year 1783, with Notes and Other Illustrations*, vol. 20 (London: T. C. Hansard, 1816) for rights as Englishman, 29; for property rights argument, 3–4.
⁸ Francis Hargrave, *An Argument in the Case of James Sommersett, A Negro, Lately Determined by the Court of King's Bench; Wherein It Is Attempted to Demonstrate the Present Unlawfulness of Domestic Slavery in England, to Which Is Prefixed a State of the Case* (London: W. Otridge, 1772) 5–6.

10 *Though the Heavens Should Fall*: The Mansfield Decision (1772)

Events sailed into history on October 1, 1769, when Stuart took Somerset with him on a business trip to England, arriving in London on November 1, 1769. His business concluded, Stuart prepared to return to Virginia when, to his dismay, Somerset "absolutely refused" to return to American slavery, citing British law.[9] The law to which Somerset referred consisted of a set of legal precedents in 1637, 1692, 1701, 1702, and 1769. The Mansfield Decision of 1772 was no bolt from the blue but followed precedents long set in British law.

As early as 1637, John Rushworth recorded the legal decision against "whipping" as "painful and shameful" in a case of "*Flagellation* for slaves" brought against "one Cartwright" who had bought a Russian slave, whom he would "scourge" regularly. For his abusiveness, Cartwright was "questioned," with the case resolved by the pronouncement that "*England* was too pure an Air for Slaves to breathe in," interpreted legally to mean that there were no slaves in England (italics and capitals in the original).[10]

Following this precedent, in 1692, the then-Lord Chief Justice of the King's Bench, John Holt, declared that "so soon a negro lands in England, he is free," a decision he repeated in 1701, adding in 1702, that "there is no such thing as a slave by the law of England."[11] Hitchhiking on Rushworth and Holt, in 1769, Granville Sharp successfully argued that "no man" (or by extension, woman) could "lawfully be detained in England *as a slave*" because England had "no law" allowing anyone to be enslaved. Each person "must necessarily be allowed" to hold "*superior property*" in "his own *proper person*," that is, each person alone owned him- or herself (italics in the original).[12] American settlers were already dodging Holt's very clear decision when they began legally euphemizing their slaves as "servants."[13] As the first governor of the Northwest

---

[9] "The Negro Case," 12 George III, 21.

[10] John Rushworth, *Historical Collections; The Second Part, Containing the Principal Matters, Which Happened from the Dissolution of the Parliament on the tenth of March, 1628, until the Summoning of Another Parliament Which Met at Westminster, April 13, 1640; with the Account of the Proceedings of that Parliament and the Transactions and Affairs from the Time until the Meeting of Another Parliament, November the third Following, with Some Remarkable Passages therein during the First Six Months*, Part 2 (London: By J. D. for John Wright at the Crown on Ludgate Hill, 1680) 468.

[11] Horace Greeley, John F. Cleveland, and John Fitch, *A Political Text-Book for 1860, Comprising a Brief View of Presidential Nominations and Elections: Including All the National Platforms Ever Yet Adopted; Also, a History of the Struggle Respecting Slavery in the Territories, and of the Actions of Congress as to the Freedom of the Public Lands, with the Most Notable Speeches and Letters of Mssrs. Lincoln, Douglass, Bell, Cass, Steward, Everett, Breckenridge, H. V. Johnson*, Etc. Etc., *Touching the Questions of the Day; And Returns of All Presidential Elections Since 1836* (New York: Published by the Tribune Association, 1860) 50; Akhil Reed Amar, *America's Constitution: A Biography* (New York: Random House Trade Paperbacks, 2005) 257.

[12] Granville Sharp, *Extract from a Representation of the Injustice and Dangerous Tendency of Tolerating Slavery, or Admitting the Least Claim of Private Property in the Persons of Men in England* (London: Joseph Cruikshank, 1769) 7–8.

[13] Mann, *President by Massacre*, 13–17; for instance, Fordham noted the Kentucky habit calling the slave a "servant," Elias Pym Fordham, *Personal Narrative of Travels in Virginia, Maryland, Pennsylvania, Ohio,*

Territories and then as Governor of Indiana, William Henry Harrison worked mightily through the "servant" angle to legalize slavery in the Old Northwest, despite federal Ordinances outlawing it there.[14]

The niceties of British law were lost on Stuart. Outraged, he essentially kidnapped Somerset on November 26, 1771, smuggling him aboard the vessel *Ann and Mary*, then idling in the Thames River, and making a deal with Captain John Knowles to sell Somerset in Jamaica in revenge for his disobedience.[15] Somerset was not friendless, however. On December 3, 1771, British abolitionists Thomas Walkin, Elizabeth Cade, and John Marlow joined in an affidavit attesting to the unlawful confinement of "James Sommersett" in the hold of the *Ann and Mary*. Filing a writ of habeas corpus with the King's Bench Court on behalf of the imprisoned Somerset, they requested that Somerset be produced, preferably in one piece. The writ was duly served upon Captain Knowles, who complied on December 9, 1772, by delivering up Somerset. At the same time, affidavits were produced by Stuart and two compatriots, proving that Stuart had bought Somerset for his slave in the colony of Virginia.[16]

Mansfield extended the habeas corpus from early December, 1771, until January 12, 1772, the second day of the first 1772 Hilary term (January 11–31, 1772). When the case resumed on February 7, objections were heard with arguments continuing till after Easter, April 19, 1772, the case running into June, 1772.[17] Following Jerome Nadelhaft, David Olusoga believes that Mansfield was dragging his feet with the continuances, but Mansfield was juggling regular court terms (Michaelmas, Hilary, and Easter terms) and Christian festivals.[18] The British holiday of Michaelmas was upon the country (running from September 29th to Christmas, December 25th), while the continuance till January 12th allowed for New Year's celebrations, Easter, and travel time around them both, in the age of horse-drawn carriages. Thus, although Mansfield was well aware of the implications of the case and purportedly tried to coax Somerset and Stuart into settling out of court (a

---

Indiana, Kentucky; and of a Residence in the Illinois Territory, 1817–1818 (Cleveland: A. H. Clark & Co., 1906) 125.

[14] Mann, *President by Massacre*, 11–17, *passim*.

[15] Hargrave, *An Argument*, 4; for the date of departure, Hargrave, *An Argument*, 6; for quotation, Hargrave, *An Argument*, 7; for date of kidnap, Hargrave, *An Argument*, 7–8.

[16] Hargrave, *An Argument*, 3–4.

[17] Hargrave, *An Argument*, 4. February 7, Hargrave, *An Argument*, 8; continuance after Easter, Hargrave, *An Argument*, 33–34.

[18] David Olusoga, *Black and British: A Forgotten History* (London: Macmillan, 2016) 131.

common practice), that is not the same thing as deliberate foot dragging.[19] In fact, in the person of a Black great-niece of whom Mansfield was reportedly fond, he might have harbored a predisposition in favor of Somerset.[20] (Perhaps that is why, according to Stuart, Mansfield even nudged Stuart to resolve the case by freeing Somerset.[21])

In the proceedings, Somerset was primarily represented by two attorneys ("Serjeants-at-law"), William Davy and John Glyn, with friendly briefs also proffered by Francis Hargrave, who made his reputation on the case, along with the noted Irish lawyers, John Alleyne, and John Philpot Curran.[22] Attorneys for Stuart were William Wallace and John Dunning.[23]

In the final analysis, it was the decision, not the timing that was contentious. In finding that Somerset was a man, Mansfield had essentially acceded to Hargrave's argument that, as a relationship, slavery was artificial, not natural, and therefore (as Holt had had it long before Mansfield) slavery had to be manufactured as a sort of monstrosity under the law. Even then, Hargrave argued, slavery had no moral standing under "Natural Law."[24] In the late eighteenth century, "unnatural" was a code word for depraved perversion leaning toward the sexually disgusting, so that Hargrave was doubly rebuking slaveholders as kidnappers and sexual predators. This was why Stuart's lawyer, Dunning, responded by invoking the husband–wife bond as his own example of an artificial yet innocent relationship, albeit one that had to be created.[25] At the time, marriage was sacrosanct, unquestionably god-given, so that Dunning here implied that slavery was the same. Dunning also took care to undermine Rushworth's 1637 verdict, proclaiming that "neither the air of English is too pure for a slave to breathe in, nor the laws of England have rejected servitude," meaning that, if there were no English law recognizing slavery, there was also no English law *prohibiting* slavery.[26]

---

[19] Jerome Nadelhaft, "The Somersett Case and Slavery: Myth, Reality, and Repercussions," *The Journal of Negro History*, vol. 51, no. 3 (July 1966): 198.
[20] Alfred W. Blumrosen and Ruth G. Blumrosen, *Slave Nation: How Slavery United the Colonies and Sparked the American Revolution* (Naperville, IL: Sourcebooks, Inc., 2005) 8.
[21] Nadelhaft, "The Somersett Case," 198.
[22] Hargrave, *An Argument*, 8. For Curran's involvement, see John McLean, Dissent, Dred Scott Decision, in Benjamin C. Howard, *Report of the Dred Scott Decision of the Supreme Court of the United States, and the Opinions of the Judges Thereof in the Case of Dred Scott* versus *John F. A. Sanford, December Term, 1856* (Washington, D.C.: Cornelius Wendell, 1857) 141; for Hargrave's reputation, Nadelhaft, "The Somerset Case," note 16, 199.
[23] Hargrave, *An Argument*, 9; Olusoga, *Black and British*, 130.
[24] 1 Lofft 11–12, 98 *ER*, 505–506; "Natural Law," 1 Lofft 3, 500; as a legislative creation, Nadelhaft, "The Somersett Case," 196.
[25] 1 Lofft 12, 98 *ER*, 506.
[26] 1 Lofft 12, 98 *ER*, 506.

The real key to Hargrave's argument was not about relationships but about establishing that Somerset was "a man." That he was may seem obvious today, but in the eighteenth-century European mind, declaring Africans to be "men" immediately conferred on them rights equivalent to those of Europeans.[27] Hargrave, therefore, stressed that only a man could "bind himself to serve by contract for life," a claim in line with Sharp's 1769 dictum.[28] This flew in the face of the entire colonial enterprise, which granted "golden" supremacy, in the Platonic sense, to any and all "whites," so long as they lived in a British colony.[29] As top of the heap, Euro-settlers could not be owned, but they could own "lesser" others. Should Africans also be declared "men," Euro-supremacy and slavery, in particular, stood to be upended.

Thus, on June 22, 1772, Mansfield did the unthinkable: He decided in favor of Somerset.

No latte liberal, Mansfield fully grasped the consequences of his ruling for both England and its American colonies. Bankruptcy topped the list of Mansfield's reported concerns, with slaveholders standing to lose £50 per freed slave.[30] One hundred slaves freed equaled £5000, or about $13.2 million in today's currency. There were supposedly 14,000–15,000 slaves who stood to be freed.[31] This was one reason why Mansfield was said to have prefaced his pronouncement by crying, "*Fiat justitia, ruat cœlum*" ("let justice be done, though the heavens should fall!").[32] He boldly ordered that Somerset be "discharged," meaning that Somerset was to walk out of the court, a free man.[33]

An academic dispute arose in the mid-twentieth century about the wording of the Mansfield's decision. The best-known record of the case comes from Capel Lofft, whose documentation of the King's Bench cases from 1772 to 1774 is the only one extant for that time period. Lofft was an ardent abolitionist, so in his famous 1966 article on the Mansfield decision, Jerome Nedelhaft suggested that Lofft had stuffed the arguments of Somerset's ardent lawyer, Hargrave, into Mansfield's mouth. Moreover, Nadelhaft noted that

---

[27] Greene, "'Slavery or Independence," 29–30.

[28] 1 Lofft 11–12, 98 *ER*, 500–501.

[29] Mann, *President by Massacre*, xiii-xiv; Plato, *The Republic*, ca. 360 B.C.E., trans. Richard C. Sterling and W. C. Scott (New York: W. W. Norton, 1985) 415a–415e.

[30] Nadelhaft, "The Somerset Case," 197–98.

[31] Nadelhaft, "The Somerset Case," 198.

[32] Simon Gikandi, *Slavery and the Culture of Taste* (Princeton, NJ: University of Princeton Press, 2011) 92. The legal precept, *fiat justitia, ruat cœlum*, is attributed to Governor Lucius Calpurnius Piso Ceasonius and is short-handed as "Piso's justice." Geoffrey Rivlin, *First Steps in the Law* (Oxford, GB: Oxford University Press, 2015) 93.

[33] "Historical Chronicle, June, 1772," in *Gentlemen's Magazine and Historical Chronicle*, vol. 42, no. 6 (1772): 293–94; "Negro Case," 12 George III, Howell, 82.

10 *Though the Heavens Should Fall*: The Mansfield Decision (1772)

Lofft's account was not published until 1776, implying that the passage of time between 1772 and 1776 might have blurred Lofft's memory.[34] Nadelhaft, therefore, preferred the wording of an earlier, one-paragraph account of the ruling that appeared in the *Gentleman's Magazine* in June, 1772, soon after the decision.

According to Lofft, Mansfield declared, "The state of slavery is of such a nature that it is incapable of being introduced on any reasons, moral or political, but only by positive law." No such English law authorizing slavery existed, however. Following instead the precedents of Rushworth, Holt, and Sharp, Lofft's Mansfield found that slavery was not "allowed or approved by the law of England" but was "so odious, that nothing can be suffered to support it." Therefore, Mansfield concluded, the "black must be discharged."[35]

The *Gentleman's Magazine* offers essentially the same outline of the case, albeit in a frustratingly brief summary. Of the kidnapping of Somerset, the *Magazine* has Mansfield declaring, "So high an act of dominion was never in use here," i.e., in England, and "no master here was ever allowed to take a slave by force to be sold abroad" for recalcitrance or "any other reason whatever." Thus, Mansfield "could not say" that Stuart's cause was "allowed or approved by the laws of this kingdom; therefore, the man [Somerset] must be discharged."[36] The only substantial difference between the two versions is the omission in the *Magazine* account of Mansfield's direct reference in Lofft to slavery's existence by "positive law," but the *Magazine*'s reference to a lack of British law approving Stuart's actions intimates reference to the claim. The extreme compression of the whole case to a single paragraph necessarily strips the flesh from around the *Magazine*'s recital.

Nadelhaft's only other evidence of mouth-stuffing was speculative, consisting of conclusions drawn from Lofft's abolitionist sentiments and Lofft's publication Four years after the decision. If Lofft shortened Dunning's and Wallace's arguments on behalf of Stuart, then the *Magazine* did not record any arguments at all. As for the 1776 publication date, Lofft was recording two years' worth of court proceedings (1772–1774), and there is no evidence that he was not recording from life for plenary publication later. It would not have been unusual for preparing a fair copy, typesetting, copy editing, and publishing to occupy a year or so, delaying the appearance of Lofft's accounts till 1776. Most importantly, the result remained the same in both Lofft and the *Magazine*: Somerset walked out of court a free man. Whether the

---

[34] Nadelhaft, "The Somerset Case," 201.
[35] "Negro Case," 12 George III, Howell, 82.
[36] "Historical Chronicle," 293–94.

decision's wording was "the man" or "the black," both accounts agreed that Mansfield's finding required that Somerset be discharged. Interestingly, at the time, the *Magazine*'s use of the word "man" for Somerset would have been more controversial than Lofft's use of the word "black," while the *Magazine*'s heightened language describing the seizure of Somerset as an act of unexampled high dominion rivaled any bias expressed in Lofft.

Mansfield had spoken, but no one seemed pleased. Abolitionists in the colonial north expressed disgust that Mansfield had not gone further with his order. Benjamin Franklin waxed snide, noting the "hypocrisy" of England. On the one hand, it continued the "detestable commerce" by legally "promoting the Guinea trade" (i.e., African slavery) while on the other hand, it "piqued itself on its virtue, its love of liberty, and the equity of its courts, in setting free a single negro."[37] For his part, the editor of the *North American Review*, Edward Everett dismissed Mansfield's decision as a half-measure. Mocking Rushworth's 1637 pronouncement that "the air of England" was "too pure for a slave," Everett observed that England had no apparent trouble "resorting to the labor of slaves" when it came to crops like tobacco and cotton that could not be grown in Norfolk, England (as opposed, say, to Norfolk, Virginia).[38]

On the pro-slavery side, planters were downright volcanic in their reproaches. Of the 24 surviving colonial newspapers, 22 reproduced arguments in the case at length as it went along, the clear implication being that it would impact slavery in the colonies.[39] In 1774, a pamphlet of "Fugitive Thoughts" appeared, purportedly by "A Black Settler" in South Carolina, with both puns (fugitive and black setter) conjuring up southern Slaveholder fears of slave escapes. Declaring that Mansfield would "complete the Ruin of many *American* Provinces," by engendering a "general Manumission of Negroes," Mansfield was derided as "badly calculated for the Meridian" of the Americas (capitalizations and italics in the original).[40]

Hysteria reigned, and not just because American colonists (and not a few English citizens) mistakenly believed that Mansfield had freed *all* the slaves, not just Somerset.[41] This conclusion rested on more than just a feverish overinterpretation of events; it rested on the 1766 Declaratory Act of Parliament,

---

[37] Benjamin Franklin, *The Writings of Benjamin Franklin*, ed. Albert Henry Smyth, vol. 5 (New York: The Macmillan Company, 1906) vol. 5, August 22, 1772, Benjamin Franklin to Anthony Benezet, 431–32.
[38] Edward Everett, "On the Complaints in America against the British Press: An Essay in the *New London Monthly Magazine* for February, 1821," *North American Review*, vol. 13, no. 32, New Series, vol. 4, no. 1 (July, 1821): 45–46.
[39] George William Van Cleve, *A Slaveholders' Union: Slavery, Politics, and the Constitution in the Early American Republic* (Chicago: University of Chicago Press, 2010) 33.
[40] Greene, "'Slavery or Independence," 27.
[41] Nadelhaft, "The Somersett Case," 193, 196, 199.

10 *Though the Heavens Should Fall*: The Mansfield Decision (1772)

which required laws in the American colonies to comport with British law in England.[42] Parliament held the power to overrule any colonial law that it saw as incompatible with British law. If forceable transport of slaves was illegal in England, as Mansfield ruled, then what would happen to the slaves transported in and around the American colonies? Mansfield, himself, was not oblivious of the potential blowback should he decide for Somerset. In 1771, he fretted about the "consequences" should "masters" like Stuart "lose their property by accidentally bringing their slaves to England."[43]

The depth of slaveholders' paranoia can be seen in a story in the *South Caroline Gazette*. On September 15, 1772, the *Gazette* ominously reported that "two hundred blacks and their ladies" banqueted in London to celebrate the liberation of the slaves.[44] In response to such a thought, horrifying to planters, the pro-slavery polemicist Edward Long wrote a point-by-point rebuttal of the Mansfield Decision. Following his learned arguments from history and law, Long's pearl-clutching clincher was to describe the West Indies as so "destructive to Europeans in those climates," that "Negroes" from "Guiney" were an "absolute necessity." The "utter inaptitude" of Europeans to withstand all that heat meant that they either had to continue African slavery or "abandon" their plantations, an unimaginable option.[45]

American slaves were as aware of the Mansfield decision as were the slaveholders, with slaves initiating their escapes to British soil as soon as Mansfield's decision hit the papers.[46] One "servant" named Dublin told his fellow slaves that his "Uncle Sommerset" had written to let him know that "Lord Mansfield had given them their freedom." Dublin took his clothes and left his sometime master sputtering in ire at his audacity.[47] Following the decision, escaped slaves inundated London, which soon saw 15,000 "starving and freezing exslaves" who had fled "plantations in the Americas."[48]

The frenzy did not die with the Treaty of Paris (1783). Still fuming in 1788 that British law had legally recognized Africans as "men" with human rights, at the convention to ratify the US Constitution, Patrick Henry maintained

---

[42] Blumrosen and Blumrosen, *Slave Nation*, 30.

[43] Blumrosen and Blumrosen, *Slave Nation*, 8.

[44] *South Carolina Gazette* and *Country Journal*, Tuesday, September 15, 1772.

[45] Edward Long, *Candid Reflections upon the Judgement Lately awarded by the Court of King's Bench in Westminster-Hall on what Is Commonly Called the Negroe-cause, by a Planter* (London: T. Lowndes, 1772) respectively, pp. 16–17, 21.

[46] Blumrosen and Blumrosen (2005, pp. 24–25).

[47] Alan Gilbert, *Black Patriots and Loyalists: Fighting for Emancipation in the War for Independence* (Chicago: University of Chicago Press, 2012) 8.

[48] George O. Roberts, "The Sierra Leone Experience with Foreign Assistance," *Journal of African Studies*, vol. 3, no. 1 (Spring, 1976): 85.

that slaves, "as well as every other property of the people of Virginia" was "in jeopardy"—now from the proposed US Constitution![49] (Article 1, Section 9 of the Constitution cut off the importation of slaves as of 1808.) In 1862, 90 years after the Mansfield decision, the redoubtable *De Bow's Review* continued to froth over the "inconsistency and effrontery" of the Mansfield decision.[50]

The American pandemonium over Mansfield explains some of Thomas Jefferson's wild language in his draft of the Declaration of Independence. England had pressed slavery on the colonies in the first place, Jefferson pouted, thereafter "exciting those very people" (meaning African slaves) "to rise in arms among" the Euro-colonists "to purchase that liberty of which" George III had originally "deprived them … by murdering the people upon whom he ha[d] obtruded them" in the first place![51] This convoluted verbiage was too much even for Jefferson's fellow slaveholders, who were aware that it would alienate necessary northern confederates favoring abolition. In the toned-down, final version of the Declaration, Jefferson primly accused George III of having "excited domestic insurrections" against the Revolutionaries, a charge so vague that most modern Americans have no idea that it refers to the Mansfield decision.[52]

In the end, *fecit caelum ruinam*; Mansfield did make the heavens fall, for immediately as his ruling hit American shores, editors, pamphleteers, abolitionists, and slaveholders ran mad, largely denouncing his decision. Within two years of his decision, the American colonies had declared their Independence from Great Britain; within three years of his decision, the battles of Lexington and Concord had been fought; and within four years of his decision, pitched warfare had erupted between the Revolutionaries and the Crown. By the end of 1782, a mere decade later, the colonies had broken free of England, retaining their "peculiar institution" of slavery for another 80-odd years.

---

[49] Speech by Patrick Henry, June 24, 1788, in Jonathan Elliott, ed., *The Debates, Resolutions, and Other Proceedings, in Convention on the Adoption of the Federal Constitution as Recommended by the General Convention at Philadelphia on the 17th of September, 1787, with the Yeas and Nays on the Decision of the Main Question*, 5 vols. (Washington, D.C.: Jonathan Elliott, 1828) 2: 432.

[50] "Somerset's Case," *De Bow's Review*, vol. 32, Nos. 3–4 (March–April, 1862): 171.

[51] Thomas Jefferson, *The Writings of Thomas Jefferson*, ed. Albert Ellery Bergh, 20 vols. in 10 (Washington, D.C.: Thomas Jefferson Memorial Association of the United States, 1903–1907) vols, 11–12, in vol. 12, vii.

[52] "Declaration of Independence: A Transcription," National Archives: America's Founding Documents, last reviewed July 24, 2020, accessed 6/28/21; https://www.archives.gov/founding-docs/declaration-transcript

Bibliography

Amar, A. R. (2005). *America's constitution: A biography*. Random House Trade Paperbacks.

Blumrosen, A. W., & Blumrosen, R. G. (2005). *Slave nation: How Slavery United the colonies and sparked the American revolution*. Sourcebooks.

Declaration of Independence: A Transcription. National archives: America's Founding Documents. Last reviewed July 24, 2020. Accessed 6/28/21. https://www.archives.gov/founding-docs/declaration-transcript

Drayton, W. H. (Ed.). (1855). A letter from freeman of South Carolina, to the deputies of North America, assembled in high congress at Philadelphia. In Robert Wilson Gibbs. *Documentary History of the American Revolution, 1764–1776: Consisting of Letters and Papers Relating to the Contest for Liberty, Chiefly in South Carolina, from Originals in the Possession of the Editor, and Other Sources*. 1774 (pp. 11–38). Appleton & Co.

Elliott, J. (Ed.). (1828). *The Debates, Resolutions, and Other Proceedings, in Convention on the Adoption of the Federal Constitution as Recommended by the General Convention at Philadelphia on the 17th of* September, 1787, *with the Yeas and Nays on the Decision of the Main Question*. 5 vols (Vol. 2, pp. 430–40). Jonathan Elliott.

Everett, E. (1821). On the complaints in America against the British Press: An essay in the *New London Monthly Magazine* for February, 1821. *North American Review, 13*(32) (New Series. Vol. 4(1)), 20–47.

Farrow, A., Lang, J., & Frank, J. (2005). *Complicity: How the north promoted, prolonged, and profited from slavery*. Hartford Courant Company.

Franklin, B. (1906). *The Writings of Benjamin Franklin*. (Albert Henry Smyth, Ed.) (7 vols). The Macmillan Company.

Freud, S. (1961). *Five lectures and psycho-analysis*. W. W. Norton.

Fordham, E. P. (1906). *Personal narrative of travels in Virginia, Maryland, Pennsylvania, Ohio, Indiana, Kentucky; and of a residence in the Illinois territory, 1817–1818*. A. H. Clark &.

Gikandi, S. (2011). *Slavery and the culture of taste*. University of Princeton Press.

Gilbert, A. (2012). *Black patriots and loyalists: Fighting for emancipation in the war for independence*. University of Chicago Press.

Greeley, H., Cleveland, J. F., & Fitch, J. (1860). *A political text-book for 1860, comprising a brief view of presidential nominations and elections: Including all the national platforms ever yet adopted; also, a history of the struggle respecting slavery in the territories, and of the actions of congress as to the freedom of the public lands, with the most notable speeches and letters of Mssrs. Lincoln, Douglass, Bell, Cass, Steward, Everett, Breckenridge, H. V. Johnson, etc. etc., touching the questions of the day; and returns of all presidential elections since 1836*. Published by the Tribune Association.

Greene, J. P. (January, 2000). 'Slavery or independence:' Some reflections on the relationship among liberty, black bondage, and equality in revolutionary South Carolina. *The South Carolina Historical Magazine, 101*(1), 15–35.

Gresham, M. (1917). *Life of Walter Quintin Gresham, 1832–1895* (Vol. 2 vols). Rand McNally & Company.

Hargrave, F. (1772). *An argument in the Case of James Sommersett, A Negro, Lately determined by the court of King's Bench; wherein it is attempted to demonstrate the present unlawfulness of domestic slavery in England, to which is prefixed a state of the case*. W. Otridge.

Hill, F. T. (1908). *The story of a street: A narrative history of Wall Street from 1644 to 1908*. Harper & Brothers.

Hirschfeld, F. (1997). *George Washington and slavery: A documentary portrayal*. University of Missouri Press.

Historical Chronicle. (1772, June). *Gentleman's Magazine and Historical Chronicle, 42*(6), 289–294.

"The Negro Case." (1816). 12 George III. In Howell, T. B. *A Complete Collection of State Trials and Proceedings for High Treason and Other Crimes and Misdemeanors from the Earliest Period to the Year 1783, with Notes and Other Illustrations* (Vol. 20, (pp. 1–80). T. C. Hansard.

Jefferson, T. *The Writings of Thomas Jefferson*. Ed. Albert Ellery Bergh. 20 vols. in 10. Thomas Jefferson Memorial Association of the United States, 1903–1907.

Lofft, C. Somersett arguments. 1 Lofft 1, 98 *ER* 499.

Long, E. *Candid reflections upon the judgement Lately awarded by the Court of King's Bench in Westminster-Hall on what is commonly called the Negroe-cause, by a Planter* (pp. 1-78). Library of Congress. Accessed June 25, 2021., from https://www.loc.gov/resource/rbcmisc.lst0082/?sp=3

Mann, B. A. (2019). *President by Massacre: Indian-killing for political gain*. Praeger, An Imprint of ABC-CLIO.

McLean, J. (1857). Dissent. Dred Scott decision. In B. C. Howard (Ed.), *Report of the Dred Scott Decision of the Supreme Court of the United States, and the Opinions of the Judges Thereof in the Case of Dred Scott versus John F. A. Sanford, December Term, 1856* (pp. 135–70). Cornelius Wendell.

Nadelhaft, J. (1966). The Somersett case and slavery: Myth, reality, and repercussions. *The Journal of Negro History, 51*(3), 193–208.

Olusoga, D. (2016). *Black and british: A forgotten history*. Macmillan.

Plato. (1985). *The Republic. ca. 360 B.C.E.* (R. C. Sterling & W. C. Scott, Trans.). W. W. Norton.

Rivlin, G. (2015). *First steps in the law*. Oxford University Press.

Roberts, G. O. (1976). The Sierra Leone experience with foreign assistance. *Journal of African Studies, 3*(1), 83–100.

Rushworth, J. (1680). *Historical collections; The Second Part, Containing the principal matters, which happened from the dissolution of the parliament on the 10th of March, 1628, until the Summoning of Another Parliament Which Met at Westminster, April*

13, 1640; with the Account of the Proceedings of that Parliament and the Transactions and Affairs from the Time until the Meeting of Another Parliament, November the 3rd Following, with Some Remarkable Passages therein during the First Six Months*, Part 2. By J. D. for John Wright at the Crown on Ludgate Hill.

Sharp, G. (1769). *Extract from a representation of the injustice and dangerous tendency of tolerating slavery, or admitting the least claim of private property in the persons of men in England*. Joseph Cruikshank.

Singer, A. J. (2008). *New York and slavery: Time to teach the truth*. SUNY, Excelsior Editions.

Somerset's Case. (1862). *De Bow's Review*, 32(3–4), 171–187.

South Carolina Gazette and Country Journal. Tuesday. September 15, 1772.

Van Cleve, G. W. (2010). *A slaveholders' union: Slavery, politics, and the constitution in the early American Republic*. University of Chicago Press.

Wiecek, W. M. (1974). Somerset: Lord Mansfield and the legitimacy of slavery in the Anglo-American world. *University of Chicago Law Review, 42*(1), 86–146.

Index

A

Aboriginal Australians: as a set of monkies
  Aborigines Protection Boards to protect Aboriginals from hostile whites, 263, 265, 266, 268, 269, 271
  blood quantum, definition of
    the earlier they are exterminated [the] better, 261
  frontier conflicts between Aboriginal and colonists, 263
  "full-bloods" and "half castes", 264, 265, 268, 269, 272
Aborigines Protection Act (New South Wales), 1909, 269, 270
Adams, Will, former slave, 147, 213
Affirmative-action programs, 157, 161
African-Americans, ix, xvi, 2, 5, 33, 45, 83–107, 170, 171, 173, 178, 180, 201, 204, 205, 208, 216, 232, 233, 238, 241
Air conditioning, lack of, in prisons, 2, 6, 7, 297

Alcindor, Yamiche, encounter with Donald Trump, 97, 98
Amazon Valley
  "All of us here realize we're fucking the environment
    any alternative means to survive, 289
    It's not like we want to – it's that we haven't found, 289
  Cities grow as the rainforest withers" Manaus, 287, 288
  clearing of land accelerates deforestation, 286
  forests to sugar-cane fields, 286
  gold mining in, and deforestation, described, 288–291, 295
  Hydroelectric dams in, 288
  Lush forests to ashes, changes in climate, 285
  Mato Grosso, rainforest to dryland savannah, 288
  Venezuela, Columbia, Peru, Paraguay, and Argentina, 290

American Civil Liberties
Union, (ACLU)
called a "liberal white supremacist"
organization, 209
speakers shouted down on freedom
of speech issues, 186
American Indian Movement (AIM)
protests of Whiteclay beer stores,
184, 185
American Party of 1849 (Know
Nothings)
deportation of foreign "beggars,"
and criminals, 85
elimination of all Catholics from
public office, 85
exploitation of ethnic hatreds, 85
naturalization period of 21 years, 85
reject women's suffrage as
unnatural, 85
used immigrants as political targets,
which has persisted, 85
Anarchy in the United States?, 14, 154
Angelou, Maya, on Donald Trump's
words and behavior, 95
Antifa (anti-fascists), blamed by Trump
for agitation, 14, 25, 40, 41
Anti-Islamic rhetoric as hate
speech, 198
Arbery, Ahmaud, vii, 57, 58
Armed forces, U.S., considering a
coup?, 17, 33, 154, 291
Arradondo, Medaria, Minneapolis
police chief, at Chauvin
trial, 12, 64
Australia
"black Saturday" fires in Victoria
State, killed 173, 293
destruction of habitats koalas,
kangaroos, velvet worms,
293, 294
fires, sizes of, 283
"mega-diverse" array of species, 294
record heat during fires, 293, 296,
299, 306

Australian federal and state
governments, xvii, 253
Australians, Aboriginal, xvii,
253–254, 268
Australia, penal populism in, x, 111
Awá tribe's efforts to stem wildfires, 278

B

Baker, Andrew, Hennepin County
medical examiner, Chauvin
trial, 16, 18–20, 22, 40, 42,
44, 50, 65
Barr, William, U.S. attorney general, 14
Bayne, Sally, 169
Bear Heels, Zachary, died in police
custody, 23
Biden, Joe, U.S. president, 37, 47,
57, 72, 212
Birth of a Nation, and cultural
ignorance, 149, 202
Black codes, denial of basic rights to
Blacks, 11, 144
Black community permanently
disenfranchised, 144
Black community, unemployment rate
twice national average, 1930s
inclusive society undermined by
ideology of white supremacy,
141, 148
Blackface, history of, 11, 195, 200–204
Black Lives Matter, organizes rallies
after Floyd's murder
Black Lives Matter Plaza, within
sight of the White House, 23
"moves the needle" in the national
conversation over race
relations, 26
Black prisoners, sentencing
inconsistencies, 1, 2
Black shootings by police, viii
Blacks, stereotypes as inferior, lazy,
dangerous, sub-human
animals, 11

Blacks, two thousand elected to
   political offices throughout the
   South after Civil War, 147
Blackwell, Jerry W. Re: Floyd: "It's
   homicide", 60, 62
Black World War I veterans,
   lychings of, 149
Blake, Jacob, 15, 45–47, 58
Blake, Jacob, Jr., shot by police officer
   Rusten Sheskey, in
   Kenosha, Wisc
   Kenosha's African-American
      incarceration rate 80 per cent
      higher than Milwaukee, which
      itself has the third-highest rate
      of major U.S. cities, 45
Bolsonaro, Jair
   blames actor (and environmentalist)
      Leonardo DeCaprio for fires,
      xviii, 275, 280, 281
   calls COVID-19 "a little flu",
      xviii, 307
   cuts Environment Ministry's budget
      24 per cent, 280
   cuts funds for National Indian
      Foundation, 277
   "God is Brazilian", xviii, 276
   Manifest Brazilian destiny, 276
   mimics Donald Trump in reaction
      to COVID-19 et al.,
      xviii, 44, 307
   re-enacting the United States'
      westward movement, 277
   urges extermination of Brazilian
      Indians, 276, 277
   vaccines will turn people into
      crocodiles, Bolsonaro
      assets, 281
   wiping out protections of Native
      peoples in Brazil's vs.
      Constitution, 277
Bolton, Johnny Lorenzo, fatally shot by
   police near Atlanta, 30

Bowser, Muriel mayor of Washington,
   D.C., tells Trump to get
   troops out, 23
Brazil, fires in, 279
Brazil's wild northwest, the "world's last
   great settlement
   frontier", 276–278
Brooks, Rayshard
   controversy over shooting, 141, 174,
      187, 210
   killed in Atlanta, 21, 22
Brown, Andrew, Jr.
   evolution of policing that's now
      terrorizing communities of
      color, 70
   killed by police in Elizabeth City,
      N.C., 71
Brown, Kate, governor of
   Oregon, 39, 40
Brown, Mildred, and husband,
   founders of Omaha Star,
   172, 177
Brown, Will, lynched in Omaha (1919)
   on suspicion of having sex
   with a white woman, 55,
   170, 176
Brown, Will, of Omaha, lynched,
   1919, 55, 170, 176
Bryant, Ma'Khia, killed by police in
   Columbus, Ohio, 51, 69
Budde, Marianne, 18
Bull Connor-led opposition to MLKing
   and civil-rights
   movement, 156
Burbank, Christopher and Matthew
   Collins, charged in death of
   Manuel Ellis, 73
Bus boycott, Omaha, Nebraska, xiii,
   172, 173, 177
Bush, George W., 9-11, Obama, and
   the continuing struggle
   for racial equality, 95,
   160, 245

C
Canada, Penal Populism in, 111, 123n5
Capitol, U.S., invasion of, January 6, 2021, x
Carbon dioxide, ability to hold heat, xviii, 275
Carpetbaggers
   took advantage of chaos for their own economic gain, 143
Carrington, Thomas, xv
Castile, Philando
   family receives a $4.5 million almost five years after his death, 28
   shot to death in Minnesota, 28
Cattle Ranching (Amazon); carbon sink to source, 285
Chambers, Ernie
   represents North Omaha in Nebraska Unicameral, 23, 176
Chauvin, Derek
   charge raised to first-degree murder, 12
   Chauvin found guilty of murdering Floyd, 72
   defense testimony begins in trial, 64
   Sixty-four people were killed by police (in the U.S.) in 19 days after Chauvin trial ended, 68
   with three others charged with 2d degree aiding and abetting murder., 23
   trial, closing arguments, 66
Cherokees, Trail of Tears, Andrew Jackson, 35
   Aborigines Protection Boards to protect Aboriginals from hostile whites, 263, 265, 266, 268, 269, 271
Churchill, W., 38
Civil Rights Act (1964) and Voting Rights Act (1965), 154
Civil Rights, the Vietnam War, and Street Chaos, 153–157

Civil War, U.S.
   Aborigines Protection Boards to protect Aboriginals from hostile whites, 263, 265, 266, 268, 269, 271
Civility, attempts to legislate, 199
Climate change, xvii, xviii, 100, 253, 277, 278, 281, 282, 284, 285, 293, 295, 296, 299–301, 303–306
Climate change, role of coal, xvii, 253, 295
Climate change, role of wildfires
   Carbon sink to carbon source, 284, 285
Clinton, Bill, calls MAGA (e.g. Donald Trump) "racist", 92
Clinton, H., 90, 92, 99, 103, 131, 161
Code of Ethics for professional journalists, 193
Coe, Joe. Killed and lynched in Omaha (1890), on rumors of kidnapping a Black girl, xiii, 170
Cohen, Michael
   releases a book, Disloyal: A Memoir, 45
   Trump's former attorney and "fixer", 45
Cold War, 154, 159
Collins, Susan, U.S. Senator, 106
Colonialism, 195, 206
Confederate battle flag ("Stars & Bars")
   NASCAR forbids display of it at stock car races, 25
   as proud display of Old South heritage, 9
Conquest, racial and cultural, xviii, 93
Consciousness-raising, 193
Cook, Capt. James, 38
Coronavirus, x, 3–5, 7, 15, 26, 36, 42, 98, 277, 289
COVID-19 virus, and vaccines against

death rates of, in prisons, 8, 22
Crouch, Roslyn, rap sheet, 4
Crum, Ben, lawyer, 70
Cultural appropriation (or misappropriation), 194, 197, 199, 200
Cummins Unit, 2

D

Daley, Richard, Chicago mayor, 155
Daniels, Stormy, characterized by Donald Trump ("horseface"), 99
Darwin, Charles Robert
   "fittest' as synonymous to 'civilization'.", 262
   influence on Galton's ideas, 255, 265
   Origin of Species (1859), 256
   "survival of the fittest", 262
David, Christopher, roughed up in Portland, Oregon, 39
Death Penalty, in Japan, xi, 111
Decolonization Café, 20
Deforestation, Brazil
   behavior of loggers, miners and ranchers, 281
   1995 and 2005, forest loss in the Brazilian Amazon reduced8, 278
   2008-2009, deforestation slows, 278–281
   2019 Deforestation shoots upward again, 279, 281
Democratic Party (U. S.)
   aid to Ku Klux Klan, before and after Civil War, 10, 11, 149
   architects of racist "southern strategy", 157, 161
   become allies of the Black community, 157
   by 1972, exodus of white supremacists was complete, 157
   with Republicans, an unexpected political realignment, 1870s, 149–153
DePorres Club (Omaha), organizes lunch-counter sit-in, late 1940s, 172
Dewey, Thomas
   Upset by Harry Truman, 1948, 152
Discrimination, ended in U.S. military, 1948, 151
Dixiecrat movement, viii
Dixon, George, Zip Coon, 200
Donovan, La Bella, shot in the face by Trump agit-prop. Portland, OR, 41
DuBois, W.E.B., viii, 144, 236
Durkan, Jenny (Seattle mayor), tells Trump "Make us all safe. Go back to your bunker", 19

E

Eisenhower, Dwight, 154
El Centro de la Raza (Seattle)
   listed in the National Register of Historic Places, 20, 172
Elizabeth City, N.C., 71
Elliott, Mike, 66, 299
Ellis, Manuel, killed by police in Washington State, 72
Emancipation Proclamation, 36, 143, 144n1, 151, 158
Enlightenment, the, xi, 112, 132, 136
Environmental issues, critique of, 283
Ernst, Joni, Republican U.S. senator, Iowa, 40
Esper Mark T., Brooklyn Center's mayor, 66, 67

Eugenics movement (literal Greek for "good birth") in Australia
   400,000 cases in Germany, 254
   60,000 court ordered sterilizations in the United States, 254
   applied with seriousness by U.S. President Woodrow Wilson to the Grand Wizards of the Ku Klux Klan, 256
   Australian Constitution excluded Aboriginal Australians as citizens, 267
   commonly accepted premise among European theorists, 259
   critical hereditary trait in a color wheel of white superiority, 258
   eugenics driven vision of superior race which crystallized as the White Australia Policy, 266
   morally endorsed conquest of Aboriginal Australians, 259
   narcissistic self adulation of the white "race", 258
   omission from national population censuses, 116
   Plato recommended a state-run program to improve "guardian class", 257
   political and academic ignorance of, xvii, 253
   pseudo-scientific thinking, 257
   "racial purity" with which eugenics was received worldwide before during the 1930s, 256
   state systems which regulated human reproduction, xvii, 253
   studies of are scarce in Australia, 254
   that the superior race was white, 258

F

"Fake News" (Trump, Donald), 37, 107, 212, 280
Fashion industry, sports mascots, and cultural misappropriation
   designers assert that this is "culture appreciation", 197
   Native American-style feathered headdress, high-heeled moccasins, 196
   Prince Harry (U.K.) and Australian art motifs, 196
   sports mascots
      names and games, 25
   Victoria's Secret model Karlie Kloss, 196
Fathi, David, 7
Fetchit, Stepin, 11, 201
Fillmore, Willard (Whig)
   campaigned under the banner "Americans Must Rule America.", 85
   a lifelong racist and nativist, 85
Fiorina, Carly, encounter with Donald Trump, 98
"Firenadoes," California, Australia, and Brazil, 282, 298–300
Fire seasons begin earlier and extend longer, *see* Climate change
Fires This Time, 275–307
First Amendment, xiv, 17, 19, 40, 191–222
Floyd, George
   $27 million award to family, 60
   arrest of, 22, 56, 63, 64, 67, 68
   being Black and breathing a capital offense?, 23
   brutality of murder, viii, 13, 73
   cell phones and murder of; spread worldwide on Internet, 51
   death's resemblance to lynching, 65
   demand for complete submission; repression was complete, 65

excessive force, definition at trial, 61
fake $20 bill, 12
funeral held in Houston, Texas, 24
(longest consecutive string of protests in United States history), 24
mass marches in support of, around the world, size and scope, viii
Minneapolis police officers fired, viii, 12, 57
Minnesota Freedom Fund, reported that a million people had donated $30 million, 26
murder lights a fuse, 12
neck crushed by Derek Chauvin, 60
Philonise Floyd, George's brother, 63, 69, 72
trial of Chauvin, number of witnesses and pieces of evidence, 66
Fort [Lewis] Benning
argued "that African-Americans were not really human and could never be trusted with, 33
full citizenship, 33
Fort Bragg, 9
Fort Hood, 9
Fort Lawton (Seattle), occupation of, by American Indian activists, 19
Fort Lee, 9
Founding Fathers, United States, xii, xiii, 141, 142
Frampton, Thomas, 4, 5
Frazier, Darnella, testimony at Chauvin's trial, 61
Freedmen's Bureau
established schools and brought educational opportunities, 145
Frey, Jacob, Minneapolis Mayor
hissed off stage for supporting Minneapolis police force, 24

G

Galton, Sir Francis
eugenic ideals that ultimately killed Australians, 255
forgotten man of Australian history, 255, 256
founder of the eugenics movement in Australia, 255
intellectual imperialist who left a legacy, 273
mentioned as an alumnus of Cambridge University in the same company as Darwin and Charles Dickens, 256
Tailors Armani suit for Darwin's monkey in Hereditary Genius (1869), 256
"we plant our stock all over the world", 259
Garvey, Marcus, advocates Black nation (Liberia) in Africa, 172, 176
Gerrymandering, 88, 161
Gingrich, Newt, 159, 160, 198
Goldwater, Barry, opposition to the civil-rights movement, 156
"Gone With the Wind" pulled from movie streaming services, 25
Gonzalez, Mario A, killed gruesomely one day before Chauvin was convicted, 68
Goodson, Casey, Jr., fatally shot; Subway sandwich mistaken for a gun, 52
Greene, Ronald, 56, 57
Gugino, Martin, peace worker, shoved to sidewalk in Buffalo, N.Y., 25

H

Hansen, Genevieve, testimony at Chauvin's trial, 61
Hate speech, 21, 197–198

Hayes, Rutherford B., U.S. president, 148, 182
Hill, Karissa, 51
Hill, Maurice, killed for carrying a cell phone $10 milion settlement, 51
Hoard, Rosina, teaching Blacks to read, 145
Hooks, John
"You've kept your foot on our neck for 401 damn years", 32
Houston Women's Group, 103
Humphrey, Hubert, 155
Hurricane Katrina, and prisoners in New Orleans, 4

I

Identity politics, xiv, 25, 192
Immigrants, European, xviii, 149, 239
Imprisonment rates, Anglophone world, xi, 111
Incarceration, costs, 6
Islamophobia, Xenophobia and Terrorist Stereotypes, 244–246

J

Jackson, Andrew, U. S. president
bets lives of slaves in poker games, 1, 35
Jackson's vice president, John C. Calhoun, poised to leave Union, 143
Jackson, Jesse; Trump and racial fears, 90
James River (Virginia), first importation of slaves, 1619, 158
Jefferson, Martha, 207, 208
Jefferson, Thomas
freedom of expression, and, 220
Sally Hemings, and, 34, 208
as slave owner, 34, 207
"Jew codes," Third Reich., viii
Jim Crow laws, end of, beginning in late 1940s, 11, 151
Johnson, Andrew, U.S. president, impeachment of, 144, 234
Johnson, Lyndon B., U.S. prersident, 153, 154
Jones, Kenneth, killed at traffic stop in Omaha, 53

K

Kaepernick, Colin; Donald Trump and, 96
Kelete, Dawit, Kills one person by ramming Black Lives Matter car, 21
Kemp, Brian, governor of Georgia, 58
Kennedy, John F.
assassination of, 154
liberal agenda, 153
we all breathe the, 21, 23
Kennedy, Robert, assassination of, 154
Kenosha, Wisc. explodes in violence after police shooting of Blake, Jacob, Jr.
demonstrations spread to Chicago, Seattle, Madison, Wisconsin Portland, Oregon, New York City, Minneapolis, and other urban areas, 13
King, Martin Luther, Jr.
assassination of, 158, 173, 177, 180
Kizzee, Dion, killed by police, while on a bicycle for a misdemeanor, 48
Koalas, millions killed in Australian fires, 297
Krasner, Larry, district attorney, Philadelphia, compares Trump to Hitler and Mussolini, 42

Krugman, Paul, 9, 299
Ku Klux Klan, Black Hawks, violence against the Black community
  disrupted gatherings of the Republican Party, 146
  unofficial arm of the Democratic Party by the end of the 1860s, 146

L

Lack of accommodations for prayer times during Ramadan, 188
LaMere, Frank, crusade against Whiteclay alcoholism, 186
Langenfeld, Dr. Bradford T. Wankhede, E.R. doctor who pronounced Floyd dead, 64
Lee, Robert E., 9, 10, 16, 32, 35, 144n1
Lemon, Don, 97
Levitsky and Ziblatt, *How Democracies Die*
  four key indicators of authoritarian behavior, 107
    denial of the legitimacy of political opponents, 107
    readiness to curtail civil liberties of opponents., 107
    rejection of or weak commitment to democratic rules, 107
    toleration or encouragement of violence, 107
Lewis, John, "conscience," U.S. House of Representatives, 10, 33, 43, 285
Lexington, Nebraska
  32 languages in small schools, 180, 187, 322
Lies, by Richard Nixon, during 1968 U.S. presidential campaign, 173

Lightfoot, Lori, mayor of Chicago, 52, 53
Lincoln, Abraham
  ends the "vile system" of slavery?, 143
Lincoln, Abraham, and slavery, vii, 14, 36, 43, 45, 50, 142–144, 149, 150n18, 153, 157, 158, 160, 170, 180, 185, 315n11
Lincoln Pictures, 170
Lindsay, John, "limousine liberal"?, 87
Living conditions, Blacks, Minneapolis, viii, ix, 12, 13, 16, 22, 24, 27, 28, 39, 46, 51, 57, 60, 61, 63, 64, 66–68, 70, 71, 74, 233–235, 238
Locke, John
  Reason brings an end to tyranny, 114
  World without reason gives rise to "despotical power", 113, 114
Lopez, Carlos Ingram, 27
Lunch-counter sit-in, Omaha, Nebraska, xiii
Lynching
  service revolver as new lynching rope, viii, 2, 60

M

Madison, James
  on freedom of expression and the First Amendment, 220
Malcolm X
  assassination of, 154
Maniguaelt-Newman, Omarosa, Trump calls her "a crazed, crying low life" and a "dog", 99
Martin Luther King, Jr. visits, 1958, viii, xii, 154, 158, 160, 177, 180
Martin, Trayvon, 15

Mass media
  experiences to do with sickness, madness, criminality, sexuality and death, 123
  individuals more reliant on media rather than other people to inform them about the world, 124
  separation of daily life from contact with those experiences, 123
McClain, Eligah, killing of
  asserting that McClain's case be re-opened, 31
  thousands of protestors assemble in Aurora, Denver, and elsewhere, 31
  two million people signed petitions, 31
McConnell, Mitch, Senate Majority Leader, gaming Supreme Court nominees, 88
McCormack, Michael, Deputy Prime Minister, blamed Australian fires on exploding horse manure, 302
Meatpacking jobs leave Omaha, 172, 173
"Middle Passage" between Africa and the slave markets of Eastern North America
  fetid conditions below decks, 35
Milley, Mark, 17
Minstrel shows, mass media, stereotypes, 11, 200, 201, 203
"Mis-gendering" regarding an individual's preferred name, pronoun, re: gender stereotypes", 199
Morales, Evo, president of Bolivia, 51, 291
Morrison, Scott, xviii, 275, 296, 299–303, 306

Mosques near Omaha; non-Muslims protest, 92, 187, 188
Mosques on the Prairie
  conflicts over parking lot, 187
Multnomah County (Portland, Oregon) elects Mike Schmidt district attorney
  Schmidt dismisses charges against roughly half of the protesters, 43
Muslim religious groups see anti-Islamic rhetoric as hate speech, 198

N

National Association of Black Journalists, 98
National Cathedral, racist stained-glass windows, 10
Nationalism and free speech, 195
Nationalistic rhetoric, x, xii, 166
Natural resources, Australia
  coal, the world's main source of climate change, xvii, 253
  uranium, xvii, 253
Nazi atrocities
  spurs need to protect human rights in penal law, 116
  Universal Declaration of Human Rights (1948), and, 116
New Deal, in the Black community
  Black community and Eleanor Roosevelt, 151
New Zealand, Penal Populism in, 111, 112, 119–125, 136
Nixon, Richard, U.S. president
  lies about N. Vietnamese intentions, 1968 campaign, 155
  "silent majority" predicated upon racial prejudice, 158
  strategy of coded ambiguous speech ("dog whistles"), 156

Index

O

Obama, Barack, timeline of slavery, 1619 to 2008
  elected 45 years after ML King's "Dream" speech, xiii
  election
    in
    2008 did not lift the U.S. from its racist past, 142
    questioning Obama's parentage, 161
    racist rhetoric aimed at, 161, 281
    U.S. society in 2008 nowhere nearly "post-racial", 142
Obama, Michelle
  "When they go low, we go high", 103
Obama's sense of reason followed by Trump
  "era that stretches to FDR just came to an abrupt and ugly end.", 131–136
  a surge of racial hate, abuse, and intolerance, 131
O'Brien, Timothy, author of Trump Nation: The Art of Being the Donald, 89
O'Dell, Nancy (TV host): Trump: "I did try and f**k her", 99
O'Donnell, Rosie. Trump calls her "very unattractive" and "a fat pig", 99
Omaha, Nebraska
  acute poverty in Black community, 172
  Black and Latino/a populations rise, xiii, 170, 178
  bus boycotts in, 173
  chronology of Black community in, 176
  citizens Committee for Civil Liberties, 177
  Ku Klux Klan forces Little family out of city, 172
  Little, Rev. Earl, Malcolm X's father, viii, xiii, 154, 172, 176, 177
  loses several thousand meatpacking and railroad jobs, 172
  lunch-counter sit-in, late 1940s, xiii
  Malcolm X born in, as Malcolm Little, 172, 177
  Martin Luther King, Jr. visits, 1958, 177
  Omaha Star, 171, 172, 177
  protests *vis a vis* George Floyd murder, 2020, 12, 23, 28, 38, 43, 50, 55
  race riot and lynching, Will Brown, 1890, 55, 170, 176
  riots, 1966, 1968, 15, 173, 174, 177, 180
  segregation in, 170, 171
  Strong, Vivian, killed by police, followed by riot, 27, 44, 51, 59, 68, 72
  United Meatpacking Workers of America, integration of, 171
  Wallace, George, visit, followed by riot, 173, 180
Omaha, North, vibrant music and entertainment culture, 170
Omar, Ilan
  addressing community concerns, 238
  born in Mogadishu, Capitol of Somalia, 1981, 234
  early life, 95
  feminist context of her racial, gender, ideological, and religious identities, 230
  first Somali elected to a state legislature (Minnesota), xvi
  first Somali refugee elected to the U.S. Congress, xvi
  Minneapolis, Minnesota's Somali community, 235

Omar, Ilan (*Cont.*)
  naturalized U.S. citizen, Somali Muslim woman, and African refugee, 229, 239
  Omar's experiences explain how African American women experience gender, race, age, class, and other prejudices, 232–233
  one of the first two elected Muslim Congresswomen [with Rashida Tlaib (D-MI)], 230, 241, 242
  Palestinians and Israelis, 242, 244
  President Donald Trump's tweets slur her, xvi, 45, 242, 243, 246
  pushing gender role boundaries within the Somali community, xvii, 230–232, 240
  Trump doubles down with false allegations that Omar celebrated the 9-11 attacks, 246
  Trump erroneously asserts Omar belittled the 9-11 attacks, causing a surge in death threats, 246
  Trump labels Somalis in U.S. as terrorists, 234, 245
  Trump's move away from liberal democracy toward authoritarian rule, xvii, 229
  white supremacists and nativists resented her, xvi
Osaka, Naomi, political activist and tennis star, 47

P

Paine, Thomas
  "The most formidable weapon against error…is reason", 114
Peat fires, Indonesia, 292
Pelosi, Rep. Nancy, 16, 41, 104, 242, 243
Penal Populism
  "authoritarian populism" and, 119
  chemical castration of child sex offenders, in Japan, xi, 111
  contradicts reason in the development of penal policy, xi, 112
  democracy and death penalty said to be antithetical, 18, 107
  democratic structures *vs.* demands for security, 113
  deterrent effect?, xi, 112
  dramatically rising imprisonment rates, xi
  fears of difference, of otherness, strangers, foreigners, immigrants, et al., 128
  "law and order" as political rallying cry; a new kind of victimhood, 127, 128
  penetration into mainstream society, 112
  political populism, relationship with, 112, 126
  Pratt: populism no longer restricted to the penal sector, 125
  punitive approach to law breaking, xi, 111
  rise of global insecurities and anxieties, 122, 123
  terrorists, and, 113
  undermines the very kernel of modern punishment, xi, 111
  vigorous use of death penalty, xi, 111
Pettibone, Mark, Trump's reaction felt like fascism, 39
Pettus, Edmund, Bridge, Pettus' life, 10
Phillips, Abby, 35, 98, 142, 284
Plato, 257
Pleoger, David, Chauvin's supervisor, 61
Police killings, Blacks *vs.* whites, 27, 50, 51

Political correctness, xiv, 191–222
Politics of race
   by 1948, had reached a crucial crossroads, 149
   continue to be a defining feature of this republic, xiii, 167
   paramount in American discourse, 141
Ponca Trail of Tears (1877); forced removal of
   Dundy, Elmer Federal District Court Judge, 184
   Dundy's ruling creates precedent for a Native person as a human being, 184
   51-day march, 183
   Lawrence, James, Indian agent, 183
   malaria kills many marchers, 183
   map-makers mistakes, 181
   number of houses, et al. torn down, 32
   Standing Bear, et al. return to Omaha from Indian Territory in winter, 35, 181, 183
   Tibbles, Thomas Henry records journalistic accounts, 183, 184
   Treaty of Fort Laramie, 1868, 181
Populism, political
   anti-democratic 'strong man' politics, 125, 132
   democracy no longer seen as a gift of modernity, with guarantees of good government, 127
   immersed in racism, nativism, xenophobia, and conspiracy theories, 87
   threatens an end to Reason itself, the foundation stone of modernity., 112
   undefined appeals to "the people", 85, 87
Portland, Oregon, daily demonstrations for months
   conflicts spread to several large cities, 15, 42
   creative protest tactics, e.g. "Wall of Moms," et al., 39, 40
   crowds grow into thousands during summer of 2020, 14, 40
   "feds" leave city by end of July, 2020; demonstrations continue, 40–42
   Seattle support rally, July, 2000, 14, 24, 40, 45, 49
Post-racial society (Idea used against affirmative action), xii, 158, 161, 165, 167
Press, freedom of, xv, 213, 221
Price, Jonathan killed by officer Shaun Lucas in Texas, 49, 93, 219
Prison incarceration rates, worldwide, 2–5, 24, 59
Prison system, United States
   COVID-19 common in, 2
   criminal justice complex, 129
   medical conditions, 2
   medications commonly prescribed, 2, 6
   prison terms as death sentences, 2, 7, 50
   race of prison inmates, 17, 176
   young Black men in, vii, 45
Prisoners, adjustment problems following release, 11
Protests, Floyd murder, effect on public opinion, 66
Prude, Daniel, died of asphyxiation by seven police officers, 12, 13, 48, 63–65
Punishment
   punishment with "more humane and constructive methods", 118
   reason and anti-reason, 113–119

340 Index

Q
Queen Araweelo (agitation against a patriarchal society; gender equality), xvi, xvii, 231–247

R
Racial Hygiene Association (Australia, founded 1926), 267, 267n56, 267n57
Racial politics in U.S. history, xii, 142, 167
Racism
  engrained nature of, 9
  politics of, xii, xiii, 141–144, 167
Rainbow Family, 196
Ralph Waldo Emerson, quoted by Trump
  When you strike at the King…you must kill him.", 106
Reason
  defeat of Reason, of rationality, science, truth, objectivity, consistency, 132
  development of punishment, 117
  resurgent anti-Reason drives penal development, 118
Reconstruction
  blacks aided by Republican Party, 86, 144, 146, 150
Reeves, T., 9
Reid, J., 37
Reinoehi, Forest, killed by police near Lacey, Washington, 44
Republican Party (United States), as absorbed by Donald Trump (c. 2016)
  addiction to counter-majoritarian tactics, 88
  census-gaming, 88
  with Democrats, an unexpected political realignment, 1870s, 149
  exploits fears of Black takeover, 159
  extreme partisan gerrymandering, 88
  minority-rule tactics, 88
  One-time "Party of Lincoln," now apologists for Southern white supremacy, 157
  opposes school desegregation, 159
  "Party of Lincoln", 149, 153, 157
  in South, after Civil War, aid to Blacks, 11
  voter suppression, 88
Rich, Jonathan, last prosecution witness at Chauvin trial, 68
Rittenhouse, Kyle, shootings in Kenosha, Wisc., 46, 47
Rivers, Doc, Philadelphia 76rs basketball head coach, 47
Robert E. Lee's surrender, Civil War, 144
Romney, Mitt, U.S. Senator
  "entitlement speech": stereotypes of Blacks, 166
  says poor are lazy and dependent upon the government, 166
Roosevelt, T.
  alienated African American voters in the South, 86
  believed that he was fighting graft and corruption, in favor of "the people", 86
  used populist ideas in 1912 as Progressive Party candidate, 85, 86
Rose, Charlie, fired on allegations of sexual misconduct, 220
Rosenblum, Ellen, Oregon attorney general, 41
Ross, Courteney, George Floyd's former girlfriend, at Chauvin trial, 63
Ryan, A., 97, 98

S

Safe spaces, xiv, 191, 193, 194
Sao Paulo, smoke in, 286
Science, rationality, and criminal justice, 115
Scientific racism, xvii, 253–254, 260
Scurry, Jena, Minneapolis Police dispatcher, at Chauvin trial, 63
Seattle's "No Cop Co-op"
  "Peoples Republic of Capitol Hill", 18
  Police break it up, 18
  Shootings at, 20
Security by state intervention
  eradicating "five giant evils: Want, Disease, Ignorance, Squalor, Idleness", 133
  reduction of risk and insecurity, 134
Sedition Act (1798)
  Madison, John, views on, 220, 221
Sexism, ix, 83–107, 194, 244
Sharpton, Rev. Al, 70, 72
Sheskey, Rusten, Kenosha, Wisc. police, killer of Jacob Blake, Jr., 45
Silva, Jorge, 288
Slaves, Slavery
  blacks attacked after Civil War emancipation, 146
  founding Fathers, and, xiii, 141, 207
  freedom in name only, 146
  history of, vii, ix, xix, 1
  slave owners said to be not the immediate cause of the Civil War, 142
  slave trade (North Atlantic, 1500-1800, 25 million transported), 27, 37, 206, 208
  U.S. Supreme Court, and, 314
  violence that occurred after 1865, 146
  white supremacists, and, 11, 141, 142, 146
Smith, Winston Boogie, shot dead by deputies of a U.S. Marshall's Fugitive Task Force., 74

Social cohesion unravels as support rises for severe punishments, 123
Social Darwinism
  provided a neat explanation which absolved whites from any blame for decline of the Aborigines, 263
Somali Community, 234–235
Sondland, Gordon, fired by Trump for impeachment testimony, 106
South Carolina Declaration of Secession, and slavery, 143
Southern Strategy, *vis a vis* Ronald Reagan and Donald Trump, 156
Soviet Union, 154, 159
"The Squad"
  Trump told Omar, Tlaib, Ocasio-Cortez, and Pressley to "go back" from where they had come, 100
Stability, erosion of
  new threats, e.g. terrorism, new cancers, credit-card fraud, 122
Stalin, Josef, xv
Standing Bear Trial, 176
States' Rights Democratic Party, 149, 152, 154
Statistical summary, 59, 102, 103, 124, 178, 257
Statues and other remembrances removed, debates about
  Colston, Edward, 37
  Columbus, Christopher, 32, 33, 40, 44, 51, 52, 69
  Davis, Jefferson, 16, 32
  Grant, Ulysses S., 33
  Jackson, Andrew, 276, 277
  Jefferson, Thomas, xv, 4, 16, 32, 34, 43, 158, 181, 203, 207, 208, 322
  Juan de Oñate y Salazar, 32
  King Leopold II of Belgium, 37

Statues and other remembrances removed, debates about (*Cont.*)
   Lee, Robert E., 10, 16, 32, 35, 144n1, 239, 288
   Milligan, Robert, 37
   Rhodes, Cecil, 37, 38
   Rizzo, Frank, 32
   Roosevelt, Theodore, x, 33, 43, 50, 83–86, 90, 133, 150, 151
   "Stonewall" Jackson, 32
   Theodore Roosevelt IV, argues for removal of TR's statue, 33
   Wayne, John, 38, 70
   Wilson, Woodrow, 34, 86, 162, 256
Stereotypes
   "All in the Family," Archie Bunker, 203
   Amos'n Andy (1928-1960)
      most popular radio program of all time, 202
      NAACP tried to block it (1951); Emmy Award in 1952, 202
   Aunt Jemima, 201
   "Birth of a Nation," D.W. Griffith, 149, 202
   black comedians, 201
   Black men as lazy, xii
   "Blacksploitation" films, 203
   BLM "moving the needle" in the national conversation over race relations, 26
   breakfast meal named after Robert W. Lee, 27
   changes in reception over time, re: "Negro," "Colored", 86, 173, 204, 272
   mass media, stage shows, and, 123, 124
   movies, all-Black casts, 202
   Mutual of Omaha's Plains Indian, 26
   silent movies and, 202
   stereotypical images "retired", 26, 27
   "Sweet Sweetback's Baadasssss Song" (1971), 203
   Uncle Ben's rice, 27
   vaudeville as the dominant form of American mass entertainment, 201
Sterling, Alton, fatally shot in Baton Rogue, LA, 28
"Stolen blackness" (e.g. Stephen Foster to Al Jolson, from Benny Goodman to Elvis Presley and the Rolling Stones), 195
Systemic racism, 44

T

Taft, William Howard *vis a vis* Theodore Roosevelt, 86
Taylor, Breonna
   Chief Steve Conrad retires, 28
   Conrad fired after fatal shooting of David McAtlee, 28
   nationwide protests seeking prosecution of officers, 28
   officers invade Taylor's apartment *vis a vis* mistaken warrant seeking Jamarcus Glover, 10 miles away, 29
   state attorney general clears officers, provoking more demonstrations, 29
   Taylor killed by Louisville police, 29
   Taylor's boyfriend Kenneth Walker shoots back, 30
   Taylor's family files wrongful death lawsuit, wins $12 million, 28
   two officers, including killer of Taylor, fired, 29
Teaching of "critical race theory", 14
Tea Party Caucus, Republican Party, revival of vicious white supremacy, 158

Tea Party, re destruction of British-
owned tea in Boston's harbor
(1773), 162
Thornton, Jesse, victim of lynching, 10
"Three-fifths compromise", 142, 167
Thurmond, Strom
  became face of continued racism and
bigotry, 152
  States' Rights Democratic Party
(Dixiecrats), 152
Till, Emmett, 54, 65, 69
Tobin, Martin, pulmonologist, at
Chauvin trial, 65
Toledo, Adam, killed by Chicago
police, 67
Trigger warnings, xiv, 191, 193, 194
Trump, Donald
  acumen at riling audiences during
his rallies, 166
  advocates statues for his father, 14
  African-American and Latino
workers' opposition, 94
  appeal to white nationalists, xii, 166
  appeal to Whites without college
degrees, 93
  approval rating among black women
at 3%, 102
  attitudes toward people of color,
women, and liberals, x, 83
  believes that Article II of the
Constitution grants him
absolute power, 106
  Biden, Joe, opinion of, 16,
26, 49, 106
  birther movement, *vis a vis* Barack
Obama, 89, 90
  Black vote totals for, 102
  blasts BLM members as assassins of
American culture and heritage
and "leftist fascists", 44
  calls all protesters "animals", 50
  Calls BLM activists "hoodlums and
anarchists", 24, 36
  Calls Hillary Clinton a "nasty
woman", 103
  calls upon Army to suppress
demonstrations vis a vis
George Floyd, 14
  Casts himself on Mount
Rushmore, 43
  Central Park Five, 89, 96
  coalition based on false promises, 94
  collateral damage of his policies are
Blacks, other communities of
color, and women, 107
  compliments himself on record vis a
vis Black Americans, 204
  "The country's real race problem is
bias against white
Americans", 44
  crude attacks on anyone who
opposed him, 91
  dismal poll numbers, 37
  disparages Muslim and Latino/a
immigrants, xii, 167
  "dog-whistle" politics, 91
  egomaniacal and narcissistic
personality, 88
  erroneously accuses demonstrators
of pulling down statues of
Jesus Christ. exclusion African
Americans and women, 36
  and his "base", x, xii
  impeachments of, 103, 104, 106
  itching for a fight (always!), 17
  journalists who stood by truth
    Facebook (2004) and Twitter
(2006) allow alt-realities, 130
    seen as "the lowest form of
humanity", 129
    Trump's "post-truth" news and
views, 130
  lack of commitment to
constitutional democracy, 107
  life of privilege and societal
advantage, 88

Trump, Donald (*Cont.*)
  "Make America Great Again," ideological basis, 90
  Neo-Nazis and Ku Klux Klan, appeal of, 92
  News media bias against Daniel Trump, 129
  normalizing the politics of insult, x, 91, 94
  Orwellian, alt facts, 129
  populist messages of insult and criticism, 84
  populist rhetoric, insults, and racist language to create a frenzy with his base, x, 83
  posing with a *Bible*, 18
  promotes wall with Mexico, xii, 167
  reactions to increasingly multiracial society, 89
  Republicans fear him so much that they will ignore the rule of law, 106
  "shithole countries", 101
  sneers at George Floyd's Funeral, 23, 24
  tapped into the same racial angst that Nixon had mined 48 years earlier, 166
  "Tell me one country run by a Black person that isn't a shithole", 45
  as threat to democracy, 96
Trump, Fred, 89
Trumpian Law and Order, 18
Tyler, Rick, and, 91
unemployment rates and hyperbole, 23, 101, 105, 179, 216
uses the National Prayer Breakfast to lash out at enemies, 105
view of first impeachment, 84
views of women and African Americans, ix, 83, 88, 95, 96
whiteness as "Americaness", 96
Truth and lies
  "fake news", xv, 37, 107, 212, 217, 280
  "when truth is abandoned, then everything can be a lie", 130
  yellow journalism, 210
Tulsa, Oklahoma
  "Black Wall Street;" dimensions of, xiii
  mass bombing of Americans by Americans, 54
  Tulsa's "red summer", 55
  white-spurred race riot (1921), 55
Tuskegee Airmen, 151

U

Uncle Tom's Cabin and Black stereotypes, 200, 201
Underground Railroad, passes through Omaha, 169
United Nations Declaration on the Rights of Indigenous Peoples, 195
United States of America, Penal Populism in, x, xi
Uranium, in Australia, xvii, xix, 253

V

Vietnam War, 15, 153–157
Villela, Vicente, 27
Vindman, Alexander, fired by Trump for impeachment testimony, 106
Voting Rights Act (1965), ends Jim Crow laws, 154

W

Wallace, Gov. George
  appeal to white supremacists, 155
  attempt to blocks Black students from U. Alabama, 1962, 155

visits Omaha, Nebraska, 1968, riot follows, 173
Wallace, Walter, Jr., killed in Philadelphia, 58
Washington George, as slave owner, 34, 207, 313
Washington Post, list of errors by Trump, critiqued, 214
Washington, D.C., protestors' "autonomous zone", 21
Waters, Maxine, 97
Wealth, inequity of, Blacks vis a vis whites, 1, 25
Wheeler, Ted, mayor, Portland, Oregon; two Black teenagers killed near Vancouver, WA, 58
Whiteclay, Nebraska: The Economics of Keeping American Indians Drunk, 184
White Extinction Anxiety, 164–167
White guilt, 206
White nationalist violence, Charlottesville, Virginia, 2017, 198
White nationalists synonymous with white supremacists, 167
White privilege, 88, 205, 210, 236, 238
White racism, 203
White shaming, xiv, xv, 191–222
White supremacy
  names of U.S. Army bases, 9
White, Tom, attorney vis a vis Whiteclay case, 185
Wildfires
  Australia, xviii, xix, 293, 294, 304
  "black Saturday" fires in Victoria State, 293
  Bolsonaro asserts that environmental groups set fires, 281
  Brazil, fires ravage wetlands, 283
  California, xviii, 275, 282
  Chile, xviii, 275, 292

  cool and wet rainforests burn, 293
  decrease in Earth's supply of oxygen, 282
  devastates plants, animals, and habitats, 282, 294, 295
  "Earth's lungs" ruined, 278
  Gergis, Joelle, as a sign of things to come, 293
  greenhouse gases, and, xviii, 275, 281–283
  Greenland, xviii, 275, 291
  Russia (Siberia), xviii, 275, 291
  wildfires envelop Australia, 293
Williams, Archie, 3
Williams, Donald, testimony at Chauvin's trial, 62
Wilson, Woodrow, 34, 86, 256
Womble, R. Andrew, N.C. state prosecutor, 71
Women worldwide protest Donald Trump's election, 95
Woodward Report (Yale, 1975), 194
Wright, Daunte
  death sparks several rights of rioting in Brooklyn Center, 66
  funeral of, 66, 67

Y

"Yale" as Ivy League university
  founded on the riches of slave-trader Elihu Yale, 36
  Morse, inventor of the telegraph and Morse Code, 36
  Six of Yale's residential colleges named after slave owners, including John C. Calhoun, 36
  Slaveholders included New England firebrand preacher Jonathan Edwards, and F.B., 36
  smuggled slaves to Europe in cargo holds, 36

Yanomami
    COVID-19 pandemic arrives, 290
    gold miners kill, 290
    pollution, disease, death, and greedy human beings intent to rip and run, 290
Yellow Journalism
    defined, 210
    invasion of an individual privacy, 211
    Pulitzer's New York World and Hearst's New York Journal, 211, 212
Young, Anjanette, shot to death in Chicago, 52

Z

Zimmerman, Lt. Richard, high-ranking officer, Minneapolis PD, at Chauvin trial, 64

The manufacturer's authorised representative in the EU is Springer Nature Customer Service Centre GmbH, Europaplatz 3, 69115 Heidelberg, Germany. If you have any concerns regarding our products, please contact ProductSafety@springernature.com

Printed and bound by CPI Group (UK) Ltd, Croydon, CR0 4YY

23/03/2026

02076748-0002